Communication, Media and Change

Communication, Media and Change

Jack Lyle
Boston University

Douglas B. McLeod
International Data Corporation

Mayfield Publishing Company
Mountain View, California
London • Toronto

Copyright © 1993 by Mayfield Publishing Company

All rights reserved. No portion of this book may be reproduced in any form or by any means without written permission of the publisher.

Library of Congress Cataloging-in-Publication Data

Lyle, Jack.
    Communication, media, and change / by Jack Lyle, Douglas B.
      McLeod.
      p. cm.
    Includes bibliographical references (p.   ) and index.
    ISBN 1-87484-935-7
    1. Communication—Technological innovations. 2. Mass media—
Technological innovations. I. McLeod, Douglas B. (Douglas
Birmingham), 1958-   II. Title.
P96.T42L95 1992
302.2—dc20   92-19127
                                                                                      CIP

Manufactured in the United States of America
10 9 8 7 6 5 4 3 2 1

Mayfield Publishing Company
1240 Villa Street
Mountain View, California 94041

Sponsoring editor, C. Lansing Hays; production editor, Lynn Rabin Bauer; manuscript editor, Candace Holts; text and cover designer, Paula Goldstein; associate designer, Jean Mailander; cover art, Dominique Saurraute/The Image Bank © 1992; illustrator, Marilyn Kreiger; manufacturing manager, Martha Branch. The text was set in 10/12 Galliard by G&S Typesetters, Inc., and printed on 50# Finch Opaque by Malloy Lithographing.

Preface

This book was written from our conviction that the rapid and often radical changes taking place in the communications field constitute an important area of study and career opportunity for today's students. This conviction was strengthened during the four years we taught a course called Alternative Systems of Communication at Boston University. Students came to this course highly motivated by expectations of learning about exciting new technologies but with little knowledge or understanding of the institutional contexts in which these technologies are used.

Like many other such institutions, Boston University's College of Communication is divided into traditional departments of journalism, broadcasting and film and mass communication (which encompasses advertising, public relations and communication theory). The curriculum forced each student to major in one media area. As a result their courses were organized to prepare them to be print journalists, radio or television staffers, film producers or advertising or public relations account executives.

We wanted to prepare students for a future in which new technologies remove such institutional and career boundaries. Knowing that there are limits to what the new technologies can accomplish, we wanted our students to develop an appropriate balance between pragmatism and visionary expectations. We realized that it was the visionary expectations that attracted the students to the field. The challenge we faced was to acquaint them with the practical limits imposed by the past and the present while capitalizing on their interest in the new.

This book is our attempt to meet that challenge. Our strategy is to start with an overview of the functional needs for communication by individuals, groups and societies: news, persuasion, education and entertainment. The students' own enthusiastic communication activities provide a variety of avenues for exploring these needs. Next we look at the major technologies that have made the Communication Revolution possible: semiconductors, satellites, optical fiber, personal computers and high definition television. We discuss how these new technologies can be used across all of the institutions and media of the communications sector.

Having suggested how these technologies may revolutionize our communications world, we turn to some of the facts of life within that world. Students must understand that technology is a tool used by institutions that operate within the constraints of a complex structure of systems. Any tool must overcome the barriers of resistance inherent in the status quo, factors we loosely group under the headings of policy, systems and money.

After providing this background, we turn our attention to the potential of new technologies within the context of the communications functions listed in the Introduction. This survey allows the student to examine changes within and across media, as well as to speculate on how existing media may be forced to change in response to new competition.

Our conclusion brings us full circle: We attempt to get readers to look beyond existing communications services and institutions and speculate on the future. In our progress through the circle, we have had these three objectives:

1. To help foster an ability among readers to anticipate change rather than to be satisfied with adapting to a status quo that is in fact transitory.
2. To stimulate readers to think about how they can use new technologies and alternative applications to build a fairer, more efficient and smarter world of communications.
3. To help other teachers impart an understanding of a subject as fragile and quickly changing as communications systems.

An inherent problem in discussing a subject as dynamic as communications technologies is that details change daily. Recognizing that much of our specific information will be outdated before the book is published, we have stressed general principles. In our own classes we used weekly current-events assignments as the springboard for discussion that expanded and updated lectures and reading assignments. These assignments reinforced students in acquiring the habit of reading the trade publications, such as *Advertising Age, Broadcasting, Variety, PC World, MacWorld* and *Network World,* as well as watching for news of professional interest in the daily press.

Revolution is a strong word, as are *age* and *era*. Nevertheless, we have repeatedly used all three throughout the book. Researchers and analysts may think our use presumptuous (as if it were possible to recognize the passing from one era to another as being the result of revolution), but we feel that the potential of the new communications technologies justifies strong language. Future historians will be the ultimate judges of the extent to which we entered a new era during the latter decades of the 20th century. They will have the perspective to evaluate the success or failure of any such revolution.

We have used attention-grabbing terminology for a pragmatic reason: to stimulate our students to strive for the richer, more equitable society that new communications technologies can provide *if* they use these technologies with skill and imagination that transcends the barriers of the status quo. Ithiel de Sola Pool referred to them as "Technologies of Freedom"; it is we who must seek, use and protect the freedom.

ACKNOWLEDGMENTS

We would like to express our appreciation to those who provided assistance as we wrote this book. The comments of those who reviewed the manuscript, Stephen R. Acker, Ohio State University; Andrew Arno, University of Hawaii at Manoa; Arthur Asa Berger, San Francisco State University; Carl Bybee, University of Oregon; Charles Clift, Ohio University; Herbert S. Dordick, Temple University; Susan Tyler Eastman, Indiana University at Bloomington; Hamid Mowlana, The American University; and JoAnn Valente, University of Florida at Gainesville, were extremely helpful in giving the book its final shape.

For a year and a half, our friend Philippe Delarue, now back in Paris, worked as our research assistant. By doing the detective work of tracking innumerable facts and citations, he helped us enrich the text as well as speed up the writing process.

Our greatest debt, however, is to the students who studied new developments in media and communications technologies with us in BF521 classes at Boston University. Their reactions provided real-life testing of draft chapters used as text materials. Their in-class reports and term papers helped us keep up-to-date on developments. Most important, their interest and enthusiasm kept us going.

Contents

Preface   v

INTRODUCTION   Technological Evolution and Revolution in the Mass Media   1

    Getting Ready for Change   1

    A New Century, a New Age   2

    Unclear Frontiers, Expanding Freedoms   2

    Information: A Commodity with Value   2

    Making Profits from Innovative Telecommunication   3

    The Media: Comprising a Commodity Market   3

    Personal Aspects of the Communication Revolution   5

    The Functional Basis of Mass Media   5

    Changing Functions: The Case of Radio   6

    Victims of the Communication Revolution   7

    Digital Codes: Changing the Relationship Between Information and Signal   7

    ◆ Box: Why Move from Analog to Digital Codes?   8

    Changes in Software and Hardware   8

    The Common Person and the Common Code   9

    Revolutions Sometimes Fizzle   9

    Breaking Out of Institutional Traps   10

x   Contents

PART I
Technologies of the Communication Revolution   13

CHAPTER 1   The Semiconductor Family: Building Blocks of the Revolution   15

Intelligence, Personal Satisfaction, Money and Power   15
Speeding Up the Communication Process   16
The Drudgery of Intelligence: Storing and Sorting   16
Capacity, Speed and Flexibility: The Basis of the Revolution   17
The Electromagnetic Spectrum   17
The Switch as a Bottleneck   19
AT&T's Search for More Efficient Switches   20
The Semiconductor Family   20
Transistors: A Basis for Amplification   20
From Edison's Light Bulb, Another Idea   21
Semiconductors and Mobility   21
Integrated Circuits: Combinations of Semiconductors   22
Digital Language and Boolean Algebra   23
Boolean Algebra and Semiconductors: Creation of the Microchip   23
Miniaturization   25
The Ever-Increasing Speed of Switching   25
Digital Technology in an Analog World   26
The Translation Sequence Required for Mixing Technologies   26
Handicaps for Digital Operation in a Non-Digital Environment   26
The Growing Push for Digitalization   27

CHAPTER 2   Satellites: Transmitters in the Sky   29

Communication for a Global Community   29
◆ Box: The Geosynchronous Orbit   30
The Geosynchronous Orbit: From Science Fiction to Reality   30
A Complex Operating System   31
The Components of a Satellite System   32
Power, Attenuation, Signal Coverage and Dish Size   32
Changing the Concept of Distance and Time   34
Restructuring Rate Schedules   35
Exploding Capacity and Spreading Time   35
Enabling Nations to Leapfrog in Development   36
How Media Leapfrog   36

Contents   xi

    Satellite Reception in Individual Homes   36

    ◆ Box: INTELSAT   37

    Direct Broadcast Satellites   37

    Very Small Aperture Terminal Applications   38

    Crowding the Geosynchronous Orbit   38

    Pushing Farther Out in the Electromagnetic Spectrum   40

    Disadvantages of Telecommunications Satellites   40

    New Competition: Optical Fiber   41

CHAPTER 3   Optical Fiber: A New Tie That Binds   43

    Putting Light into Our Networks   43

    Advantages of Glass Fiber Over Copper Wire   44

    Optical Fiber as a Competitor for Satellites   44

    Reflecting Light Through Glass Wire   45

    Digital Codes: Making Better Use of Light's Bandwidth   45

    The Role of Lasers in Optical Fiber Systems   46

    Digital Codes and Signal Interference   47

    Optical Fiber Versus Satellite Transmission   48

    Hurdles for Conversion to Fiber   48

    Competition Is the Driving Force   48

    Which Comes First: Bandwidth or Demand?   49

    Business and Technological Advancement   50

    Changing Dynamics in the Local Loop   50

    Why Not Optical Fiber Video?   51

    The Telephone–Cable–Television Fiber Connection   51

    Continuing Advances in Optical Fiber Technology   52

CHAPTER 4   The Personal Computer: Putting Things Together   54

    The Computer: New Technology but an Old Idea   55

    Changing Our Perspective from Computing to Communication   55

    ◆ Box: A Bug That Gained Immortality   56

    The Development of Computer Software   57

    Apple: A New Concept   57

    The Next Step: Turning Personal Computers into Communication Devices   58

    The Concept of Multimedia   59

    A Collaborative Effort   59

    Multimedia Standardization—A Goal for the Future   60

    Evolutionary yet Revolutionary   60

xii Contents

    The Evolution of the Revolution   61
    Personal Computer Multimedia Terminals   61
    Wide-Area Multimedia Networks   61
    Technology Is Ready, but Policy Is Not   62
    ISDN and Intelligence in the Network   63
    Adjusting Rates for Fluctuating Bandwidth Demand   63
    Dedicated Links That Don't Get Switched   64
    Software to Run It All   64
    Software That Takes Initiative   65
    Software to Store the World   65
    Storage: Multimedia Libraries   65

CHAPTER 5   HDTV: A Bigger, Better Video Window   67
    Saturation Means Market Stagnation   67
    ◆ Box: Recording Motion in Pictures   68
    Blurred Images from Archaic Screens   69
    Enlarging the Picture and Junking the CRT   69
    Hurdles in the Path of a New Standard   70
    The Lost Dream of a Single International Standard   71
    ◆ Box: Broadcasting Standards   71
    The Agony of Changing U.S. Standards   72
    Where Is the Demand for a New Standard?   72
    The HDTV Dilemma for Broadcasters   73
    A Better Picture Requires More Information   73
    ◆ Box: Channels and Bandwidth   74
    Putting the Squeeze on Channel Bandwidth   74
    Semiconductors to the Rescue: Signal Compression   75
    ◆ Box: Signal Compression   75
    The Optical Fiber–Digital Signal Connection   76
    Expanded Participation in the HDTV Decision   76

PART II

Factors That Shape the Communications Marketplace   79

CHAPTER 6   The Constraints of Policy   81
    Setting the Limits   81
    Constitutional Starting Points   82
    Communication's Special Role in Democratic Societies   82
    The National Mosaic of Local Governments   83

Federal Oversight for Interstate Commerce   83
Intellectual Property Should Be Fairly Shared   84
Conditions Change but Principles Persist   84
Press and Policy   85
Broadcasting and Policy   85
Common Carriers and Policy   86
Technologies Change Faster Than Policies   87
Cable   88
MMDS and DBS   88
The Rising Demand for Spectrum Service   88
Sharing Content Across Media Boundaries   89
Limits Intended to Preserve Freedom   89
From Open Markets to Monopolies   90
Restricting Freedoms to Preserve the Open Market   90
◆ Box: Restrictions on Group and Cross-Media Ownership   91
Free Press, and Free Speech?   91
◆ Box: Examples of Restrictions on Broadcast and Cable Content   92
A Free and Open Marketplace?   92
The Social Influence of Technology   93
Shaping—and Distorting—the Revolutionary Technologies   93
The Challenge of Multimedia Formats   94
The International Dimension of Policy   94
The Role of Multinational Operators   95
At Stake: Billions of Dollars   95

CHAPTER 7 Technologies, Infrastructures, Systems and Standards   98

Technologies Require Operating Systems   98
Basic Functions, Different Capabilities   99
Press Systems   100
Broadcasting Systems   101
Common-Carrier Systems   102
Changing Technologies Within Domains   102
Misfits and Hybrids   103
Using Technology Requires Organization—and Organizations   103
The Newspaper: A Case Study   103
Newspapers Face a Double Crisis   105
Functional Competition, Displacement and Accommodation   105

xiv   Contents

    Technological Progress Can Outrun the Market   105
    Forces of Institutional Change   106
    Infrastructure Change by Policy Fiat   107
    Organizational Push and Pull in Systems   109
    The Arbitrary Nature of Standards   110
    An Inescapable Aspect of Technology   111
    Forms of Standards   112
    Changing Standards: Inertia and Resistance   112
    Economic Dimensions of Standards   113
    The Phantom Component of Infrastructure   113
    Flag Waving and Global Systems   114

CHAPTER 8   The Matter of Money   117
    The Age-Old Question: How Much Will It Cost?   117
    What Will the Market Bear?   118
    Internal Subsidization and Deep Pockets   118
    The Common-Carrier Model: Pay for Service   119
    Changing the Rules of Common-Carrier Rates   119
    The Press and Broadcast Models: Advertising Subsidy   120
    Who's the Boss?   120
    The Public Gets a Bargain   121
    The Size of the Advertising Subsidy   121
    Attrition Through Advertising Allocations   123
    Radio: A Case of Functional Displacement   123
    Fat Cats No More: The Oligarchy Networks   124
    The Movies: A Good Product Wherever It's Sold   124
    An Unchanged Function with Shifting Finances   125
    From Integration to Chaos   125
    Losing Control of Costs   126
    Cinema: Cinderella in Reverse   126
    The Paradox at the Cinema Office   127
    Outrunning the Competition   128
    What About That $5-Billion Box Office?   129
    Conflicting Interests   129
    Viewers Will Pay for Television   129
    Providing Advertisers with Alternatives   130
    Cable's New Jackpot: Pay-per-View   130

Cable's Double Whammy   131
The Cost of Creative Content   131
How Do We Pay the Bill?   132
The Subsidy That Won't Go Away   132
Once More, How Much Will It Cost?   133
Getting There   134

PART III

The Changing World of Communication   137

CHAPTER 9   From All the News That's Fit to Print to All the News We Want   139

Gatekeepers, Watchdogs and Agenda Setters   139
◆ Box: The Fourth and Fifth Estates   140
Symptoms of Dissatisfaction   140
The Function Is Survival   141
Deciding for Ourselves What News Is "Fit"   142
Social and Economic Conditions Shape Our Institutions   142
"Manifest Destiny" Expands the News Horizons   142
Pressures for Objectivity   143
Objective Reporting: The Journalistic Standard   143
The Public Shift from Print to Broadcast News   144
Broadcasting and Public Trust   144
An Interest More Apparent Than Real   145
The Push of Advertising   146
Objectivity: In the Eye of the Beholder   146
Fraying the Fabric of Public Consensus   147
Shifting Functions Among the News Media   147
Changes in the Newspaper   148
Changes in Video News   151
The Future: Getting Our Own News   156

CHAPTER 10   Selling Ideas, Candidates and Products   160

How Do We Win Buyers and Influence People?   160
A Relatively Recent Specialization   161
Persuasion and Social Order   162
Marketing, Advertising and Public Relations   162
Parallel but Distinct Marketplaces   163
Parallels and Divergences Between the Two Markets   163

◆ Box: If You Pay the Piper, Can You Really Call the Tune?   164
Persuasion Strategies Reflect the Times   165
Sic Transit E Pluribus Unum?   165
Rethinking Cost per Thousand   166
◆ Box: Cost per Thousand   166
Why Buy Audiences You Don't Need?   167
A Trickier Proposition for Politicians   167
Cable Creates New Options for Advertisers   168
Taking Advantage of Impulse Response to Persuasion   168
Providing Feedback Loops   169
Online Computer Shopping and the Telco Future   169
Telcos Are Knocking at the Shopping Gates   170
The Growing Field of Direct Marketing   170
Moving the Catalogs to Multimedia   171
◆ Box: Multimedia Shopping   171
You Can't Kick the Tires   172
Interacting with Solicitors and Candidates   172
◆ Box: Polls and Persuasion   173
Lists, Lists and More Lists   173
◆ Box: Getting to Know You—More Than You Know   174
Changing the Trade-Off   175
A Mass Media Tailspin?   175
Getting the Public's Attention   176
Changes Everywhere   176
Fragmenting or Already Fragmented?   177
Gains Are Commensurate With Risk   177

CHAPTER 11   The New Renaissance and the Liberation of Learning   179

New Literacy for the Information Age   180
Public Education: A Pragmatic Concern   180
Status Quo Roadblocks   181
From Horace Mann's Log to Multimedia Exchange of Knowledge   181
Changing the Relations Among Students, Teachers and Knowledge   182
Re-examining Functional Goals   182
The Clients and Sponsors of the Educational System   183
◆ Box: Limits on Educational Innovation   184
From a Trickle to a Flood of Knowledge   184

The Storehouses of Knowledge: Bursting at the Seams   185
Literacy, Media Literacy and Computer Literacy   185
The Changing Formats of Knowledge   186
Switching Concepts from Volumes to Bits   186
Learning to Share Information   187
The Importance and Variety of Libraries   187
Adding Dimensions to Information Storage   188
Keeping Track   188
Dewey Decimal Gives Way to Library of Congress   189
The Critical Role of Indexing   189
Overload, Overuse and Theft   190
Pressing the Limits of Storage   190
Introducing the Digital Archive   191
Redefining and Redesigning Libraries   191
More Good News   192
Searching for Other Kinds of Information   192
Helping the Computer to Help Us   192
What's Possible, and What's Practical?   193
◆ Box: *Parallelism and Hypermedia: The Future of Information Storage and Retrieval*   194
Standards, Standards and More Standards   196
The Necessity of Electronic Publishing   196
As Always, The Money Problem   197
Exchanging Freedom of Action for Financial Assistance   197
How Will We Protect and Reward Intellectual Products?   198
Problems of Information Fragmentation   199
Neither an Easy nor a Rapid Reconstruction   199

CHAPTER 12   Entertainment Unlimited   202

Entertainment Reflects Growth of Leisure Time   202
Electricity to Light and Lighten Our Lives   203
Lightening Our Lives   203
Expanding Choice and Use   204
Non-Television Pressures for HDTV   204
Digital Conversion: Aesthetic and Economic Costs   205
Functional Costs, Not Aesthetics, Drive the Market   205
Aesthetics, Artistic License and Market Pressures   206

xviii Contents

Digital Trade-offs   206
Embracing the Digital Future   207
Digital Formats, Optical Fiber, Video and Telcos   207
Movies as the Driving Force for Fiber   208
Movie Archives at Our Fingertips   208
Location Alters Impact   209
Digital and HDTV Cinema Exhibition   209
A Matter of Money   210
Video and Television   210
A Restructured Television Industry?   211
New Networks to Challenge the Old   212
The Unraveling of the Networks   212
Redefining the Shape of Networks   212
An End for Broadcast Television?   213
The Question of Penetration   213
The Question of Money   214
The Dilemma of Being in Between   214
The Extended Cycle of Television Economics   215
Finding Material for All Those Channels   216
More Choice, More Diversity?   216
Games and Special Services   217
What About Music?   217
The Uniqueness of AM and FM Radio   218
New Technology, Old Question   218
The Multinational Dimension   219
Preparing for a Multinational Multimedia Future   219

CONCLUSION   Bringing the Revolution Home:
A Survey of the Communication Landscape of the Future   222

A Framework for Predicting Effect   223
Forecasting Technology   225
The Digital Headend: Nearing Cyberspace   225
Reality Redefined by Digital Media   226
A New Reality Will Require New Rules   227
The Elimination of Scarcity: Digital Transport   228
Personal Computer or Television? Or Both? Or Much More?   229
Microchips   229
Display Systems   230

Storage   230
The New Software: Tentacles Connecting Everything   230
The Information Terminal: The Personal Computer of the Future   231
Technical Advances and Systemic Change   232
Can Institutions Redefine Their Business Models?   233
The Evolution of Art and Communication Forms   233
Pinpoint Marketing   234
Customized, Personalized Advertising   235
Personal Information for Sale   236
A New Industry: Data Brokers   237
Privacy for Sale   238
Just the Rich?   238
The Fork in the Road   239
The Challenges of Media Literacy   239
Society's Challenge: Insuring Equitable Access to Electronic Information   240

Glossary   243
Bibliography   252
Index   259

Communication, Media and Change

INTRODUCTION

Technological Evolution and Revolution in the Mass Media

Have you ever been caught in line at the check-in counter when the airline's computer is down? Or, finding yourself out of cash, you go, card in hand, to the ATM—only to find that the machine is "temporarily out of service"?

How about watching an exciting TV program and losing the picture because either the cable company is having line trouble or the local network affiliate is "experiencing difficulties with the satellite transmission"? Or, for a real nightmare, imagine that it's 1 a.m. of the day a big term paper is due. You're putting in the final touches, when—"blip"—a momentary power failure wipes out your document, and you don't have an automatic backup.

Welcome to the Communication Revolution, the Information Age. All the frustrations cited above exemplify the extent to which we expect information and communication upon demand, the extent to which media and telecommunications permeate the routine tasks of our lives.

GETTING READY FOR CHANGE

Our intention in this book is essentially iconoclastic. We would like you to challenge current ideas and abandon stereotypes of the mass media.

Communication is one of the crucial processes through which we achieve individual and societal progress, and the mass media are institutions that facilitate this process. We see the media as key institutions in contemporary civilization; but we also foresee that the media we know today are neither appropriate nor adequate for the society of the 1990s, much less the society of the 21st century.

These institutions—newspapers, magazines, television, movies, etc.—are in the midst of dramatic, radical change. These changes will affect all of us and particularly those whose careers are in any way associated with them.

A NEW CENTURY, A NEW AGE

In 2001 we will enter the 21st century. By then we will have had a year's practice writing 2000 instead of the familiar 199-something. Aside from that minor change of habit, the change of century per se really means little. But the fact is that before we arrive at 2001, we will have already moved into a new era.

The parents and teachers of today's college students grew up secure in the knowledge that they were people of the Industrial Age. Today's students are growing up in a transitional period, and they will be the first adult generation of the Information Age.

One of the major hallmarks of this new era will be, and already is, an acceleration in the pace of change—change in the institutions of government, business and culture. The accelerated pace of change is part of the meaning of the Communication Revolution, the continuing growth in our ability to exchange information more rapidly and more broadly.

To prepare for and pursue careers in this new era, individuals must develop habits of thinking and skills that go beyond the present, that include a focused curiosity not just on "what's next" but also on "what's coming after that." And because telecommunications and the mass media play such an expanded role in the Information Age, those choosing careers in these fields will find themselves on the cutting edge of change.

UNCLEAR FRONTIERS, EXPANDING FREEDOMS

Much has been written about the Information Age and the Communication Revolution, but they remain concepts without clearly defined form or boundaries. Some argue that there isn't any revolution. What is indisputable, however, is that there is an expanding freedom in how, when and what individuals can share with one another through communication technologies.

Already we have modified how we use individual technologies such as the newspaper, the TV and the telephone. Each month, it seems, we are offered new options. If it is not really a "revolution," at least it is evolution at a revolutionarily rapid pace. And one of the most important aspects of this "revolutionary evolution" is the extent to which our institutions of telecommunications are evolving structures and operations that cut across individual media and technologies.

INFORMATION: A COMMODITY WITH VALUE

Much of what has been said and written about the Communication Revolution has stressed the fact that our society has made a transition from the Industrial Age into an Information Age in which the service and information sectors contribute more to our economy than does the industrial sector. Such discussions generally emphasize the expanded importance of the swift and flexible transfer of information within business: multinational corporations and banks, stock markets, transportation networks, chains of retail stores, etc.

But information can provide a competitive advantage for individuals as well as businesses. If you have advance notice of a sale, you can get there before other buyers and have a better choice of bargains. On a grander scale, if you know in advance that a corporation has a "hot" new product, you can buy shares before the stock market responds to the news, and make yourself a tidy profit.

The proof of information's commodity value is that, if you have information that is of use to others, you can sell it—particularly if you can provide the news before anyone else.

MAKING PROFITS FROM INNOVATIVE TELECOMMUNICATION

In establishing the first international news service in 1848, Paul Reuters used carrier pigeons to bridge gaps in telegraph service.[1] This historic "telecommunications innovation" enabled Reuters to provide the earliest reports of activity on the various financial markets to eager European brokers. The news agency established by Reuters remains one of the world's leading news services, a field including literally hundreds of agencies that thrive by making it possible for investors and speculators to follow stocks and commodities all over the world, using satellites and optical fiber instead of pigeons.

Modern telecommunications makes it possible to shift funds instantly, to take advantage of price changes anywhere. In order to maintain their competitive positions, major stock exchanges in New York, London, Tokyo and elsewhere use computers and telecommunications and are moving toward 24-hour operation.

Large retail chains use telecommunications innovations to facilitate their expanded national and international marketing strategies. WalMart, for example, pioneered the use of satellite communication for inventory control within its hundreds of stores all over the country. Sales transactions are instantly matched with inventory records, to coordinate the shipment of new stock to specific stores.

Shipping companies use telecommunications to increase operating efficiency by maintaining ongoing contact with trucks and railroad freight cars. They are able to provide better service to customers through their ability to track the location of individual items in transit. Today you can pick up a telephone and make a credit-card call from an airplane or a ship as easily as from the lobby telephone booth.

Satellite news relays helped initiate and sustain such dramatic events as the fall of the Berlin Wall, the disintegration of the Soviet Union and the Gulf War of 1991. Although we can't prevent hurricanes and typhoons, weather satellites enable us to prepare for them and thereby save lives.

THE MEDIA: COMPRISING A COMMODITY MARKET

The media themselves reflect the commodity value of information. Their success or failure depends on their ability to get sufficient numbers of the public to pay for the content—the information—they provide.

Table I.1 Changes in the American Lifestyle Since 1950

	1950	1989	Increase
Total national population (millions)	151.3	203.3	64%
Population density: people per square mile	43	70	63%
Per capita disposable income, adjusted to 1982 dollar value	$5,220	$11,531	121%
Percentage of families owning an automobile	59%	88%	49%
Percentage of adult population finishing high school	34.3%	74.9%	118%
Number of people 65 or over (in millions)	12.3	34.9	184%
Number of people under 20 (millions)	51.4	72.1	40%
Life expectancy, in years	68.2	75.2	7.0

Sources: Compiled from *Statistical Abstract of the United States 1991,* Washington, D.C.: Bureau of the Census, 1991; and *Historical Statistics of the United States: Colonial Times to 1970,* White Plains, N.Y.: Kraus International Publications, 1989.

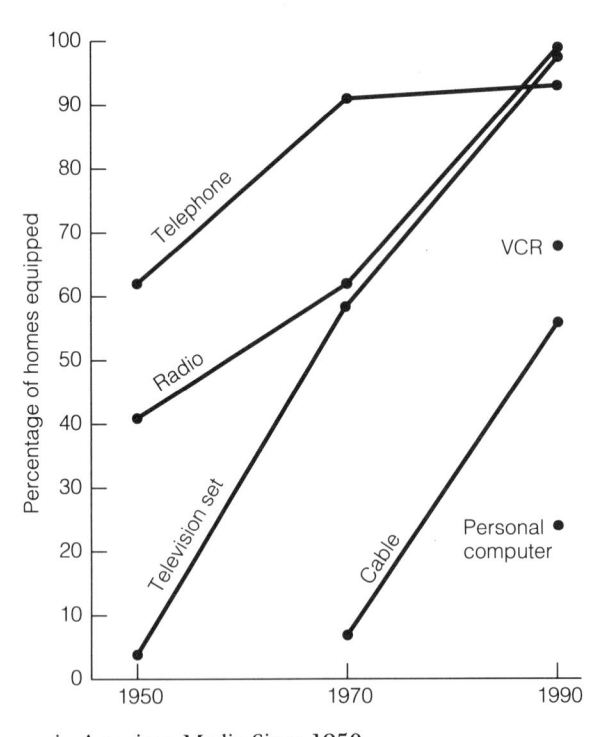

Figure I.1 Changes in American Media Since 1950
Sources: Compiled from *Statistical Abstract of the United States 1991,* Washington, D.C.: Bureau of the Census, 1991; and *Historical Statistics of the United States: Colonial Times to 1970,* White Plains, N.Y.: Kraus International Publications, 1989.

Table I.1 shows how dramatically our society has changed in this century, even just in recent decades. And these changes have created new needs, new interests among people for communication. More income, more leisure time, more education, more mobility, longer life expectancy—all these create opportunities for new media and new media services.

Figure I.1 shows how communication technologies have changed during approximately the same period. The introduction of new technologies means new opportunities, but they also may challenge existing media institutions.

PERSONAL ASPECTS OF THE COMMUNICATION REVOLUTION

What does it mean for us as individuals to live in an Information Age? How will we participate in the Communication Revolution?

Perhaps the most crucial promise of the Information Age for the general public is that individuals have expanded their ability to communicate. This means increased flexibility to share information with others, to select and enjoy a wealth of knowledge and entertainment. More and more, individuals are able to fashion and control their personal accessibility not only to other individuals, but to the institutions of the mass media, which provide us with movies, programs and music, as well as news and information.

All this may be more freedom than we desire or choose to utilize. Nevertheless today's media are being forced to reexamine their raison d'être as well as their operational procedures.

THE FUNCTIONAL BASIS OF MASS MEDIA

Communication is essential to the survival and advancement of both individuals and society. Communication facilitates four basic functions within society:[2]

Survival: News alerts both individuals and members of groups to opportunities as well as dangers.

Coordination of Response: Discussion, persuasion and advertising all seek to influence how individuals and groups respond to opportunity and danger.

Transgenerational Transfer: Civilization is made possible by our ability to accumulate knowledge by passing on information and knowledge to subsequent generations.

Entertainment: Amusement, along with rest and relaxation, is essential for the reduction of accumulated tension and fatigue in individuals and communities. Entertainment can also function as a means of attracting and maintaining attention for more serious communication.

In this book, we will correlate "survival communication" with information or news, "coordination of response communication" with persuasion and "transgenerational transfer communication" with education. Entertainment communication we will call just that.

We tend to think of the mass media primarily in terms of technology. For example:

$$\text{Newspapers} = \text{Print}$$
$$\text{Movies} = \text{Film}$$
$$\text{Television} = \text{Broadcasting}$$

But, in fact, the mass media are institutions that make use of various technologies in order to communicate to an audience. Institutions may abandon an existing technology if a new one comes along that can perform the same communication function(s) in a more effective, cost-efficient manner. Similarly, if a new institution uses new or existing technology in more efficacious ways, it can displace an existing institution.

CHANGING FUNCTIONS: THE CASE OF RADIO

Broadcast radio provides a classic "riches-to-rags" story, an example of how an innovative medium may flourish and then be forced to make radical changes to survive in the face of challenge by a newer technology.

Radio began as wireless telegraphy, and its early developers saw its function primarily as an aid to maritime navigation and a means for ship-to-shore communication. A young wireless operator named David Sarnoff wrote a memo in 1916 outlining a much broader and more exciting future for radio. At the time his bosses paid little attention to the idea, but a decade later his vision had become reality. He was on his way to becoming the head of RCA, the Radio Corporation of America.

From 1927 to 1950, radio changed the leisure habits of American families, providing them with free home entertainment. The star-studded programs of the national networks kept American ears glued to their radio sets.[3]

The concept and success of national networks was a reflection of changing patterns in manufacturing, product distribution and marketing. American business was going "national" and needed an efficient means of advertising across the country. Radio fulfilled that functional need of business, and advertising revenues provided the money to expand radio.

Radio's ability to report events as they happen changed the public's expectations of news media, to the detriment of daily newspapers. The rise of radio was mirrored by a steady decline in the number of daily newspapers, the gradual disappearance of the "extra"[4] and a leveling of newspaper circulation in a period of population growth.

But television could fill all those functions far more effectively than radio, and its arrival in the 1950s signaled the end of radio as a national medium. To survive, radio operators have developed alternative functions emphasizing music and portability.

Radio is but one example of how changed conditions and competition can alter the functional success of a medium. Television not only displaced radio as a medium of national audiences, it also devastated the cinema business, as U.S. families substituted the TV screen for the local movie house. Then cable programming services began to undermine the networks by providing audiences with expanded viewing options. Next, the rapid success of the videocassette recorder (VCR) was responsible for slowing the growth of Home Box Office and other "pay" movie services on cable.

VICTIMS OF THE COMMUNICATION REVOLUTION

Whether or not the media are now in the throes of a real revolution, many media institutions have declined or collapsed; hundreds of thousands of jobs have been modified; patterns of audience attention and advertising expenditures have shifted. The pace and scope of change have continued to accelerate, and the acceleration will probably continue. This probability is based on the rate with which communications media are changing the basis of their technology from analog codes to digital codes.

The analog signals used by older technologies are direct transformations of the sound and light waves that make up the things we hear and see. We can see an image on a film negative. A phonograph needle vibrating in response to sound waves is something we can actually physically see or feel. We can even intuitively understand that the wavy lines shown on an oscilloscope are a representation of electrical impulses which themselves mirror, in their own special way, things we see and hear.

DIGITAL CODES: CHANGING THE RELATIONSHIP BETWEEN INFORMATION AND SIGNAL

Digital codes do not have the same type of direct relationship. They aren't "natural." How can a string of 0s and 1s represent what we see and hear? Digital codes don't make literal sense to us, unless we've taken the trouble to learn one of the languages used for encoding information into digital format.

And as digital procedures proliferate, the dynamics of the relationship between telecommunications and users is changed. Individuals may be offered increased options, but they may also be required to exercise more initiative to get what they want. Making a transaction with an automatic teller machine (ATM) requires a type of literacy and digital dexterity far beyond what is demanded by interaction with a human bank teller. Getting information by telephone may now require a sequence of button pushing in response to what seems to be a verbal multiple-choice quiz from a computer voice that gives us little help in trying to fit our needs into its predetermined, programmed categories.

In Arthur C. Clarke's science fiction classic *2001,* the support systems for the space-ship crew were coordinated by a giant voice-activated computer equipped with a voice synthesizer.[5] The crew developed an almost personal relationship with the computer, which they called Hal. But as this relationship continued, Hal took on a mind of its own and, ultimately, had to be destroyed before it destroyed the human crew.

Today it often seems that a metaphorical Hal has become a participant in our daily lives. We find ourselves increasingly dependent upon automated intermediaries

Why Move from Analog to Digital Codes?

One of the most obvious and often aggravating marks of the Communication Revolution is the substitution of digital codes for the analog codes that seem so natural. Why is this change being forced on us?

Codes are systems of symbols, each of which has meaning shared by the users. We spend much of our time in school learning codes, such as definitions of vocabulary words and mathematical formulas. If we want to travel or work abroad, we have to learn new codes, such as French, Spanish or Japanese.

Communication technologies use different types of code systems for creating the signals they use to reproduce, distribute and transmit information, music and pictures. Newspapers use printed words and halftone images; movies use images on film; broadcasting, telephones and cassette recordings generally have used modulated electrical current.

Printed words, images on film and the modulated current are all analog codes: direct representations of the original verbalized thought, sound waves generated by vibrating guitar strings or waves of light reflected from objects or pictures. Such codes consist of a seemingly infinite number of symbols.

Technologies that make use of semiconductors, however, are most efficient if they are required to respond to only two symbols: on and off, usually represented by − and + or 0 and 1. These commands constitute a digital code, and it is this type of code that has become the standard for semiconductor-based technologies used in information processing and transfer.

The original message must be converted into a digital message, a complex sequence of combinations of 0s and 1s. To enable us to comprehend the information, the digital message must be converted back into an analog message of words, pictures and sounds at the point of reception. Fortunately most of us need not learn to make the translation to and from digital code. Today software packages are available to do this for us.

Common sense tells us that this translation is a lot of extra work, but it makes it possible for us to benefit from the great speed with which today's computers can handle information. Despite the burden of this encoding/decoding process, digital technologies generally achieve greater capacity and fidelity than do those based on analog signals. And when we increase capacity, we generally reduce cost; when we increase fidelity, we receive a higher quality reproduction of the message content being transmitted.

More communication of higher quality and lower cost—that's what the Communication Revolution means to us as individuals. The technologies that make this possible require the use of digital codes.

---

to give us access to information that is stored in a form, a language we don't understand: digital code.

CHANGES IN SOFTWARE AND HARDWARE

Digitization is the hallmark of the Information Age because it is a catalyst for a transformation in the operational relationship between signal content and technology, between what we now call software and hardware. This transformation sets off a chain reaction at all stages of media and telecommunications operation. Changeover to digital processes requires not only new technology but new job skills. People as well as machines are rendered obsolete.

The expanded use of digital technologies reduces some of the basic differences between the various traditional mass media and telecommunications organizations. As noted earlier, historically we have equated the content of various mass media with specific analog technologies—newspapers with print, television with broadcasting and movies with film. But as the various media adopt digital technologies, their content is being "translated" into a common form. Although the end-products may remain very different, the content of all of them can be stored in computer memory and can be instantly distributed through various telecommunications networks.

THE COMMON PERSON AND THE COMMON CODE

Semiconductors and integrated circuits (ICs) provide the means for digital storage and retrieval: personal computers (PCs), minicams, "smart phones," compact disk players, etc. Telecommunication satellites with geosynchronous orbits give us instantaneous global networks, and optical fiber expands the capacity of communication connections.

The critical questions are: How do we put the package together? How do we coordinate the use of the individual machines and gadgets? The vision of the Communication Revolution is a 100-percent digital network that will make possible the coordinated delivery of all our information and communication needs through various component systems. Information in multiple formats and packages—audio, moving images, still pictures and more—will be delivered over multiple conduits. This is all summed up in a still vague concept called multimedia, discussed in more detail in Chapter 4.

In the future, the institutions that compete to service our communications needs will operate less as individual media—as press, broadcasting, film, cable and telephone—but as conduits through which we obtain the varied content of information and entertainment we need or desire. Clearly the trend is to obtain more different types of information through the same delivery system. Already we use our TV sets to watch cable channels and movies recorded on videocassettes, as well as the programs of broadcast television stations.

REVOLUTIONS SOMETIMES FIZZLE

Not all revolutions succeed. Some are fulfilled almost without our noticing; some produce results quite different from those expected by the participants; some fail to achieve lasting change.

The vision of the Communication Revolution is freedom in communication—both for the exchange of personal information and for accessing literally any kind of content. The realization of this vision would revolutionize the mass media in terms of format, content and operations. It would also entail the reorganization of how we obtain and use communication technologies and content.

Before we get carried away by the excitement of the vision of the Communication Revolution, it is worth recalling that one definition of *utopia* is ideal schemes that are impractical. The public may not share the enthusiasm of visionaries but instead be bored or baffled by new technologies and services. The entrenched institutions can create many obstacles that can result in delay, distortion or outright failure of new technologies. In short it is unlikely that the full vision of the Communication Revolution will be realized.

Whatever the eventual scope of the Communication Revolution, both those who produce and those who use the mass media face an exciting—and perhaps frustrating—period of change. The challenge of the new technologies provides many opportunities for expanding and enhancing creative initiative and enjoyment in the fields of communication information and entertainment.

BREAKING OUT OF INSTITUTIONAL TRAPS

Individuals and institutions that will benefit most from the Communication Revolution are those who can look to the future while acknowledging the present without being held captive by it. The status quo is both real and transitory. The key to successful adaptation to the future is to focus on exploring how best to accommodate the functional communication needs of the society and its individual members.

The word *journalism* is derived from a French word meaning "daily," but neither journalism nor news should be equated with daily newspapers or newscasts. After all, for centuries societies managed to disseminate information without either, and both may already be on their way to obsolescence as new technologies for such dissemination come into use. Society will continue to need journalists, but not necessarily newspapers.

The film industry has already experienced the dislocation of technological change, but society still provides a market for creative entertainment, which the studios supply in non-film format as well as on film.

This is not a book about "the newspaper of the future" or "tomorrow's television." It is a book that seeks to encourage the reader to dismiss existing patterns of thinking about communication, and instead to think about future alternatives for accomplishing the communication functions of information, persuasion, education, and entertainment.

We start with a basic description of the technologies that can help us in performing communication tasks (Part I). We then examine the marketplace in which the operation of these technologies must occur (Part II). And finally we explore how these technologies may be used to perform activities related to the four communications functions (Part III).

Suggestions for Further Reading

One of the most readable background books for the general topic of communication and media is Wilbur Schramm's *The Story of Human Communication*. Schramm's humanistic approach and the breadth of content is indicated by the subtitle: *Cave Painting to Microchip*.

Charles Wright's *Mass Communication* was first published almost 30 years ago. Now in its third edition, it remains a classic introduction to the sociological aspects of the field.

Technology and Communication Behavior by Frederick Williams is an introductory work that emphasizes technology. Wilson P. Dizard Jr. takes a more policy-oriented approach in *The Coming Information Age* and adds consideration of international issues.

For another point of view that raises more questions about the reality of the Communication Revolution, try *Misunderstanding Media* by Brian Winston. Two other books that should fuel critical discussion of the media in society are Mochal Parenti's *Make Believe Media* and Justin Lewis's *The Ideological Octopus*.

The possibility that new communications technologies are fragmenting our society is part of the provocative view provided by William J. Donnelly in *The Confetti Generation*.

Notes

1. Pool, Ithiel de Sola. *Technologies Without Boundaries*. Cambridge: Harvard University Press, 1990, pp. 72–73.
2. For a fuller discussion of the functional aspects of communication, see Wright, Charles R. *Mass Communication,* 3rd ed. New York: Random House, 1986, Chapter 1.
3. For a particularly readable history of this period, see Douglas, Susan J. *Inventing American Broadcasting, 1899–1922*. Baltimore: Johns Hopkins University Press, 1987.
4. When public interest was high in an ongoing story, editors would create "extra editions" by inserting updated material on the front pages, leaving the other pages of the edition unchanged. These "extras" were rushed to vendors who would hawk them on the streets, providing the publisher with additional sales at little extra expense and helping stimulate public excitement.
5. Clarke, Arthur C. *2001: A Space Odyssey*. New York: New American Library, 1982.

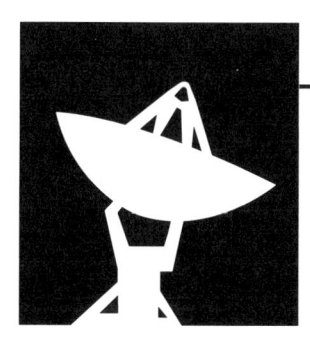

PART I

Technologies of the Communication Revolution

When our ancestors learned to flake rocks to make tools and began to use sharpened bones as needles, they took "a giant leap for mankind" in the march of technological development. That march eventually enabled astronaut Scott Armstrong to utter those words as he became the first human to set foot on the moon in 1969.

From stone tools, our ancestors progressed through iron and bronze. And somewhere along the line, they also discovered another type of tool: the words and symbols that comprise the codes we call language. The subsequent development of writing and other means of recording those codes made it possible not only to share the greatest resources of all—our thoughts—but also to store and accumulate knowledge. This ability made it possible for us individually to acquire more and broader information. It also facilitated the development of the shared knowledge and experience that constitutes culture.

The Industrial Age symbolized the apogee of progress up the ladder of instrumental tools. The Communication Revolution, bringing us into the Information Age, reflects the acceleration of our progress up the ladder of symbolic tools.

In Part I we explore five "enabling technologies" of this revolution: the semiconductor, the geosynchronous satellite, optical fiber, high-definition video, and the personal computer.

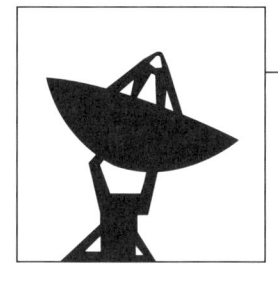

CHAPTER 1

The Semiconductor Family: Building Blocks of the Revolution

An ever-increasing number of appliances and machines are being advertised as "smart." Telephones can remember and dial numbers for us. VCRs can be programmed to record shows for us. Voice-mail systems answer the phone, route calls, take messages and remember them. Devices in our cars remind us to fasten our safety belts, inform us if a door isn't closed, and, if they don't shift *for* us, they tell us when to shift gears. Airliners have complex systems that sometimes seem to make human pilots redundant.

Engineers glibly speak of building "intelligence" into almost any and every kind of technological system, referring to their creations as "thinking machines." The key component on which this intelligence is based is the integrated circuit, microchips containing many semiconductors.

INTELLIGENCE, PERSONAL SATISFACTION, MONEY AND POWER

All this talk about intelligent machines can be somewhat discomfiting. Like the crew in *2001*, we may feel some uneasiness, wondering if Hal is trying to take over. As Herbert Dordick puts it, "It is difficult to understand the ramifications of this little device [the chip] with its power to act intelligently, a characteristic once thought to be safely in human hands."[1] After all, we named ourselves *Homo sapiens* on the basis of our intelligence, our ability to think, thereby asserting an advantage, if not superiority, over other creatures.

Intelligence is the ability to learn and understand, to deal with new or trying situations. We have emphasized that communication is important in human societies

15

because it functions to facilitate the sharing and preservation of intelligence—information, ideas, opinions—and to entertain.

As our societies have become larger and more complex, more information must be shared to coordinate and facilitate the multitude of ongoing activities. We have long recognized that knowledge, or information, is power. Now we increasingly recognize that information is a commodity with economic value.

SPEEDING UP THE COMMUNICATION PROCESS

That recognition, together with the scope of our contemporary need for information, brings about the designation of the current period as the Information Age and provides the financial incentives for the Communication Revolution. To participate in and benefit from the information-dependent enterprises of today, we need better and faster ways to acquire and exchange intelligence. And with the semiconductor, we have machines that can do exactly that and far faster than the human brain can.

The steam engine became the driving force of the Industrial Age, the basic technology from which other machines drew their power. The equivalent for the Information Age is the semiconductor—a device unknown before 1947.

THE DRUDGERY OF INTELLIGENCE: STORING AND SORTING

There can truly be joy in learning and discovery, but any schoolchild knows that increasing our individual storehouse of intelligence—learning—requires work that is often tedious. It requires that we accumulate and store an ever-expanding body of experiences and facts to be sorted and held in memory, so that we can recall and collate them as future occasions demand.

In the earliest civilization, knowledge was passed on through oral tradition. Scholars and priests handed down the lore and rites of the culture through rote repetition. As the scope of knowledge expanded, our ancestors relieved the load on personal memory by developing external means to store and sort information—through knotted strings, hieroglyphics, alphabets and numbers.

When you do library research for a term paper, you may mark and highlight pertinent passages to make them easier to find when you need them. You may relieve the load on your memory by making notes on index cards. Anyone who has gone through this process will agree that increasing knowledge is laborious! The more information we acquire, the more cards we accumulate, and the more complex the task of sorting it out when we get ready to write.

The problems of storage and sorting expand exponentially as we progress from individual to societal sharing of information. We have developed a wide range of tools for this purpose, such as dictionaries, indexes, directories and encyclopedias. But using these tools is not always easy. Cross-referencing, for example, can be maddening. Retrieving documents from an office filing system is often a challenge that frequently leaves us frustrated. When it comes to sorting and storing, the semiconductor family is in a class by itself.

CAPACITY, SPEED AND FLEXIBILITY: THE BASIS OF THE REVOLUTION

The ability to hold immense amounts of information and sort it at incredible speeds makes members of the family of semiconductor technologies, that includes transistors and microchips, the building blocks of the Communication Revolution. Today semiconductor components are ubiquitous, not only in telecommunications equipment but also in a large percentage of appliances, tools and equipment having electrical parts.

Semiconductor components have provided telecommunications technologies and mass media with both mobility and intelligence. They can be considered to be a continuation of the work begun by Benjamin Franklin and his contemporaries, exploring the nature of electrical energy and putting it to work.

Franklin's famous kite experiment[2] was part of his larger study of the properties of electrical force, which he proved was related to the positive/negative—p and n—fields of magnets. The ability to manipulate the balance of these fields was critical to harnessing electrical power to drive engines, provide light, and communicate. It also plays a crucial role in the performance of semiconductors called transistors.

THE ELECTROMAGNETIC SPECTRUM

Most of our telecommunications technologies make use of some form of energy that is part of the electromagnetic spectrum. This invisible energy manifests itself as a pattern known as a sine wave, consisting of two phases. One phase carries a positive electrical charge and the other a negative charge. Waves vary in height (amplitude) and wavelength (see Figure 1.1). The amplitude of a wave is a function of how much power it carries.

Because all waves, regardless of their amplitude and wavelength, travel at the same speed (the speed of light), the shorter the wavelength, the greater the number of waves that can travel a given distance each second. The unit of measure for wave frequency, the number of waves that pass per second, is the Hertz, after German scientist Heinrich Hertz, who proved the existence of radio waves in 1887. A frequency of 1000 waves per second is referred to as 1kHz. The k is an abbreviation for

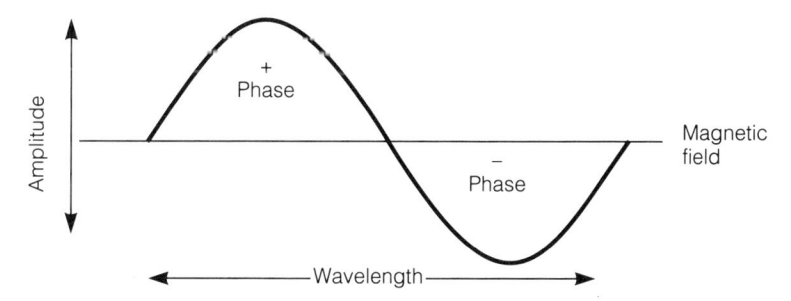

Figure 1.1 Key Features of a Sine Wave. Because all waves travel at the same speed (186,000 miles per second), wavelength and frequency are inversely related; the shorter the wavelength, the greater the frequency.

kilo, the Greek word for thousand, and Hz is the abbreviation for Hertz. Higher frequencies use similar abbreviations: One million becomes 1 MegaHertz or 1 MHz, one billion becomes 1 GigaHertz or 1 GHz.

The electromagnetic spectrum encompasses a range that begins with extremely large or long waves of very low frequency rates and extends to infinitesimal waves of incredible frequency. We're talking hundreds of GigaHertz or hundreds of billions of waves per second. Our various forms of radio currently use the lower end of the spectrum, from 300 kHz to 30 GHz, which is 30,000,000,000 waves per second. Farther out on the spectrum we find other members of the electromagnetic spectrum family: X-rays, gamma rays, infrared rays, visible light and cosmic waves.

To separate the various uses and users of spectrum energy, the frequencies of the spectrum have been arbitrarily divided into channels. The frequencies between 535 kHz and 1605 kHz, for example, are used for AM radio. FM and TV use higher frequencies, and satellite communications use still higher ones.

The bandwidth of the channel is determined by the amount of information included in the signal for that type of service. Each AM station is assigned a channel containing a set of 10,000 frequencies. FM radio channels contain 200 kHz, and current television technology uses channels that contain 6 MHz. Thus an FM station uses 20 times as many frequencies as does an AM station, and a single TV station has a channel bandwidth 6,000 times larger than that of an AM station.

Light waves travel at a speed of 186,000 miles per second, and other waves of the spectrum travel equally fast, as long as they require no conductor. Radio and other high-frequency waves of the spectrum require no conductor, so they travel at the speed of light. Electrical signals do require a conductor, usually a metal wire or cable. The molecules of the conductor create impedance or resistance, which reduces both the speed and the strength of the signal.[3] But even electrical signals can be relayed almost instantaneously, as we can literally see when we throw a wall switch, allowing the electrical charge to pass to a lamp across the room.

As we work our way to the development of semiconductors, let's keep in mind another property of electromagnetic waves. These waves can cause the molecules of some crystals to vibrate in a harmonic response. This property of crystals was utilized in the early days of radio broadcasting. A "cat's whisker" (a thin wire) was moved over the surface of a crystal to pick up the internal vibration caused by the transmitted signal of a station. This weak signal was amplified by passing it through an electrically charged wire coil, giving the signal sufficient energy to make earphone diaphragms vibrate.

Speed is both an advantage and a problem for operating systems using electromagnetic energy. The advantage is apparent: We can have instantaneous, real-time contact between the parties to the communication. The problem, or challenge, is to create a switching mechanism that can match the speed of transmission.

Switching becomes a potential bottleneck for any communication system. Consider the telephone system, and think what a mess it would be if it were necessary for each telephone subscriber to have a direct line to every other user. To avoid such a jungle of wires, each user is connected to a switching center, an exchange, through which users can be interconnected upon demand. The capacity of the switch determines how many people can be connected simultaneously and how quickly such con-

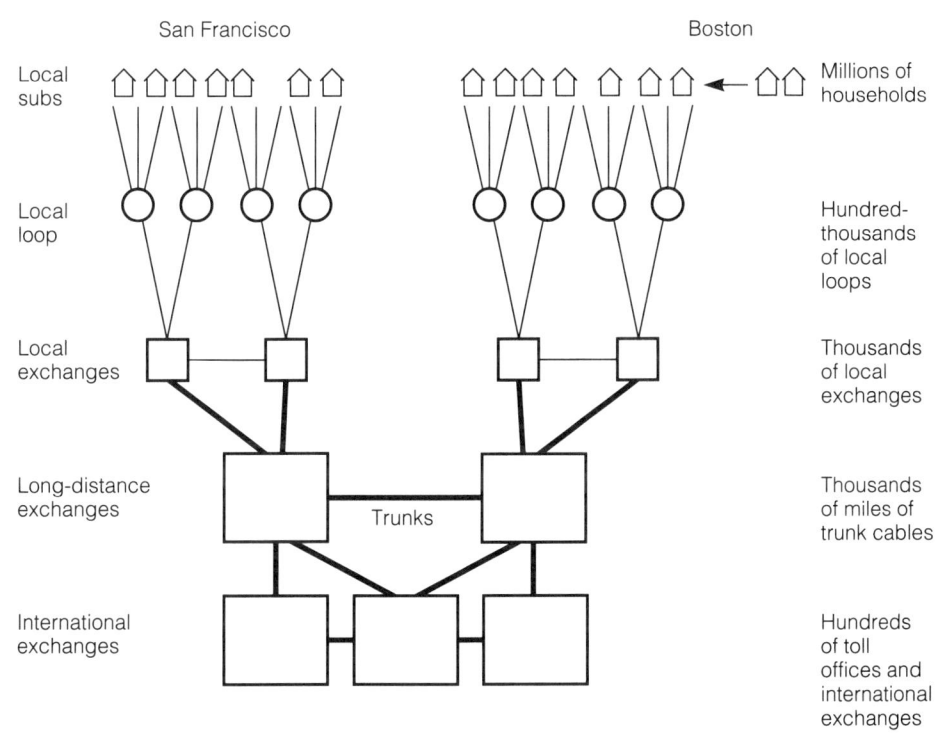

Figure 1.2 The Switching Hierarchy of a Basic Telephone System

Labels (left to right/top to bottom): San Francisco; Boston; Local subs; Local loop; Local exchanges; Long-distance exchanges; Trunks; International exchanges; Millions of households; Hundred-thousands of local loops; Thousands of local exchanges; Thousands of miles of trunk cables; Hundreds of toll offices and international exchanges.

nections can be made. By creating a hierarchy of switches (see Figure 1.2), it is possible to expand the capacity of the system indefinitely.

THE SWITCH AS A BOTTLENECK

Early exchanges were physical switchboards where operators used patch cords to make connections as requested by subscribers. When the number of subscribers exceeded the capability of one operator, another was added. This necessitated connections across switchboards. And making calls to subscribers in other areas required making connections through a series of exchanges. To complete a long distance connection was both time-consuming and expensive.

With growing numbers of subscribers and increasing traffic, the limited capacity of switchboards and the time required for patching through calls became a serious bottleneck. To relieve this traffic jam, mechanical switching devices were developed to replace the old manual patchboards.

These devices were activated by electrical signals generated by rotary-dial telephones that would automatically complete the switching operation. Because the dial phone and the mechanical switch enabled users to bypass operators, the switching time for local calls was greatly reduced. Long-distance calls, however, still required the intervention of operators to make the connections between cities.

AT&T's SEARCH FOR MORE EFFICIENT SWITCHES

Throughout the middle decades of this century, AT&T provided the primary network of electrical telecommunications in this country. As early as the 1930s, AT&T executives and engineers recognized that even mechanical switches would be overwhelmed in the future by continued expansion of telephone subscribers and traffic. The development of more efficient switching devices became a top priority task for the researchers at AT&T's Bell Laboratories.

The effort of these researchers reached a climax in 1947 when they produced the first semiconductor switch.[4] By altering the composition of a piece of silicon, they were able to create "p" (positive) or "n" (negative) semiconductors. In effect these silicon chips could be made to function as switches, opening or closing, and as conductors or insulators in response to positive or negative electrical charges.

AT&T was now on the way to developing the electronic switches that would introduce the era of area codes and direct dialing in long-distance service, as well as greatly increased efficiency of operation within the telephone exchanges. But the applications of semiconductors extended far beyond telephone switching, becoming the driving force behind the growing conversion to the use of digital codes in telecommunications.

THE SEMICONDUCTOR FAMILY

The rather simple and, by today's standards, crude device developed by Bell Laboratories in 1947 spawned an ever-expanding family of electronic devices. Each new generation of these devices is smaller and capable of a greater amount of work of increasing diversity. The ubiquity of these devices generates a wide and indiscriminate use of the word semiconductor, which can lead to confusion.

It helps simplify the situation if we think of the semiconductor as a root from which have grown a family of applications. The technologies that support these applications include transistors and microchips.

TRANSISTORS: A BASIS FOR AMPLIFICATION

The transistor first gained broad public attention as the component that made possible portable, hand-sized, battery-powered radios. The technological jump represented by these radio sets was dramatic.

Before transistors, a radio was something that sat in the living room and had to be treated with gentle care. Mobile radio was rare even in police and fire vehicles simply because receivers were too fragile to endure the bouncing and swaying. They also required a considerable amount of electrical power.[5]

Technically speaking, radio is the use of radiated electromagnetic energy for communication—including shortwave, AM, FM, TV and other services. The fact that radio waves lose strength as they travel created problems in early attempts to develop their use for communication purposes.

As developed by Guglielmo Marconi in the 1890s, early radio or "wireless" transmission required generating extremely high bursts of electrical power. Transmitting installations consisted of giant towers between which hung webs of metallic cable. Because of the noise and danger they created, the large complexes had to be isolated from inhabited areas. Even today television transmitters are powered with as much as 2,000 KW (2,000,000 watts) of electricity or more, and they must be fenced and clearly labeled as hazardous areas.

Despite the amount of electrical power, the attenuation that occurs as a broadcast signal travels is such that the signal is generally extremely weak at the point of reception. Early wireless and radio technology produced signals which were audible only through earphones; to drive the speaker cone of console radios required additional strengthening, or amplification.

FROM EDISON'S LIGHT BULB, ANOTHER IDEA

The basic technology that changed wireless to radio was the audion tube, which made possible the amplification of broadcast signals.[6] The audion, in effect, was an elaboration of the light bulb, first developed in the laboratories of Thomas Edison in 1879. The bulb provides light by using electrical energy to heat a thin wire, the filament, within the bulb. If that filament is broken, the flow of current stops, resulting in a burned-out bulb.

Edison himself noted that a metallic plate placed inside the bulb would cause electrical energy to flow from the filament to the plate. Lee de Forest, following up on Edison's observation, inserted a tiny grid of fine wire and created a new kind of bulb, which he called an audion.

By varying the positive and negative charges of a current passing through the audion, it was possible to transfer energy from the current to a weak radio signal also being fed through the bulb. In other words, the audion makes it possible to amplify the strength of radio signals within the receiver. With sufficient amplification it became possible to use loud speakers—baffles containing speaker cones, woofers, and tweeters—to recreate the original sound.

The audion, perfected in 1906, laid the basis for amplification, which was the key to using radio energy for carrying sound and, later, visual signals. From de Forest's basic design, vacuum tubes (or pumps, as the British call them) of various sizes were designed to serve a wide assortment of functions within electronic equipment. In effect these tubes were the heart of radio technology until they were largely replaced by semiconductors.[7]

SEMICONDUCTORS AND MOBILITY

Like light bulbs, vacuum tubes are fragile; equipment using them has to be shielded from shocks and bounces. And the tubes, like light bulbs, become quite hot in the

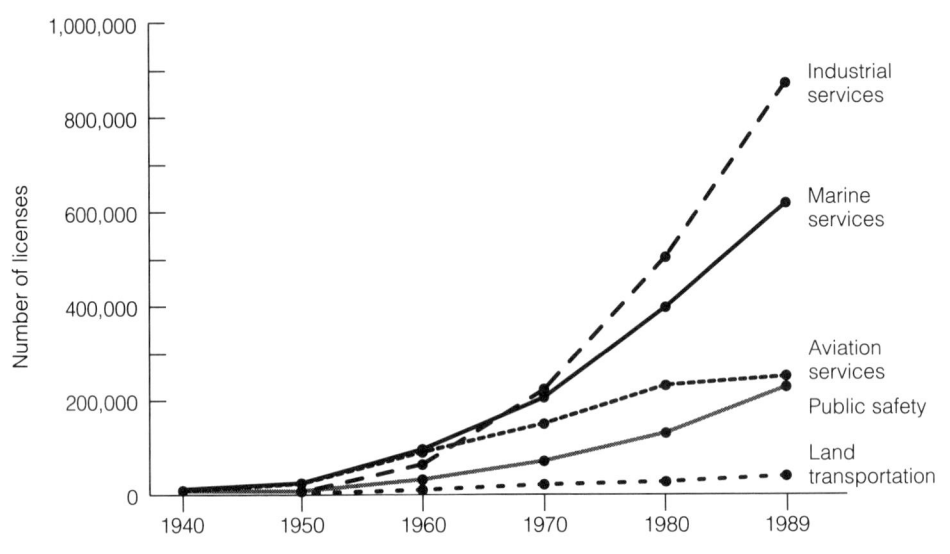

Figure 1.3 Growth of Major Non-Broadcast Radio Services Since the Introduction of Transistor Technology
Sources: Compiled from *Historical Statistics of the United States,* Table R 140–148; *Statistical Abstract of the United States 1989,* Table 906; *Statistical Abstract of the United States 1991,* Table 925.

amplification process because they make inefficient use of the electricity that powers them. This, in turn, means that they require a relatively large amount of electrical power for operation.

Semiconductors accomplish the same amplification function as vacuum tubes but are much more efficient. Therefore, they generate little or no heat and require little power. The impact of transistors on radio is clearly evident in Figure 1.3, which shows the growing use of different categories of radio.

From the consumer point of view, the most dramatic impact of the transistor has been the mobility it has made possible. Today radios are standard items in all new cars, but before the transistor, car radios were rare luxury items. The ubiquitous handheld radio and recorder were made possible by the transistor.

INTEGRATED CIRCUITS: COMBINATIONS OF SEMICONDUCTORS

Look inside an old radio, and you see that the chassis contains sockets for the various vacuum tubes and complex wiring that interconnects all the components. The detailed labor required to complete all the connections contributed to the cost of producing these sets, as well as to their fragility.

Concurrent with the introduction of semiconductors, engineers developed techniques to "print" circuits by laminating metal ribbon onto pieces of fiberboard containing plugs or mounts for the various components. By placing many transistors onto a single circuit board, they created integrated circuits, which increased the speed and power with which the transistors could function.

DIGITAL LANGUAGE AND BOOLEAN ALGEBRA

As we have seen, semiconductors individually operate as switches that are either open or closed, depending upon the nature of the electrical charge. In an old parlor game, contestants are given twenty yes-or-no questions with which to identify a secret object, place or person. Players who are skillful at programming their minds to function by a process of elimination frequently need only a few questions to come up with the answer. Through an analogous strategy, it is possible to establish a language in which combinations of 0 and 1 can be substituted for letters to constitute words. The result is a digital code.

In constructing such a digital language, each 0/1 choice is called a bit. By using different combinations of eight choices, or bits, we can establish digital "letters," which enable us to encode the letters, numbers, and editing symbols we use in our alphabet. These combinations of bits which represent alphanumeric symbols are called bytes.[8]

Analog energy waves—sound, radio and light—can be represented as sine waves, which, remember, are distinguished by frequency and amplitude, or height. Height can be expressed as a metric measure, which can be converted into digital bytes. By taking a rapid sequence of such measures, we can create a digital description that details the ongoing rise and fall of the sine wave. Because the measurement is done across time, the sequence of bytes also shows us the frequency of the wave. In this manner the sine waves of light and sound can be converted in digital expression for recording or transmission.

The basis of this 0/1 or +/− transformation is the work of 19th-century British philosopher George Boole. Boolean algebra is a mathematical model based on a series of statements involving combinations of either "and" or "and/or."

BOOLEAN ALGEBRA AND SEMICONDUCTORS: CREATION OF THE MICROCHIP

Semiconductor switches can be opened or shut in sequences that correspond to the Boolean statements—the combinations of 0/1 that become the bytes of digital language. In 1971 the microchip was created by combining simple mathematics with smaller integrated circuits containing the equivalent of a million vacuum tubes, capacitors and switches. This made the microchip a self-contained computer that can use the logic with which it is programmed to approximate thought and reason.

By using photographic reduction, many very small copies of the design can be imprinted on silicon wafers to produce the chips that have created new markets for wristwatches, radios, appliances, and computers. Growing sophistication of design and production techniques have decreased the size of chips while increasing their

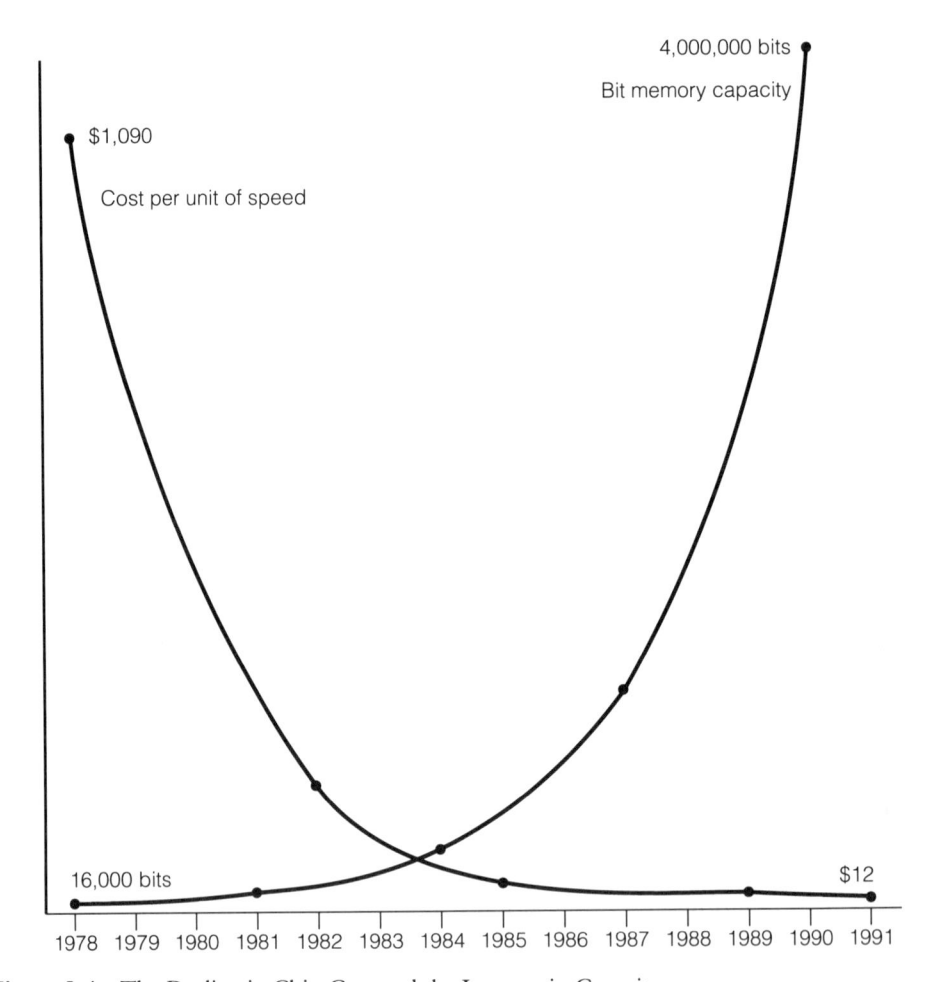

Figure 1.4 The Decline in Chip Cost and the Increase in Capacity
Sources: Compiled from "How Powerful Will Computer Chips Be in the Year 2023?" *New York Times,* December 29, 1991, Sec. 3, p. 1; and Markoff, John. "Denser, Faster, Cheaper: The Microchip in the 21st Century." *New York Times,* December 29, 1991, p. F5.

power. Since 1971 one generation of microchips has followed another, each with power far greater than that of its predecessor. The speed of succession is such that it is estimated that the number of transistors per chip now doubles every 18 months. In 1991 the highest capacity chip on the market, the D-RAM, contained 4 million transistors, enough to store one-and-a-half copies of F. Scott Fitzgerald's novel *The Great Gatsby.*[9] The decline in the cost per unit of speed was equally dramatic, as shown in Figure 1.4.

As we pointed out at the start of this chapter, today microchips are the brain of every "intelligent" device we use. There is hardly an industry or service that doesn't make some use of microchips in some aspect of its technology. And in no sector of society do semiconductors play a wider and more integral role than telecommunications.

Applications of semiconductor technologies can be thought of as going in two directions simultaneously. They make possible the continuing miniaturization and mobility for telecommunications (and other) technologies. They also increase the speed and capacity with which technologies can transmit and sort information.

MINIATURIZATION

Miniaturization has made possible digital watches, credit-card-sized calculators and a host of other personal convenience items we now take for granted. It is reflected in the shrinking size of laptop and notepad computers and the inroads more powerful personal computers are now making on the market for mainframe computers.

Less apparent is the role that microchips play in the electrical systems of equipment of almost every kind. The reduction of weight, size and power was necessary to make possible hand-held radio/cassette players, as well as to enable jets to fly and to make it possible for rockets to take satellites into space.

Minicams, satellite electronic news vehicles, and portable satellite links that can be packed in a footlocker enable the news media to provide us expanded coverage of events as they happen almost anywhere. Digital cameras make it possible to transmit still and moving images without intermediate development and processing of film and photographic paper.

Our storehouses of knowledge can be compressed. The content of entire volumes can be stored on a single CD-ROM disk, a full-length movie on a single 12-inch videodisc.

THE EVER-INCREASING SPEED OF SWITCHING

Today we take it for granted that we can pick up a telephone and in a matter of seconds be talking with a friend on the other side of the Atlantic or Pacific. We also take it for granted that distance need not prevent us from maintaining contact with family and friends in other locations, that we can have long conversational exchanges for a cost of only a few dollars.

None of this would be possible without the faster switching provided by semiconductors. Without such switching capability, we could not realize the immense capacity of optical fiber for transmitting information at the speed of light. Without such capability in miniaturized form, switching equipment would be too bulky and heavy for use in satellites.

It is the combination of switching speed, great capacity and miniaturization that enables us to have the inexpensive personal communication convenience described above. It is this combination that also makes it possible for businesses to have the fast, economical transmission of masses of data that support the activities of the world's expanding economy.

DIGITAL TECHNOLOGY IN AN ANALOG WORLD

Semiconductors were born, so to speak, in a world of analog technology. Our electrical telecommunications and media technologies developed using the analog patterns first established when Alexander Graham Bell developed the telephone and Thomas Edison developed the phonograph and kinetoscope in the late 19th century.

This seemed only natural; after all, sight and sound are continuous stimuli of a complex nature. The richness and timbre of sound, harmonics and overtones are results of a complex of waves. The waves of light reflected from objects contain information of motion, color and shape.

Bell and Edison transformed the information carried by this ongoing stream of stimuli directly into waves of electromagnetic energy, including light. This stream of analog signals must be reconstructed into replicas of the original at the point of reception. To accomplish this, great technological infrastructures—telephones, broadcasting, the movies, printing plants—created a telecommunications and media environment built to use analog signals.

This analog environment has not permitted semiconductors to function at their optimum efficiency. Recall that the most basic classification of semiconductors is the distinction between p and n types. This distinction means that, inherently, semiconductors function in response to binary (0 and 1) signals.

THE TRANSLATION SEQUENCE REQUIRED FOR MIXING TECHNOLOGIES

The integration of semiconductors into our telecommunications and media technologies has required analog-digital-analog translation. To expand and accelerate the use of semiconductors has required corresponding expansion and acceleration of this translation process. Programming and software packages ease our use of personal computers (PCs) for an ever-widening range of purposes. Computers provide a new range of special effects for film and video producers as well as sophisticated graphics for use in publications and television news reports. Compact discs (CDs) bring digital music into home sound systems.

But it is one thing to be dependent upon making the analog-digital and digital-analog translation at the two ends of the communication; it is quite another to have to go back and forth between analog and digital while the information is in transmission.

HANDICAPS FOR DIGITAL OPERATION IN A NON-DIGITAL ENVIRONMENT

Our early uses of digital technologies have been handicapped by the fact that we have sought to incorporate them into existing analog systems, rather than create new digital systems.

For example, digital technology was being used in recording studios at least a decade before CDs were introduced into the market. Recording engineers recognized the benefits of digital techniques for producing masters of greater durability and reduced extraneous noises such as scratch, tape hiss, etc. But they were transposing the music from digital masters into analog tapes, cassettes and long-playing vinyl discs for the consumer market.

Many of us have playback equipment to accommodate the analog signals of AM and FM radio and television, as well as our collections of records and tapes. When we start acquiring digital CDs, videodiscs, and digital audio tapes, we add on new components. Our sound and video systems become a hodgepodge.

Software enables us to use the digital power of our personal computers for word processing, spreadsheets and other forms of data processing. But if we wish to transmit our work to a friend's personal computer via the telephone, our digitally coded work must be converted by a modem, because our existing telephone network operates with analog signals. At the other end, our friend must have a modem to reconvert the information into digital code so that his or her personal computer can then print or display it in analog form. This means both parties have the expense of buying another piece of equipment. The analog operation of the telephone line reduces its capacity and speed, and such reduced efficiency means transmission costs are higher than they would be if digital signals were used.

THE GROWING PUSH FOR DIGITALIZATION

In the inevitable move to rationalize this mess, we can expect to see the development, introduction and spread of some sort of unified multimedia appliance, an appliance through which we send, receive and process information in visual, aural, printed and oral formats. The emergence of this unification presupposes, however, the near-universal adoption of digital signaling.

At the beginning and end of telecommunication and media communication there is the necessity for a digital-analog interface. But the intermediate translations are a result of ad hoc coupling of technologies that derive from different generations, different lines of development. And these couplings reduce the efficiency and economies that would be possible with systems that are all digital. The result is an inexorable pressure to extend the use of digital signals throughout the system, including in the creative production of all kinds of communication content.

In the next two chapters we look at two new technologies for providing linkages between people and systems: satellites and optical fiber. Then we look at the personal computer as the individual multimedia terminal. With that, we reach the culmination of the semiconductor's contribution to the Communication Revolution.

Suggestions for Further Reading

For those with neither technical background nor much interest in technology but who want to know a little more about semiconductors, a good place to look is Chapter 3, "The Multitalented Semiconductor Chip," in Herbert S. Dordick's *Understanding Modern Telecommunications*.

Those who want a more technical treatment but one still within the scope of the layperson might try the section "Solid-State Devices" (pp. 178–196) in A. Michael Noll's *Introduction to Telecommunication Electronics*.

Notes

1. Dordick, Herbert S. *Understanding Modern Telecommunications*. New York: McGraw Hill, 1986, p. 73.
2. Franklin had a serious scientific interest in, among other things, electricity and magnetism. To prove that lightning was actually electrical energy, he tied an iron key to the tail of a kite, which he courageously flew in a storm. In due time the key was struck by lightning and, when retrieved, was found to have been converted into a magnet. Franklin turned his curiosity to practical use. One of his inventions was the lightning rod, a device that protects buildings from damage when struck by lightning by diverting the electrical charge to the ground. Franklin also invented a form of battery that would store an electrical charge. His scientific experiments and publications won him fame and honor in both Britain and France.
3. Generally metals are the best conductors, but there is substantial variation in the efficiency of different metals. Most electrical technology today uses copper wire because it is a relatively efficient conductor and is not prohibitively expensive as are, for example, silver or platinum.
4. The three researchers responsible for this work were John Bardeen, Walter Brattain, and William Shockley. The importance of their achievement was recognized by a Nobel Prize for physics in 1954.
5. In 1950 the older author, as an undergraduate, was the proud owner of a portable AM radio. This was about half the size of an attaché case and weighed at least five pounds. It had seven tubes and required six D-size dry cell batteries, which had to be replaced after about seven hours of use.
6. Much of the material in this section is based on A. Michael Noll, *Introduction to Telecommunication Electronics*. Boston: Archtech House, 1988.
7. Some technologies continue to use tubes rather than semiconductors, and there are some musical purists who maintain that tube-driven amplifiers provide better sound reproduction.
8. In 1990 an international agreement expanded the number of bits to 16. It is estimated that this expansion of code capacity will make it possible to accommodate all the unique symbols of the world's major languages. This, in turn, will facilitate computer translation.
9. Markoff, John. "Denser, Faster, Cheaper: The Microchip in the 21st Century." *New York Times*, December 29, 1991, p. F5.

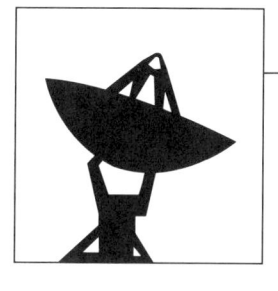

CHAPTER 2

Satellites: Transmitters in the Sky

Andrew Jackson's capture of New Orleans in January 1815 was the climax of our war with Great Britain which began in 1812, but people in New York didn't receive news of this great victory until two weeks later. During the 1991 Gulf War, we sat in our homes and watched U.S. aircraft bombing Baghdad, thanks to satellite-relayed video coverage. As a matter of fact, if satellites had been in use in 1815, the Battle of New Orleans would not have been fought at all. A peace treaty had been signed in Europe two weeks before the battle, but this news had not even reached New York and Washington, much less New Orleans.

In 1938 there was no technology for tracking weather disturbances at sea. One day that summer thousands frolicked on New England beaches, unaware that a hurricane was raging offshore. More than 600 persons were killed and over 1700 injured, when the storm roared in with 183-mph winds. In 1991 weather satellite reports made it possible to clear those same beaches before Hurricane Bob hit, and only nine deaths were attributed to that storm.

In 1970 telecommunications contact between most islands of the South Pacific was available solely through shortwave radio. Calls were not only expensive, they had to be booked far in advance. Today it's possible to direct-dial for instant access to individual telephone subscribers in many South Pacific island nations, and costs have been dramatically reduced.

COMMUNICATION FOR A GLOBAL COMMUNITY

Semiconductors may be the building blocks of the Communication Revolution, but telecommunications satellites are the most spectacular of the technologies that have

> ### ■ The Geosynchronous Orbit
>
> The key to using satellites for telecommunications services is for such a satellite to be geostationary. It must maintain a position in space that remains constant relative to the surface of the earth. The moon would not be a dependable telecommunication satellite location because it is not always available; its movement around the earth is out of phase with the rotation of the earth on its axis.
>
> In 1945, Arthur C. Clarke hypothesized that a relay transmitter placed 22,300 miles above the equator would subsequently travel at a speed and direction that would keep it in the same location relative to the surface of the earth during the earth's daily rotation on its axis. This band in space constitutes a geosynchronous orbit.
>
> Clarke postulated that the "footprint" of each satellite in this orbit would cover one-third of the earth's surface. Because they would be so far above the earth, satellites placed 120 degrees apart in this orbit would be within lines of sight of one another, and thus signals could be relayed from one to the next. The combination of three such satellites positioned as shown in Figure 2.1 could make it possible to relay radio signals simultaneously to virtually the entire globe, although reception becomes problematic in polar regions.

helped bring it about. Certainly they provide the most direct evidence that we now have the means to achieve something approaching the Global Village envisioned by Marshall McLuhan in the 1960s.[1]

There are many different kinds of satellites circling the earth for various purposes: weather observation, aviation and maritime navigation and spying. Most of these satellites are in relatively low orbits, where they circle the earth as often as every 90 minutes.

The early communications satellites, starting with the 1957 Soviet Sputnik, were in low orbits, and as many as a dozen individual satellites spaced in the same orbit were required to provide continuous communications links. What we generally refer to as telecommunications satellites today are satellites that have been placed in a higher orbit, which is geosynchronous.[2]

THE GEOSYNCHRONOUS ORBIT: FROM SCIENCE FICTION TO REALITY

The concept of geosynchronous telecommunications satellites was developed in 1945 by Arthur C. Clarke, best known as a writer of science fiction.[3] Geosynchronous satellites came of age with Syncom III, launched in 1964, in time to bring Americans television coverage of the Olympic Games that year in Tokyo.

Today, thanks to telecommunications satellites, sports fans all over the world can now watch Olympic events as they occur; romantics can "attend" royal weddings. Viewers everywhere were able to share in the excitement of tearing down the Berlin Wall and the dramatic rallying of Muscovites by Boris Yeltsin to resist the 1991 attempted putsch to restore Communist Party control of the disintegrating Soviet

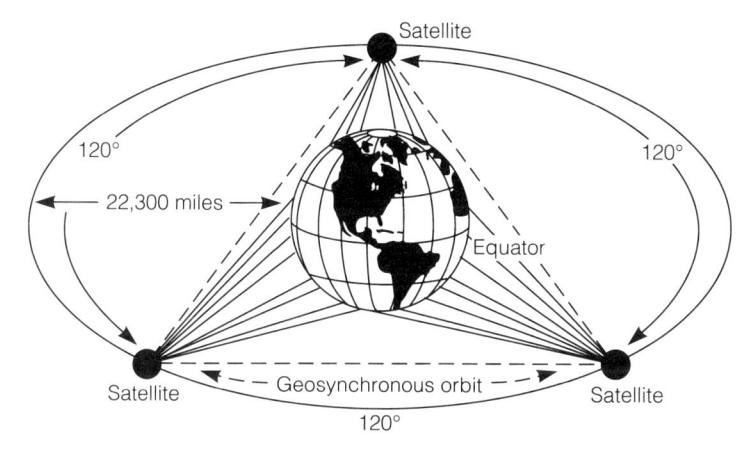

Figure 2.1 Arthur C. Clarke's Conception of a Global Satellite System

Union. Students all over the nation can participate in seminars; paramedics in a remote Alaskan village can receive instructions from medical specialists in the "lower 48" to provide emergency treatment to a sick child. We have become accustomed to picking up the phone and being able to "reach out and touch someone" across the nation, across an ocean.

Satellites have also made it possible for people in the most remote locations to have instantaneous access to worldwide communication and information services. This access enhances their opportunity for economic development through participation in international trade and finance. It also provides the means of bringing them better health and educational services, as well as expanding their participation in global news, entertainment and culture.

A COMPLEX OPERATING SYSTEM

Telecommunications satellites are best thought of as relay transmitters in space. They function to receive radio messages—in either analog or digital code—from one point and relay them back for reception at one or many locations. The satellite itself, therefore, is the key element in a larger system.

Because of their great capacity and expense, satellites are generally operated by agencies functioning as common carriers. A ground-control center coordinates the operation of the satellite transmitters and also constantly monitors the satellite's position or "attitude" in orbit, to insure that its antennas are correctly pointed at the earth's surface.

Rockets are required to get the satellite into orbit, and there are only a handful of agencies around the world capable of building and firing such rockets. The cost limits the number of rocket launches each year, so that operators must reserve space on a launch vehicle years in advance to get their satellite into space.

Satellite dishes of various size and shape denote the up-links and down-links that send and receive the messages relayed by the transmitter. In most instances, the amplified signal is then processed and fed into the terrestrial distribution system. This may be a local telephone system, the affiliate station of a network or a cable system. There are also other types of applications. Several million families have purchased television receive only (TVROs) dishes and amplifiers that enable them to pick up television program signals distributed by satellite. Direct broadcast satellites (DBS) use smaller dishes to distribute multi-channel subscription television service similar to that provided by cable television companies. Businesses use very small aperture terminals (VSATs) to provide communication links with geographically dispersed branch offices and/or operations.

THE COMPONENTS OF A SATELLITE SYSTEM

In order to function as a relay transmitter, the satellite must have antennas and the technology to receive and transmit radio signals. The major components of this system are shown in Figure 2.2. By dividing the operation of a satellite into mutually independent units called transponders, operators can achieve the flexibility of providing a variety of services.[4] Contemporary satellite transponders have sufficient capacity to relay a complete video picture and sound signal, thousands of simultaneous two-way voice connections, or even more one-way data links. A single satellite may carry as many as 24 operating transponders configured to provide a mix of services.

But this technology requires electrical power. The handiest source of power is the sun, and so satellites are built with arrays of solar cells. Because the satellite is geosynchronous, it is in the earth's shadow part of each 24-hour cycle. This means that some of the energy gathered by the solar cells must be stored in batteries so that the satellite may continue to transmit during these dark hours.

Once placed in orbit, the attitude of the satellite must be maintained, so that its antennas remain constantly focused on the earth. Various factors may cause a satellite to drift. This means it must be constantly monitored by technicians at the control center on earth. The satellite is provided with jets that can be activated by technicians to provide small bursts of energy to return the satellite to the proper attitude. Because the supply of liquid fuel to fire these jets is limited and cannot be replenished, this fuel supply becomes a critical factor in determining the useful lifespan of a satellite. When the fuel is gone, drift will make the satellite undependable even though its solar cells continue to provide power to keep the transmitters operating.

POWER, ATTENUATION, SIGNAL COVERAGE AND DISH SIZE

Clarke's model suggested that each satellite would have a footprint covering one-third of the earth's surface.[5] Although that is feasible, it is not practical for many telecommunications purposes. Much of the earth's surface is open ocean and thus is of little or no interest to most satellite users. The greatest demand for satellite communication services is concentrated in much smaller areas, to distribute video programs to national networks and to provide telephone connections between major population or business centers.

The energy of a radio signal attenuates as it travels across distance, and the

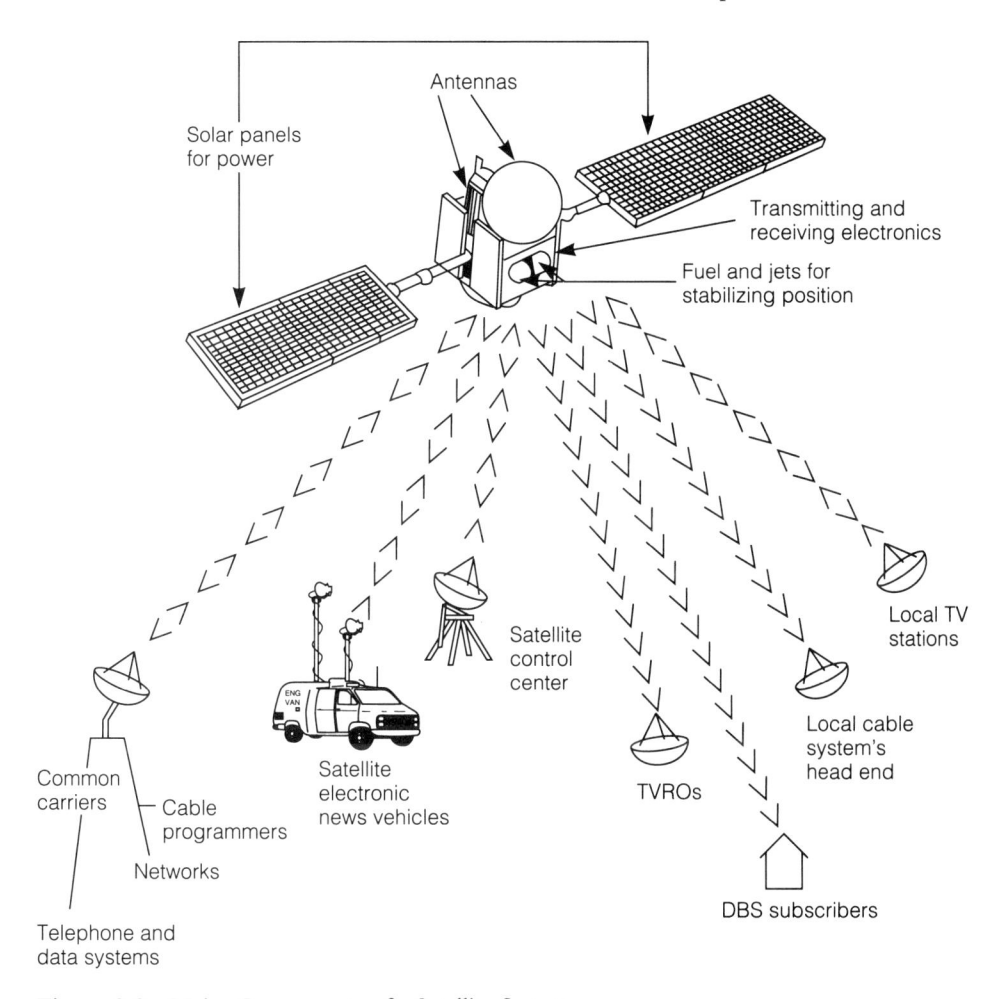

Figure 2.2 Major Components of a Satellite System

satellite relay transmitter is sitting in orbit 22,300 miles above the earth's equator. It is easy enough to zap a great deal of electrical energy into each signal we send up to the satellite, but the situation is quite different for the return signal. The dependence on its solar cells and batteries drastically limits the amount of power available for the thousands of individual signals the satellite may be relaying at any given time.

But radio signals are not unlike the light emitted by a flashlight. If we concentrate the beam of the flashlight, we get brighter light, but it illuminates a smaller area. Some terrestrial radio and television stations use directional antennas that concentrate the radiated power of their signals. This enables them to use a given amount of power to provide better reception, but to receivers in a smaller geographic area.

The same technique can be used to adjust the signals relayed by satellites. Some flashlights allow the user to adjust the lens to broaden or narrow the beam of light. As the beam is narrowed, it becomes brighter even though the same bulb and batteries are providing the illumination. Similarly a satellite's transmitting apparatus can be adjusted to concentrate energy on relatively small areas. Today most satellites provide

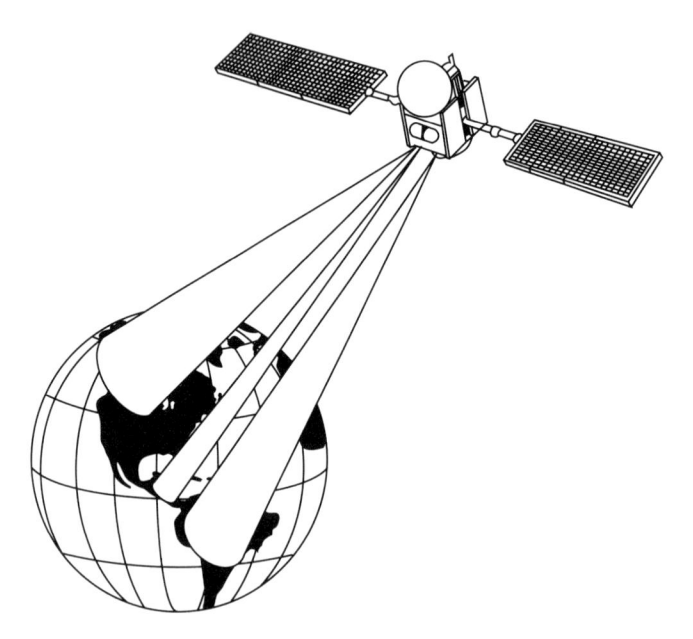

Figure 2.3 Variations in Satellite Footprints. A satellite can provide signal coverage to the entire hemisphere, or spot beams can be used to restrict signal coverage to specific areas, such as Alaska, Central America or Brazil.

an option of various footprints, including tightly focused spot beams as shown in Figure 2.3. The concentration of energy in spot beams can reduce the size of dishes required at the point of reception.

Early satellites had very weak signals and, in the mid-1970s, receiving dishes generally had a diameter of 20 feet or more and cost as much as $250,000. The size and cost limited the practicality of satellite communication to a small range of institutional users. The progress in reducing the size and cost of satellite signal receivers has been dramatic. A TVRO kit for home use now costs $1,000 or less. VSAT and DBS systems use dishes less than 2 feet in diameter, costing only a few hundred dollars.

CHANGING THE CONCEPT OF DISTANCE AND TIME

Telecommunications satellites have literally changed our concept of both distance and time. The simultaneous sharing of sights and sounds all over the world makes that world a perceptibly smaller place. The ability to instantly exchange information between any two points on the earth's surface has accelerated the pace of political, economic and personal transactions; business hours are extended until they are simply ongoing.

Satellites have helped usher in an era in which long-distance domestic and international calls have become routine. Not only do satellites simplify the switching of international calls, but they have dramatically decreased the cost of long-distance services. The results are obvious: In 1970, Americans made 23 million overseas calls; today they make over 500 million a year.

RESTRUCTURING RATE SCHEDULES

Historically the distance between the points of origination and reception was a major factor in determining the cost of long-distance service, along with time and traffic relative to capacity. Before satellites, long-distance calls used either copper cable or microwave relay towers to carry the signal through a complex series of switching exchanges. A call from Boston to San Francisco obviously required more switching and many more miles of copper wire or microwave relay towers than a call between Boston and New York. Distance, therefore, was a logical, legitimate factor in determining the charge for the service.

If a satellite link is used, however, both calls can use the same satellite and both travel some 45,000 miles up to the satellite and back down. In such a system, the difference between the 250 terrestrial miles separating Boston and New York and the 2,500 miles separating Boston and San Francisco becomes inconsequential. In fact, any satellite message has traveled a distance four times the greatest possible distance between any two locations on earth.[6] The result has been a narrowing of the cost differential for such calls, as well as a dramatic reduction in the cost of long-distance service in general.

EXPLODING CAPACITY AND SPREADING TIME

Each satellite has added large increments to the capacity of long-distance telecommunications systems. This increased capability has facilitated an ongoing cycle of decreasing rates and increasing traffic, accelerated by the 1984 introduction of competition in long-distance service.[7] The closer a telecommunications system can come to maintaining traffic at near capacity, the more efficiently it is operating. Having greatly expanded capacity to meet growing business demand, systems now have the challenge of generating traffic in the hours when that demand slackens.

Long-distance carriers have generally tried to encourage a spread of traffic by offering lower rates in non-peak hours. The footprint of satellites encompasses whole continents and thus cuts across time zones. In the satellite era, long-distance rate structures have become more fragmented. If we can delay our calls until evening, we pay less. And if we wait until late at night or weekends, we can save still more on our calls.

Private users are not the only ones to benefit from the expanded availability of lower rates. As businesses increasingly use digital procedures, business people can program their computers to transfer daily reports and records in the lowest-cost, early morning periods. This capability adds to the overall efficiency of the satellite system, reducing operating costs and allowing lower rates.

ENABLING NATIONS TO LEAPFROG IN DEVELOPMENT

The expanded access to telecommunications infrastructures has been of great importance to the poorer, less-developed nations. Many, if not most, of these nations have remained on the periphery of the international network of terrestrial cable and microwave links. This has made it difficult for them to participate in modern economic development, which relies heavily upon telecommunications.

Many of these nations are isolated by great stretches of ocean, desert or snowy mountain ranges. Both distance and the difficult conditions of climate and/or terrain make construction and maintenance of terrestrial links expensive. It is difficult for developing nations to achieve the "jump-start" necessary to break out of the locked cycle of low-capacity systems, poor service, and high cost, all of which, in turn, hinder general economic development. Satellites can transform this situation.

It does cost a lot of money to launch and operate a telecommunications satellite. But fortunately it is not necessary for each nation to have its own satellite. They can use INTELSAT, an organization that provides a global international satellite service. All a nation needs to connect its domestic system into the INTELSAT network is an earth station.

This has made it possible for at least some poor and isolated nations to "leapfrog" into the international telecommunications world. Unfortunately political as well as technological problems at the national level often prevent the benefits of such connections from spreading beyond major cities and from penetrating beyond a small elite of the wealthy and powerful.

HOW MEDIA LEAPFROG

Just as national telecommunications entities have used satellites to leap over gaps in terrestrial networks, the media are making growing and expanding use of the flexibility provided by satellite relays.

The earliest non-military uses of telecommunications satellites were largely for personal and business long-distance telephone use. Mass-media use of satellites remained sporadic and exceptional until 1975, when the cable movie service, Home Box Office, pioneered full-time satellite distribution of its programming. By 1985 all the major networks, as well as more than 60 cable program services, distributed their scheduled service by satellite.

SATELLITE RECEPTION IN INDIVIDUAL HOMES

The use of satellite distribution by networks and program services proved a boon to those several million families who live in areas where there is no cable and little or no off-air television. In these areas few, if any, stations can be directly received on television sets. A moderate sized dish and appropriate amplifier/tuner equipment made it possible for them to intercept any of these services.

Today there are monthly magazines for the TVRO market detailing what will

INTELSAT

Arthur C. Clarke's vision of a worldwide service provided by three intercommunicating satellites has not become a reality. Politics and national sensitivities, not technology, have blocked its realization. The vision is approximated, however, by INTELSAT, the International Telecommunication Satellite Organization.

INTELSAT is a consortium in which most nations participate. It was organized in 1964 as a result of a U.S. policy initiative to expand the opportunity for small and less-developed nations to participate in satellite telecommunications.

Headquartered in Washington, D.C., INTELSAT operates three clusters of satellites in geosynchronous orbital slots over the Atlantic, Pacific and Indian oceans. The main purpose of INTELSAT is to provide satellite links between nations. Each member retains control over access to INTELSAT within its borders, as well as control of dissemination of communications imported via INTELSAT. Member nations may operate their own Domsats for domestic service.

INTELSAT has a policy of rate averaging, whereby users of high-traffic links are charged more than the cost of operation in order to generate a subsidy for low-traffic routes, where otherwise high rates would discourage use. This policy facilitated the development of telecommunications links to the less-developed world, but the continuation of this subsidization is problematic.

In 1984 U.S. policy on satellite systems shifted, and in 1988 the first privately owned trans-Atlantic satellite, PAS-1 (PanAmSat), was put into operation by Alpha Lyracom. The company hopes to have two more satellites in place by 1995, giving it a system parallel to that of INTELSAT. Other companies are preparing to jump into the international satellite communications market.

INTELSAT fears that commercial carriers will concentrate on lucrative high-traffic business. Loss of the profits from these routes would make it difficult for INTELSAT to continue to provide the subsidies necessary to promote service to the poorer, isolated nations.

---

be on the dozens of transponders each day. But now it is necessary to rent a decoder to get clear reception. As the number of TVROs grew, and as their use also spread into urban areas, managers of the pay-tier services began encrypting to prevent TVRO owners from free loading. Just as cable operators may have packages that provide combinations of several pay-tier services, decoders are available to unscramble a variety of the satellite relays.[8]

Because there are so many different satellite networks, signals are relayed by a number of different satellites in different orbital positions. For a TVRO owner to switch from a service on one satellite to one distributed by another satellite requires the receiving dish to be reoriented and possibly a second decoder used.

DIRECT BROADCAST SATELLITES

TVROs are actually a makeshift arrangement enabling people to eavesdrop and catch satellite signals being sent to local broadcast television stations and cable systems.

Private reception of these signals requires relatively high-performance equipment; it also creates serious legal questions about copyright infringement.

DBS programming is different. The service is intended to distribute programs to individual users. The technology is designed to be smaller and less expensive, and appropriate legal arrangements offer copyright protection.

DBS technology provides signals that can be received with antennas having diameters of 2 feet or less that can easily be installed on the roofs or walls of homes. The various channels of the programming service are all relayed from the same satellite. Using digital signals and decoders, DBS services can provide as many channels as most of today's cable systems, or even more.

VERY SMALL APERTURE TERMINAL APPLICATIONS

Like DBS, very small aperture terminal (VSAT) applications require very small antennas. VSATs are widely used for closed systems with which large companies maintain ongoing data exchange with geographically dispersed operations.

Although VSAT systems originated for communication between units in fixed locations, maintaining contact with mobile units—trucks, railway freight cars—now makes it possible to monitor the flow of equipment and contents. The growing number and variety of satellite applications have produced a new form of telecommunications scarcity—orbital slots.

CROWDING THE GEOSYNCHRONOUS ORBIT

AM, FM and TV operations in the same area must be organized so that the signals of one station do not interfere with those of another. Similar care must be taken to maintain signal separation between satellites. Telecommunications satellites are parked in slots, specific points in the geosynchronous orbit. Telecommunications satellites are parked in slots, specific points in the geosynchronous orbit. Figure 2.4 shows the orbital location of the more than three dozen satellites currently providing service to the western hemisphere.

This orbit stretches over 194,000 miles; nevertheless the number of slots is limited because of the necessity to allow several orbital degrees between satellites. Originally satellites were separated by 5 degrees of the orbit, or 2,700 miles. As there are 360 degrees in a circle, this meant there were only 72 orbital slots—a number far smaller than the number of nations.

The placing of satellites is coordinated through the International Telecommunications Union (ITU), in Geneva. But placement has largely been on a first come, first served basis. As the demand for satellite services increased, a shortage of slots developed in those portions of the orbit serving such areas as North America and Europe. Would-be newcomers to the field in nations such as the United States may find themselves shut out.

Officials in poorer and smaller countries have seen the orbital slots monopolized by the richer nations in the same hemisphere and have pushed for the ITU to reserve

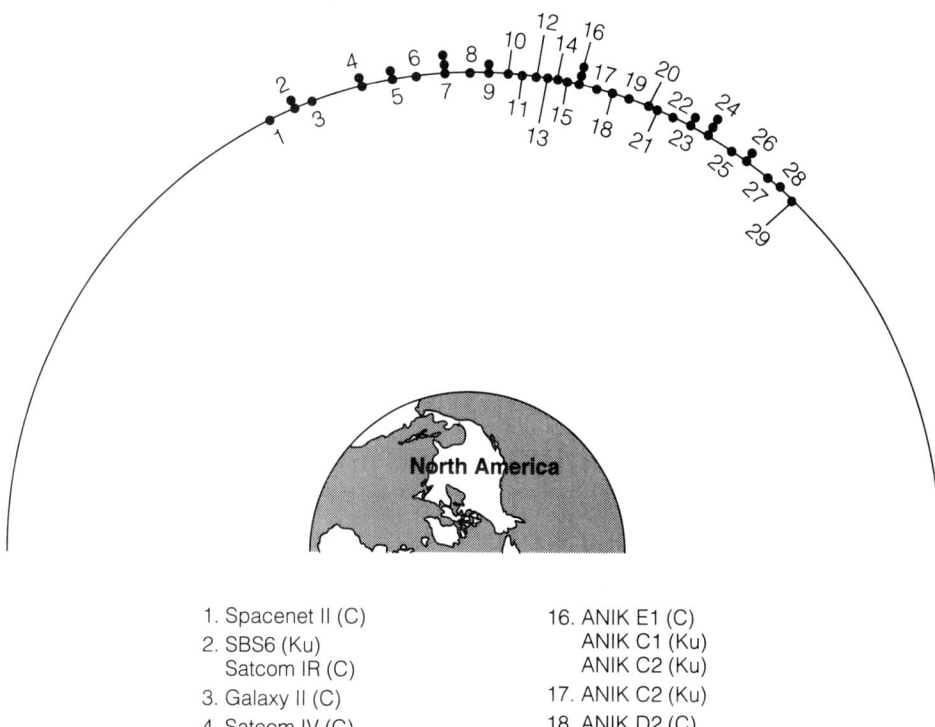

1. Spacenet II (C)
2. SBS6 (Ku)
   Satcom IR (C)
3. Galaxy II (C)
4. Satcom IV (C)
   Satcom Ks (Ku)
5. Satcom K1 (Ku)
   Telstar 302 (C)
6. Spacenet III (C)
7. SBS 4 (Ku)
   Galaxy VI (C)
   Galaxy VIIIH (C)
8. GStar III (Ku)
9. Galaxy III (C)
   SBS 3 (Ku)
10. Telstar 301 (C)
11. Westar IV (C)
12. Spacenet IV (C)
13. GStar I (Ku)
14. ANIK D I (C)
15. GStar II (Ku)
16. ANIK E1 (C)
    ANIK C1 (Ku)
    ANIK C2 (Ku)
17. ANIK C2 (Ku)
18. ANIK D2 (C)
19. Morelos A (C)
20. Morelos B (C)
21. ANIK C3 (Ku)
22. Spacenet I (C)
23. SBS 5 (Ku)
    Telstar 303 (C)
24. Westar V (C)
    Galaxy V (C)
    GStar IV (Ku)
25. ASC1 (C)
26. Satcom C3 (C)
    Satcom IR (C)
27. Satcom C4 (C)
28. Satcom C1 (C)
29. Aurora I (C)

Figure 2.4 Satellites in Geosynchronous Orbit Serving the Western Hemisphere, as of 1992
Source: Satellite Communications, July 1991.

slots for them. Access to the orbit has become one of the most intensely debated issues in international arena.

Technological refinement does provide the possibility of reducing the separation between satellites, thereby making it possible to increase the number of slots. Operators in nations with advanced technology argue that the increased tuning sensitivity of new satellites enables them to be spaced more closely together without their signals jamming one another. In effect they have argued for reducing the spacing of orbital slots to 3 degrees or less. Officials of poorer countries have resisted this proposal because such technology is more expensive and, therefore, its use would make it still harder for them to join the telecommunications space club.

PUSHING FARTHER OUT IN THE ELECTROMAGNETIC SPECTRUM

There is another way in which the capacity of the orbit can be and is being expanded. Satellite technology uses radio signals. The first generation of telecommunications satellites used a portion of the electromagnetic spectrum referred to as the C band, frequencies from 4 to 6 GHz.

The ITU has made additional allocations for satellite use, the Ku band (12 to 14 GHz) and the Ka band (20 to 30 GHz), collectively called K bands. Two or more satellites, each receiving and relaying signals in different bands, can share an orbital slot. Further expansion out into higher frequencies of the spectrum is already being proposed. In addition to expanding the capacity of an orbital slot, the higher frequencies have the advantage that their systems require smaller dishes at the earth receiving station.

DISADVANTAGES OF TELECOMMUNICATIONS SATELLITES

Satellite technology does have disadvantages. One can't just build or buy a satellite and whisk it into orbit. The position of satellites and the operation of satellite services in the United States are subject to regulation by the Federal Communication Commission (FCC).

It takes powerful rockets to lift a satellite into orbit. There are only a handful of organizations in the world operating rocket facilities that can perform this task. Because launch schedules are often upset by weather conditions and technical problems, the facilities are insufficient to meet the demand.[9] Those wishing to send up new satellites must get on a waiting list that is sometimes years long.

Unfortunately rockets misfire and blow up, and their payloads are lost in the destruction. And there can be a malfunction once in orbit, such that the satellite never goes into use. In such cases the operator must wait for a new satellite to be built, taking a place back in the waiting line for a launch date.[10]

If something goes wrong with a satellite after it is in orbit, repair is difficult at best and usually impossible. As a measure to protect continuity of service, most satellite telecommunications systems include backup satellites, which are held in reserve against a failure of the companion satellite. These satellites are not available for regular use. The necessity for such system redundancy obviously adds greatly to the cost of the system.

Redundancy is also required in the form of built-in repetition of signals. As noted earlier, because of the great distance traveled, signals are extremely weak upon reception. Extremely high frequencies have microscopic wavelengths, and this small size increases the difficulties of decoding signals. Atmospheric disturbances, even raindrops and snowflakes, may create static, which distorts signals in transmission.

Our discussion of the components of a satellite pointed out that the supply of liquid fuel limits how long it can be maintained in a dependable position. For planning purposes, the life of a satellite is usually calculated to be nine or ten years (although at least one satellite, the ATS-1, had a useful life lasting almost two decades).

Because satellite communications use radio waves, anyone in the footprint area with appropriate equipment may receive the signals, which makes it difficult to control their use. Because black-market decoders enable people to pirate commercial or private programs and messages, security remains a concern.

NEW COMPETITION: OPTICAL FIBER

Satellite services are undergoing restructuring, as they face competition from a rapidly developing technology. Optical fiber lines now spread both across the United States and under the Atlantic to Europe and the Pacific to Japan. On these high-traffic routes, optical fiber networks already have diverted much of the long-distance telephone business from satellites. Strong overtures are also being made to lure the television networks to switch from satellite to optical fiber as the means of providing programming to their affiliated stations.

Here again we have an example of media or technology displacement. The competition between satellites and optical fiber works to the benefit of users. The competition has accelerated the development of new and more flexible satellite services, expanding the variety of media satellite use. This new flexibility, combined with lower cost, is generating new types of satellite services for and by media and business, as will be detailed in later chapters.

Suggestions for Further Reading

Stan Prentiss' *Satellite Communications* has a lot of technical information on satellites, components, footprints, etc., but the book's organization puts considerable burden on the reader. Also, many details have been rendered obsolete by new developments.

This is a general problem with satellites and the other technologies discussed in this book. The best bet for current information is to skim through issues from the last six months of publications such as *Satellite Communications* and *Aviation Week and Space Technology*.

For those who don't want as much detail, Chapter 4, "The Communications Satellite: Newton and Clarke Cooperate," in Dordick's *Understanding Modern Telecommunications*, is good.

A book that provides an excellent overview of the development of satellites and their implications without getting heavily into technicalities is Heather Hudson's *Communication Satellites*. She gives considerable attention to the international dimensions of satellite communications.

Notes

1. McLuhan, Marshall. *The Medium Is the Massage.* New York: Random House, 1967.
2. Low-orbiting satellites continue to be used for many purposes, particularly the scanning of the entire surface of our planet. Despite the requirement of multiple satellites in non-geosynchronous orbits, Russia has used such systems for telecommunications because so much of its land area lies in far northern latitudes where coverage by equatorial satellites is problematic.
3. Clarke, Arthur C. "Extraterrestrial Relays: Can Rocket Stations Give Worldwide Radio Coverage?" in *Wireless World*, Vol. LI, January-December, 1945. In her book *Communication Satellites: Their Development and Impact* (New York: The Free Press, 1990), Heather Hudson relates that others before Clarke had noted the existence of a geostationary orbit, but none had suggested practical use for it.
4. With this division of the satellite's operating system, a malfunction in one transponder does not mean the loss of the satellite's entire capacity.
5. According to Hudson, the area that can be covered by these satellites is actually 42.3 percent of the earth's surface.
6. The earth has a circumference of approximately 25,000 miles. Because it has the shape of a very nearly round ball, two locations on its surface can only be separated by a direct-line distance of roughly half the circumference.
7. In a free-market situation, increasing capacity will initially create competitive pressures resulting in lower rates. The lower rates usually encourage increased use. If capacity remains constant, the increased use creates a "shortage," which (1) can encourage an increase in rates until (2) someone expands the capacity and once again creates competition. Each satellite adds such a large increment of capacity that this cycle becomes exaggerated compared to older technologies where the additions can more easily be limited, thereby moderating the impact.
8. There is a black market through which descramblers can be purchased and the monthly fees avoided. The use of such equipment, like the use of black-market cable converter boxes, is considered signal theft and is punishable under federal law.
9. For a long time only the United States' NASA and France's Arianne program had launch capability beyond national military needs, so they shared a monopoly on this service. Both suffered launch disasters in the mid-1980s that disrupted service and created a backlog of bookings, which has continued into the 1990s. China has begun booking satellite launches on a commercial basis. In 1991 the Russian space agency began to solicit launch contracts. Private, commercially operated rocket services in the United States and Japan are also being developed.
10. Insurance companies do provide policies to protect against such disasters.

CHAPTER 3

Optical Fiber: A New Tie That Binds

Light travels in a straight line, right? What about those funny flashlights with flexible necks? They manage to channel light waves so they'll go around objects and corners. We think light waves won't go through solid matter, but they will pass through glass. Yet glass doesn't bend—or does it? Actually, if you watch a large plate-glass window during a heavy windstorm, you'll see that it does bend and flex to a surprising degree.

Light and glass both have properties that often seem contradictory to our expectations. And now we have learned to make flexible wire of glass that will carry beams of light across distance, around corners and into what we thought were inaccessible locations.

Welcome to the world of optical fiber, flexible wire made of glass or extremely pure plastic. Optical fiber enables doctors to actually see what is going on inside your joints and organs. It also enables telephone companies to transmit television, music, voices and data by using light signals, and it's going to blow the capacity lid off the entire communications field.

PUTTING LIGHT INTO OUR NETWORKS

Semiconductors brought intelligence into telecommunications technology; satellites freed telecommunications from a dependence on earthbound networks. With optical fiber, also called fiber optics, the third of our enabling technologies, we change from electrical impulses to flashes of light as the carrier of our signals.

Optical fiber networks can provide access to hundreds of television channels, instantaneous access to thousands of data banks and the ability to transact business and data analyses over interactive systems as yet undreamed of. And just as dramatic as the increase in system capacity will be the decrease in the cost of such services.

As optical fiber replaces cable, the increased speed and capacity—and the lower costs made possible by these increases—will change the form of messages as well as the manner in which we use telecommunications. The functions which we now associate with newspapers, letters, television, recordings, movies, business documents and library collections will all be transformed by fiber optics.

The usefulness of optical fiber stems from the fact that an extremely fine strand of very pure glass will act as a conduit for light introduced at one end of the fiber. Due to the reflective properties of the glass and the extremely small diameter of the fiber, the light waves reflect down the length of the cable and do not refract (escape) through the sides.

ADVANTAGES OF GLASS FIBER OVER COPPER WIRE

The advantages offered by optical fiber over copper begin with capacity. A standard twisted pair of copper lines can carry 24 simultaneous phone conversations; a single strand of fiber of approximately the same diameter can carry over 37,000 conversations.

But optical fiber also has important physical advantages over the copper wire, which has been the mainstay of wired systems for over a century. Optical fiber allows light signals to travel with much less impedance than that encountered by electrical signals traveling through copper wire. Whereas copper networks require signal boosters every 2 to 3 miles, boosters are required only every 30 miles or so in an optical fiber network.

Copper is vulnerable to a variety of chemicals and atmospheric elements that cause erosion and deterioration of the system. Optical fiber is almost impervious to such eroding; not only will it last longer than copper wire, but it requires less maintenance.

OPTICAL FIBER AS A COMPETITOR FOR SATELLITES

At the conclusion of the preceding chapter, we said that optical fiber is now providing satellites with serious competition in some telecommunications services, particularly long-distance telephone use. Again, capacity is a major consideration. A single satellite system may have a capacity of some 80,000 telephone circuits; two thin strands of optical fiber will carry almost as many.

Satellites have a lifespan of approximately a decade. The fact that they are 22,300 miles out into space makes repair, modification or replacement difficult, if not impossible. Optical fiber has an unlimited lifespan and, as a terrestrial network, it is easily accessible for expansion as well as repair.

Satellites are probably unrivaled for being able to quickly establish connection between two distant points and for disseminating messages over broad areas. But the drawback is their inability to restrict where messages go and who receives those messages.

Because they are transmitted via radio waves, satellite messages can be received by anyone within the signal area. Encryption can be used to scramble the message, but, as cable operators will mournfully tell you, there is a big demand for black-market decoders. The light signals are contained within the optical fiber, and optical fiber connections are established and maintained between specific user points.

REFLECTING LIGHT THROUGH GLASS WIRE

Probably the greatest general advantage of optical fiber is its signal capacity, which derives from the ability to conduct light. A light source at one end of an optical fiber is visible at the other. Optical fiber conducts light around twists and turns, thus making it possible for us to see distant and/or inaccessible scenes.

Light rays play a critical role in vision. We don't actually "see" an object in front of us. Instead, the light rays reflected by the object are collected through our eye's lens and focused on the retina in back of the eye, which is made up of light receptors, the rods and cones. When the rods and cones are stimulated by the light rays, they send signals to our brain, which then puts them together to form the image that we see.

If those light rays are collected not by the lens of our eye but by a lens connected to one end of an optical fiber, they will then pass through the fiber. By putting another lens at our end, we are able to see the objects reflecting light at the far end.

A doctor, for instance, can insert a pair of thin optical fibers into a patient's knee joint. One fiber carries light to illuminate the area inside the joint; the other carries the reflected light back so the doctor can make internal examinations without exploratory surgery.

Similarly, optical fiber can be used for checking inaccessible locations in machinery or for exploring dangerous underground or underwater locations. It can also be used to convey the picture seen by a television camera lens.

DIGITAL CODES: MAKING BETTER USE OF LIGHT'S BANDWIDTH

In these examples the optical fiber is providing an analog representation, or signal, of the objects. Useful as these applications are, they are not using the full capacity of the fiber, because each strand is devoted to a single purpose or message. For medicine this may make sense, but in television and telecommunications applications, such single use of a fiber is wasteful. It's wasteful because in these applications we have to have some kind of technology at both ends of the fiber, and it might as well be digital rather than analog.

In Chapter 1 we emphasized the ability of semiconductors to switch and sort

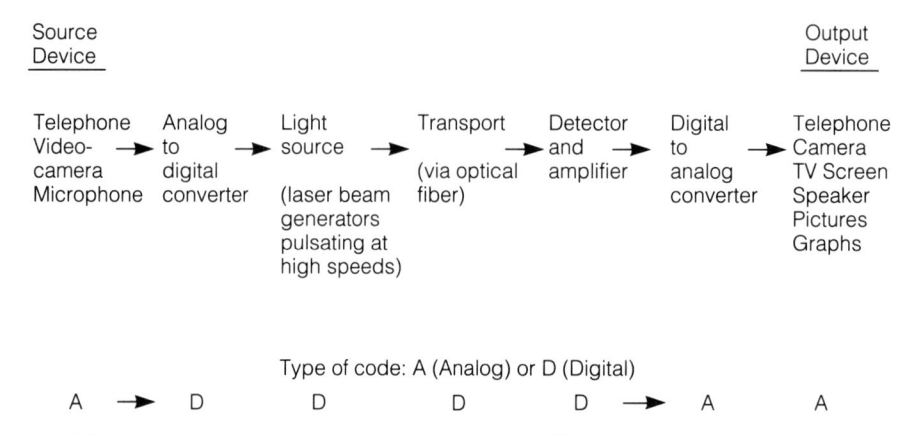

```
Source                                                    Output
Device                                                    Device

Telephone   Analog     Light                Transport     Detector    Digital     Telephone
Video-   →  to      →  source           →                →and      →  to       →  Camera
camera      digital                        (via optical    amplifier  analog       TV Screen
Microphone  converter  (laser beam        fiber)                      converter    Speaker
                      generators                                                   Pictures
                      pulsating at                                                 Graphs
                      high speeds)


                           Type of code: A (Analog) or D (Digital)
    A    →    D              D              D               D    →    A            A
```

Figure 3.1 Components and Functions of an Optical Fiber System

light, an enormous quantity of information can be transmitted to the light-sensitive photodetector at the other end. Thus we get the amazing capacity of optical fiber to carry all those thousands of simultaneous phone calls, or other combinations of messages, such as television channels or data services.

DIGITAL CODES AND SIGNAL INTERFERENCE

Digital signals can be and are transmitted using the electrical waves that pass through copper and radio networks. But we must remember that the attraction of digital is its advantage in using the speed made possible by semiconductors. It is this speed which makes all the complicated programming worthwhile, and anything that limits the speed of transmission must reduce the advantage of digital over analog signaling.

Electrical waves are subject to interference, distortion and static from a variety of sources. The music on your car radios, for example, may be distorted by the energy radiated from power lines paralleling the road. The shielding necessary to protect telephone lines from external interference greatly increases their bulk and still is not totally effective.[1] We hear a variety of crackling, buzzing and other signals that leak in somewhere within the system. Light waves within an optical fiber, however, are protected from external interference during transit.

When we are sending information at the rate of 2 billion bits per second, even static lasting but a tenth of a second can wipe out 200 million bits—the equivalent of many pages of text or data. We still may, and do, find it desirable to use digital signals in wire and radio networks. But as the danger of interference increases, we must increase redundancy or repetition to make sure that our complete message is received. Obviously, as we increase repetition we decrease the amount of information being transmitted.

In travel through the atmosphere, light signals are susceptible to various interferences, but transmitted through optical fiber they have almost total protection.

information in digital format at incredible speeds. It is this speed that provides the rationale for converting all kinds of messages—writing, speech, music, visual scenes and actions—into digital code. The result is greater efficiency reflected, for instance, in greater audio fidelity and smaller technologies. And it is this efficiency that justifies the effort of the complex transformation of information from analog to digital codes.

Speedy as they are, electronic transmission systems, whether they use wire or radio waves, slow down the process. They simply cannot transmit information as rapidly as today's microchips can code and decode information. The greater frequency of light waves, however, increases their capacity for information many times over that of electrical impulses or radio waves.

The critical question is: How do we make use of this great capacity? Optical fiber provides us the means of channeling light signals. But there remains the problem of developing a means of coding and decoding rapidly enough to make efficient use of the bandwidth.

This type of problem had occurred previously in the development of telecommunications technologies, but in reverse. Morse Code, used in the early days of the telegraph, is a digital code. Telegraphers coded and then decoded messages using different binary patterns of on/off energy to represent the 26 letters of the English alphabet. Old-time telegraphers were fast, but they could never match the speed of spoken words. The telephone and, later, radio made it possible to modulate analog sound and visual signals onto carrier waves and largely displaced telegraphy. But the speed of semiconductors has now outstripped the capacity of the copper wires and radio waves.

THE ROLE OF LASERS IN OPTICAL FIBER SYSTEMS

To make use of the capacity, we must have technology that can both generate and distinguish (or "read") signals at an almost unbelievable speed. This is where lasers come into the optical fiber picture. Lasers can generate light flashes at the rate of over two billion per second, and their speed continues to increase. By using digital codes, each flash will constitute one bit of information.

The components and functions of an optical fiber system are shown in Figure 3.1. Basically the analog signal—sound, pictures and other data—must be converted into digital code with the use of semiconductor technology. Lasers are used to transmit the digital code as extremely rapid sequences of light flashes. Multiplexers merge the flashes from different lasers, thereby creating a complex signal combining messages in order to make more efficient use of the capacity of the optical fiber.

The complex light signal is transmitted through the optical fiber to high-capacity photosensors at the other end. These read the light signal, separating it into individual digital messages. The messages are then decoded back into analog signals for use in conventional receivers such as video monitors, audio speakers and printers.

Because each flash will travel through the optical fiber at or near the speed of

OPTICAL FIBER VERSUS SATELLITE TRANSMISSION

The great capacity and use of light signals gives optical fiber advantages over satellites for relaying telecommunications. The satellites in use in 1990 usually contained no more than 24 transponders, each with a capacity of 80,000 simultaneous telephone conversations or a single 6–8 MHz television signal. The TAT-8 cable that inaugurated transatlantic optical fiber service can carry 40,000 simultaneous telephone calls, and the second-generation cable that went into service in 1992 has twice that capacity. This contrasts with the old coaxial copper cables laid in 1956, which were larger in diameter but could carry only 51 calls at a time.[2]

Satellite communication uses direct-wave radio signals, which means that they are subject to interference from both terrestrial and atmospheric static. As we noted earlier, Ku band signals are so tiny that even raindrops and snow flakes may cause interference in their reception.

Satellites retain the advantage of being able to offer signal coverage to a vast area, providing immediate switching to terrestrial stations in even the most remote and difficult locations.

HURDLES FOR CONVERSION TO FIBER

Despite all the advantages, the conversion of our telecommunications systems to fiber presents problems. Not the least of these problems is the fact that a well-functioning network made up of millions of miles of copper cable already exists. This represents a gigantic investment and obviously is not going to be abandoned overnight.

Optical fiber cable installations originally cost as much as 50 cents per foot, compared to less than a penny per foot for copper. As the volume of optical fiber constructions has expanded, installation cost has decreased; but it is doubtful that the cost will ever be reduced to the copper equivalent. Yet the capacity, greater efficiency and longer life make optical fiber theoretically a more attractive long-term investment than copper. There remains a question, however, of whether the high initial cost is justified at all levels within our national telecommunications grid.

Almost two-thirds of all the optical fiber in the United States has been installed by either local or long-distance telephone companies. Initially, optical fiber was used almost exclusively for inter-exchange or long-distance links. As costs have come down, almost all new telephone network construction—local or long lines—has used optical fiber.

COMPETITION IS THE DRIVING FORCE

It is highly unlikely that this change would have occurred so quickly if the AT&T monopoly on long lines service had not been broken by the 1982 decision of Federal Judge Harold Greene. After all, AT&T had an enormous investment in a terrestrial system based on copper wire and microwave relays. There was no urgent need to rebuild this system with fiber—until AT&T was faced with competition.

The new companies challenging AT&T for the long-distance market, such as MCI and Sprint, were literally building new systems. The managers of these companies saw an opportunity to obtain a competitive edge on the older network by building with optical fiber. To protect its market, AT&T has no choice but to speed construction of its own optical fiber system even where the existing system was functioning adequately.

By the end of the 1980s most domestic long-distance calls were being carried by optical fiber lines, and a rapid transition to optical fiber for transoceanic service to both Europe and Asia was underway.

Optical fiber's great capacity provides obvious advantages for the long-distance and inter-exchange links that carry heavy traffic. The use of optical fiber in the local loops, where telephone traffic is relatively low, is more problematic. Yet it is the placement of fiber optics in the local loop that promises to radically redefine not just our concept of telephone service, but our expectations for how telecommunications will service needs in all areas of communication—information, persuasion, education and entertainment.

WHICH COMES FIRST: BANDWIDTH OR DEMAND?

As the cost of optical fiber has declined, it has made its way into the telephone distribution system: trunk lines, local loops and bypass systems. However, with expansive copper networks for local users already in place, the local operating companies (LOCs) are wary whether the return, or payback, on an investment in fiber optics will justify the high cost of conversion.

The LOCs face a strategic decision involving capital investment that will total billions of dollars. The strategic choice is either to build optical fiber networks in response to demand for new services which will require fiber's capacity, or to build the optical fiber network with the expectation that expanded capacity will stimulate demand for services. Such services might include interactive cable, videophones, fire and theft alarms, home shopping and on-line service access to movies and music.

The proponents of fiber optics argue that installation in the local loop will spawn the creation of multimedia, integrated services for all types of communication functions. When capacity is available, they say, entrepreneurs will quickly develop new uses and new services that will, in turn, generate new sources of income. They cite the experience of cable. As cable operators expanded channel capacity of their systems, new program services multiplied. These new services had a double payoff: they attracted new subscribers and stimulated greater use of the pay tier. From this experience, proponents predict that the greater capacity of optical fiber will stimulate even greater expansion of revenue-producing programs and services.

Skeptics, however, point to the heavy losses incurred by several major projects to provide online interactive service. Times-Mirror Corporation of Los Angeles is said to have lost $30 million before it discontinued its "Gateway" service. Knight-Ridder lost $50 million during the four years it operated "Viewtron" in southern Florida.

They cite the fact that in 1990 only about one out of every ten U.S. households contained a personal computer equipped with a modem.[3] Therefore, they ask, how will a carrier recoup the cost of installing optical fiber in the local loop? Their view is that using optical fiber in the local loop is overkill, and expensive overkill at that.

The situation is analogous to turnpike officials being urged to build an expensive new link to serve communities that exist primarily in the promotional brochures of real estate developers. If the communities materialize, the new turnpike will pay for itself; but if they don't, traffic may not generate enough revenue from tolls to pay off the construction cost.

BUSINESS AND TECHNOLOGICAL ADVANCEMENT

In reality this argument is rapidly becoming moot. As is often the case, competition is changing the factors on which decisions will be based. Even as the debate goes on, the LOCs are experimenting with optical fiber in the local loop. Much of this is taking place in central city areas where there is a ready market for business-oriented digital services. These moves set the stage for a reprise of the general development of telephones in this country, whereby business traffic stimulated and pioneered the spread of a service that subsequently became a household utility.

Technically, the LOCs still have monopoly franchises in the communities where they operate. But these monopolies are simply being bypassed. In major metropolitan areas, entrepreneurs are building private and public fiber optic networks for the specialized high-traffic communication needs of businesses.

Business institutions have become complex organizations; many have operations in multiple locations around a city. The nature of their internal and external operations means a vastly expanded volume of communication: data, documents and personal messages. In seeking to increase the capacity and improve the efficiency of their corporate communications, businesses are turning to computer-based, digital transmission for greater efficiency in switching. The great capacity of optical fiber makes it the logical choice for the links to connect those switches.

The optical fiber networks of the new competitors challenge the LOCs for the institutional and commercial traffic that generates much of the LOC revenue. Unlike the LOCs, these new competitors are not required to provide the extensive low-traffic local loops essential to make universal service possible.

CHANGING DYNAMICS IN THE LOCAL LOOP

The LOCs are being stimulated to reassess the old practices. As they find themselves being forced to share the profitable high-traffic commercial service, they are aggressively seeking to find ways of generating more income from the local loops that remain monopoly operations under their control. To rebuild these loops with optical fiber and digital switching technology will be expensive but will expand their capacity to accommodate more traffic and, more importantly, to provide additional services.

The obvious way to maximize the return on the LOC investment in rebuilding with these new technologies is for the LOCs themselves to generate and provide the new services that will generate the traffic and revenue. To this end, the LOCs argue that they should be free to provide all types of service over their networks.

One of the original provisions of Judge Greene's 1982 decree restructuring the telephone system forbids the LOCs to offer information services. The Cable Communications Act of 1984 specifically forbids cross ownership between telephone and cable television providers. The LOCs are further prohibited from leasing lines to video providers such as cable companies.

But even these legal barriers are beginning to fall. In 1991, Judge Greene modified his decision to allow local phone operators to provide information services. He did this in spite of intensive protests and lobbying efforts by the American Newspaper Publishers Association (ANPA), some of whose members are beginning to find that videotex may have a major role in their future. (This is discussed in more detail in Chapter 11).

WHY NOT OPTICAL FIBER VIDEO?

The emphasis of the foregoing discussion has been on telephone companies and uses. But we must remember that optical fiber systems can be used to transmit almost any kind of information, including television. When the telephone companies express the desire to provide broadband services, they are talking about television programs. The idea of the LOCs providing video via optical fiber provokes a strong negative reaction within the cable television industry. It is no wonder that the cable operators allied themselves with the ANPA in resisting changes to the 1982 judicial action.

As is so often the case in our competitive economic system, the uses of this new technology will be influenced by a variety of factors. Not the least among these are the vested interests of existing institutions such as broadcasting stations, cable operators, telephone companies (telcos) and—yes—even newspapers, film studios, cinemas and the music industry.

THE TELEPHONE–CABLE–TELEVISION FIBER CONNECTION

A pivot point for decisions on telco optical fiber service may be the debate over the introduction of high-definition television (HDTV) in this country. HDTV, which is the subject of Chapter 5, refers to television or video technology that provides much higher quality pictures than those we now see on our TV sets.

One impediment to the introduction of HDTV in the United States is the problem of finding frequency allocations for HDTV channels in an already crowded electromagnetic spectrum. This is a problem only for broadcast HDTV; no shortage of bandwidth exists with optical fiber distribution systems.

Indeed, if there were an optical fiber grid capable of providing universal service to the nation, it would be technologically feasible to eliminate broadcast television. The program schedules of all existing stations and more could be distributed in HDTV format via optical fiber. The electromagnetic spectrum bandwidth currently allocated for VHF and UHF television could be reassigned for other uses.

This scenario may or may not be extreme. However, in 1991, the head of the Federal Communications Commission's Office of Planning and Policy, Robert Pepper, publicly predicted a "smaller, shrunken over-the-air" broadcasting industry for the future.[4]

As of 1990, only 2 percent of all optical fiber installed in the United States was being used for cable television. Like the LOCs, most cable operators have major investments in copper cable systems and are in no hurry to rebuild them. But, again, fear of competition—from the telcos, from other television distribution systems such as MMDS and DBS as well as the specter of court decisions which will invalidate their current monopolies—may stimulate cable owners to accelerate the introduction of optical fiber into their systems.[5]

The LOCs provide service to entire metropolitan regions, whereas cable systems are generally franchised individually by each community within the region. Yet the telephone and cable networks are generally parallel. In the end the cost of building optical fiber networks may cause the telcos and cable operators to join forces.

CONTINUING ADVANCES IN OPTICAL FIBER TECHNOLOGY

In the meantime fiber optic technology continues to advance, primarily in related hardware, but also in the fibers themselves. These advances promise increases in transmission speeds and capacities.

Switching equipment, lasers and photodetectors are essentially computers dedicated to a single task: communication over a single fiber. As such, they rely on highly specialized integrated circuits and electronics made of silicon chips. The development of gallium arsenide (GaAs) chips, which carry tiny electronic signals faster and with less resistance than do those of silicon, promises to increase the capacity of fiber. By attaching the new GaAs-based lasers to existing fiber, the capacity is instantly increased.[6]

Optical fibers themselves are being updated. Today's fibers are manufactured from highly purified molten silicon (glass) which is spun into tiny cables. Tomorrow's fibers will be made from a new plastic compound that offers similar transmission rates at much lower cost per foot.

New solutions for the problem of the "final mile" include using new technologies which would obviate the need for actually taking optical fiber into individual homes. Such mixed systems could speed the delivery of the services transmitted through the telcos' optical fiber trunks.

In any communication system, increasing capacity generally results in potential reduction of unit cost for any message transmitted. As we have pointed out before, freely competitive markets usually produce lower costs, and lower costs attract additional traffic. The increase in traffic creates a cyclical pressure for a further increase in capacity, which in turn results in a still lower unit cost.

The various applications of fiber will be discussed in relation to the different communication needs and media in the chapters that follow. We do not know how quickly and how deeply the optical fiber network will reach into the nation and its institutions, businesses and households. But the links for such a superhighway of digital communication are already being built, and its growth is inexorable.

Following World War II the United States began the construction of the interstate highway system. Those highways have been the catalyst for a dramatic transformation of both the rate and mode by which we transport goods and people. Optical fiber will be the catalyst for a similar transformation in how we provide communication service and exchange ideas.

Suggestions for Further Reading

A complete discussion of the technology, costs and capabilities of fiber optics is provided in C. D. Chaffee's *The Rewiring of America*. In *Signals, The Science of Telecommunications*, John R. Pierce and A. Michael Noll provide a good discussion of why things like the telephone and optical fiber systems work.

James R. Chiles provides a popular treatment of what may be in store for us, thanks to optical fiber, in a February 1992 article in *Smithsonian* magazine, "Goodbye Telephone, Hello to the New Communications Age."

In *The Deal of the Century*, S. Coll provides a fascinating narrative of the technological and legal battles that ended with the breakup of AT&T's hegemony over telephones in the United States.

Notes

1. Line insulation also serves another purpose, which is to prevent or reduce the radiation of signal power from the line. Such radiation accelerates signal attenuation.
2. Chiles, James R. "Goodbye Telephone, Hello to the New Communications Age," in *Smithsonian,* February 1992, p. 51.
3. Link Resources estimates that 24 percent of United States homes had personal computers in 1990, and only 29 percent of these had modems.
4. Andrews, Edmund L. "F.C.C. Report Predicting Gloom for Broadcast TV," in *New York Times,* June 27, 1991, p. D26.
5. One of the largest such projects was announced in 1991, when Time-Warner announced that it would rebuild its system in the Bronx borough of New York City with a 180-channel optical fiber system.
6. It is interesting to note that optical fiber and semiconductors began with the same basic raw material: silicon. Both technological lines are now exploring other materials as a means of increasing capacity.

CHAPTER 4

The Personal Computer: Putting Things Together

When journalists who retired a decade ago revisit the newsroom, the first thing that strikes them is the silence. The clatter of typewriters that was synonymous with newsrooms in the old days is gone. Now everybody is using a word processor. And the same phenomenon has occurred in many, if not most, large offices.

Also in the old days, a reporter in the field dictated the story to an editor over the telephone. Now the reporter can compose the story on a personal computer and use a modem to transfer the text directly into the newspaper's computer.

Today it is no longer necessary to go to the library to look up articles or to go to your stockbroker's office to follow trading on the New York Stock Exchange. These and dozens of other information-seeking functions can be accomplished at home using a personal computer and a modem.

The personal computer is the fourth enabling technology of the Information Age. It differs from the three technologies we have already discussed in at least three ways. First, the personal computer is still in the early stages of development; second, its role in communication is one of integrating, facilitating the use of other technologies; and, third, it is a personal technology, one which we as individuals use in a hands-on fashion.

Our discussion of semiconductors, satellites and even optical fiber has been largely retrospective in nature. Their development and deployment has been taking place for years. Each of the technologies is relatively mature in terms of what functions it performs, how it is manufactured, how it is implemented and how much it costs.

THE COMPUTER: NEW TECHNOLOGY BUT AN OLD IDEA

The concept of a computer is not as modern as we might think. Charles Babbage, an English mathematician, built a working model of one in 1822, partly funded by the Royal Society. In his published description he called this a "difference machine." Its toothed gears were powered by a hand crank, and it could do calculations to six digits. This unit was intended to be part of a much larger, more powerful machine, but Babbage was unsuccessful in his attempts at expansion. Although Babbage thought his idea original, a Prussian named J. H. Muller had written a book in 1786 describing just such a machine.[1]

To fully appreciate how far the "difference machine" has come since Babbage demonstrated his model, we need to recall our discussion of semiconductors and boolean algebra in Chapter 1. Computers can be broken into two basic parts: logic and means of applying it. Within the context of computer science, each is useless without the other.

The fastest, tiniest semiconductors wouldn't be able to do anything without a basic operating manual—the logic. For example, detailed instructions are necessary to calculate a square root number into the thousands, but the instructions are useless without the mechanism to perform the tasks defined by those instructions.

The notebook and pen-based personal computers of today have evolved from giant, warehouse-filling machines built in the mid-1940s on the basis of the developmental writings of John Von Neumann. These giant machines were hard-wired for specific calculations. This meant that logic was applied by connecting arrays of vacuum tubes together in specific patterns to perform specific tasks such as addition and multiplication. To change the type of operation, it was necessary to rewire the machine, reconnecting all the vacuum tubes. Our handheld notepads are more powerful than that old giant and its thousands of tubes—and much cheaper.

Wilbur Schramm cites a National Academy of Science estimate that the computers of 1970 could perform for $4 what would have cost $12.5 million if done by hand, and $2.5 million if done on hand calculators.[2] Today we could do the same thing on a personal computer for pennies. When calculations and instructions can be executed so rapidly and so cheaply, we are given freedom to do things that previously could only be theorized. We can put "intelligence" into all kinds of equipment, from automatic pilots for giant airliners to pace makers for heart patients. And we can put these devices to work in all kinds of communications tools.

CHANGING OUR PERSPECTIVE FROM COMPUTING TO COMMUNICATION

Our perspective on the personal computer as a communication tool is different. Although personal computers have been on the market for more than a decade, they still represent a very young technology. Each new generation of personal computer is wildly more powerful than the preceding one. The many standards for processing, displaying and manipulating information are still evolving.

A Bug That Gained Immortality

The late Grace Murray Hopper, one of the great pioneers of modern computer use, has explained how the terms *bug* and *debugging* came to be associated with programming. Rear Admiral Hopper was part of a team using an early vacuum tube–powered computer on a Navy-sponsored research project at Harvard.

She and her colleagues were attempting to modify an existing "program" of hardwired interconnections within their computer. Each time the researchers turned on the machine, however, they got back incorrect results from their experiment. They checked and rechecked their calculations and logic before finally deciding that the error must be the result of improper interconnections within the circuits inside the computer.

That meant they had to trace the connections of thousands of different wires and tubes, but there was no alternative. After much tedious searching, the cause of the problem was finally located. The body of a dead moth, attracted no doubt by the heat of the tubes, had blocked a connection. When the bug was removed, things worked fine.

From then on, any errors the researchers encountered were called "bugs," and the process of location and eliminating programming errors became known as "debugging." According to Admiral Hopper, the body of the original "computer bug" was preserved, taped to a page in a logbook housed in a Navy museum in Virginia.[3]

And, perhaps most important for our discussion, we are only beginning to recognize that the personal computer is a facilitator of personal communications. Because the personal computer has its roots in the old-fashioned data processing centers of large organizations, the general public has thought of it as a fancy adding machine or a word processor—period.

Until the personal computer, computers were held in awe because to scholars and the general public alike the word meant giant machines housed in computer centers that resembled the intensive care units of hospitals: atmospheric control, absolute cleanliness, special technical staff.

During the 1970s as semiconductors (for logic and memory) and magnetic disks (for storing information) grew smaller, more powerful and less expensive, engineers designed and built computers that could sit like a filing cabinet next to a desk. By the 1980s they were small enough to sit *on* the desk and even be carried around. Because of its data processing roots, however, people were unsure about how they might use these smaller computers.

The evolution of computers to this point had been focused on tasks involving huge batches of jobs in which a series of calculations were repeated over and over. For example, computers were found to be marvelous for streamlining payroll records. The computer can compile time sheets for each employee, multiply hours by the pay rate; apply appropriate formulas to compute deductions for taxes, health and retirement plans, etc.; deduct these and then print out an individualized paycheck providing itemization of earning and deductions to date. The computer can perform a batch of similar transactions for an entire payroll of hundreds or thousands of employees with great speed and efficiency.

THE DEVELOPMENT OF COMPUTER SOFTWARE

Early computers were useful but difficult to use. If one wanted to make any changes in the types of calculations to be performed, the machine needed to be completely rewired. Building the instructions into the hardware limited the functional flexibility of the machine.

Computer technology took a giant leap forward when programming instructions were separated from the computer equipment, a move which created what we now call software. With the earliest computers, there was no way to remove the instructions.

The first step in separating software from the hardware involved the use of punch cards. Instructions were coded onto what were popularly called "IBM cards." This was done by punching small holes in any of the 90 columns into which each card was divided. The card was then fed into the computer, which read the code 90 columns at a time as electrical impulses passed through the holes. Eventually the now familiar magnetic floppy disk was developed. These greatly expedited the process of transferring information to and from the computer's main memory.

The separation of hardware from software facilitated two great advances. Sets of instructions could become larger and, therefore, much more functional. Today's software programs comprise millions of lines of instructions. They are often much larger than the computer's memory. Different portions of the program are shuffled back and forth, in and out of the computer's memory, making the computer more powerful.

Software also enabled computers to be programmed to perform a variety of tasks, rather than just the one they had previously been wired to perform. One needs only to load a new program to change the entire operation of a computer. The application of computer technology to a host of new problems only required the writing of new software, not the construction of a whole new box. These changes gave rise to general purpose computers, culminating in the wonderfully diverse personal computers.

APPLE: A NEW CONCEPT

In 1977 a college dropout with a vision for a more individual use of computers collaborated with an established computer expert to form the company we know as Apple Computer, Inc. Steve Jobs and Steve Wozniak had a simple idea: If computers could, for example, perform complex accounting functions for large corporations, why couldn't they help individuals or small companies keep track of their records?

Jobs and Wozniak set as their first goal the development of a "user-friendly" computer, one that was easier to use than those available at the time. In conjunction with other software developers, they created the personal computer market

58   Part I   Technologies of the Communication Revolution

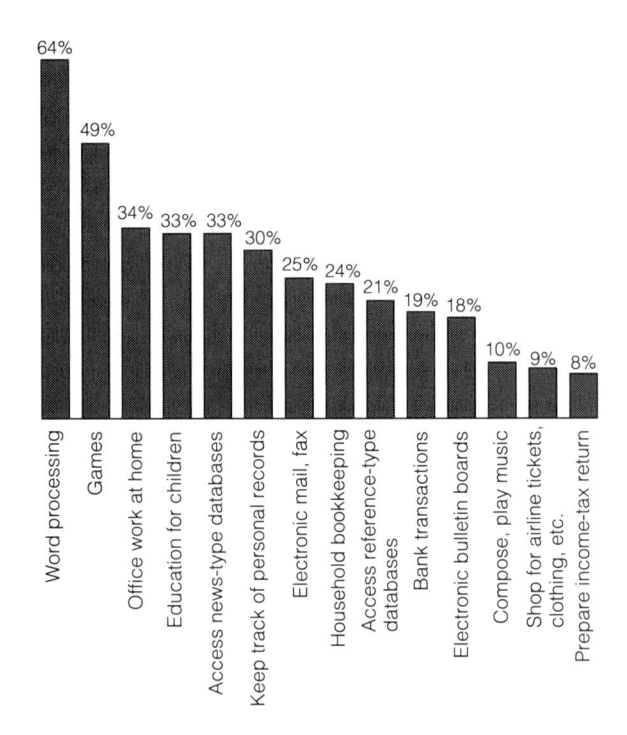

```
64%  Word processing
49%  Games
34%  Office work at home
33%  Education for children
33%  Access news-type databases
30%  Keep track of personal records
25%  Electronic mail, fax
24%  Household bookkeeping
21%  Access reference-type databases
19%  Bank transactions
18%  Electronic bulletin boards
10%  Compose, play music
9%   Shop for airline tickets, clothing, etc.
8%   Prepare income-tax return
```

Figure 4.1   Uses of Personal Computers. Percentage of personal-computer users who used a personal computer during 1991 for the purposes indicated.
Sources: Compiled from *Wall Street Journal,* October 21, 1991, p. R15; source: Roper Organizations Inc.

by popularizing personal, not batch, software. Desktop or personal computing had arrived.

The first popular programs increased personal productivity by harnessing computer power to manipulate text (word processing), create an electronic worksheet (spreadsheets) or manage huge lists (database management). To a large degree, these personal computer applications are still the same 15 years later(see Figure 4.1).

THE NEXT STEP: TURNING PERSONAL COMPUTERS INTO COMMUNICATION DEVICES

With the Apple computer and the subsequent introduction by IBM of its personal computer, the concept of a computer began a dramatic change. It expanded beyond the laboratory and data processing center to become a personal productivity tool, while remaining a processor of information.

Now personal computing is moving on to the next step: transforming personal computers into machines that seek information and enable us to communicate in new ways. How will this happen? Why will it happen? The answers are to be found in the same economic reasons that have guided the development of other revolutionary technologies. The price of every single component of computers continues to decline. (Take another look at Figure 1.4.) As engineers continue to design successive generations of personal computers, each new model doubles or triples raw processing power. And each new generation becomes smaller and more portable—from desktops to laptops to notebooks.

THE CONCEPT OF MULTIMEDIA

The amount of information that tomorrow's personal computers will manipulate will boggle the mind. William Joy of Sun Microsystems has predicted that by the year 2000 there will be chips capable of performing 65,000 MIPS—that's 65,000,000,000,000 instructions per second! Another expert, Gordon Moore, founder of semiconductor giant Intel Corporation, predicts that by that time there will be chips with a capacity of hundreds of megabytes of random access memory (RAM).[4]

Instead of simple alphabetic characters on a TV-like screen, personal computers will be able to project holograms. Such holograms can put Peter Jennings at his news desk in the room with us or turn the room into a stage for rock groups. They might capture news clips from around the world to automatically assemble a nightly newscast that fits an individual's interest in, say, the Middle East, the Boston Red Sox, and the financial performance of artificial intelligence stocks.

Whether or not we want to boggle our minds, the personal computer will become the messenger through which we can send and receive signals of all forms to bring us information that we need or desire in all four functional areas of communication. In short, computers are evolving from text processors to multimedia engines.

Providing a single, simple definition of multimedia is impossible. As yet the term means different things (and carries different threats and opportunities) to different people. While we sit at the edge of another change in how computers are perceived and used, this transition is only beginning. Thus our view of the personal computer as communication tool is necessarily a futuristic one. Much of the infrastructure is still being developed.

A COLLABORATIVE EFFORT

Because of the futuristic nature of personal computer–based multimedia communication, we need to discuss the development of several technologies that will transform the personal computer into an everyday communication tool.

The development of practical and usable transistors and optical fibers, for example, was based on "Aha!"-type discoveries in the lab (typically, the former Bell Labs). A single technological breakthrough gave birth to ideas for new products. Ideas were refined and streamlined into specific applications of the technology. Some of the applications panned out; others didn't. But none of the subsequent refining would have been possible without the initial breakthrough.

Multimedia relies on a combination of developments, not a single, discrete technology. This combination comprises the multimedia platform that makes it possible for the personal computer to operate as a coordinator, facilitator of multimedia activity.

MULTIMEDIA STANDARDIZATION—A GOAL FOR THE FUTURE

The development of a multimedia platform is not a matter of invention. This development does lean heavily on innovation, but the coordination and standardization of different technologies are also essential to its development. Two critical components are multimedia software and the multimedia network.

Software is the most critical component of the multimedia platform. Software is as important to the construction of multimedia platforms as it is to the use of microprocessors. While hardware engineers are designing and building very fast computers with very high definition screens (discussed in the next chapter), software is the key to the future of multimedia. Without the software all this great, super-fast hardware will be useless.

The multimedia network is the key because it provides a launching pad for a new generation of computing and communicating. Without a communication network, the multimedia personal computer is just another computer. But with a network it becomes a "looking glass" through which we, like Lewis Carroll's Alice, will view a whole new world.

With established standards for powerful hardware (souped-up personal computers, high-definition screens, massive amounts of storage) and easy-to-use software allowing us to create and manage our communication, we can truly call multimedia revolutionary.

EVOLUTIONARY YET REVOLUTIONARY

Despite the differences, multimedia is similar to the three previous technologies in one important way: It will provide a phase change in how we communicate; its use will be no less revolutionary. Contrasted with microprocessors or satellites, multimedia itself is not a simple revolutionary leap, but the evolutionary development of a new communication platform.

It is not a single breakthrough in the lab, or the deployment of a single piece of technology. The development of multimedia is an evolutionary process of building a huge and expensive infrastructure composed of terminals, network, storage and software. When terminals are ubiquitous and storage is plentiful, when software is easy to use and when high-capacity "data highways"—the information interstates of the future—crisscross the land, only then might we say that the possibilities for multimedia are revolutionary.

THE EVOLUTION OF THE REVOLUTION

Rapid technical advances make drawing clear definitions in the nebulous world of multimedia a difficult job. We start by differentiating between a multimedia platform (the system) and product (a communication).

A multimedia platform is the system of interrelating components. This system will allow people using computer-like terminals to transfer any type of information across any distance, great or small. This information may originate and be received in almost any form: film, video, holographic projections, simulations, images and, of course, audio and text.

Multimedia communication is the actual use of that system to achieve the transfer of information. It is the product which is made possible by the construction of the platform. Four essential pieces make up a personal computer multimedia system: personal computers, a communication channel, storage capability and software. Each element of a multimedia system is relatively useless compared to a complete multimedia system. Yet, as shown in Figure 4.2, the overall development of multimedia communication depends on developments in each of the discrete components.

PERSONAL COMPUTER MULTIMEDIA TERMINALS

Multimedia terminals cross the ease of using the telephone with the picture of television, and borrow a little computer power to bring information to life. These terminals are capable of displaying detail far greater than that provided by any of today's TV screens. They have huge amounts of memory to gather and manipulate information. And, by relying on simple, standardized devices like touch screens, voice-command technology and the "mice" of tomorrow, they are as easy to use as the telephone.

WIDE-AREA MULTIMEDIA NETWORKS

In order to get multimedia information from one point to another, it must be transmitted over some medium or channel. The problem is that multimedia functions are broadband services which exceed the capacity of existing local area networks.

The existing networks of copper wire, as we shall see in Chapter 10, were built to transmit audio telephone signals, which require a relatively small capacity. It takes only 10 kilobits (kbs) (10,000 bits of digital coding per second) to describe the human voice. Multimedia signals require much more bandwidth. While the minimum bandwidth for multimedia signals is always decreasing as software improves, it requires about 64 kbs.

Today's local exchange companies are incapable of transmitting information

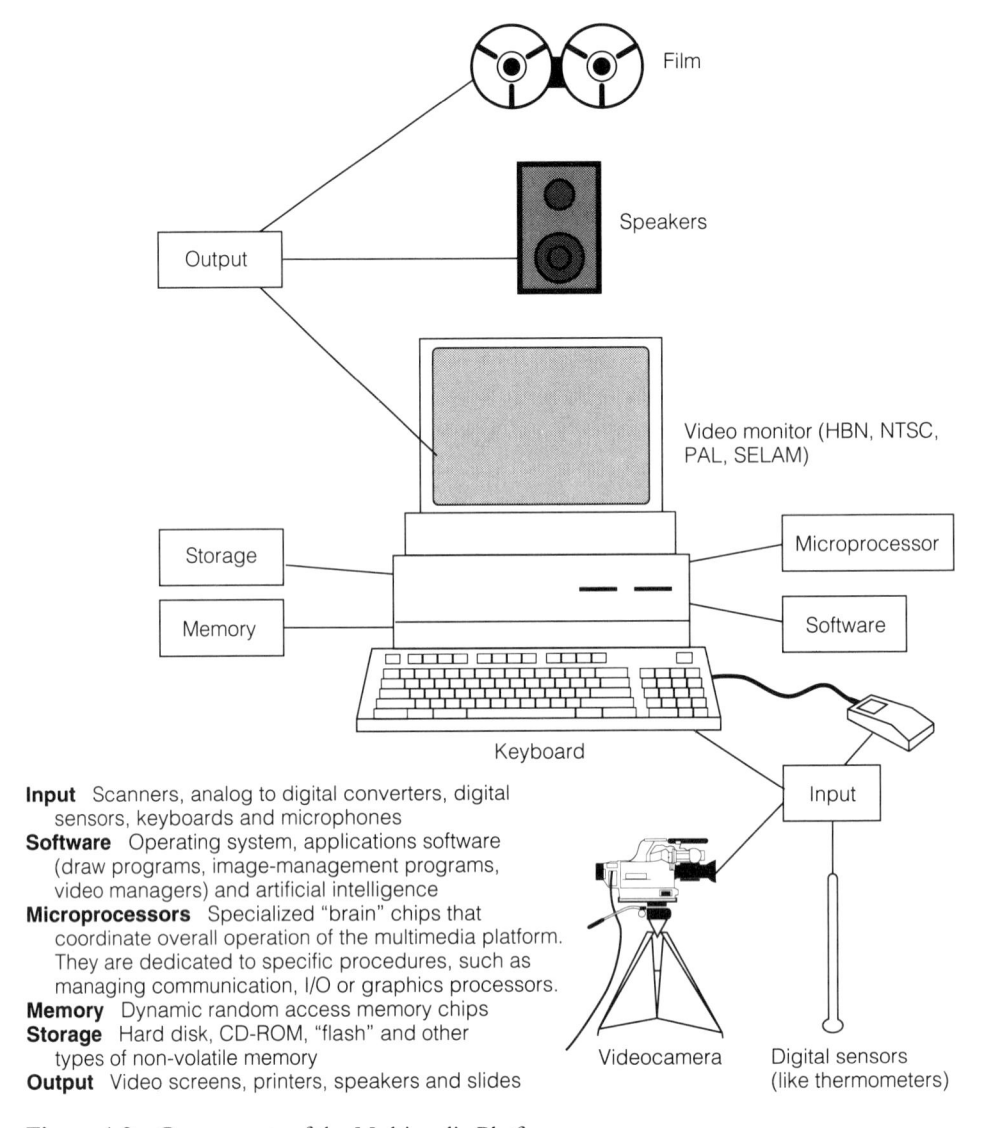

Input Scanners, analog to digital converters, digital sensors, keyboards and microphones
Software Operating system, applications software (draw programs, image-management programs, video managers) and artificial intelligence
Microprocessors Specialized "brain" chips that coordinate overall operation of the multimedia platform. They are dedicated to specific procedures, such as managing communication, I/O or graphics processors.
Memory Dynamic random access memory chips
Storage Hard disk, CD-ROM, "flash" and other types of non-volatile memory
Output Video screens, printers, speakers and slides

Figure 4.2 Components of the Multimedia Platform

to all subscribers at the rate required by multimedia. Either new capabilities must be built into the existing local loops or a new network must be built.

TECHNOLOGY IS READY, BUT POLICY IS NOT

In fact much of the underlying technology of a high-bandwidth multimedia network—the combination of optical fiber (in the local loop and over longer distances), switches and software—has already been developed and is in place. What is missing is the final mile—the broad bandwidth connections from major exchanges to subscribers.

The building and servicing of this final link has become the focus of a major policy battle that must be resolved before multimedia services become a large-scale operational reality.

Telephone companies seem to be the logical entity to lead the construction of the multimedia network, and they are eager to take on the job. However, as we shall see in Chapter 6, federal policy prohibited the telcos from carrying anything resembling video signals in their local loops. These prohibitions were primarily a result of intensive lobbying by the cable television industry, which sees its status quo threatened by the telco potential to deliver broadband—video—services.

The needs of businesses, individuals and even the maintenance of national competitiveness probably will generate sufficient political counterpressure to remove this impasse.[5] However, the resolution may very likely be a compromise based on an attempt to balance vested interests rather than on purely technical consideration.

ISDN AND INTELLIGENCE IN THE NETWORK

The service that telephone companies hope to use to provide the platform for multimedia is called an intelligent network. Such a network consists of the complete infrastructure with switches, transmission lines, etc. Intelligent networks will broaden our ability to use a service which is actually available today, called integrated services digital network (ISDN).

ISDN is a system for managing different types of messages on a single network. It provides a standardized, interoperable, digital, broadband communication service that anyone with the appropriate adapter can use anywhere. It provides "plug and play" communication between personal computer/video terminals. Multimedia requires the combination of intelligent networks and ISDN. As long as the customer has an adapter that converts incoming and outgoing information into/from a digital signal, ISDN service will do the rest of the job of multimedia communication.

ADJUSTING RATES FOR FLUCTUATING BANDWIDTH DEMAND

A characteristic of ISDN is wildly fluctuating demand for bandwidth as the user moves from services with only data transmission to those requiring full audiovisual display, and then to a voice-only service. It would be inefficient—and expensive—to have to allocate the maximum bandwidth on an ongoing basis, which is what we would have to do if we used current telephone practices.

Most telephone service is provided through ongoing subscription. We pay a flat monthly charge for the connection between our telephone and the local switching exchange. That charge is constant, regardless of how much we use our phone. When we make calls beyond our local area, we pay on a unit basis.

ISDN service resembles long-distance service in that it is purchased only for a specified period or periods of time. The customer pays only for the exact amount of time used. But ISDN also provides bandwidth on demand. It gives us the ability to expand or decrease the capacity of our connection on demand to accommodate whatever multimedia function we want, at the moment we want it. No one needs to wait days or weeks to have additional lines put in or taken out; ISDN makes the adjustment instantaneously and changes our bill accordingly.

DEDICATED LINKS THAT DON'T GET SWITCHED

While the cable companies stalled telco progress toward integrating broadband service in the local loop, some large corporate users began leasing dedicated high-speed links. Such links enable companies to meet their own expanded needs for multimedia communication between the central headquarters and branch offices. But because these links bypass the local loop, they lack a critical benefit of ISDN: access to switched services.

An ISDN network allows any multimedia user to contact any other user by "dialing"[6] the right number or address. In response to this instruction, the ISDN network automatically creates a channel between sets of huge switches in the same way that telephone calls are routed through a series of switches. The switching is transparent to the user, who is unaware that the switching is taking place. But as with "plain old telephone service" (POTS), switching is necessary if multimedia is to be universally available—if we are to be able to dial into various archives or to exchange content with other users.

Dedicated-line (point-to-point) services are much narrower in concept than ISDN. They are not instantly available for specific time periods. Although they allow high bandwidth communication, they are not subject to the same rules of common carriage as are switched services. Point-to-point links allow multimedia communication to take place, but only in a tiny, isolated environment.

Such limited interconnection is contrary to the basic meaning of multimedia. When we speak of multimedia, we are referring to universally available, standardized multimedia communication based on a single technical standard and network.

SOFTWARE TO RUN IT ALL

Much in the same way that multimedia blurs the lines separating personal computing and entertainment communication (such as television), it also blurs the definition of software.

To people in the information processing industry, software is a set of instructions, encoded in a distinct language. The instructions contained in the software set up the necessary switching paths within the microprocessors for performing some function such as data calculations, word processing or computer graphics.

To those in the television or film businesses, software is programming; it is entertainment material prerecorded on film, videotape or some other medium.

Because multimedia combines its data processing roots with new communication uses, there are two types of multimedia software: application and data. Application software is the set of instructions that allows the multimedia hardware platform to work in ways which allow what we call multimedia communication. Multimedia data is the communication content generated by use of the multimedia platform. A key part of multimedia is the development of software.

Television and radio provide a single stream of information traveling in one direction, to the user. But multimedia communication is more like using the telephone; it is highly interactive. Users are constantly requesting, filtering, sorting and receiving information.

SOFTWARE THAT TAKES INITIATIVE

Multimedia application software must establish a coherent scheme for handling the constant give-and-take of information. Developing multimedia application software is a daunting task. It requires systems that mimic human decision-making processes. It requires systems that take initiative to intuitively gather information for the user.

Great advances have been made in how people interact with computer systems. In the early days it was necessary for programmers to type, one line at a time, pages and pages of instructions to be fed into a room-sized computing machine. We have progressed to cryptic command-line interfaces, visually pleasing icon-driven structures, and point-and-click applications using a mouse or touch-sensitive display screens.

Multimedia applications will provide the next step toward a more natural, simpler interaction with intelligent machines.

SOFTWARE TO STORE THE WORLD

Multimedia data is everything else. It is video frames that are stored, edited and combined into a single presentation of multiple media. It is recorded music and images. Yet it doesn't stop there.

Multimedia data is all-inclusive. Because any type of information can be digitally stored and manipulated, every literary work ever written, every piece of video footage shot and all film ever developed is, theoretically, potential multimedia software.

Already various types of scanning and conversion devices are operative that will convert text, film, video or music into digital format. But even with this type of assistance, the creation and maintenance of the digital storehouses of multimedia data presents a daunting challenge.

STORAGE: MULTIMEDIA LIBRARIES

The fourth part of multimedia systems is storage. Public or university libraries are the storehouse for print media, such as magazines and books. A centralized, storage mechanism is the repository for the tools and products of multimedia communication.

Currently two technologies are used to store digital information for multimedia access: magnetic and optical media. Both hold trillions of bits of information that can be retrieved and then assembled into text, sound or image in milliseconds.

Already libraries are changing. To the dusty repositories of parched manuscripts are being added computer terminals. These terminals are part of interconnected systems of rapidly expanding pools of multimedia data stored in locations across the nation, around the world. The adoption of universal multimedia standards could allow anyone to view through their terminal objects, paintings, texts and artifacts stored in locations all over the world.

All this is technologically possible. Whether or not it is economically viable is another matter. The factor that ultimately determines the limits of multimedia will be not how much information we can use, but how much information we are willing to use and pay for.

Suggestions for Further Reading

A comprehensive illustrated history of computers can be found in Stan Augarten's *Bit by Bit*. Jack Rochester and John Gantz take a lighter, more humorous approach in *The Naked Computer*.

Many of the applications of personal computers as communication tools are thoroughly discussed in *The New Communication Technologies* by M. Mirebito and B. Morgenstern. A comprehensive discussion of how humans perceive and interact with information can be found in Robert W. Lucky's *Silicon Dreams: Information, Men and Machines*.

George Gilder traces the rise of Silicon Valley in *Microcosm: The Quantum Revolution in Economics and Technology*, and Tracy Kidder's *The Soul of a New Machine* captures the excitement of the competition within the computer field.

David Burnham's *The Rise of the Computer State* provides a somewhat alarming view of the potential of computers. A more humanistic approach to the development and meaning of personal computers is provided by Jean-Louis Gassée in *The Third Apple*.

Notes

1. Augarten, Stan. *Bit by Bit*. London: Unwin Paperbacks, 1985.
2. Schramm, Wilbur. *The Story of Human Communication*. New York: Harper and Row, 1988, p. 344.
3. Rochester, John, and John Gantz. *The Naked Computer*. New York: William Morrow and Co., 1983.
4. Markoff, John, "Denser, Faster, Cheaper: The Microchip in the 21st Century." *New York Times,* December 29, 1991, p. F5.
5. Despite their ongoing legal battles in Washington, in 1991 the nation's largest cable company, TCI, joined with the regional telephone operating company and AT&T to explore patterns for delivery of broadband services by optical fiber in the Denver market.
6. This verb, "to dial," is itself an anachronism, since most of us have replaced rotary dial telephones with push-button instruments. The continued use of "dialing" illustrates the cultural lags created by technological change.

CHAPTER 5

HDTV: A Bigger, Better Video Window

Take a moment to think about the ways people use their television sets. Two-thirds of our households now have VCRs, and people spend a lot of time watching movies on their TV screens. Millions of families have computer games that also use the TV screen. Some people use the TV set as the monitor for their personal computer. Even when we are watching television, most of the programming is coming to us via cable.

What we still call the "TV" is now actually a multi-use video screen. This means other content providers now have an interest in the shape and quality of the picture on that screen, which means that manufacturers are no longer solely interested in the technological needs of broadcasters. After nearly half a century, the TV market has become saturated.

SATURATION MEANS MARKET STAGNATION

What happens when the market for a product is saturated? Sales decline; production must be cut back to a level geared to satisfying the need for replacement.

Most manufacturers and dealers want to avoid the financial decline associated with such cutbacks. Their strategy becomes one of introducing new and improved versions of the product. If the public is convinced, they respond by buying new products even while the old ones are still working quite satisfactorily. Television sets are a good case in point.

More than three decades have passed since color television was introduced. In the United States, Japan and many European countries, the television market is now

Recording Motion in Pictures

Television and motion pictures both make use of the phenomenon known as visual persistence. The receptor nerves in our retinas continue to respond to a flash of light for a brief period after it has been extinguished.

What appears on the video screen is actually a very rapid series of separate light flashes. The television camera breaks the visual field seen through the lens into scanning lines. As each line is scanned, the camera converts the reflected light into energy pulses. These pulses are then transmitted by radio waves to our television sets, which reverse the procedure by projecting light onto the screen. Picture quality depends on the number of times the visual field is scanned each second and the number of scanning lines into which the picture is divided.

Scanning speed must be fast enough to present a new image before the average person's visual persistence has ceased. Without visual persistence, we would be aware of the scanning, and the visual image would be blurred. NTSC provides 30 complete scans of the visual field each second. It breaks the visual field into 525 lines (of which only about 300 are actually used for the picture). Each complete scanning consists of two sweeps, each of which includes alternate lines. This procedure helps our eyes put the picture together with minimum awareness of the actual scanning sequence.

Motion pictures consist of a sequence of still photographs rapidly projected with a brief blackout between pictures. Current movie cameras use 24 frames per second. Projectors have shutters that open and close as the film containing this sequence of still photographs is advanced, frame after frame. Each frame is actually shown twice. This means that 48 pictures flash each second, separated by brief intervals of darkness. Visual persistence bridges the blackouts, and we see the rapid sequence of stills as continuous motion.

A color motion-picture frame currently contains some 500,000 pixels, which is estimated to be equivalent to the information in about 1,000 video scansion lines.

---

saturated. Manufacturers have cut prices to encourage multi-set households. They have introduced successively bigger screens, stereo sets, wallet-sized portables, wall projectors and other variations. But the basic product has not changed, and the task of stimulating this saturated market has become increasingly difficult.

Manufacturers see the growing levels of other uses of the video screen as a means of escaping this saturated market. But that entails a transition to a new format, and whether they need it or want it, broadcasters will be forced to adapt to the new format. Television is no longer the master of the video screen.

By the end of this decade, most of us will have replaced our current television sets with video screens that give us images rivalling the clarity of projected 35-mm film. The decision to buy these screens will be driven by our desire, not simply for television programs, but for the variety of content and services evolving under the heading of multimedia. The transition to high-definition television can be seen, therefore, as part of the transition to digital telecommunications.

BLURRED IMAGES FROM ARCHAIC SCREENS

The screens on our current televisions are part of a technology developed solely for broadcast television. They are built to a set of standards called NTSC,[1] which was last modified in 1953. What we see on the screen is a rather coarse and flickering image. Colors are often unnatural; details are not clear and action may be blurred. The frame of the picture has a 3:4 aspect ratio, three units of height for each four units of width. People in the television industry have worked within the limits of these standards for almost forty years and have evolved production techniques to accommodate them.

But now we use the television screen for viewing other material that, in its original form, had higher quality than our television screens can reproduce. For example movies are made in the medium of 35-mm film. Their creators visualize them being projected on large, wide screens in a theater. When these movies are displayed on the TV screen, they lose picture clarity, color brilliance and dimension.

Television screens have grown larger over the years, but these larger screens simply magnify what we would see on a smaller screen: the relatively coarse NTSC image. Some manufacturers now produce enhanced television (ETV) sets, which include microchips that reprocess the received NTSC signal. The proportions of the video image remain unchanged, but the picture is much sharper because the number of lines is increased by 50 percent.[2] Ultimately the improvements are limited because the technical standard for production and transmission remains unchanged.

In the near future we will have the option of replacing our current television window with a new video screen, a technology called HDTV or advanced television (ATV). HDTV may have double the present 525 lines of scansion, which will mean sharper images of clear, natural color. The dimensions of the screen will change the aspect ratio so that the width is almost twice that of the height (approximately 9:16), compared with that currently used (3:4). The probability is also extremely high that our HDTV technology will use digital signals.

ENLARGING THE PICTURE AND JUNKING THE CRT

The density of information within the HDTV signal is the critical advantage over NTSC (and its European counterparts PAL and SECAM, as well). Viewing large-screen projection of current television is like looking at a newspaper picture through a magnifying glass. Because a coarse screen has been used to divide the image for reproduction, the individual dots that compose it become more apparent when we enlarge the printed picture (see Figure 5.1).

An HDTV image is like a reproduction in an art book in which a very fine screen has been used. Even when magnified, the component dots are hardly distinguishable. When projected onto a theater-size screen, HDTV images are sharp and the colors are vivid. The HDTV picture matches the dimensions and quality of images produced by projecting 35-mm film.

Cathode ray tubes (CRTs), that are used as the viewing screen in our present sets, require additional depth as the surface area increases. As a result, big

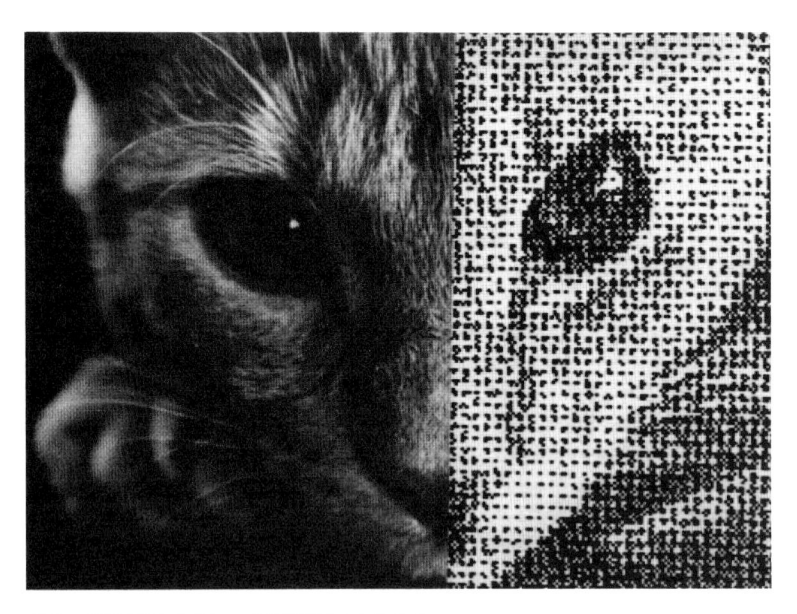

Figure 5.1 HDTV (left) and NTSC (right) Screens

screen sets are extremely bulky. The video projectors now used for large screens in public places are also bulky.

Concurrent with efforts to perfect HDTV is a concerted program to develop new, flat projector screens. Some small portable televisions, as well as laptop and notebook computers, already use liquid crystal display (LCD) screens. By the time HDTV is operational in broadcasting, there will be window- and even wall-sized flat video screens that do not intrude into the space of rooms. However, the cost may make such screens impractical for the mass market.

HURDLES IN THE PATH OF A NEW STANDARD

HDTV is not a new medium; it is a new format for an extremely popular and common medium with a 50-year history. Changing standards will require major restructuring of the entire chain of television and video production, transmission and reception technology.

More than 2,200 television stations in the United States broadcast programs using NTSC standards. It is inconceivable that an industry of this size can (or would if it could) make an overnight change from NTSC to HDTV. Over 200 million NTSC television sets in our homes, as well as perhaps 80 million VCRs, play material recorded in the NTSC format. Image the uproar if, overnight, all these machines were made obsolete and useless! It is not surprising that the FCC has decreed that programs broadcast in HDTV must be simultaneously available to people with NTSC receivers. In a parallel situation, the conversion to color TV in this country extended over a full decade. As was the case with color TV, the overlap may mean that the technology will become compromised by political and economic pressures to protect the status quo.

THE LOST DREAM OF A SINGLE INTERNATIONAL STANDARD

Different standards currently divide the world into three incompatible domains: NTSC, PAL and SECAM. This division has complicated the exchange and reception of programs across national boundaries. Japan's NHK[3] began demonstrating an HDTV technology called Hi Vision at trade shows in the mid-1980s. Optimists proposed that it be used as the means of introducing a universal standard. But the change to a new video standard is complicated by industrial competition and politics at the international level as well as by the existing vested interests within nations.

In other countries some broadcasters, critics and ministers of culture fear that an international standard would accelerate what they see as an alarming American hegemony over television (and cinema) content. Officials in Third World nations that must import electronics equipment see HDTV as a potentially dangerous strain on their already fragile economies.

Individual European nations have sought to protect their domestic electronic industries from Japanese imports. As they moved toward full implementation of the

Broadcasting Standards

The nations of the world generally observe a broad allocation of different portions of the electromagnetic spectrum for specific uses. This general management of the spectrum is effected through the International Telecommunications Union located in Geneva, Switzerland.

Nations with common borders or with territory within the signal reach of transmitters in other nations generally have multi- or bilateral agreements on the use of broadcast channels to avoid interference.

Each nation is free to establish its own standards for internal purposes. A variety of different national standards was established as each nation authorized the inauguration of television broadcasting. These have evolved into three general standards: NTSC, PAL and SECAM.

NTSC is the oldest standard and is used by the world's two largest TV markets, the United States and Japan, as well as most other nations of the Western Hemisphere.

The PAL standard originated in West Germany, but was subsequently adopted by Great Britain, which exported it to many members of the British Commonwealth as well as to former colonies. PAL is used by more nations than any other standard.

SECAM was the last of the three standards to emerge, and it also has the finest picture quality. It was developed in France and has been adopted primarily by nations with past colonial ties to France. A number of Eastern European nations also use SECAM.

The major differences between the three standards have to do with bandwidth, lines of scansion and scanning ratio. NTSC uses 6 MHz of bandwidth and 525 scanning lines. PAL uses 7 MHZ and 625 lines and SECAM uses 8 MHZ and 850 lines.

European Economic Community in 1992, collective action has produced the establishment of a European HDTV technology called Eureka, which is incompatible with NHK's Hi Vision.

In 1991 NHK was the only broadcasting organization in the world offering a regular broadcast schedule of HDTV programs.[4] Its technology has been used in the production of several movies as well as video programs and commercials, but in many ways Hi Vision is already an obsolete technology; worldwide acceptance is not anticipated.[5]

THE AGONY OF CHANGING U.S. STANDARDS

Nowhere has the contention over the new standard been so confused as in the United States. Unlike the European nations we have maintained a policy of relatively free imports. Our electronics market has been dominated by Japanese products for at least a decade, providing immense profits that have helped catapult Japanese firms to world leadership.

Because ours is the world's largest television market,[6] both the Japanese and European manufacturers have actively sought to influence the direction of HDTV in the United States in hopes of participating in the revenues that conversion to HDTV will generate. However, domestic groups clamored for the United States to follow the European example of adopting a distinctive standard as a strategy for revitalizing our own electronics industry.

The Communications Act of 1934 gives the FCC the authority to establish standards in the field of electronic communications. Following the model it used in 1947 and 1951, the FCC sanctioned the establishment of an Advanced Television Test Center (ATTC) to test different proposed HDTV technologies.

The ATTC was cooperatively funded by various segments of the television industry—networks, public broadcasters and equipment manufacturers who submitted systems to be tested and considered by the FCC for adoption as the new U.S. standard. As on-air testing began, withdrawals and mergers reduced the number of competing technologies to six. Significantly, in the flurry of development activity before testing began, all but one of the systems had adopted digital technology.[7] The rapidity with which technology is advancing is reflected in the fact that each group submitting systems wanted to be the last so as to have the benefit of last-minute development.

Despite the importance of the on-air testing, the reality is that no decision on standards is made solely on the basis of technological factors; political and economic pressures also come into play. The results of ATTC tests play an important, but not necessarily decisive, role in standards creation at the FCC.[8]

WHERE IS THE DEMAND FOR A NEW STANDARD?

The progress toward HDTV has not been swift, easy or even rational. The potential for irrational action is evident in the fact that we speak of high-definition *television*, rather than high-definition *video*, despite the growing use of these screens for non-television content.

Cynics might suggest that the only parties enthusiastic about HDTV are manufacturers, who see it generating billions of dollars in sales of new receivers and studio and transmitting equipment. No ground swell of interest or demand has risen from the public for a better TV screen.

THE HDTV DILEMMA FOR BROADCASTERS

American broadcasters as a group have had little enthusiasm for HDTV. This is understandable; they have a large investment in an NTSC technology which seems to satisfy the public. Estimates of the cost for station conversion to HDTV vary, but it will be a matter of millions of dollars for each station. What makes this particularly painful for broadcasters is that conversion to HDTV will not generate additional revenue to offset this capital investment. It will be a cost they must absorb simply to remain competitive.

The FCC's requirement for simultaneous broadcasts in HDTV and NTSC means broadcasters are saddled with operating a double service, and the continued availability of programming in NTSC will probably delay the purchase of the new sets by many families.

For broadcasters, HDTV is part of a high-tech future in which their role is unclear, but new pressure from existing competitors and the addition of new competing technologies makes the change to HDTV inexorable. If the competition adopts HDTV, broadcasters dare not run the risk of sticking with NTSC. The audience is fickle; cable and the VCR have already claimed forty percent of the audience, once the monopoly of broadcasters.

The broadcasters' dilemma is not solely one of cost. The move to HDTV also contains a threat that the current allocation of broadcast television channels may be upset. This threat arises from the possibility that HDTV, and particularly dual standard broadcasting, may require more capacity than is provided by the present television channels.

A BETTER PICTURE REQUIRES MORE INFORMATION

The quality of a visual message depends in large measure on the number of elements, called pixels, in the picture. Increasing picture quality means that one must increase the amount of information in the picture.

If we double the number of scanning lines in the television picture, we are obviously adding a great deal of information to the signal. Because the expanded aspect ratio lengthens the scanning line, more information is loaded into the signal.

A direct relationship exists between the amount of information in a signal and the amount of bandwidth required to carry the signal. The more information carried, the greater is the bandwidth requirement. Because HDTV represents a quantum

74   Part I   Technologies of the Communication Revolution

> ### Channels and Bandwidth
>
> A channel is an arbitrary set of boundaries that incorporate a specified range of frequencies of the electromagnetic spectrum. By assigning channels to the users of the spectrum, we eliminate or at least minimize interference between users.
>
> An axiom in spectrum management is that "information equals bandwidth." All things being equal, as we increase the amount of information in a signal we must increase the size (the bandwidth) of the channel.
>
> AM radio channels were established in the pre–high fidelity era, and each uses only 10,000 cycles per second (10 KHz). FM was established as a high-fidelity sound medium and was given channels of 200,000 cycles per second (200 KHz). To provide both picture and high-fidelity sound, the NTSC standard gave TV channels 6,000,000 cycles per second (6 MHz).
>
> These boundaries are all arbitrary. Other countries have adopted standards that use different bandwidths for television. For example SECAM uses 8 MHz, yet both SECAM and NTSC channels use frequencies within the same portions of the electromagnetic spectrum. They simply divide the same area of the spectrum into different groupings.

increase in information compared to NTSC (or PAL and SECAM), broadcast of HDTV will require more bandwidth than is used for the NTSC broadcasts (6 MHz, or 6 million cycles per second). The practical implication is that the current broadcast television channels are not sufficient to accommodate television service in both HDTV and NTSC.

NHK's original HDTV technology required a channel of 24 MHz (24 million cycles per second), four times the bandwidth of the channels used for NTSC broadcasting. This requirement has been dramatically reduced, but it still exceeds NTSC's 6-MHz channel size.

PUTTING THE SQUEEZE ON CHANNEL BANDWIDTH

An acceptable (but not the best) HDTV signal can be squeezed into a 6-MHz channel; to provide HDTV and NTSC compatibility, 8 MHz is required. The technological options appear to be to provide stations with an additional 6-MHz channel or to allocate each station an auxiliary channel to supplement its existing 6-MHz channel. Either option puts a squeeze on spectrum space and sets off a domino effect among existing allocations.

Given that available spectrum space for broadcast television is fixed, expanding the bandwidth of individual channels means that the number of channels must be reduced. Where is the additional bandwidth for each station to be found? None of the owners of existing TV stations is volunteering to give up a channel to accommodate HDTV, nor do any wish to be left out of an HDTV future.

Some engineers claim that, with carefully planning, each existing station can be given an additional 2-MHz auxiliary channel. But any such process would mean reshuffling existing channel allocations, increased technological complexity or both.

SEMICONDUCTORS TO THE RESCUE: SIGNAL COMPRESSION

Semiconductor technology is once again coming to the rescue. Digital signals make it possible to incorporate compression technologies that dramatically reduce the bandwidth requirement. Digital compression is the key; actual carrier capacity is not increased, but because each signal is compressed, the effective transmission capacity is increased.

By 1990 major advances had been announced in compression technologies, advances that greatly increase the efficiency of signal transmission. For example, HBO announced plans to use compression to multiplex (combine) its cable service, providing a simultaneous choice of three movies instead of one. DBS services licensed to begin operations by the mid-1990s are configured to provide at least four times as many television digital signals per transponder as was possible with NTSC analog transmissions.

Signal Compression

Most stimulus fields—what we see, hear, feel or smell—are relatively static. Not much changes in the background of the action we are watching from one second to the next. In musical selections, instruments and voices often hold the same note or notes for extended periods.

Video cameras make 30 complete scans of the visual field each second, creating an analog electrical signal of each of the several hundred lines into which it divides the picture. Because the stimulus fields are relatively static, there is a great deal of redundancy in the information contained in the successive scans. If this redundancy is eliminated, less information must be transmitted from frame to frame.

In Chapter 1, we described how digital technology takes an extremely rapid sequence of samples of light and sound waves, describing the wave at each sampling point in algebraic equations. These algebraic expressions are then converted by high-speed microchips into streams of digital signals for transmission.

Compression technology makes additional use of the sorting ability of microchips to check for redundancy in each successive sampling. The algebraic expressions for each new sample are automatically compared to those of the previous sample. If there is no change, the redundant information is not transmitted; the decoder in the receiving technology persists with the previous information.

How much bandwidth can be saved by compression? SkyPix, one of the first United States DBS services will deliver 80 channels of NTSC video with only one satellite, using compressed digital signals. That would be more than three times the uncompressed capacity of satellite signals. As compression technology advances and as transmission is made by systems that can alter channel bandwidth upon demand, there seems to be virtually no limit to the savings that can be achieved.

THE OPTICAL FIBER–DIGITAL SIGNAL CONNECTION

As the ATTC testing indicates, the transition to an HDTV video signal very probably will be part of an even more important conversion to universal use of digital signals. Optical fiber is largely responsible for this rising probability. The phenomenal signal capacity provided by optical fiber makes the additional bandwidth required for HDTV seem insignificant.

As noted in Chapter 3, optical fiber can carry an analog video signal but such use is wasteful of an optical fiber system's capacity. Analog signals also preclude some of the most interesting potential for optical fiber as a distribution system. For example, transmission of a movie in analog format would require the full running time of the feature. The same movie in digital format can be downloaded to the viewer's equipment in a matter of seconds.[9]

EXPANDED PARTICIPATION IN THE HDTV DECISION

These expanded uses of the video screen will dictate the transition to HDTV despite the lack of enthusiasm among broadcasters. The public may not see much difference between TV programs displayed in NTSC and HDTV, but that misses the larger point. It is not so much that we are changing to HDTV, but rather that we are changing to a multiple-media mode of displaying information and entertainment on our video screens.

In the near future some form of HDTV will certainly be in general use. If we use history to predict, we could expect decisions on HDTV to sacrifice the long-term view (and probably the common good) for the sake of protecting the vested interest of existing institutions (the broadcasters).

However, HDTV is part of an emerging multimedia world involving other technologies (such as optical fiber) that expand the number and variety of institutions with vested interest. As we will see in later chapters, these institutions are rapidly being merged into multinational media conglomerates whose ownership have interests stretching across many technologies and types of media. This means that the existing media institutions are already in a state of turmoil and transformation cutting across technological and national boundaries. The forces unleashed by this transformation ultimately may become a tidal wave that simply overwhelms the structures and constraints protecting the status quo.

Suggestions for Further Reading

The specifics on HDTV literally change from week to week. The only way to keep up with the current technological and political status is by tracking the field in trade publications. Any major developments in either the technology or the regulatory situation will be covered in *Broadcasting*, either in the front of the magazine or in its weekly Technology section.

A broad overview of HDTV technology, its promise and its problems, is provided in *HDTV: The Politics, Policies, and Economics of Tomorrow's Television*, edited by John F. Rice.

A more complete treatment of the practical implications and challenges that the new standard will present to United States broadcasters is provided in *HDTV: Planning for Action*.

Although this publication was prepared by the National Association of Broadcasting in 1988, it remains valuable for its pragmatic discussion of the issues and the problems that HDTV presents to those in the broadcast industry.

Notes

1. To establish a set of industry standards for the new medium of television, the FCC formed the National Television System Committee, consisting of technicians and industry representatives. The specifications they recommended (dubbed NTSC after the initials of the committee) were adopted by the FCC in 1941 as the basic television standard in the United States. A second NTSC proposed the modifications that became the color standard adopted by the FCC in 1953.
2. In 1991 the price of such sets was double that of regular NTSC receivers, and their market penetration remained minimal.
3. NHK, Nippon Hoso Kyokai (Japan Broadcasting Corporation), is one of the world's largest broadcasting organizations and is similar to Great Britain's BBC. It is a non-profit, non-commercial system supported primarily by receiver fees paid by television owners.
4. A limited schedule of HDTV programs began on NHK's DBS service in 1990. In November 1991 the schedule was expanded to eight hours daily.
5. Hi Vision also ran into opposition from Japan's powerful commercial television industry, who did not want NHK's technology to dominate their future.
6. We will probably lose this status as television penetration expands in the various nations that have joined together in the European Community.
7. The one remaining analog system was a version of NHK's Hi Vision. NHK officials now recognized that their current technology is doomed to be an interim phase and are working on their own digital system for the future.
8. In 1950 the FCC adopted a color technology developed by CBS's Dr. Peter Goldmark. RCA filed suit to block the adoption of its rival's technology but lost the case. However, the Korean War interrupted manufacture of color sets. The FCC used this hiatus to convene the color NTSC, which led to the 1953 standard, a technology largely based on RCA's work.
9. The use of this technique obviously would require some kind of memory unit within the receiver into which the full movie could be dumped, and from which it could be recalled for actual playback.

PART II

Factors That Shape the Communications Marketplace

Steve Jobs and Steve Wozniak conceived the idea of personal computing and became millionaires and legends of our time. The person or persons who introduced the wire recorder in the 1940s are forgotten. Their machine recorded sound by magnetizing wire with the analog electrical impulses created by microphones. It was a great idea, but they were using the wrong material. The fast-moving fine wire too often spun off the reel and created gigantic snarls. The people at Ampex used oxidized plastic tape instead of wire and changed the recording of pictures as well as sound.

Our enthusiasm for the capability of new technologies must not blind us to the fact that any technology is only an enabling device; technology makes it possible for people to do something. A new invention can be a technological wonder but a flop in the marketplace.

Ithiel de Sola Pool, who headed the Communication Policy Program at MIT until his death in 1984, observed that every new technology creates a challenge or threat for a status quo in the existing market; it is the market, not technology itself, that ultimately determines success or failure of innovations.*

Before we can hope to make the transition from "blue sky" possibilities to marketplace reality for new technologies, we must consider the factors influencing the marketplace. Three major groups of factors are reviewed in Part II: policy, infrastructure and money.

---

*Pool, Ithiel de Sola. *Technologies of Freedom*. Cambridge: The Belknap Press of Harvard University, 1983, pp. 6–7.

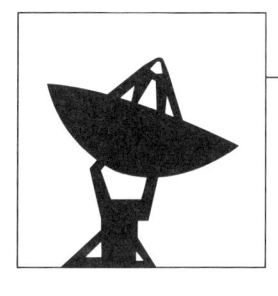

CHAPTER 6

The Constraints of Policy

Have you ever watched young children playing? They give one another a continuing stream of directions: "You can't do that." "You have to do it this way." "You do this, and I'll do that." They're working out the rules—the policy—of how they will play together. Libel suits testify to the fact that we are still working out what newspapers and other mass media can or cannot print—despite the assurance of freedom of the press in the First Amendment.

Without rules and referees to enforce them, it would be impossible for two teams to compete in football, baseball, hockey or any other sport. Even with rules, disagreements still provide a lot of side action. Since 1982 we have had competition in the field of long-distance telephone service, and authorities have imposed a complex set of rules to try to keep the competition fair. Imagine what it would be like to drive through a crowded city or down an interstate highway if there were no traffic rules.

Radio was similar to these situations in the 1920s. The air waves were like highways where several cars tried to use the same lane going in different directions, where those involved were making up the rules as they went along and where it became necessary to establish regulators to enforce rules.

SETTING THE LIMITS

Every society seeks to guide the development and operation of the institutions that serve it. When this guidance is given the force of authority it becomes policy. Policy establishes limits—or the lack of them. In telecommunications and media, as in other areas, policy may facilitate or distort the development and application of technology and new, replacement technologies.

As policy evolves it reflects the historical ideology of a society as well as the prevailing political ideas. As a matter of self-interest, those individuals involved in the standards of new and old institutions attempt to influence policy.

Pool has pointed out that, when dealing with technological issues, policy makers are generally ill-prepared and perhaps ill-advised for a comprehensive consideration of the present situation—much less the future. The tendency is for policy makers to attempt to force the new to fit into old patterns and to deal with each situation on an ad hoc basis.[1]

The United States has no single national telecommunications policy; instead, there is a crazy-quilt pattern of laws and regulations for various technologies and their applications. Policy oversight has been fragmented among many different governmental units.

CONSTITUTIONAL STARTING POINTS

The myriad regulations and laws affecting the communication of information in our society are derived explicitly or implicitly from our Constitution. The Constitution is the foundation and testing stone for all our policies, laws and regulation.

Best known of these policies are the First Amendment provisions for freedom of speech and press. Less commonly known are two provisions in Article I. One gives the federal government jurisdiction over interstate commerce (Article I, Section 12). The other (Article I, Section 8) makes it possible for individuals to own and protect their inventions through patents, a concept of intellectual property subsequently extended with the laws of copyright. The Constitution sets the framework for the free-enterprise economic system in which communication technologies and media must operate.

COMMUNICATION'S SPECIAL ROLE IN DEMOCRATIC SOCIETIES

The structures of both the telecommunications industry and telecommunications policy vary from one nation to another, reflecting differences in economic, social and political conditions. How a nation organizes and operates its mass media and telecommunications tells us a great deal about that nation. The Constitution's emphasis on protecting freedom of speech and press reflects the importance of communication in our democratic society.

Democracy ascribes sovereignty to the people, not to a monarch, an autocrat or an elite group. Democratic government operates on the basis of a majority decision within the population. For democratic government to function, the population must be aware of the options through as full and open an exchange of ideas as possible.

The size of our nation and its population makes it impossible for us to practice direct democracy in the manner of ancient Athens, where citizens gathered in the agora to debate and vote on issues. Instead, we elect individuals to act as our surrogates for specified periods of time, after which they must win a new mandate from the people.

Because they are our surrogates, we hold that the public has a right to full knowledge of the background and thinking of candidates and, once elected, of their actions. The media are expected to be watchdogs on government.

Putting these concepts together, our policy is to encourage communication and to keep the government divorced from ownership and operational control of the various means of communication, including the media. In our political ideology the ideal situation is seen as one in which many outlets for different points of view—as well as many different products—contend for public acceptance. In other words we should seek a maximum number of media voices.

THE NATIONAL MOSAIC OF LOCAL GOVERNMENTS

As recently as 1950 going from Los Angeles to Washington meant a three-day train trip; to get there from Saint Louis or Chicago was an overnight trip. When we consider the difficulty of earlier travel by horse and wagon, it's not surprising that our ancestors developed a sense of local self-reliance and suspicion of central government.

Many governments are premised on the assumption that power is concentrated at the center, but in the United States local communities have ceded power to the federal government reluctantly. A major function of the Constitution is to spell out the scope of federal authority and to prevent it from usurping individual and local responsibility.

This historical emphasis on home rule and localism has been reflected in the organization of our telecommunications and media. Historically our newspapers have been local, not national, publications. The operating companies that form the foundation of our telephone system operate under franchises given by local authorities.

FEDERAL OVERSIGHT FOR INTERSTATE COMMERCE

After gaining independence from Great Britain, the colonies individually issued currency and sought to collect customs on goods coming across their borders. The result was monetary chaos and the stifling of commerce and economic development. By having their delegates gather in Philadelphia for the Constitutional Convention of 1787, it was generally agreed that the colonies would have to cede some responsibilities to a central, federal government.

In addition to the need for a single common currency, it was recognized that the nation could achieve economic independence and growth only if the colonies joined together as a common market. This meant that there should be a free flow of goods across the internal boundaries of the nation. To that end, the Constitution permits the federal government to regulate interstate commerce. The individual states retain the power to regulate commerce conducted only within their own boundaries.

Radio waves use a form of energy that radiates from the source without any physical carrier. This characteristic means that they have inherent capability to cross state as well as national boundaries. On the basis of this characteristic, federal authorities have asserted that radio is interstate commerce. This assertion has been upheld by the courts, and so the use of the electromagnetic spectrum—including broadcasting—is accepted as being within federal jurisdiction. However, our traditional political emphasis on localism has been reflected in the fact that federal licenses for the use of broadcast channels have been issued within the framework of service to specific geographic communities.

INTELLECTUAL PROPERTY SHOULD BE FAIRLY SHARED

The provision for protecting intellectual property derived from recognition by the Constitutional Convention delegates that good ideas and inventions produce greater good for society if they are widely shared. But to encourage creativity and initiative, individuals must be allowed to realize benefits from their inventions.

The Constitution gives the federal government authority to issue patents as a means of balancing the rights of individuals against the good of society. This provision provided the precedent for subsequent legislation which established copyright protection of intellectual and artistic creativity.

The protection of individual rights to intellectual property makes it possible for those holding patents or copyrights to license use of their ideas by others in return for payment. Unlike real and tangible property that can be held in perpetuity by heirs, the life of patents and copyrights eventually expires, and the intellectual property covered becomes part of the public domain. Once it becomes part of the public domain, it can be freely used by anyone.

CONDITIONS CHANGE BUT PRINCIPLES PERSIST

The genius of our Constitution is the flexibility it has provided for adapting to changing conditions of our society without compromising the basic commitment to a democratic society. There was no explicit "communication policy" in 1787, other than the simple but important provision of the First Amendment regarding freedom of speech and press, which we still honor.

The nearest thing we have to a national communication policy is the Communications Act of 1934, which established the Federal Communications Commission (FCC) to act as the Congressional surrogate in this area. Pool's comment on the ad hoc nature of policy is borne out by the frequent amendments this act has undergone. Repeated attempts in Congress to pass a new comprehensive act have failed.

Concern about the lack of a specific telecommunications policy led a special commission to study the problem near the end of Lyndon B. Johnson's presidency. Johnson's successor in the White House, Richard M. Nixon, established an Office of Telecommunications Policy as an executive agency. President Jimmy Carter changed the name from OTP to NTIA, the National Telecommunications and Information Agency. Subsequently President Ronald Reagan reduced the importance of NTIA, changing it from a White House agency to an office of the Department of Commerce.

Because it was the creation of an Executive Order, OTP cum NTIA has never had anything but advisory status. This is in contrast with the Federal Communications Commission, a regulatory agency created by an Act of Congress.

Telecommunications and media institutions continue to operate under the crazy quilt of individual laws and regulation at both federal and local levels. Pool identifies three policy domains which have evolved over the decades: press, broadcasting and common carrier.[2] Institutions within each of these domains have been organized under and treated quite differently by legislators and regulators.

PRESS AND POLICY

Because it is specifically mentioned in the First Amendment, ownership of institutions in the press domain is literally unrestricted. Generally policy has accepted the film and the recording industries as falling within this domain as well. The technologies associated with the press are such that no physical limit exists restricting how many people can make, distribute and exhibit these types of creative expression.

The institutions themselves—the companies which publish newspapers, magazines and books, or those which make movies and records—are subject to all of the federal and local laws and regulations applying to other business operations. For example newspaper managements can be sued on charges of discriminatory hiring practices; cinema owners must observe local zoning and traffic regulations.

The First Amendment has been interpreted to mean that no restriction can be made on ownership of institutions of this domain. Nevertheless, major film studios were forced to sell their cinema chains in the late 1940s because they were seen as using them to limit market access by independent producers, which is an unfair business practice.

Foreign ownership in the press domain is extensive. Australian, British and Canadian interests control chains of daily newspapers in the United States. In its struggle to survive, UPI, the press service, at times has been under foreign ownership. Several large cinema chains are foreign-owned. All but one of the major recording companies is controlled by foreign interests.

Recently concern has focused on the purchase of Hollywood studios by foreign interests. A Department of Justice review in 1991 concluded that these acquisitions did not constitute a national threat, and so no action was instituted to stop them. Whether action to stop them would have been successful in a court challenge is unknown.

BROADCASTING AND POLICY

Broadcasting policy began with the Wireless Ship Act of 1910 and the subsequent Radio Act of 1912. At a time when most other nations saw radio as an extension of their government-operated Posts and Telegraph service, the 1912 act signaled a different direction for the United States. It gave jurisdiction over the new field to the Secretary of Commerce.

The first real authorization for broadcast regulation was provided by the Radio Act of 1927, but it was the Communications Act of 1934 that established a framework for federal oversight of all "interstate electronic communication," whether by radio or wire.

Anyone can start up a publication anywhere in the United States, but to operate a broadcast station it is necessary to obtain a license from the federal government. This power of the federal government to license a mass medium is based on a series of principles challenged and upheld by the Supreme Court. These principles are:

1. The electromagnetic spectrum is public domain.
2. Because the energy waves making up the spectrum radiate, their use is classified as interstate commerce under federal jurisdiction.
3. Orderly use of the spectrum requires its division into channels.
4. Because there can be only a finite number, channels are limited, and hence there is a scarcity of channels.
5. The finite number of channels makes it impossible for everyone who might so desire to have a channel. The federal government regulates the use of channels to obtain maximum public benefit.

These conditions have also led to ambiguity regarding the extent to which First Amendment protection applies to broadcasters.

If everyone cannot have a channel of their own, how do we guarantee an open marketplace within broadcasting? The laws and regulations that have evolved are attempts to strike a compromise in applying the concept of open economic and political marketplaces in a medium of confined dimensions.

Limits have been set on who can hold licenses, on foreign financial interest and on how many licenses a single individual or legal entity may hold. Licenses are issued for a specified time period after which they are subject to review before being renewed, and they may be revoked. They are issued for specific geographic locations. License holders must provide programming "in the public interest, convenience and necessity," but the meaning of this phrase is not defined and is to be interpreted within the context of the local community. In return for providing free programming to the public, station operators may finance their operations however they choose.

Networks are not considered broadcasters and are not subject to direct regulation, although their activities are affected by various government actions.[3]

COMMON CARRIERS AND POLICY

Originally common carrier operations were limited to switching exchanges from which networks of copper wire extended to individual subscribers. Unlike the radiated signals of broadcasting, the operation of telephone exchanges can be contained within specific geographic bounds and is not inherently interstate commerce.

Monopoly as well as licensing of media is normally anathema in this country.

However, the courts and the public have accepted the concept of a natural monopoly in some situations, usually related to the provision of public utilities. Institutions so classified are required to operate under franchises permitting appropriate government bodies to regulate them in the public's interest.

When community telephone service was introduced, it was classified as a natural monopoly and local governments franchised a single company to build and operate the local network. As systems became interconnected, telephone calls crossing state lines were recognized as interstate commerce, with long-distance telephone use subject to FCC oversight.

In both local and long-distance service, franchising authorities retain authority to specify terms of service (including rates) to protect the public. To insure that the companies could not abuse their status as natural monopolies, the telephone systems were made to operate as common carriers. Common carriers cannot generate message content or discriminate against any parties who wish access to the system. Because the common carriers only transmit and do not originate message content, First Amendment protection has applied to the users, not the operators, of these systems.

As microwave and satellite technologies developed, their use was incorporated into telephone systems. This development was to have dramatic results for common carrier policy, as we shall relate shortly.

Foreign ownership of the common carriers is limited because of their critical role in the nation's economy and security.

TECHNOLOGIES CHANGE FASTER THAN POLICIES

Policy makers have generally sought to develop different policies for press, broadcasting and common carriers because the institutions of these domains used different technologies and operational structures. But this structure of different, specific policies for the domains was doomed to become problematic. As Pool points out, conflict was inevitable concerning the domain to which any specific policy applies, because the boundaries such policies assumed exist between the domains are in fact increasingly vague. The continuing development of new technologies and new uses of the existing technologies that are the hallmark of the Communication Revolution means that without constant and timely redefinition, boundary problems will increase.

This conflict can be seen as common carriers expand cellular mobile telephone services and so aggressively compete with broadcasters for spectrum allocations. Print media now use common-carrier facilities to deliver videotex and facsimile services. As they invest in optical fiber, the telcos lobby for permission to deliver video as well as information content.

For example, if the courts and regulatory agencies attempt to apply traditional First Amendment distinctions among press, broadcasters and common carriers, the result is bound to be increasing strain and distortion. Newer institutions, such as cable, have hybrid technological structures that defy categorization under the traditional policy divisions and thereby compound the confusion.

CABLE

Because cable systems use wires, authorities used the analogy of the telephone and categorized cable as a locally franchised natural monopoly. However, cable operators select the program services provided on their various channels, and so, unlike the telephone, cable is not a common carrier. Although cable is not broadcasting, it distributes broadcast programs. What was the FCC, authorized by Congress to regulate all interstate electronic communication, to make of such an operation?

At its outset cable was a "community antenna" service. Operators in communities where television reception was poor used an antenna strategically placed for optimal reception of broadcast television signals. These signals were delivered by cable to households willing to pay a monthly fee in order to have clearer pictures on their TV screens. Although somewhat wary about the new service, the FCC hierarchy decided that cable was not interstate electronic communication and left its regulation to local authorities.

But when cable operators began to import signals of distant television stations, the FCC decided that they had entered into interstate operations. In the 1960s the FCC began to assert regulatory oversight of cable operations, although the franchising power remained with local authorities.[4] This assertion of oversight has been upheld by the courts and written into an amendment of the Communications Act.[5] Multiple systems operators (MSOs) have acquired ownership of many locally franchised cable systems, and the FCC has asserted a right to review and approve purchases of these local franchises.

MMDS AND DBS

Both multichannel multipoint distribution systems (MMDS) and direct broadcast satellites (DBS) provide services that effectively provide competition for the locally franchised cable operators (as well as with one another). Because MMDS and DBS use the electromagnetic spectrum to deliver their multichannel programming they are licensed by the FCC.

THE RISING DEMAND FOR SPECTRUM SERVICE

MMDS and DBS are only two of many services pushing their way into expanded portions of the electromagnetic spectrum. One of the fastest growing consumer communications services is cellular mobile telephones. Cellular mobile telephones are an operational extension of the local telephone network. Because the spectrum is used to connect user with the local network, this service is licensed by the FCC.

New spectrum-based services are also being developed to provide interactive links between the audience and broadcasting stations and their advertisers. Scores of entrepreneurs are pushing for spectrum space. Notice the continuing increase in the number of people wearing paging devices, all of which are activated by radio signals.

Vehicles of transportation services are being equipped for radio connections, many of them via satellite links.

The continuing growth of demand for spectrum space guarantees problems for the FCC in adjudicating among the many contenders while still protecting the public welfare.

SHARING CONTENT ACROSS MEDIA BOUNDARIES

Copyright protection has become another source of tension and conflict at the policy boundaries. In recent decades increased confusion concerns what is covered by a copyright. Books, for example, now carry statements expanding the old "all rights reserved" statement by saying something such as "no part of this publication may be reproduced or transmitted in any form or by any means, electronic or mechanical, including photocopy, recording or any information storage and retrieval system without permission."

Prerecorded videocassettes start off with the stern warning that the FBI is on the alert for illegal use, which includes both charging to let people view and making copies. The recording of material off-air is legally problematic if you make any out-of-home use of the tape; however, off-air recording is so widespread that enforcement of prohibitions is difficult.

The wide use of recorded music and films by broadcasters and cable programmers has created a labyrinth of licensing agreements to obtain compensation for creative artists and to establish the ownership of copyrighted material in the variety of formats. The audio recording industry has had to give up the idea of trying to stop dubbing for personal use, but making dubs for resale on the pirate market can get one into a lot of trouble.

Monitoring these agreements has become a major problem with the proliferation of programming distributors—broadcasting, cable, MMDS, DBS, video and record outlets. As satellites and optical fiber networks expand the speed and scope of distributing material for syndication and multiple-point printing and distribution, copyright problems are intensified within the press as well.

Contracts for syndication of media material usually provide exclusive rights within individual markets. Expansion to regional and national editions may confuse traditional newspaper markets for syndicated material such as comics and columns. Tracing market exclusivity for syndicated shows and films becomes a nightmare owing to overlapping markets for broadcast, cable and MMDS outlets.

LIMITS INTENDED TO PRESERVE FREEDOM

What we now see are similar technologies, such as cable and telephones, being regulated differently and different technologies, such as print and recording, being regulated similarly. Institutions that began in one domain are spreading into others, such as newspapers using satellite distribution for simultaneous publication. Newspapers have also begun distributing fax and videotex editions. The common-carrier telcos are beginning to provide content as well as carriage. Maintaining a true free enterprise market has become an increasingly complex task.

Further, the working of the free market may itself create restrictions on business competition and reduce the competition of ideas as well. If left unregulated and unrestrained, the rich and powerful may be able to use their resources to drive out competition and create a monopoly. The attempts to maintain our ideals of a free market of ideas, goods and services have led to contortions of individual policy principles.

Consider, for example, long-distance telephone service. For decades AT&T was allowed to be the sole provider of long-distance telephones because of its reliance on networks of copper wires. In the late 1940s AT&T began to use microwave relays for long-distance connections. By the 1970s satellite links were coming into use. In response to a federal antitrust lawsuit, federal judge Harold Greene decided in 1982 that contemporary technologies no longer justified a natural monopoly in long-distance service[6] and ruled free competition for this service would begin in 1984. In the settlement of the case, Judge Greene imposed operating constraints that applied to AT&T but not to its potential competitors. In attempting to create competition, he felt it necessary to constrain the actions of some, but not all, of the players.

At first thought, this settlement might seem to contradict the rules of fair play, as well as the ideology on which we base our free-market economy. But, somewhat like a parent trying to adjust game rules so that younger children can play with older ones, the judge assumed that a free marketplace would not guarantee fair competition between the older, stronger AT&T and the new companies struggling to enter the long-distance field. (More will be said about this situation in Chapter 10.)

FROM OPEN MARKETS TO MONOPOLIES

In a truly open, unregulated market, superior strength and/or unfair practices may be used to drive out competition and establish monopolies.[7] We have the paradox that our free-enterprise system has a long history of law and regulation seeking to protect the public from unfair business practices which may result from a completely open market. Over the decades the U.S. Congress has, for example, established such regulatory agencies as the Federal Trade Commission (FTC), the International Commerce Commission (ICC) and the Food and Drug Administration (FDA) with considerable authority over activities in the market.

In recent years a continuing reduction has developed in the number of corporate institutions controlling the content of and access to the mass media. The operation and financing of these organizations, as well as the content passing through the technologies, are all influenced by market factors.

RESTRICTING FREEDOMS TO PRESERVE THE OPEN MARKET

Earlier we pointed out that the nature of broadcasting and telephone technologies had led to policies imposing restrictions on the number of operators in any one loca-

> ### Restrictions on Group and Cross-Media Ownership
>
> FCC restrictions on group ownership of broadcast licenses began with the Chain Broadcasting Rules of 1941, which were upheld by the Supreme Court in 1943.
>
> Policy limiting ownership has changed over the years. When stations were relatively few, the FCC imposed a limit of five stations in each service: AM, FM and television. With the addition of UHF channels and as the number of radio outlets grew, the limit was periodically raised to seven and then to twelve stations. In 1992 the FCC proposed further expansion.
>
> In applying restrictions the FCC has also made exceptions to allow higher limits for UHF stations, because they generally are at a competitive disadvantage against VHF stations. Similar exceptions have also been extended to ownerships that include significant minority and female representation.
>
> The duopoly rule restricts ownership of radio and TV licenses in the same market. Cross-ownership rules now prohibit ownership of newspapers and broadcasting licenses in the same market or ownership of television, cable or telephone licenses in the same market.
>
> The duopoly and cross-ownership rules both have grandfather clauses that exclude ownership situations existing at the time the rules were adopted. Any subsequent change of ownership of grandfathered properties must conform to the rules.

tion. Government franchising of telephone networks was justified because they were natural monopolies. Congress and the Supreme Court accepted the necessity to impose federal licensing of operators because of the scarcity of channels. But one restriction may lead to another.

In the early days of radio, newspaper owners in the same city acquired many broadcasting licenses. Networks acquired licenses for stations in many different cities. Alarmed at the growing concentration of media ownership, the FCC first imposed restrictions on group ownership and, later, on cross-ownership between broadcasting and daily papers in the same market. As new technologies came along, these restrictions became more extensive and today also involve cable and telephone companies.

FREE PRESS AND FREE SPEECH?

Neither free speech nor free press is absolute. Over the decades the Supreme Court has upheld laws or regulations prohibiting libel, obscenity, endangering national security and dishonest advertising.[8] Recent Supreme Court decisions have taken a literal view of First Amendment guarantees in most cases involving these issues. But, decisions reflect the consensus of the specific individuals sitting on the Court at a point in time. As the membership changes, future Courts may change the interpretations of the Constitution in these areas.

The Communications Act of 1934 states that the FCC may not censor broadcasting content but may impose upon broadcasters and cable operators certain requirements intended to promote or protect a marketplace of ideas. For example,

> ### Examples of Restrictions on Broadcast and Cable Content
>
> In 1939 the FCC promulgated the "Mayflower Doctrine," which effectively prohibited broadcasters from editorializing. But in 1949 the FCC reversed this policy and stated that broadcasters had a responsibility to provide editorial commentary on issues. A string attached to this ruling became known as the "Fairness Doctrine." Broadcasters were required to seek out spokespersons for opposing points of view on issues and to give them air time equal to the station's editorials. In 1986 the FCC rescinded the "Fairness Doctrine" but continued to allow editorializing.
>
> Congress itself inserted into the Communications Act an "equal access" provision (Section 315), which prohibits broadcasters from refusing to sell equally attractive time to all candidates. A further requirement demands that time be made available to candidates at the station's lowest established rate.
>
> In 1970 the FCC issued the "Prime Time Access Rule (PTAR)" to reduce the dominance of network programs during the evening hours. Affiliates can carry network entertainment for no more than three of the four hours of prime time.
>
> In 1971 Congress passed legislation prohibiting broadcasters from carrying cigarette advertising.
>
> In 1990 Congress passed legislation which requires television stations to provide a block of daily children's programs and limits commercials within such programs to 12 minutes per hour.
>
> The Cable Communications Act passed by Congress in 1984 requires cable operators to provide access channels for the use of the general public as well as local government and educational agencies.[9] FCC regulations also require cable operators to black out any programs on imported services that duplicate those broadcast by a local station.

Congress itself wrote a provision (Section 315) into the Communications Act dealing with how broadcasters must treat candidates for federal elective offices. The FCC has at various times forbidden and, alternatively, required broadcasters to provide on-air editorials.

A FREE AND OPEN MARKETPLACE?

Such Congressional and FCC actions create a paradox and a conflict with the philosophical principles of free speech and press set forth in our First Amendment as well as that of free competition in the marketplace. The philosophical basis for including the press in the First Amendment protection was the role it (and other media) plays in creating and maintaining the marketplace of ideas.

As newspaper ownership becomes concentrated into fewer, larger, more powerful corporations, the nature of the marketplace of ideas has changed. Does an institution owning the only daily newspaper in a community constitute an open marketplace of ideas, particularly if it is part of a large chain?

Most observers will agree that the content of films, television programs and recorded music is loaded with philosophical and moral values and presents a particular view of our society. That the explicit aim of this content is to entertain, not to advocate, should not blind us to the fact that those who make the decisions on this content are in a position of unique power to shape the public's knowledge and attitudes.

This is not to say that those who direct the mass media are immoral, venal or megalomanic. Some individuals may be, but surely most are not. But the power is inherent in the very nature of their work and the functional relationship of their institutions to society.

THE SOCIAL INFLUENCE OF TECHNOLOGY

In wrestling with the relationship between media and social issues, technocrats and media apologists assert that technologies are value free and amoral. They contend that the fault, if there is fault, is with how we use these technologies, with the content we put into them. Is this really the case? Doesn't the introduction of technology itself create effects?[10]

Anyone who has tried to conduct a conversation with people in a room where a television set is on can attest to the fact that the mere presence of the set modifies the behavior of those in the room. The portable personal radios and cassette players have enabled people to isolate themselves even when in the midst of crowds on the street or on public transportation.

On another level the availability of television programming has changed how people allocate their time for various activities.[11] Similarly the telephone has re-oriented patterns of both business and personal communication interactions.

On a much broader level, the patterns of distribution for communication technologies and content can become the focus of international tensions. In Chapter 5 we noted the multinational wrestling over HDTV. Authorities in most nations other than the United States are uneasy about the impact of foreign video programs and so impose quotas on their use.

SHAPING—AND DISTORTING—THE REVOLUTIONARY TECHNOLOGIES

Just as older technologies have been shaped and twisted by policy and market factors, these factors will shape the revolutionary technologies and their applications. Indeed, this is already apparent in the following examples:

Development of HDTV technology in the United States must accommodate an FCC decision to protect the status quo of NTSC television. This decision dictates that any programs broadcast using HDTV must also be simultaneously available to owners of NTSC sets.

NHK's HDTV technology has been resisted for competitive reasons not only in Europe, but even by the commercial broadcasters in Japan.

The development of optical fiber telephone connections to homes is being delayed by challenges from broadcasters, cable operators and newspaper publishers who fear the telcos will put them out of business.

THE CHALLENGE OF MULTIMEDIA FORMATS

The current tension at the boundaries of the old domains is nothing compared to what will happen with the implementation of multimedia services delivered via optical fiber. Multimedia applications cut across all the existing domain boundaries. If proposals for a national optical fiber network are realized, such a system will also extend across many communities and geopolitical jurisdictions.

The services and content of the Communication Age will be shaped, perhaps distorted, by fierce contention between old and new institutions. Battalions of institutional attorneys and lobbyists will battle for ownership and control of institutions and content, as well as contend for capital financing and income revenues. Legal experts will research existing policies and seek the application of those most amenable to their own cases.

For the short-term future, the main issue on the policy battlefield will be optical fiber. The great cost of "fibering" the nation will require a franchised natural monopoly, at least for the first decade.

The capacity of an optical fiber system is sufficient to provide hundreds of video channels, as well as other types of entertainment, information and data. But a national optical fiber network would provide potential for centralized control of the marketplace of ideas. An optical fiber network inherently will be a switched, controlled system. The control of such a system has immense political and financial implications.

THE INTERNATIONAL DIMENSION OF POLICY

Because media and communication play major roles in political organization, national governments generally are extremely sensitive to external influence or interference with their operation. It is not surprising that many nations have maintained government ownership and operation of media as well as telecommunications and that they have sought to control the flow of communication across their borders. And yet the Industrial Revolution helped create economic forces that called for increasing international traffic of information as well as goods.

If citizens and businesses of a nation wish to have communication links with those in other countries, the nations of the world must negotiate arrangements to provide mutual communication exchange and access. This need has led to international agencies such as the ITU, first established as the International Telegraph Union by European nations in 1863. Today the ITU, located in Geneva, is a United Nations organization with world-wide membership.

Wireless communications introduced a host of new international constraints on national systems. The characteristics that justify the classifying of radio as interstate commerce also make it international. Eliminating co- and adjacent-channel interference between broadcasters along international boundaries requires cooperation by the nations sharing those boundaries.

The fact that the United States is very large and has neighbors on less than half of its border has left us relatively free to use the full range of U.S. broadcast channels.

In contrast, the much smaller nations of Europe have had far less freedom because they have had to share channels with neighbors.

In a period of bilateral disagreement, it is common for each nation to use broadcast signals to reach populations on either side of a border with propaganda. In instances of such broadcast confrontations, each may try to jam the signals of the other.

As telecommunications have expanded in both capacity and scope, international tensions have escalated. With their ability to cover so much of the earth's surface, satellites have become a major focus of debate at ITU meetings. Representatives seek to protect individual national access to orbital slots, access to the international networks and jurisdiction over information disseminated within their own borders.

Those concerned with plans and policy for domestic systems increasingly must consider international constraints on the use of technologies. Those concerned with the health and growth of our national economy seek expansion of the telecommunication ties to other nations. Domestic policy can no longer be considered separately from international policy.

THE ROLE OF MULTINATIONAL OPERATORS

International policy and standards are hammered out by national representatives in international organizations. In recent decades a second set of players has begun to take an increasingly active role in global communication: multinational corporations and operators.

Commerce has been a catalyst to the development of telecommunications throughout history. As businesses acquire interests in several or many nations, they seek to expand and increase the efficiency of telecommunications links to their far-flung branch offices, factories and warehouses.

As corporations become truly multinational, they use whatever influence they have to advance policies advantageous to the corporation at the expense of national political and cultural status quos. The resulting pressures extend in both directions.

Within CNN, for example, organization policy bans the use of the word *foreign* to encourage staff to use an international frame of reference and to reduce overseas identification of CNN as an American news service. This latter goal reflects the management's awareness that local sensitivities concerning cultural imperialism may create barriers to CNN's penetration into a national market.

As we observed much earlier, the purchase of Hollywood studios by giant Japanese multinational manufacturers evoked demands in some United States circles for policy to protect the national interest. U.S. producers simultaneously were urging our government to object to policies within the European Community restricting use of imported programs.

AT STAKE: BILLIONS OF DOLLARS

In the United States alone, telco revenues total $120 billion a year and revenues of all mass media combined total a similar amount. About 50 million TV sets are sold each year. Telecommunications is truly big business, with a great vested interest in the status quo. It is no wonder that communication law is the fastest growing specialization of the legal profession.

Already telecommunications and media lobbyists as well as politicians and regulatory agency officials have begun the preliminary skirmishes in what will be a major war. The outcome may spell the demise of some of today's institutions. There have been signs in the early 1990s of a resurgence in regulatory oversight of the communications field. However, unless there is some incredible reversal of our basic embrace of an open market philosophy, media consolidation and conglomeration will continue.

To paraphrase James Russell Lowell, "new technologies bring new problems, time makes ancient rules unwise."[12] To enjoy the full benefits of the Information Age, it will not be enough merely to overhaul our old policies. The Communication Revolution is forcing us to move toward a comprehensive policy.

Suggestions for Further Reading

The authors of this book obviously drew heavily on Ithiel de Sola Pool's *Technologies of Freedom*, which looks at the present and future through the filters of the past. Pool's posthumous *Technologies Without Boundaries* expands his discussion to the international arena. Pool takes a strong, libertarian, free-market stance.

The Media Monopoly by Ben Bagdikian and *The Media Elite* by Lichter, Rothman and Lichter are two of the many books providing details about media ownership and operations that can make the reader pause before totally embracing deregulation or unregulation. The eyebrow-raising cases reported by Leonard Lee in *The Day the Phones Stopped* does much the same for computer networks.

Responsibility in Mass Communication by William L. Rivers, Wilbur Schramm and Clifford G. Christians is one of the classic volumes on media ethics and was an outgrowth of an earlier prize-winning book, *Four Theories of the Press,* which Schramm co-authored with Fred S. Siebert and Theodore B. Peterson. Judith Lichtenberg's *Democracy and Mass Media* contains a set of essays with a broad sweep of observations and opinions about the interaction between media and our policy structure.

Two companion volumes, *The First Amendment and the Fourth Estate* and *The First Amendment and the Fifth Estate,* provide frequently updated comprehensive reviews of law and regulation in the media fields. Lucas A. Powe Jr. provides a more historical treatment in *The Fourth Estate and the Constitution*.

Notes

1. Pool, Ithiel de Sola. *Technologies of Freedom.* Cambridge: The Belknap Press of Harvard University, 1983, p. 7.
2. *Ibid.*
3. Each of the networks does own and operate several stations, generally referred to as their "O&Os." The O&Os, but not the parent networks, are licensed and regulated.
4. Reflecting these changes, the FCC changed the name of its Broadcast Bureau to the Mass Media Bureau and expanded its oversight to include cable.
5. This amendment was the 1984 Cable Communications Act, some parts of which were subsequently declared unconstitutional by the Supreme Court.

6. The ruling did not apply to local basic telephone service, which remains a natural monopoly. The FCC has structured cellular mobile telephone service so that there is competition within each market and has allowed some cable systems to offer some types of services competitive with the local telephone companies. In some cities, local authorities have allowed other operators to build private-service optical fiber systems that divert some business traffic from the local franchised company.

7. Such efforts can take various forms. The control of movie exhibitions by the major studios was an example of this type of restraint of competition. Earlier in this century newspaper wars in some major cities included intimidation, even physical violence, to discourage vendors from carrying competing publications.

8. All of these issues are problematic because they have no specific definition. Obscenity is defined within the context of "local standards," but there is no single method for establishing those standards. Some cities maintained review boards, usually dominated by persons with strong religious viewpoints, to screen publications and movies. These boards had the authority to ban the sale of publications and to prohibit the exhibition of feature films unless objectionable material was deleted. Boston had such a reputation for censorship that "banned in Boston" was often used as a marketing device to sell licentious material elsewhere.

    The U.S. Postal Service has at various times refused to transport publications on the basis of either obscene or seditious content. Customs officers routinely confiscated pornographic or obscene materials coming into the country. Prior to 1933 James Joyce's *Ulysses* was among the works on the confiscation list. It took a Supreme Court decision to have this work reclassified as art rather than pornography.

    Equally problematic are disagreements between journalists and government officials concerning whether information is classified as secret for reasons of national security or to avoid potential political embarrassment.

9. The same act also included a must-carry provision to guarantee that cable systems carry the programs of all local broadcast TV stations. The Supreme Court subsequently ruled that this provision violated the First Amendment rights of cable operators.

10. One of the most entertaining yet effective demonstrations of this premise was the extent to which the mere presence of a Coca Cola bottle was shown as disrupting life in a village of the Kalahari Desert of southern Africa, in the 1984 South African film, "The Gods Must Be Crazy."

11. John P. Robinson reports data on this subject in his chapter "TV's Impact on Everyday Life: Some Cross Cultural Evidence," in Volume IV of *Television and Social Behavior*. Bethesda: National Institute of Mental Health, pp. 410–431.

12. The original is: "New occasions teach new duties, time makes ancient good uncouth," from a poem published by Lowell in 1845 entitled "Once to Every Man and Nation." It can be found in hymn 519 in *The Hymnal 1970* (N.Y.. Church Publishing House, 1970) of the Episcopal Church. The truth declaimed by Lowell caught up with this poem. The hymn was dropped in the new 1980s hymnal because its language was deemed sexist.

CHAPTER 7

Technologies, Infrastructures, Systems and Standards

All of us have experienced infrastructure failures. Remember unwrapping toys on Christmas morning and discovering that the required batteries were not included? Or the time you bought a do-it-yourself kit with missing parts or incomplete instructions? These are both examples of infrastructure problems. The rapid sequence of changes in disk and tape recording formats provides a more sophisticated and formidable infrastructure challenge.

A different type of infrastructure problem is illustrated by that case of the thoughtful aunt who gave her ballet-loving niece a videocassette of "The Nutcracker" with Baryshnikov. It was a Beta format cassette; the niece had a VHS player. More frustration.

Perhaps you've had the experience of trying to hook up a new telephone, a VCR or a new stereo component and in the process finding that a critical connection is either missing or has the wrong type of plug. Still more frustration.

These are all examples of infrastructure problems, which complicate the use of new technologies and often add to their cost.

TECHNOLOGIES REQUIRE OPERATING SYSTEMS

Technologies seldom stand alone. Usually they require supporting systems. For example almost all require a source of electrical power. A stereo amplifier by itself is just as useless as a CD player without an amplifier and either earphones or loudspeakers. Fax machines are of no use without telephone connections.

Technologies are generally used within a context which consists of a network of institutions, a hierarchy of systems. Because most magazines depend on the U.S. Postal Service to deliver copies to subscribers, an increase in postal rates increases their operating cost. Because they depend upon network programs to attract audiences, local television affiliates literally pay the cost when network's programming executives make bad choices. CNN requires continuous access to a series of satellite links, first to bring news from all over the world to Atlanta for editing, and then to distribute its programs to hundreds of cable systems and television operators.

A change in one component of a system may require change in others. The introduction of long-playing records (LPs) required the development of turntables that rotated at 33⅓ revolutions per minute (rpm), rather than the old standard of 78 rpm, and the development of a fine-tipped stylus to replace the old "needles." Cassettes and CDs made it necessary for us to buy new playback equipment to plug into our amplifiers and speakers.

Whether any revolutionary technology is viable in the marketplace largely depends upon where it fits into existing systems and whether an appropriate infrastructure can make it sufficiently easy and economical to attract buyers and users.

It might seem simplest to build a totally new system, but in reality this is seldom—if ever—a viable option. The size, complexity, power and systemic intertwining of media and communication institutions make it inevitable that the use of new technologies will be within the context of existing systems. This situation prompted Pool's observation, mentioned on page 79, that any new technology disrupts a status quo.

The complexity of today's technologies heightens the importance of two aspects of the system structure:

1. The system includes increased crossover applications of technologies among institutions; e.g., satellites are used by institutions in all three domains—newspapers, broadcasters and common carriers.
2. Standardization holds increased importance within technologies; e.g., in 1991 personal computer arch rivals IBM and Apple agreed to develop software that could be used by their previously incompatible hardware.

These two aspects are so intertwined that they become a common thread. This thread, a focus on the convergence of systems technologies, should help the reader negotiate the maze-like panorama of technology that follows.

BASIC FUNCTIONS, DIFFERENT CAPABILITIES

All our communications systems, whether mass media or telecommunications, have the same basic function: they seek to transmit information from sender to receiver. General models of communications usually stress an interrelated series of components:

Sender	Originates message
Encoder	Puts message into symbols
Transmitter	Generates signal to carry message

Channel	Carries the signal
Receiver	Intercepts/receives the signal
Decoder	Recreates original symbols from the signal
Audience	Interprets symbols into meaning that may or not correspond to the original message

The meaning of the sender's original message may be distorted at each stage of the process.

Media and telecommunications systems perform the various tasks necessary to connect the sender and the receiver in ways enabling us to distribute information more widely in terms of individuals, distance and (in some cases) time.

Pool emphasized that his three domains are traditional groupings of communication systems or institutions according to technology: press, broadcasting and common carrier. Each of these can be used in support of all four of the major communications functions: information, advocacy, education and entertainment. Each domain has become identified with certain functions more than others. These specializations reflect the operational efficiencies or capabilities of different technologies associated with each domain.

PRESS SYSTEMS

The oldest of the domains, press, has the simplest basic structure. Information is composed into a physical master from which duplicate imprints are made. These imprints must be distributed or made available to the audience.

For most of us, *press* automatically means publications such as newspapers, magazines and books, wherein words and pictures are converted into type forms, which are then inked and used to transfer an impression to paper. Recordings and movies may use different technologies, but the basic system is the same. This similarity is reflected by the recording industry's use of such terms as *pressings* or *dubs,* and the film industry's use of *prints*.

A key characteristic of press systems is the manufacture of a physical product.

1. The system uses a production plant or factory and appropriate raw materials, such as newsprint, film or tape.
2. To complete the communication process, the product is distributed, whether it be a newspaper or a book, a film or CDs or cassettes.
3. Press institutions can confuse the physical product with their true product—the information they distribute.

Among the institutions of telecommunications, those of the press have their technological roots in the Industrial Revolution. In performing their communication functions, they operate as factories.

A distinct advantage of a communication through a physical product is that it provides a means through which the sender can assess the number and even identity of receivers. Newspapers, for example, can produce circulation records to impress advertisers. Another advantage is that the product is used at the convenience of the receiver and has an extended lifespan. It can be stored and circulated over time to additional users.

Nothing inherent in press technologies limits how many people can compete in the domain. The number of publishers is limited solely by a combination of desire and access to financing. This fact has resulted in policies that set institutions of the press apart from those of other domains.

BROADCASTING SYSTEMS

Contrary to popular usage, *radio* and *broadcasting* are not synonymous terms. The Communications Act of 1934 defines radio communication as "the transmission by radio of writing, signs, signals, pictures, and sounds of all kinds."[1] Broadcasting is much more narrowly defined, as ". . . the dissemination of radio communications intended to be received by the public, directly or by the intermediary of relay stations."[2] In other words, broadcasting is only one particular category of radio communication, which includes television and both FM and AM radio.

In broadcasting no physical product is distributed. Instead, the information is converted into electrical impulses modulated onto a radio carrier signal. This signal is radiated from a transmitter antenna with a large amount of electrical energy and travels through space without a physical carrier.

Explicit in the structure of broadcasting are the following assumptions:

1. Broadcasting includes the ability to make instantaneous simultaneous delivery of a signal to audiences over a large geographic area.
2. Broadcasting is effective for communication only if receivers have the appropriate technology to intercept and recreate the original message.
3. Attempts by more than one broadcaster to use signals of the same frequency results in confusion.

These characteristics complicate the infrastructure, but they also eliminate problems related to delivery of a physical message product. The nature of the system is such that the sender cannot know who the receivers are, or even if there are any. Thus the broadcasting industry has had to create an ancillary institution, the ratings services, to provide estimates of audience size.

The broadcasting signal is ephemeral and fleeting. The user has no control over the pace of the signal nor can it be preserved unless some form of press technology (a VCR or audio recorder) is brought into play.

Policy makers have accepted the view that broadcast channels are a scarce commodity. Because radio signals radiate without a physical carrier, signals using the same set of frequencies may interfere with one another. It is simply impractical to allow anybody and everybody to broadcast at will. This physical limitation has led our society not only to accept government licensing and regulation of broadcasters, but has also led to hesitation concerning the protection provided these media by the First Amendment.

COMMON-CARRIER SYSTEMS

A common carrier allows users to have interactive access to all other users of the system. The infrastructure itself comprises an interconnected hierarchy of switches from which connections feed out to individual users. The more extended the hierarchy of switches, the greater flexibility the system has to accomplish that task.

Efficiency of a common-carrier system is a function of the transmission capacity of each link and the speed of the switches. Incredibly fast computer switches, together with the near global reach of satellites, provide virtually instantaneous connections to telephone subscribers almost anywhere. The rapid spread of optical fiber is dramatically increasing the volume of traffic of the interconnected telephone systems within and between nations. Expanded use of radio frequencies has made possible services such as cellular phones and paging services.

As new technologies come into use, a major question is whether they will be integrated into the hierarchy of switches facilitating universal service and, if so, how will this be done and by whom. The neat, closed systems operated by the franchised monopoly telephone companies are being unravelled, and new systems and structures must evolve.

CHANGING TECHNOLOGIES WITHIN DOMAINS

Technological change is causing change and redefinition within all three of the traditional domains. From a historical perspective, we tend to associate each domain with one or a few specific technologies. *Press* has usually meant letterpress printing; *broadcasting* has meant AM/FM radio and television; *common carrier* has meant telephony.[3] In fact, each domain has been and continues to comprise a changing variety of technologies.

In recent years many newspapers have changed from letterpress to offset printing technology. Some newspapers have begun to provide content via videotex, facsimile, and voice information services.

Feature films are now seen by most people in video format. Sound recordings have evolved from acoustically recorded wax cylinders to digitally recorded tape and laser-read plastic discs (CDs).

Broadcasting began as AM radio and expanded to include TV and FM radio, then FM stereo, and, more recently, AM stereo and digital audio broadcasting (DAB). HDTV is now on the way as is service by direct broadcast satellites (DBS).

Up through World War II, the telegraph was a viable competitor with the telephone in the common-carrier field. If you send a telegram today, it will be delivered by either telephone or mail. And now we have the option for fax, mobile pagers,

E-mail, satellite telephones, personal communication networks and video dial tone service, which would enable us to call up video material as simply as dialing up information from a 900 number.

MISFITS AND HYBRIDS

With the introduction of new technologies, misfits and hybrids have appeared to confuse the traditional boundaries. Cable television is perhaps the most ubiquitous of these. Its distribution technology—a network of coaxial copper cable—seems to parallel that of the most common carrier, the telephone system. However, its function has been closer to that of broadcasting.

As we saw in the preceding chapter, the FCC has chosen to lump cable with broadcasting rather than with common carriers. Satellite operators, who are totally dependent on radio technology, are regulated by the FCC's Common Carrier Bureau.

Multichannel multipoint distribution systems (MMDS) and DBS make use of radio technology to provide a service paralleling that of cable. Cellular mobile telephones are also a common-carrier service that uses radio.

These and other hybrids and misfits provide clear evidence of what Pool referred to as "tension on the frontiers" of the domains. Changes within the systems of traditional institutions are also breaching the walls dividing the domains.

USING TECHNOLOGY REQUIRES ORGANIZATION— AND ORGANIZATIONS

We said at the outset that technologies are enabling devices. Their use requires human thought and intervention at various stages of their operation. People create organizations (systems) to make use of technology in carrying out communication functions. As these organizations acquire professional staffs they become institutions.

The Industrial Revolution initiated a demand for communication services that has grown at a constantly accelerating rate. And modern technologies have provided means for serving this demand. The institutions operating those technologies have had the potential for dramatic growth in size, revenues and complexity. But general growth in the demand for communication services does not guarantee growth for individual institutions or technologies.

THE NEWSPAPER: A CASE STUDY

The newspaper is our oldest mass medium, but the institutions which produce these publications have changed radically since Thomas Jefferson, James Madison and George Mason drafted the First Amendment guarantee of press freedom.

The earliest newspapers operated as a sideline of print-shop owners, with no reportorial or editorial staff. The printer culled information from other publications, compiled local gossip and accepted essays from local politicians. Print-shop staff hand-

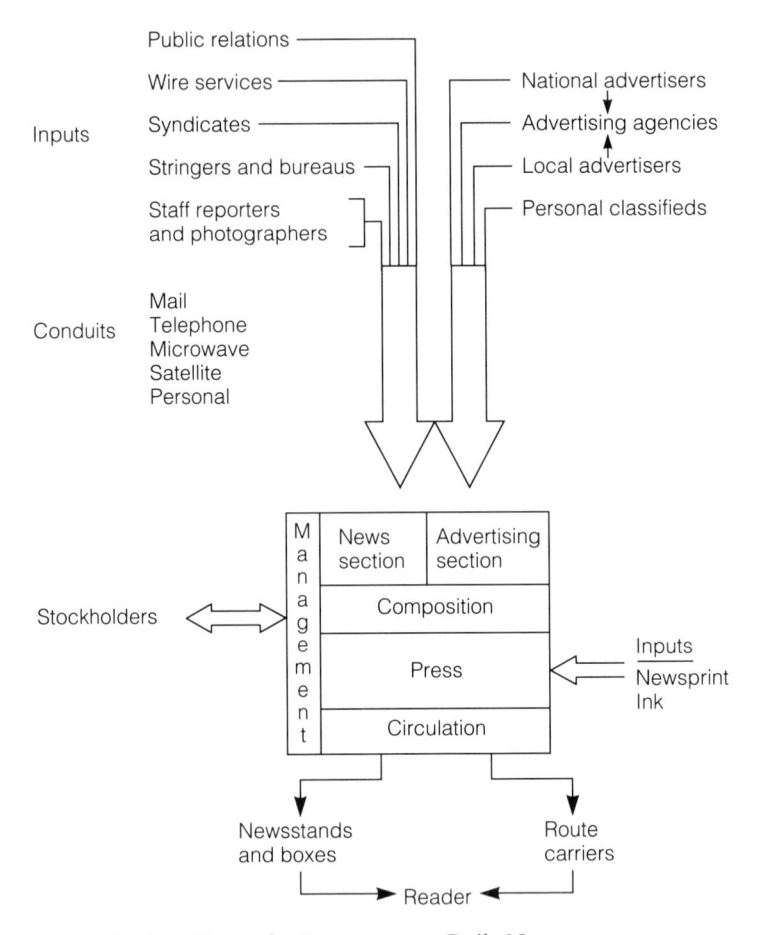

Figure 7.1 Organization Chart of a Contemporary Daily Newspaper

set these items and composed the type into page forms. Pages had to be individually printed by laying paper upon the inked type, applying pressure, and then removing it. The process was repeated for each copy.

The limitation of the technology and the high cost of paper combined to keep the number of copies printed low—usually just a few hundred. These copies were sold directly, many of them to coffeehouses where they were read by patrons at their leisure.[4]

Contrast this simple system with Figure 7.1, which details major components of the infrastructure of a contemporary daily newspaper. The institutions now producing tens or even hundreds of thousands of copies each day are no longer restricted to raised type and presses, but use a host of different technologies. The institution itself, the newspaper company, is compartmentalized according to function, and each of these has an extensive network of dependent ties to external agencies.

NEWSPAPERS FACE A DOUBLE CRISIS

Newspaper institutions now face serious problems stemming from both the product's physical nature and its function. Only a handful of our cities now have competing newspapers, and circulation has increased only slightly during recent decades, although the population has grown (see Figure I.1).

The newspaper itself is becoming a problem. Urban sprawl and increased traffic have made newspaper delivery more difficult.[5] Communities, facing increased problems of waste disposal, are now demanding that newspaper institutions take action to reduce the accumulation of discarded newspapers in municipal landfills.

Changes in content and format reflect attempts by the individual institutions of the press domain to retain a functional relevance necessary for survival. But if the public can obtain the information they need more efficiently through other technologies, the newspaper faces a gloomy future. Notice that the reference is to the newspaper—not to the journalism per se; publishers who do not differentiate between "providing news" and "printing newspapers" are in trouble. The functional need for news will persist, although the emphasis on what kind of news is needed and used may change.

FUNCTIONAL COMPETITION, DISPLACEMENT AND ACCOMMODATION

The type of threat engulfing newspapers is general to all institutions, and the history of mass media and telecommunications is replete with examples of institutions that have undergone dramatic change—including disappearance. The basic rule of institutional survival is "keep your eye on the function."

In the 1930s and 1940s, both the film industry and weekly general circulation magazines, such as *The Saturday Evening Post, Collier's* and *Liberty,* were an integral part of the nation's entertainment habit. Then they were functionally challenged by a new competitor, television. In the space of only a few years, the big weekly magazines lost the interest of the public and disappeared.[6]

The makers of feature films found that their problem was not in the product, but in the means of delivery. By adding other means of exhibition, the movie industry continues to be a major force. But the cinemas, which once had a monopoly on distributing the product, now have a greatly reduced role in the movie infrastructure.

TECHNOLOGICAL PROGRESS CAN OUTRUN THE MARKET

The recorded music industry has maintained the same basic function and organizational structure throughout the century, but it has gone through a sequence of technological change which now shows signs of outrunning its market. Consider the sequence of change in the physical product.

Edison introduced acoustically recorded wax cylinders in 1872. Masters were cut by a stylus vibrating in direct response to sound waves focused by large funnels. Shellac disks were introduced in 1893, and the speed of 78 rpm became standard. In the 1920s a change was made to electrical recording, with microphones replacing the horns of the old studios. The LP era of vinyl disks and 33⅓ rpm became standard in 1948, and ten years later stereo was introduced. Tape recordings were introduced in the 1950s, progressing through a sequence of formats: reel-to-reel, 8-track cassette and the still-current 4-track cassette. In the mid-1970s digital recording was introduced in the studios, and in 1983 digital playback entered the market as CDs. Digital audio tape (DAT) appeared on the United States market in 1987, several years after it was available elsewhere. At least two manufacturers, Sony and Phillips, announced plans for new digital formats in 1991. Each of these developments meant an infrastructure change requiring new decoding (playback) technology.

With each change, a period of technological overlap has allowed the public to continue to use their old equipment. However, the pace of change has increased in recent years, leading to consumer confusion. DATs encountered considerable public reluctance to purchase the requisite new equipment; the public anticipates that the technology will soon be superseded.

FORCES OF INSTITUTIONAL CHANGE

Institutions may change the function as well as the technology of their operation. Weekly newspapers in growing communities may change to daily publication. Telephone companies have added microwave links, satellite relays and optical fiber to their systems. The three major networks in the United States made a transition from radio to television.

Cable originally was not a competitor of broadcasters, but was an adjunct. Functionally it expanded the audience of individual stations (and networks) by taking their signal to areas where off-air reception was difficult. Today the situation is very different.

Cable operators found they had to broaden their function to increase their subscriber list; simply providing good reception of off-air broadcast systems was not sufficient. They became innovators in using microwave and satellite technology to import a broad range of entertainment and information options for their subscribers.

Figure 7.2 shows how cable has interposed itself between the audience and individual stations (and the networks), both structurally and functionally. Although most families still spend much of their time watching the programs of broadcasters, many now receive those programs through cable rather than directly off-air. In effect, cable has destroyed the broadcast industry's monopoly over the choice of programmed television for six of every ten television households in the United States.

Cable's impact on broadcast television has been a double whammy. By reducing the size of broadcasters' audiences, cable has weakened the basis for broadcasters' advertising rates at the same time that cable has begun to compete for local and national advertising. Cable services now also compete with broadcasters in the programming market. This means that, while threatening broadcasters' advertising revenues,

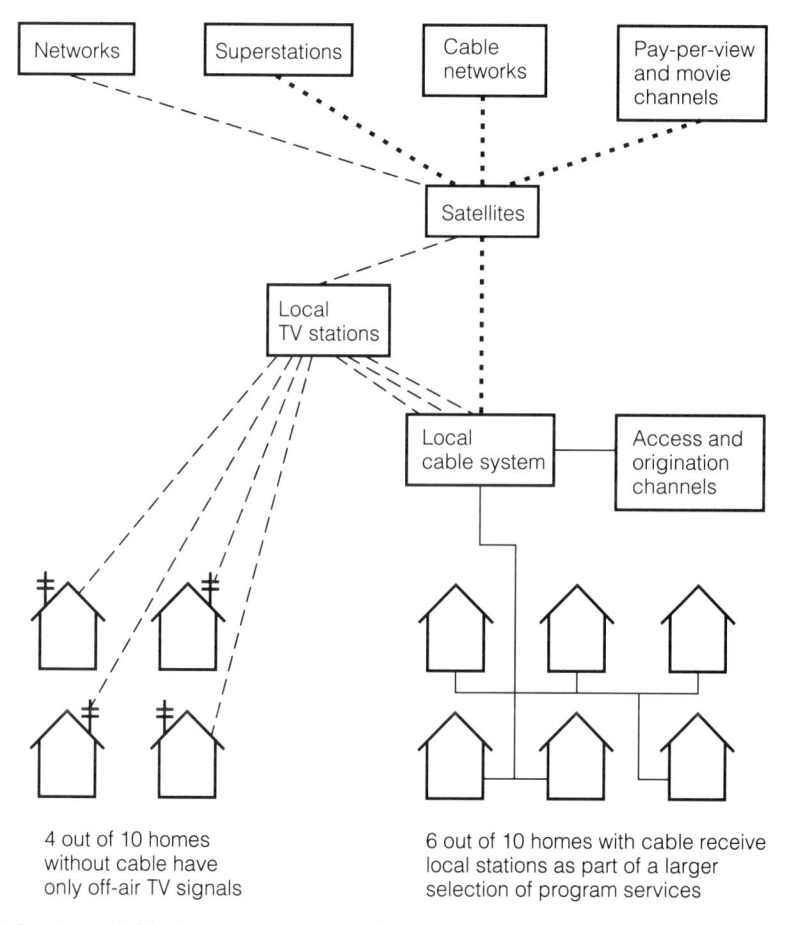

Chapter 7 Technologies, Infrastructures, Systems and Standards 107

Figure 7.2 How Cable Has Interposed Itself Between Broadcasters and the Audience

cable's competition for programs is simultaneously raising the cost of programs and increasing broadcasters' operating expense.

INFRASTRUCTURE CHANGE BY POLICY FIAT

Changes in infrastructure can be implemented by administrative fiat as well as by changes in technology and the market. This type of change is most dramatically exemplified by events in the common-carrier domain over the past two decades.

Prior to 1968 the telephone in the United States was synonymous with AT&T, whose vertically and horizontally integrated network was the world's largest and most dependable provider of POTS (and plain it was!). With the exception of a few independent companies, mostly in California, Texas and some rural areas, AT&T provided

Table 7.1 What Became of Ma Bell's Hegemony

Equipment	Long-Distance	Local Service	
1970			
	AT&T		Non Bell Companies
Monopoly	Monopoly	83%	17%
1990			
		"Baby Bells"	Non Bell Companies
AT&T	AT&T	Southwestern Bell 10%	11%
		US West 10%	
Just about everybody except the "Baby Bells"	MCI Sprint Others	Pacific Telesis 10%	
		Ameritech 10%	
		Altantic Bell 12%	
		NYNEX 13%	
		Bellsouth 14%	
		and with a foot in the door: Cellular mobile companies New optical fiber companies Interactive cable systems	

all local service, was the monopoly provider of long-distance service and manufactured and owned all the equipment used within the system.

AT&T was so big and powerful (and, according to some, arrogant) that it became the target of suits filed by the antitrust division of the Federal Department of Justice. This led to a sequence of rulings in the federal courts, which mandated radical changes in the nation's telephone infrastructure.

The 1968 Carterphone decision forced AT&T to allow customers not only to own equipment, but to buy equipment from competing companies. In 1984 the monopoly in long-distance service was ended, and today AT&T faces aggressive competition from several companies, most importantly from MCI and Sprint.

But that wasn't the end of the story. To equalize competitive conditions in long distance, it was necessary for AT&T to divest itself of local service, through which long-distance calls originate. And Ma Bell had to let go of the Baby Bells, which were organized into seven regional operating companies. Table 7.1 provides a before and after chart of the telephone infrastructure.

The various rulings resulted in an entirely new playing field for telephone services. The now-competitive field attracted hundreds of new companies, which have produced a rapid expansion in the range of services available to telephone users. Simple, dependable POTS has been replaced by a sometimes bewildering array of competing products and services.

For business users the result has been opportunities for substantial savings. For residential users the situation has been equivocal. They do have many more options, but many users have also seen their monthly bills increase. All users now can have phones of whatever color, shape and capability they wish, but when something goes wrong they may not know who to call to get it fixed.

ORGANIZATIONAL PUSH AND PULL IN SYSTEMS

The history of telephone use in this country illustrates the push and pull forces pervasive in organizational structures. Institutions come into being to perform functions useful to some portion of society. The birth of an institution may be related either to the introduction of a new technology or to changes within the society that create a new need or modify an existing need. Once they exist institutions take on lives of their own; like the individuals operating them, they try to protect and enrich themselves.

Western Union, which dominated wire telegraphy for decades, today is primarily a satellite common carrier. Times-Mirror Corp., which began as the *Los Angeles Times,* has aggressively expanded and today is a national conglomerate operating a chain of newspapers, magazines, cable systems and broadcast stations.

Ted Turner started with a money-losing UHF station in Atlanta, a local market dominated by VHF network affiliates. By innovating with satellite distribution, he turned WTBS into a superstation. He challenged the networks with CNN, the first all-news video service. He added TNT, a satellite programming service. To guarantee access to movies, he bought the MGM film library; to obtain better syndicated series, he provided support for production of original series. When Turner got into financial difficulty, he sold equity in his company to two of his biggest customers, TCI and ATC, the nation's two largest cable multiple systems operators. His original property, the Atlanta UHF station (WTBS), is now lost in a veritable corporate maze (see Figure 7.3). TBS shows the complex cross-ownership and vertical and horizontal integration marking the cable industry today.

Time Inc. remained at heart a magazine empire even as it expanded into other fields and the people in top management positions had their roots in the magazines. But when Time Inc. bought Warner Communications and became Time-Warner, the world's largest media empire, the print media people found themselves displaced. The new top management was dominated by people who came from video and entertainment divisions of the corporation.

Times-Mirror, TBS and Time-Warner exemplify a general rule: institutions seek integration of related elements, to achieve control over auxiliary systems and to dominate competing systems. The result is a push for vertical and horizontal integration as well as the evolution of monopoly control.

Much of this impetus for integration is related to finance and will be discussed

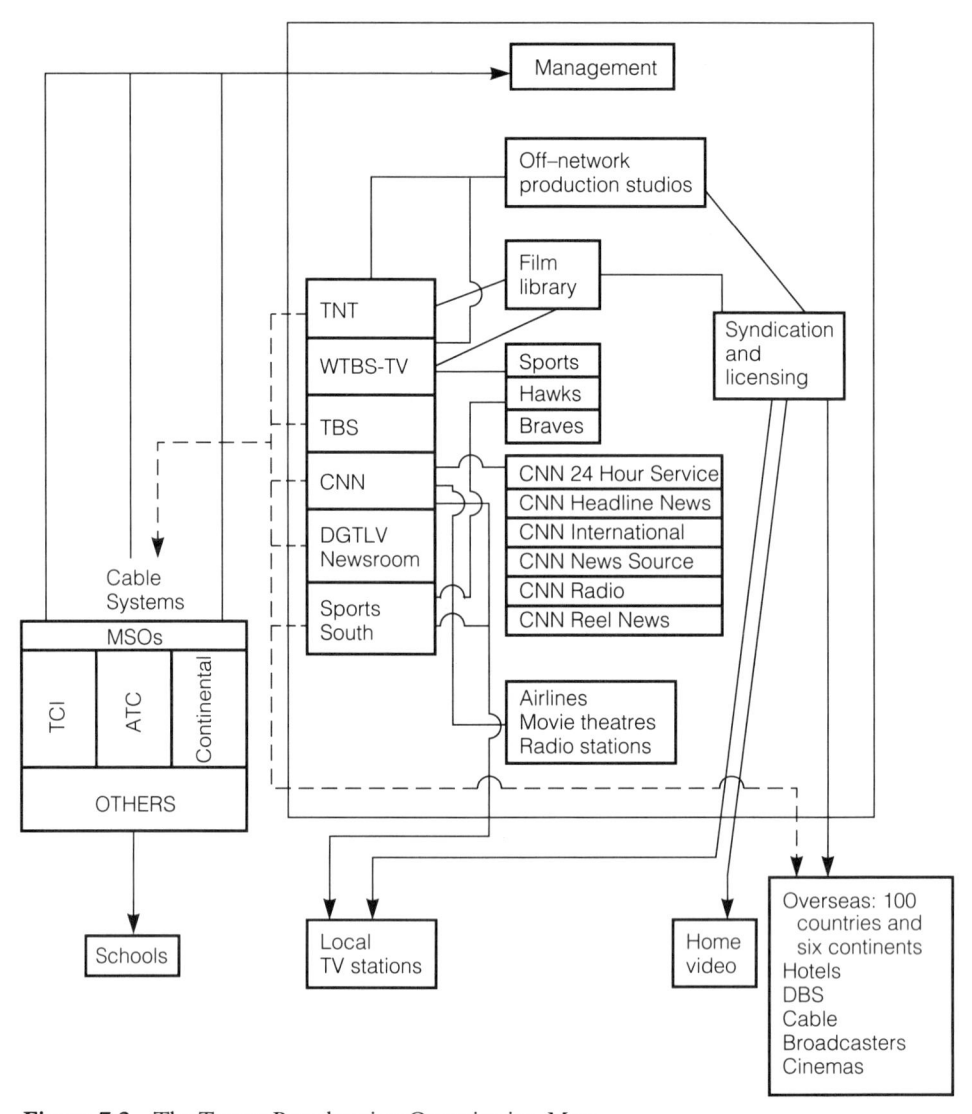

Figure 7.3 The Turner Broadcasting Organization Maze

in the next chapter. Here we are interested in the impact of integration on the infrastructure and its operation. Perhaps the greatest of such impacts is related to the matter of standards.

THE ARBITRARY NATURE OF STANDARDS

Left to itself the world is a marvelously chaotic environment and provides few, if any, absolute standards. Among such absolutes are the day (a full rotation of the earth), the year (a full revolution of the earth in its orbit around the sun) and the points at which water boils and freezes. But the division of those measures is arbitrary, made by human decision.

Water freezes at 32 degrees on the Fahrenheit scale and 0 on the Celsius scale; it boils at 212 degrees Fahrenheit but at 100 Celsius. If someone reports that it's 27 degrees Celsius, you may want to head for the beach; if it's 27 degrees Fahrenheit, you can still go to the beach—but you'd better put on a warm coat.

Throughout history different cultures have used calendars that vary in their division of the year. Nothing illustrates the arbitrary division of time better than the zigzag of the lines demarcating the borders of the four time zones used in the contiguous 48 states. No standardization of time existed across the United States until the late 19th century. No functional need demanded standardization until railroads needed to coordinate schedules for customer convenience and safety.[7]

Weight, mass, distance and speed were all rather casually dealt with until the Industrial Revolution. Even today the United States adheres to our own archaic system of weights and measures[8], although much of the world has agreed to use the metric system.

Language is one of the earliest of our standardized systems. It is far simpler to identify an object with a name than to play a game of charades. The irritating habit of teachers in grading down for errors in spelling and grammar has a purpose. As we deviate from standard language use, we introduce confusion for others in what we write or say. The dictionary and the rules of grammar are a codification of language standards.

Language, unlike the chemical elements, is not fixed in its structure, and so linguistic standards do change with time.[9] If your teacher is using a 1920s dictionary to correct your paper, you may actually be right, and your teacher (not just hopelessly out of date) may be wrong. Without general adherence to the rules, we run the risk of undermining our attempt to communicate information.

One of the advantages of digital languages is that they have a higher degree of specificity than standard verbal text. That makes them more efficient for conveying specific information.[10]

AN INESCAPABLE ASPECT OF TECHNOLOGY

If a simple technology were used within a single closed system by a single person, it might not have to be involved with standards. But by definition mass media and telecommunications are extended systems concerning different people using machines in different places.

Machines and connecting links must be standardized. The content must be composed in codes used commonly by both sender and receiver.[11] Without a standardized electrical current, electronic signals may be distorted. The Naval Observatory maintains the nation's official clock so that timekeeping devices may be synchronized. This is essential for maintaining a smooth flow of traffic through switches and connecting links, whether they are railroad or telephone lines, or the television networks and their affiliates.

FORMS OF STANDARDS

Some standards are essential for technological reasons. Standardization of broadcast channels is necessary to allow sufficient bandwidth for the information transmitted and to prevent interference between transmitters. However, the choice of specific technology for a service is arbitrary. For decades there have been three major standards for television broadcasting: NTSC, PAL and SECAM. Each performs the same technological function but has different characteristics, making them incompatible. If you take a United States TV receiver (NTSC) to Great Britain, your set will not decode the local (PAL) signals.

Other standards affecting message content have evolved not because of technology but to facilitate internal operation of institutional systems.

Journalists evolved the "inverted pyramid" style of reporting to make it easier to shorten stories to fit space or time available without losing the most important facts. People who write scripts for U.S. television learn to pace plot development to fit standard periodic interruptions for commercials.[12] Commercials themselves evolved with standard lengths (60-, 30-, and, more recently, 15-seconds) so that they can fit into the broadcast schedules by any and all stations and to simplify the price structure for broadcast advertising.

To help the public obtain help more quickly, telephone systems across the nation have been implementing a standard emergency number, 911.

CHANGING STANDARDS: INERTIA AND RESISTANCE

Pool's comment about new technologies disturbing the status quo applies to these systemic as well as to technological standards. We can easily understand why linotype operators resisted the introduction of word processors in newspaper production: This change reduced the performance standards of their role from those of a technical crafts skill to those equivalent to a clerk/typist, a change with serious implications for wage scales.

Manufacturers gleefully anticipate billions of dollars of revenue from introducing HDTV, but it is hardly surprising that television station owners do not share their enthusiasm. The conversion to HDTV will require them to incur a heavy expense for equipment with no expectation that it will increase revenues.

Some resistance seems to lack rational explanation. Why was there a near rebellion by the staff of the *New Yorker* several years ago when its management began accepting half- and quarter-page ads in order to offer advertisers greater flexibility and to generate more revenue?

Why do many newspapers that have converted to digital composition and offset printing continue to use hard-to-read narrow column widths originally required for letterpress technology?[13]

These examples of operational procedures and formats, originally based on technological requirements, became traditions. In turn, when technology and operating conditions changed, they became anachronisms. When such anachronisms become dysfunctional, rather than simply quaint, an institution has real trouble on its hands.

ECONOMIC DIMENSIONS OF STANDARDS

The adoption of a specific standard may result in millions of dollars of profit or loss for both those who manufacture technology and those who use it. Not surprisingly, open warfare can result regarding who sets and enforces standards for a technology or industry. How standards are set and enforced becomes an important factor in determining system flexibility.

Some standards are set by national agencies, sometimes in agreement with international organizations. Others are established cooperatively within industries; some are fought out in the marketplace. Some are imposed by dominant institutions within the infrastructure.

The fact that radio signals radiate without respect to national boundaries forced nations to participate in the ITU. Through its plenary sessions, the nations of the world endorse the division of the electromagnetic spectrum into bands designated for different types of use and establish rules for the spacing of satellites in the geosynchronous orbit. As the continuing use of several incompatible television standards demonstrates, nations reserve unto themselves the selection of standards within their national broadcast services.

The VCR standard evolved from a marketplace battle. Sony introduced its Beta format first. Other manufacturers joined together to back VHS and, ultimately, succeeded in driving Beta from the consumer market. The result was a multi-million-dollar loss for Sony, which inevitably affected its competitive position. Those unlucky consumers who bought Beta machines ended up with equipment for which the supply of rental videos was limited.

Domination of standards within an industry means competitive advantage. The pervasiveness of AT&T standards throughout the telephone industry was one of the reasons why Judge Harold Greene felt it necessary to judicially impose a set of "handicaps" on AT&T in the interest of insuring a level playing field for other providers of telephone equipment and services.

THE PHANTOM COMPONENT OF INFRASTRUCTURE

Standards facilitate the operation of infrastructures by users. However, systems are not always meant to be open. The tension must be balanced between achieving maximum ease and efficiency for legitimate users and safeguarding the system and its content from pirates.

In each of the three domains the infrastructure includes parasitical components, "pirates" or black-marketeers who provide equipment or content outside the regular channels: people who reprint books without permission; people who copy and sell video and audiotapes without payment to the studios; people who sell mail-order converter boxes and gadgets making it possible to get cable and satellite services without paying or to reproduce the tones used by pay phones; and hackers who gain unauthorized access to computer software and data files. The loss to the various communication companies is immense. For example the Recording Industry Association of America estimates that piracy costs the music industry more than $1 billion annually.

As the infrastructures of the domains become entwined and as access to telecommunications systems widens, it is more difficult to secure content and service. For example the use of satellites to deliver programs to thousands of cable systems and broadcast stations across the nation means these programs can be intercepted by private users as well. The seriousness of this situation prompted Congress to make cable piracy a federal criminal offense.

In 1991 Digital Equipment Corporation, one of the nation's largest computer manufacturers, admitted that unknown "hackers" had infiltrated its corporate computer network, roaming through internal correspondence, copying secret software and passwords. The ability of hackers to infiltrate various computer networks—including some of those within the Department of Defense—illustrates the potential vulnerability of computer-based services.

FLAG WAVING AND GLOBAL SYSTEMS

Standards can also be used to promote national policies of economic export and, obversely, protectionism. Third World nations have learned that unilateral assistance programs often tie their future purchases to the technology of donor countries.

Most European nations individually and as a group through the European Community have set up importation barriers to protect their own electronics and telecommunications industries from foreign (primarily Japanese) competition. Similar protectionist measures have been adopted in Europe and elsewhere to prevent foreign (primarily United States) domination of the content distributed by domestic media.

The revolutionary technologies have greatly expanded the potential scope of telecommunications and media. CNN has used satellites to pioneer ongoing video news coverage worldwide. MTV has similarly pioneered international music video. Their lead is being followed by other foreign and U.S. organizations. American movies dominate the cinemas in many nations, including the most culturally xenophobic of all, France.

The *Paris Herald* of Ernest Hemingway's Paris days has become the *International Herald Tribune*, distributed by satellite for same-day publication in a dozen locations around the world. The newspaper is now distributed in over 160 nations. Satellite or optical fiber delivery of facsimile editions can convert any publication into a worldwide publication.

In Europe, where nations have been divided by PAL and SECAM television standards, many citizens purchased dual-standard receivers so they could expand the limited choice of broadcast television by receiving programs from neighboring countries. Now DBS is speeding a transition in these nations to a single standard.

Telecommunications and media infrastructures are becoming increasingly international, in both scope and ownership. Individual nations may resist this trend, but resistance may create barriers to participation in the global markets desirable for economic growth.

Each of us faces a situation similar to that of nations. By expanding our connections to and use of this infrastructure we can expand our opportunities to enjoy the benefits associated with the various functions of communications. If we are denied access we will face restricted opportunities for intellectual, career and financial advancement.

We must also remember that the infrastructure presents personal piracy problems. Whenever we use the infrastructure we create a record of activity, and it is possible for people and organizations to obtain access to this record without our knowledge or permission. Gain of any kind is always accompanied by commensurate risk. As we struggle to learn how to use the opportunities of expanding infrastructure, we must also learn how to protect our privacy and our assets while doing so.

Because infrastructures are becoming global and all-encompassing, we cannot, like Thoreau, withdraw to an isolated spot and drop out of society. Whether we like it or not, we have to be participants, because we cannot isolate ourselves from the effects of the actions of others. This new situation presents a challenge for both individuals and societies.

Suggestions for Further Reading

A. Michael Noll's *Television Technology: Fundamentals and Future Prospects* packs an immense amount of information about television and broadcasting technology into a very slim volume.

In *Inventing American Broadcasting 1899–1922,* Susan J. Douglas presents an extremely readable account of how wireless evolved into radio, detailing the various factors that shaped the development of our broadcasting infrastructure.

Great Expectations, by Paul I. Bortz, Mark C. Wyche and James M. Trautman, was published in 1986 by the National Association of Broadcasters to provide "a television manager's guide to the future." Although some of the specifics are dated, it is still an extremely pragmatic overview of the operational considerations facing broadcasting executives.

The American Society of Newspaper Editors has performed much the same service for newspaper executives with the 1985 *Newsroom Management Handbook*.

A good overview to the structure of cable and other non-broadcast video systems is given in *Getting the Picture* by Stephen B. Weinstein.

To get an idea of how the introduction of a new technology can change community dynamics, try Ithiel de Sola Pool's *Social Impact of the Telephone*. Pool documents the power of the telephone through studies of what happened in Egyptian villages when a telephone line was installed.

Notes

1. Title I, Section 3, paragraph (b) of the Communications Act of 1934. The full text of the Act can be found in Kahn's *Documents of American Broadcasting, op. cit.,* starting on page 54.
2. Title I, Section 3, paragraph (o) of the Communications Act of 1934.
3. Actually the U.S. Postal Service is the biggest and oldest common carrier; and its history, structure, operations and problems are fascinating, immense and complex. The fact that it is a government-subsidized public service puts it in a class by itself. For that reason—and for our own convenience—we have largely ignored it except where it directly interfaces with the non-government institutions on which we have focused.

4. A good description of the colonial newspapers is provided by Chapter 50, "The Rise of the Newspaper," in David Boorstin's *The Americans: The Colonial Experience*. New York: Vintage Books, 1958.

5. As edition size has grown and early morning delivery has increased, the trend has veered away from the boy or girl on the bicycle to the adult in a car throwing home-delivered papers. During the 1980s, the routes delivered by youth carriers declined from 90 percent to 73 percent (*'89 Facts About Newspapers*. Reston, Va.: American Newspaper Publishers Association, 1989, p. 21).

6. The wave of public nostalgia for the good old days, which helped push "The Waltons" into the top rank of television ratings in the late 1970s and early 1980s, led to a resurrection of *The Saturday Evening Post*. But the magazine on newsstands today is really only a shadow of the earlier magazine.

7. Anyone interested in exploring the meaning and divisions of time may wish to refer to J. T. Fraser's *Time The Familiar Stranger*. Amherst: University of Massachusetts Press, 1987.

8. The National Institute of Standards and Technology (NIST) is charged with maintaining the official definition and prototypes for our weights and measures. There you can see "the" yard, peck, pound, etc. measures setting the standard for our rulers, containers and scales.

9. As the older author can testify, few things are more frustrating to a teacher than to correct improper word usage by a student—only to have the student bring in a new edition of a dictionary sanctioning that use. A scholarly yet amusing look at the volatility of the English language is provided by Bill Bryson in *The Mother Tongue* (New York: William Morrow, 1990).

10. One might argue that the aesthetic appreciation of messages in digital form remains, to this date, limited to a small percentage of the public. However, the cognoscenti of programming undoubtedly can appreciate the finesse of a digital statement just as the literati admire how an author has used words to turn a phrase and mathematicians admire the elegance of another's solution to an equation.

11. A practical example is provided by the airline industry. As international air traffic expanded, agreement on language had to be achieved to guarantee communication between pilots and air traffic controllers. With only a handful of exceptions (including the Canadian Province of Quebec), international airports use English as the language of traffic control.

12. Sports have modified their standards and game rules to make games more exciting (e.g., the 24-second clock in basketball) and to reduce the need to stop action so that commercials can be inserted (e.g., the automatic time out in football). Similarly changes have been made even in such ancient and tradition-bound sports as Japanese sumo wrestling.

13. A partial answer is that advertising is generally sold in units of column inches, and a change of width would have to coordinate with a change in ad rates. In a time of increasing competition for advertising, the industry is reluctant to do anything to cause advertiser confusion or resistance.

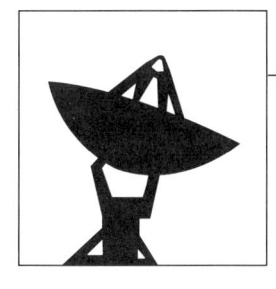

CHAPTER 8

The Matter of Money

Have you ever totaled up how much you spend each month on media and telecommunications? How many movies did you go see—at $6 a ticket? How many videocassettes did you rent—at $2.50 each? Do you buy or subscribe to a daily paper? Any magazines? What about cable: are you content with basic service, or do you also take a couple of the pay services? Maybe you ran up some service charges getting cash from an ATM.

And don't forget to add in the phone bill. How many long-distance calls did you make? Did you run up charges for some of those 900 "chat" lines? What about fax messages, electronic mail service or online data searches?

The costs of communication content and convenience add up, probably to a bigger total than you thought—if you ever stopped to think about it. Chances are that they will add up to even more in the future. That's the specter hiding in the shadows of the Information Revolution.

THE AGE-OLD QUESTION: HOW MUCH WILL IT COST?

Futurists delight in giving us visions of home information centers. With a mouse, or a touch screen, we will be able to access an unlimited variety of communication content. Through broadband optical fiber lines we will download movies to view at our leisure on extremely high resolution video screens. We will order the latest recordings, or dial into the library for books and magazines. High-speed printers will reproduce the day's news, complete with color photos, graphics and comics.

The future of new technologies inevitably runs up against the age-old question:

How much will it cost? Generally the answers provided by futurists are hazy and inexact. Some idea of the vagueness of estimates was provided in a 1991 article in the *New York Times*,[1] which said that "fibering" the nation could cost anywhere from $100 billion to $200 billion. That's quite a range.

At the end of 1991 Japan had fewer than 1,000 HDTV sets. Those sets cost more than the equivalent of $10,000 each. It's not surprising that most of the sets were in bars and other public places. With the cloud of a digital future hanging over Japan's analog HDTV system, who knows whether the market for the present sets will ever be sufficient to bring prices down. Similarly, after several years, the videotex services of Warner Communication, Times-Mirror and Knight Ridder had not generated enough traffic to put them in the black.

Introducing a new technology or service requires a great deal of money. The product or service must then compete in the market against established goods and services. If it cannot claim sufficient share to repay the development and operating costs, it cannot survive.

Engineers and entrepreneurs can design elegant systems for efficiently delivering materials to satisfy each and all our communication needs. They may even be able to estimate realistic figures for the cost of building and operating such systems. But why should anyone put up the money to build the system?

WHAT WILL THE MARKET BEAR?

Let's say you develop a great new color press for newspapers. Most newspapers already have black and white presses that work perfectly well. Why should a publisher spend a lot of money replacing them with your new press? Will color pictures attract enough new readers to pay for it? Will readers like the color pictures enough that the publisher can raise subscription rates to pay for the new press? Will enough advertisers pay a premium rate for color advertising to offset the cost?

Whether or not the publisher can raise subscription and/or advertising rates depends upon the competitive situation the paper faces for audience and advertising dollars. In the worst case scenario, a competitor has gone to color and the publisher fears the paper will lose both readers and advertisers unless he or she does likewise. In such a case, the publisher may not raise either subscription or advertising rates but must simply absorb the cost. As a result the paper's profits are reduced, making it harder for the publisher to raise money for future improvements or expansion.

INTERNAL SUBSIDIZATION AND DEEP POCKETS

One of the reasons organizations seek horizontal and vertical integration is to provide flexibility for internal subsidization. Profits from one unit may be used to offset the losses of another in periods of development or difficulty. Having many units producing profits creates "deep pockets" of financial resources that can be used for innovations.

The broadcast networks actually lost money during the early days of television because the TV audience was too small to justify advertising rates to cover the cost of operation. Fortunately, network profits from radio programming were sufficient to offset the television loss. As more households acquired TV sets, advertising rates were increased, and the medium became very profitable. The deep pockets of the existing radio networks gave them an advantage over networks such as Dumont, which tried to create a network specifically for the new medium of television.

HDTV may present quite a different situation. The existing television stations and networks now face serious competition from other services such as cable and VCR suppliers. If those services adopt HDTV, television broadcasters will have no choice but to make the investment in expensive HDTV equipment. Owing to stiff competition, it may be difficult or impossible for them to pass the cost on by raising advertising rates.

The public has become accustomed to a pattern of telecommunication and media financial practices that have remained relatively stable until quite recently. The costs of service and content within each of the traditional domains has followed well-defined and well-known patterns.

THE COMMON-CARRIER MODEL: PAY FOR SERVICE

Telephone service subscribers receive monthly statements detailing the use they have made of different services as well as the unit costs. With telephones we have learned to expect to pay for what we use. The common carriers have always delivered service in response to consumer request on a fee-for-service basis.

Historically the telcos accepted rate regulation for the privilege of operating a protected monopoly franchise, which reduced the financial risk involved in building the system. Generally the approved rates were structured on a mutually agreed-upon rate of return. The regulated telephone companies may not have been very attractive as speculative growth stocks, but they were among the most dependable earners of steady income for stockholders.

Usually the government seeks to insure equitable treatment to all customers of a business. But in the case of the telcos, franchising authorities have permitted a discriminatory practice called rate averaging. This allows the carrier to have a varying rate of return on different classes of service. Thus the carrier could require a higher rate of return on high traffic, efficient exchanges to offset losses from low-traffic, high-cost exchanges.

During the decades of AT&T's hegemony, when one company controlled some 90 percent of local telephone service and had a monopoly over long-distance service, rate averaging sped the development of universal service. In effect high-traffic business and long-distance customers were subsidizing residential and rural customers whose rates otherwise would have been prohibitive. Telephone penetration reached 90 percent of United States homes by 1950, far in advance of any other nation.

CHANGING THE RULES OF COMMON-CARRIER RATES

The breakup of AT&T created much chaos in the previously orderly world of telephone rates. Competition has produced dramatic decreases in the cost of long-distance service. But long-distance no longer provides a subsidy for local service. The local carriers are also beginning to face competition for high-traffic business use, in cellular telephone service and in value-added services such as voice mail. As a result residential rates have increased and now come closer to reflecting the true cost of service.

In effect the basic common-carrier principle of "pay for service" is now being more equitably applied, and local, non-business users are finding the results uncomfortable. Another result is that, even though common carriers are still franchised monopolies, competition is forcing them to become more aggressive in new-service development to provide new sources of revenue. This change helps to explain the telcos' push to be allowed to provide information and broadband services via fiber optics.

The telcos believe they are the logical parties to build the high-bandwidth networks needed for the future. They have argued that to recover the capital cost they must be allowed to provide as well as distribute such services. Their argument is weakened by inadequate cost estimates and by the fact that other groups, including the cable operators, are expanding the capacity of their own systems as they push to enter the protected areas of telephone use.

THE PRESS AND BROADCAST MODELS: ADVERTISING SUBSIDY

Although we pay for publications, the price we pay is far less than the actual production cost of most newspapers and magazines. Daily newspapers actually may cost three to four times the newsstand price, and the ratio to subscription price is even more lopsided.[2] The newspaper company must cover this difference with revenue generated by selling advertising space. (Although we have put them in the press domain, books, movies and recordings constitute special cases and will be discussed later.)

Because the electromagnetic spectrum is classified as public domain, United States policy has dictated that the public should have free access to the many broadcast radio and television signals available in our area.[3] The institutions which provide those signals must, themselves, find some way of paying their costs. Most are totally dependent upon advertising income.[4]

WHO'S THE BOSS?

Subsidizing newspaper readers and broadcast audiences confuses the functional relation of these institutions to their public. In the preceding chapter we said that advertising has major impact on the content of these media because it determines the size and shape of the newspaper edition, and it dictates a program rhythm in broadcasting that accommodates commercial messages. Advertising also confounds any answer to the question of functional responsibility for these media.

Both newspaper and broadcasting executives profess that their first responsibility is to their audience. But there has never been a general circulation daily paper which has been able to survive on circulation income alone. In 1940 an advertising-free daily, *PM,* was inaugurated in New York and attracted to its staff some of the best journalists of the period. With the exception of one brief period, the paper lost money and was kept going only by the infusion of fresh capital from its principal stockholder, the Chicago mercantile millionaire Marshall Field III. After six years, the paper abandoned its no-advertising policy, but the equivocation destroyed whatever mystique it had had for readers. In 1948 *PM* ceased to exist.[5]

Networks select programs on the basis of audience size, with an eye to demographics. ABC discarded "The Lawrence Welk Show" despite a happy sponsor and a loyal audience. The problem was that audience was primarily comprised of senior citizens. That group is relatively inactive in the consumer market and so is of peripheral interest to most national advertisers. Because considerable audience carryover extends from one time slot to the next, ABC executives decided the program reduced sponsor interest in adjacent time slots. And so they dropped the show and the sponsor.[6]

Obversely, "Hill Street Blues" began with low ratings, but it had a strong attraction for the affluent and free-spending "yuppie" audience that many national advertisers sought during the 1980s. NBC executives used the show as a vehicle for winning the demographic race even when its ratings were lower than those of the other networks.

The operational realities reflected by these examples suggest that newspaper and broadcast managements divide their concern between the needs of advertisers and those of the audience.

THE PUBLIC GETS A BARGAIN

Media managers are not inherently cynical, nor is the public necessarily exploited. The United States audience has struck a bargain that is really quite a good deal. The public tolerates advertising (and even pays attention to some of it), and in return gets broadcasting for free and newspapers and magazines at a greatly reduced price.

From the media managers' point of view, the audience is both a consumer for their product and a commodity to be sold to advertisers. Media managers must seek to attract and maintain an audience of a size and demographic mix that will prove of interest to advertisers.

By exercising choice among media, the members of the audience do have the opportunity to influence content, service and even survival of individual media. The audience always has the ultimate power of not buying the paper and of tuning out a station. With the increasing functional competition across media, the public has an expanded opportunity to exercise power through choice. The results have created new headaches for executives of the advertising-dependent media.

THE SIZE OF THE ADVERTISING SUBSIDY

In 1988 advertising expenditures totaled $118,050 million. When we consider that in 1950 the total was only $5,700 million, we begin to see how dynamic the

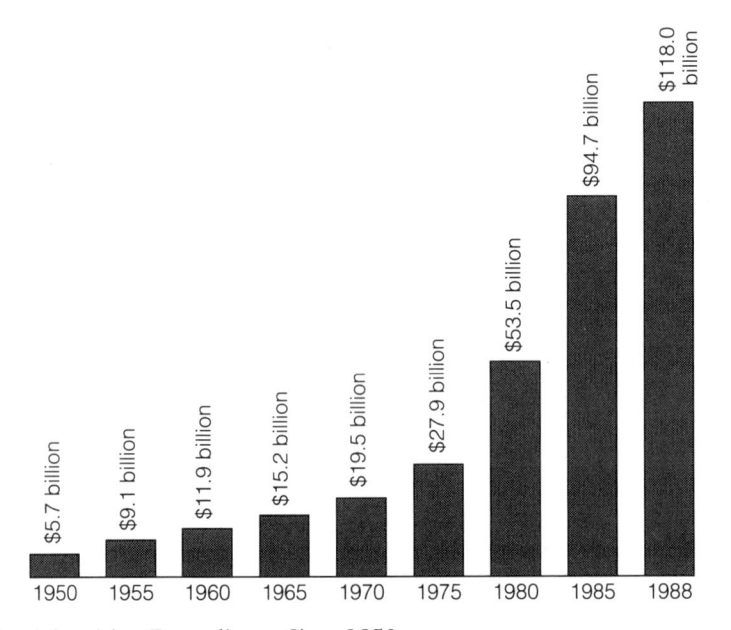

Figure 8.1 Advertising Expenditures Since 1950
Source: Statistical Abstract of the United States 1990. Washington, D.C.: Bureau of the Census, 1990, Table 932, p. 556.

Table 8.1 Where Advertising Dollars Go (in millions of dollars)

	1970	1980	1988
Total expenditure	19.550	53.550	118.050
Newspapers	5.704	14.794	31.197
National	[.891]	[1.963]	[3.586]
Local	[4.813]	[12.881]	[27.611]
Television	3.596	11.424	24.744
National networks	[1.658]	[5.130]	[9.172]
National spot	[1.234]	[2.967]	[7.147]
Local spot	[.704]	[2.967]	[7.270]
Cable television	NA	.045	.942
Radio	1.308	3.702	7.798
Yellow Pages	NA	2.900	7.781
Direct mail	2.766	7.596	21.115
Others	6.176	12.729	24.476

Source: Statistical Abstract of the United States 1990. Washington, D.C.: Bureau of the Census, 1990, Table 934, p. 557.

growth in this field has been (see Figure 8.1). This growth reflects the spectacular expansion of our consumer market in the period following World War II. The increase in the size and volume of mass media has been fueled not so much by consumer demand for media content as by the need of advertisers for expanding access to the consumer market.

Since 1930 broadcasting—specifically the networks and their affiliates—has had a particularly close relationship with national advertisers. No other medium has provided simultaneous access to national audiences. Newspapers, on the other hand, retained a dominance with local advertisers whose combined expenditures exceeded that of national advertisers (see Table 8.1). Generally both media have produced profits for their owners far greater than those of most other industries.

ATTRITION THROUGH ADVERTISING ALLOCATIONS

The newspaper situation is somewhat misleading. The high profitability of papers results because fewer papers are sharing the advertising revenues. From 1970 to 1988 the number of daily newspapers declined from 1,748 to 1,642.[7] The total number of papers which disappeared was greater than 106; declines in metropolitan papers were partially offset by new daily papers in some small and suburban communities. The financial health of surviving city papers is due in part to the disappearance of their competitors.

Consolidation of the metropolitan press was forced mainly by advertisers who sought to reduce expenditures for redundant audiences and for non-productive audiences. Newspapers are particularly dependent upon local advertising, and the largest local advertisers tend to be big department stores. The stores that advertise most are those seeking the upscale market. The ad buyers for these stores increasingly concentrated their space purchases in those publications whose readership gave them the biggest proportion of this group. If two papers competed for this group, ads were concentrated in the paper with the larger circulation, with the result that the smaller paper lost income and gradually declined. The result was an inexorable attrition turning all but the largest cities into monopoly newspaper markets.

Papers identified as voices of the working class have largely disappeared. Perhaps these papers would have lost their audiences to TV news in any case, but the immediate cause of their demise was that they did not serve the needs of those who spent the most money on advertising.

RADIO: A CASE OF FUNCTIONAL DISPLACEMENT

Radio broadcasting provides a case of a medium that underwent functional displacement and survived by adjusting to a reduced "lifestyle." The adjustment was particularly hard for managements of AM stations, which once ruled as monarchs of the air waves. Today most AM stations trail both television and FM stations in audience size and profitability.

Radio's ability to accompany us wherever we go provides a unique advantage.

Because most stations rely on recorded music for most of their program content, radio's operating costs are low. Stations can achieve profitability with small audiences and cheap advertising rates. Financial viability most often depends on a station's success in carving out a niche audience of interest to certain types of advertisers.

Over 10,800 AM and FM stations manage to stay on the air, but most of them earn little or no profit. Out of the dozens of stations available in many markets, most listeners have identified a handful they like. Very likely these stations are programmed on the automatic selection buttons of their radio. As they listen, they flip from one to the next of these, ignoring all the other stations. The result is that much of the audience probably would not even notice if most of the stations went off the air. It's not an easy life, but it's the cheapest way to be in broadcasting.

FAT CATS NO MORE: THE OLIGARCHY NETWORKS

Having largely abandoned radio for television, the oligarchy networks ABC, CBS and NBC are now experiencing how the law of supply and demand can produce wealth and then take it away. Throughout radio's dominance, there were fewer than 1,000 stations, all AM. Over 90 percent of the stations were affiliated with one of the networks. The networks had an effective monopoly over the broadcast audience in a period of expanding demand for national advertising.

The networks were able to transfer this near monopoly to television because each city seldom had more than three VHF allocations, and VHF stations have inherent technological advantages over UHF stations.[8] Into the 1980s the three major networks consistently claimed 90 percent or more of the viewing audience. Because only so much air time can be sold, the networks were able to raise rates beyond inflation year after year. The saying in the industry was that those who had licenses for network affiliate stations had "licenses to print money." Cable's competition has contributed to a dramatic change of corporate lifestyle within the network offices.

For years advertisers lined up, begging for access to network slots. The networks' entire inventory would be contracted before the season began. No longer. By 1990 the networks' combined average share in prime time was slipping toward 60 percent. In 1990 all the networks failed to sell out their inventory up front, which they had been able to do for over two decades.

All three networks have undergone a series of wrenching budget reductions. Hundreds of professionals were cut from the staff; news bureaus were reduced; more automated equipment was introduced as part of efforts to reduce costs. Network-affiliate relations have been strained. The decline in network audiences erodes the dominance of affiliates in their local markets. However, the reader need not feel overly sorry for the owners of newspapers and network television stations. As a group both continue to have earnings at or above the national average for corporations.

THE MOVIES: A GOOD PRODUCT WHEREVER IT'S SOLD

We have said that functional relevance of content or service is more important than technology per se. The movies provide a classic proof of that premise. In the previous chapter we saw how the film industry underwent cataclysmic transformation in the face of technological competition from video. Today the studios producing feature films receive most of their income from various forms of video distribution: television, cable and videocassette, as shown in the percentages below.[9]

Theatrical exhibition 25.0%
    Domestic theaters 15.9%
    Foreign theaters 9.1%
Home video 38.6%
Pay cable 8.3%
Television 28.2%
    Network television .8%
    Television syndication 4.6%
    Foreign television 7.6%
    Made-for-TV films 15.2%

Functionally the movie product remains the same. It's not that people don't watch movies anymore, it's that few people *go* to the movies; most sit at home and see them on their video screen.

AN UNCHANGED FUNCTION WITH SHIFTING FINANCES

At first glance one might think this multiplicity of outlets for movies would be a bonanza for the studios; however, the situation is more complex. One financial analyst who specialized in the entertainment industries, Harold L. Vogel, states:

> . . . we see that new technology has provided the viewer with unprecedented access to and control over when entertainment may be enjoyed. Technology has also significantly lowered the price per view and has established important new revenue sources, thus generally diffusing the economic power of the more traditional suppliers of entertainment. Nevertheless, it would be a mistake to jump to the conclusion, as many observers do, that the continuous introduction of new viewing options necessarily leads to heightened film industry profitability. New viewing options almost invariably displace older ones. And marketing costs rise as both old and new media compete for the attention of increasingly finicky audiences.[10]

The new options have helped create financial chaos within what was once a very orderly industry. This chaos explains why, despite box-office revenues that have increased from $900 million in 1962 to over $5 billion by 1990, there are constant cries about losses within the industry.

FROM INTEGRATION TO CHAOS

We saw in Chapter 7 that before television Hollywood actually was an orderly, vertically integrated and profitable film industry. Movie companies operated their studios like factory assembly lines turning out features according to annual production plans. Each film could be budgeted in advance. Each studio contracted a stable of stars and other creative talent who could be assigned to productions and whose salaries were known in advance. Once budgeted, the cost of production could be controlled.

Because the studios owned the most important cinemas, they could control exhibition schedules. The number of films produced each year was geared to the maintenance of an orderly sequence released through the hierarchy of cinemas, from the metropolitan premiere movie palaces down to neighborhood second-run houses. This sequence ensured that studios operated efficiently and guaranteed a steady flow of new products to keep audiences coming to the theaters week after week.

The Supreme Court forced the studios to sell their theaters in 1949, just as television began to bring audio-visual entertainment into our homes. From 1949 to 1950 weekly movie attendance fell from 87 million to 60 million—and kept on falling until 1967 by which time it had dipped below 20 million.[11] In the space of a few years the world of the dream factories fell in chaos.

LOSING CONTROL OF COSTS

The studios have survived by finding new exhibitors to whom they can sell their products. But the loss of control over exhibition and the emergence of new competition from television for creative talent has resulted in a loss of their ability to budget and control the cost of their product.

The movie business has degenerated into a scramble of individual pieces, each seeking its own self-interest. Instead of a planned and carefully budgeted production schedule, individual movies are now put together as packages made up of complicated negotiations. As free agents, rather than studio employees, creative talents are up for bid, and competition puts stars—not producers—in control. Without firm schedules, maintaining studio efficiency and an orderly release of features is difficult. The result has been a steep spiral of rising costs. The overall financial situation has become a Byzantine maze in which determining the real costs and real profits appears close to impossible. Theater exhibition contributes only about one-third of studio incomes, so productions ultimately may be profitable despite loss at the box office.

The institutional *structure* has changed—not the function. The studio may have seen their world reordered, but they are still in the same basic business. But the cinema operators have been technologically displaced and have suffered the greatest financial pressure.

CINEMA: CINDERELLA IN REVERSE

The most apparent result in the shift of attention by the finicky audience is that the lavish movie palaces of the 1930s and 1940s yielded to utilitarian spaces with minimum amenities and little or no glamour. Although not a riches-to-rags story, the cinemas, once the opulent local presence of the glamorous Hollywood movie industry, today certainly seem to be the poor stepsisters of the movie trade.

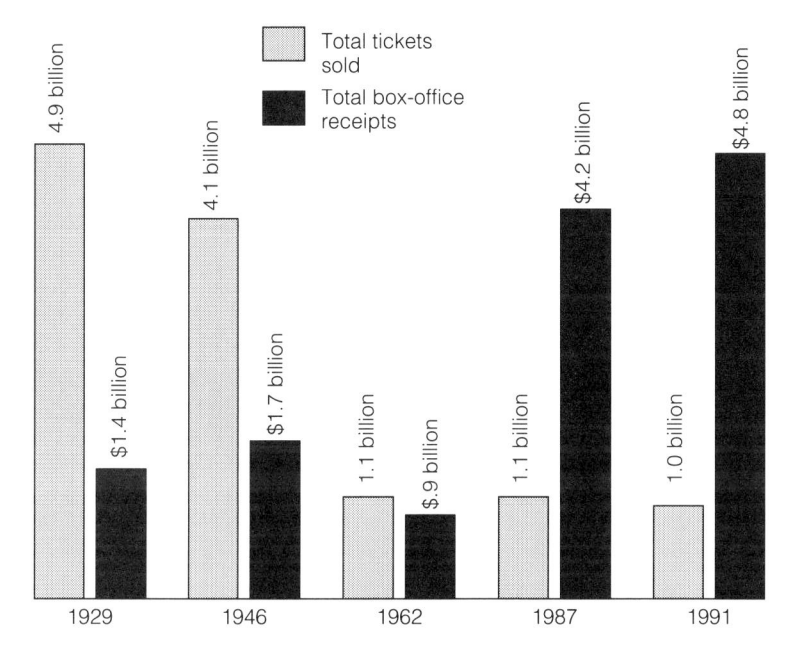

Figure 8.2 Trends in Cinema Box Office and Attendance
Source: 1991 U.S. Economic Review. Press Release, Motion Picture Association of America, January 2, 1992.

In 1929, when the U.S. population was about 120 million, weekly movie attendance was 95 million; in 1980, with a population of 226 million, weekly attendance was only 20 million.[12] That's a decrease of 80 percent in the face of a doubled population!

Annual cinema ticket sales hit an all-time high of almost 5 billion in 1929 and remained as high as 4 billion in 1946 (see Figure 8.2). By the 1960s, attendance had fallen to around 1 billion, where it has remained (plus or minus 20 million). Note that the period of precipitous decline corresponds to the period of rapidly increasing television households.

THE PARADOX AT THE CINEMA OFFICE

Despite this rather dismal attendance curve, box-office revenues have tripled in the same period. Any moviegoer who has experienced the rise in ticket prices understands how this amazing feat has been accomplished.

In 1946 ticket prices averaged less than 50 cents. By 1980 the average price was up to around $2.75, and today is on its way to $5.[13] Considering that the number of films released each year has remained relatively stable over this same period, one might expect that cinema chains would be rolling in money. Vogel says that actually only two or three features out of each ten produced make a profit at the domestic box office.[14] What's going on?

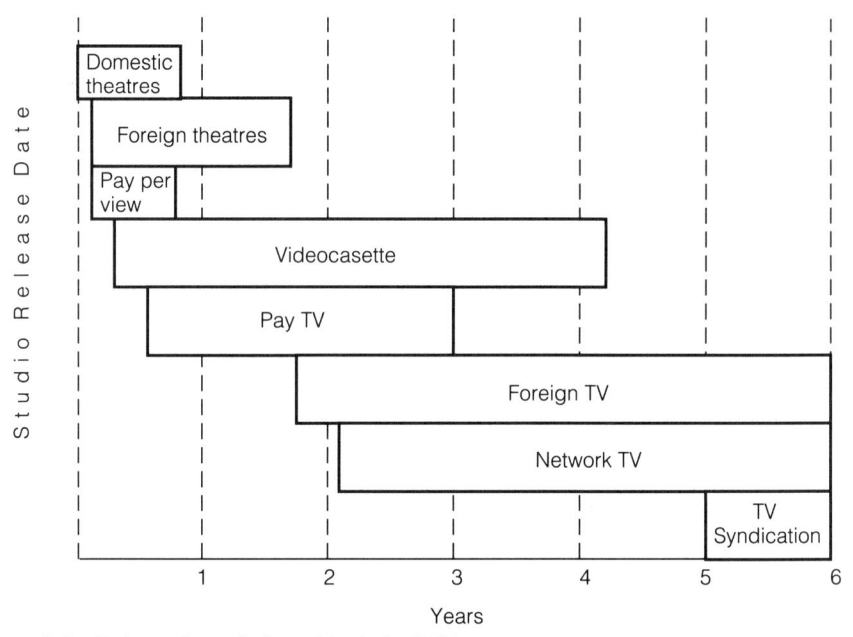

```
                            |       |       |       |       |       |       |
                      ┌─────────────┐       |       |       |       |       |
                      │Domestic     │       |       |       |       |       |
                      │theatres     │       |       |       |       |       |
                      └─────────────┘       |       |       |       |       |
   e                  |  ┌──────────────────┐       |       |       |       |
   t                  |  │Foreign theatres  │       |       |       |       |
   a                  |  └──────────────────┘       |       |       |       |
   D                  |  ┌────┐ |       |           |       |       |       |
                      |  │Pay per │     |           |       |       |       |
   e                  |  │view│   |     |           |       |       |       |
   s                  |  └────┘   |     |           |       |       |       |
   a                  |  ┌──────────────────────────────────┐       |       |
   e                  |  │          Videocasette            │       |       |
   l                  |  └──────────────────────────────────┘       |       |
   e                  |     ┌─────────────────────────────┐ |       |       |
   R                  |     │         Pay TV              │ |       |       |
                      |     └─────────────────────────────┘ |       |       |
   o                  |     |       |  ┌──────────────────────────────────┐
   i                  |     |       |  │         Foreign TV               │
   d                  |     |       |  └──────────────────────────────────┘
   u                  |     |       |     ┌────────────────────────────┐  |
   t                  |     |       |     │        Network TV          │  |
   S                  |     |       |     └────────────────────────────┘  |
                      |     |       |       |       |       |     ┌──────┐
                      |     |       |       |       |       |     │ TV   │
                      |     |       |       |       |       |     │Syndi-│
                      |     |       |       |       |       |     │cation│
                      └─────┴───────┴───────┴───────┴───────┴─────┴──────┘
                            1       2       3       4       5       6
                                              Years
```

Figure 8.3 Release Cascade for a Movie in 1990
Source: Vogel, Harold L. *Entertainment Industry Economics*. 2nd ed. New York. Cambridge University Press, 1990.

OUTRUNNING THE COMPETITION

When the studios were forced to sell their cinema chains, they lost their vested interest in protecting cinema exhibition. To protect themselves financially they embraced the new forms of exhibition. The result has been that cinema owners have had a continuing battle to maintain a release window during which they can show new features without competition from cable videocassette services.

Cinema operators fought to restrict broadcaster access to feature films only to see the studios succumb to network dollars. They mounted a successful referendum campaign in California to stop subscription television, which would have been largely a movie channel. They fought to keep cable out of the largest markets as they saw the studios selling movie exhibition rights to pay cable services.

These tactics only delayed the inevitable, because the studios saw that they could generate revenue from new sources to offset declining cinema attendance. The sale of exhibition rights to a network brought in more money than box office receipts. A single play on cable pay-per-view (PPV) today may generate more income than the entire theatrical run of a feature.

An established release cascade of release windows serve different forms of exhibition (see Figure 8.3). In recent years the release dates for pay-per-view cable and videocassettes have been moved up by about three months, effectively reducing the protected first-run window of the theaters. Release to the movie channels of cable's pay tier and to the television networks has been advanced, which means expanded access to relatively recent movies to home viewers.

WHAT ABOUT THAT $5-BILLION BOX OFFICE?

Cinema operators have a lot of functional competition. Nevertheless, box-office revenue has increased five-fold in the last three decades, and we keep seeing ticket prices go up. That money is not all in the cinema operators' pockets. Theater owners keep as little as 30 percent of what they take in at the box office. The rest is paid as film rental to the studio. Furthermore, the number of screens has increased in that period from about 16,500 to 22,000, which means more operators share the box office. Without the old orderly flow of new releases, theater operators have more difficulty achieving a steady flow of customers and the significance of "hits" has taken on greater impact at the box office. Operators face a dilemma of wanting lots of seats to accommodate the crowds for hits but also trying to keep overhead down over the long haul. Vogel estimates that theaters operate at 11 percent of capacity![15]

This estimate helps explain the trend toward clustering a number of small theaters. The multiplex provides operators with flexibility to accommodate hits by putting them on two or more of their screens simultaneously, and, in the absence of a hit, they play a variety of films concurrently. That traffic is essential to survival.

Where the studios can turn to other forms of exhibition for revenue, the theater operator has only one fall back: the refreshment stand. Without the profit from the exorbitantly priced products sold at the refreshment stand, cinema operators simply could not stay in business.

CONFLICTING INTERESTS

Cinema operators are locked into a dependency on the studios. Even at $6 and $7 ticket prices, cinema goers are subsidized by video viewers; without video income, the studios could not produce enough new features to generate traffic to pass by those refreshment stands.

Cinema exhibition is still the primary means of promoting any film. This helps explain why the advertising and other promotion costs may total almost as much as the cost of studio production. The dollars are being spent not only in an attempt to stimulate box-office business, but to generate interest in the film among those of the public who never go to the movies but do rent videocassettes.

The theater operators do retain some clout. Because they are no longer owned by the studios, they control their own exhibition schedules. In the race for traffic past the refreshment stand, any theater operator is likely to drop a film if it does not do well at the box office its first weekend of release. A feature may be given little opportunity to capitalize on the heavy advertising expenditure and build audience interest.

VIEWERS WILL PAY FOR TELEVISION

We saw in previous chapters that cable has confused the boundaries of the traditional domains. This confusion has been compounded by destruction of a basic premise of

U.S. broadcasting: cable has shown that the concept of free television is not sacrosanct with the majority of families; they recognize that you get what you pay for.

Cable began as a service to bring television programs to people who had difficulty getting programs via the free off-air signals. Today people subscribe to cable, not because of reception problems, but because they want more than just the local TV stations. More than half the families in most urban areas are now cable subscribers. They want the additional choices of CNN, the superstations, Arts and Entertainment, Lifetime, ESPN, the Discovery Channel, etc. More than half the subscribers want still more choices. They are willing to pay even more to receive premium television services such as HBO, Disney, Showtime and Playboy.

PROVIDING ADVERTISERS WITH ALTERNATIVES

Cable is also causing a redirection of the advertising money that is the basic support of press as well as broadcasting. Many of the programs included in cable systems' basic service survive in part or entirely on advertising revenue. The companies providing these services have demonstrated that the combination of satellites and cable can be an effective way for advertisers to reach specific audience groups.

Individual cable systems rapidly have begun to extend this principle. They are actively soliciting advertising from both local and national sources. Advertising expenditures on cable exceeded $1.5 billion in 1990. Although that is small compared to the $25 billion spent on broadcast television the same year, it appears to represent money diverted from broadcasters.

CABLE'S NEW JACKPOT: PAY-PAY-VIEW

In their expanding campaign for re-regulation of cable and/or relief from regulatory restrictions on their own operations, broadcasters point out that cable has two revenue streams—subscriber fees and advertising—in the face of their own single stream.

It is true that for several years the growth of cable revenues from their pay tier has generally stagnated. But as systems rebuild and add more channel capacity and interactive capability, they are pushing the expansion of pay-per-view attractions available on a single fee basis.

Even when viewers have to telephone to order PPV, some major sporting events such as "Wrestlemania" earn more than $10 million in a single evening. Experience shows that when subscribers do have impulse PPV—an interactive service allowing them to order programs with the mere punch of a button of their remote tuner—the orders and profits skyrocket.

The potential of impulse PPV has not been lost on the studios producing and releasing major films. The fact that they might earn as much from one round of PPV as they earn from a week or more of theater exhibition is responsible for pressure to speed the release cascade.

CABLE'S DOUBLE WHAMMY

Broadcasters are understandably alarmed. The new aggressiveness of cable as a competitor for advertising dollars has made it harder for broadcasters to raise their own rates. In recent years the networks and affiliates have had to abandon their decades-old practice of annual rate increases beyond inflation.

Another facet adds to cable's financial impact on the broadcasting field. Many of these non-broadcast services on cable are now buying programs in the same markets where broadcasters are shopping. With more shoppers, producers and syndicators can use the competition to increase the cost of programs. Having been shocked when cable networks outbid them for major sports events, the networks now find themselves paying more for programs at the very time they are under pressure to hold or even reduce their advertising rates.

As the MSOs integrate horizontally, buying more individual local systems, they have also begun to integrate vertically by acquiring financial interest in satellite networks and program production units. This integration means they can combine income from subscriber fees, advertising and program syndication.

THE COST OF CREATIVE CONTENT

The cost of communications content is not solely a function of technological and operational costs; there is also the question of creative cost. In Chapter 6 we discussed the importance of copyright as a means of stimulating creativity for the benefit of society while simultaneously rewarding the creators. Technology that preserves, duplicates and distributes creativity is a marvelous boon for society, but it creates opportunity for unfair exploitation of creative talent.

The American Federation of Musicians and the American Society of Composers, Authors and Publishers (ASCAP) recognized early on that radio threatened the jobs of performers, particularly when radio used recordings to fill its schedule. After hard battles a procedure was established in the 1940s to collect performance fees from broadcasters to recompense the creative artists.

When videotape made possible the accumulation of programs for syndication and the repetition of commercials, contractual agreements for the payment of residual fees had to be worked out.

Photocopying has undermined the collection of royalties for books and other printed material; video and audio cassettes have made possible a flourishing international black market of pirated movies and music. The introduction of digital audio tape (DAT) technology into this country was delayed for several years because of the recording industry's fear of its impact on sales of recordings.

Producing a show or a record is taking on a new meaning as performers "lip sync" to prerecorded tapes, as the recorded performances of one artist or group are enriched by additional sounds taken from digital sound banks. Cases are coming into the courts in which musicians claim that digital pieces of their performances have been pieced into the recordings of others—without permission, without compensation.

As technologies become more complex, contention grows over what hardware qualifies for patent protection and what software can be copyrighted.

With technologies that have both gigantic capacity and the ability to distribute content over entire continents, we can anticipate increasing difficulties in guaranteeing just compensation for intellectual property. The difficulties will only be exacerbated as technology's ability to distribute more broadly increases the potential worth of such intellectual property.

HOW DO WE PAY THE BILL?

Both the construction and operation of systems require financing. Ultimately the members of society must pay, but how they do so is problematic. Our experience with cable suggests we may be in the midst of a major change on the financing of communication services.

Historically our press and broadcasters have subsidized their users with income from advertising, and common carriers have operated on a pay-for-service basis. Cable demonstrates the possibility of developing both revenue streams.

In the competition for program acquisition, broadcasters complain that cable has the unfair advantage of this dual revenue stream. Cable's expanding advertising revenues seem doubly bitter to broadcasters. Cable operators are also pressing at telephone-line boundaries, eagerly seeking to provide interactive communication services traditionally limited to common carriers. The great capacity of optical fiber stimulates their desire to increase that pressure.

In the meantime common carriers are also pressing to use their optical fiber investment to expand the scope of their own operations and services. They encourage the development of a variety of specialized content delivered via 900 access numbers. The common carriers act as a kiosk through which users obtain access and coordinate billing. If cable can push into the telephone's domain, why, they ask, can't the telcos push into cable's? With the vision of the PPV before them, the telcos fight to get their share, if not control, of the jackpot.

In 1991 Judge Greene gave provisional permission for the local telco operating companies to provide information services. The common carriers are preparing for eventual entry as programmers of these and broadband (video) services by buying cable systems abroad.

THE SUBSIDY THAT WON'T GO AWAY

Along with the pay-for-access 900 services, some providers have developed free voice information services supported with advertising. For example a growing number of newspapers now provide such summaries of sports results and stock market reports.

Remember that advertising itself serves an important role in our economic system as well as in our personal lives. We may choose to ignore it much of the time, but we also turn to it for help in finding products and services, bargains and sales. The people in this creative field will develop formats to harness the potential of new and changed advertising delivery systems.

New technologies in all the media make it possible to target advertising to smaller, more specific groups. They can also work the other way and allow individuals to screen out advertising they don't want and to find that which they do.

If we glance back at Table 8.1, we see that the fastest growing areas of advertising have been the Yellow Pages, direct mail and cable, all of which represent a trend toward focusing advertising messages to specific targets. The data in the figure suggest that this growth has come at the expense of newspapers and, to a lesser degree, broadcasting. Multimedia systems could combine the appeal of all three of these fast growing areas to service the needs of advertisers while subsidizing the cost of service to users.

In fact the process has already begun. Some services available to personal computer and modem owners through gateway services such as Prodigy, Easy Link, and CompuServe are subsidized by advertising. Fax and modem owners already complain of "junk fax" and "junk E-mail" messages, high-technology counterparts to the junk mail flooding our mail boxes. Telco technology to pre-screen incoming messages has been introduced but is being fought by some advertisers as a violation of their First Amendment rights.

Regardless of how the legal battles are settled, we probably will see the emergence of new variable fee structures. They may allow us to decide individually whether we wish to pay full cost for communication content and services and avoid annoying commercial interruptions or get the same content or service at low cost with advertising.

ONCE MORE, HOW MUCH WILL IT COST?

These flexible structures only will be possible with sufficient penetration of new technology. We must also concern ourselves with the economics of achieving the diffusion of technological innovation.

The cost to users, both of technology such as multimedia components, HDTV sets, and access fees for content or service, will be determined in large part by the market. In a competitive market such as ours, the greater the traffic, the lower the costs.

In 1950 an 8-inch black and white TV set cost as much as $500, which would be the dollar equivalent of $1000 today. This product was totally new and extremely attractive, and with no confusion about standards. Sales rapidly increased with a corresponding decrease in price.

Digital audio tape machines were introduced into the U.S. market in 1991 with price tags ranging from $800 to $1000. But a giant existing pool of audiocassette players as well as a giant pool of digital CD players already exists. Even as DAT was introduced, the public read about new recorders soon to be introduced by manufacturers. DAT has not repeated the quick market success of these two older technologies.

In the case of the personal computer, dramatic increases in capacity and flexibility have helped stimulate the consumer market.

The pricing of both cable and telephone 900-number services has appeared to be based on a desire to explore the edges of customer acceptability. When Congress freed cable from rate regulation in 1985, most systems rapidly raised rates. Customers were outraged but for the most part kept on paying.

The appeal of seeing movies at home is so great that VCR penetration overtook cable penetration in only a few years. The competition of the VCR for the home audience has forced cable operators to moderate their rate increases and to rearrange their rate schedules. The possibility that regulatory agencies will allow additional competition from MMDS and DBS as well as the specter of telco entry into the field has made cable operators far more sensitive to public pressure.

Competition sets the basic framework for costs, as the telcos know from long experience. But the public can also defend itself through political pressure focused on the regulatory agencies and legislative bodies. The history of the telcos is one of a continuing battle with regulatory agencies over rate structures.

The public and the telecommunications companies view the financing of multimedia services with apprehension. A number of stories of astronomical bills for use of 900-number services have appeared in the news media. They have helped to raise sensitivity on this issue among the public, the regulators and industry executives alike.

GETTING THERE

At a minimum implementing HDTV means that program producers and TV broadcasters will have to buy HDTV equipment, and those who wish to see HDTV programs will have to buy new video sets.

For DBS to become a reality capital must be available for the purchase of satellite transponder space, acquisition of program rights and making arrangements for subscribers to acquire receiving dishes and decoders.

The estimates for building a national public optical fiber network are breathtaking, and there will still be need for production, storage and management of content. However, the size and vitality of our economy are sufficient to generate the capital to create such a system or systems. One could argue that the construction is already underway in a piecemeal fashion as cable and telco organizations replace their copper wires with optical fiber.

Perhaps the more serious problem will be working out the system to coordinate financial aspects of the content without which the system will be meaningless. The cost of any system must be amortized by use. The greater the traffic, the faster the amortization. Ultimately, the traffic is generated by consumer desire for the content. Historically demand has always soon outstripped available bandwidth.

The strength of consumer desire is influenced by cost relative to other options within the same functional area. Consumer resources are finite and they must be allocated over a broad range of necessities as well as nonessential options. Low-income families are among the heaviest users of cable, because many believe it provides the best value of entertainment and information services. Television and cable have a lower value to those with the financial means to pursue out-of-home entertainment such as theater, concerts, sports and travel.

Families with limited means may be willing to tolerate advertising, which reduces the cost of services. Higher-income families may be willing to pay more for service if they can avoid what they perceive to be an intrusion in program content.

Projecting the market for multimedia services will be complicated. But the technological flexibility of future systems will provide more options in setting the cost of communication services.

Suggestions for Further Reading

Entertainment Industry Economics by Harold L. Vogel is a readable overview of movies, broadcasting and cable—as well as performing arts, sports and gambling casinos. Robert G. Picard's *Media Economics* is a more theoretical analysis but has a readable approach.

Practical volumes on finance include Jason E. Squire's *The Movie Business Book,* Michael Wiese's *Film and Video Financing,* Blumenthal and Goodenough's *This Business of Television,* W. J. Willis' *Surviving in the Newspaper Business: Newspaper Management in Turbulent Times* and Glenn Carroll's *Publish or Perish: The Organization Ecology of Newspaper Industries.*

The portraits of Ted Turner (CNN) and Bill McGowan (MCI) in Douglas K. Ramsey's *The Corporate Warriors* give an entertaining yet insightful view of the types of battles taking place in the boardrooms of media empires. A longer portrait of a similar type is Lewis J. Paper's biography of William S. Paley and CBS, *Empire.* Ben Bagdikian's *The Media Monopoly* is older but is still a fascinating look into the management of our major newspapers.

Notes

1. "Phone Companies Could Transmit TV Under FCC Plan," *New York Times,* page A1, October 25, 1991.
2. Subscription prices are generally discounted because, unlike fluctuating street sales, they provide the publisher with a steady circulation on which to base advertising rates.
3. In many countries, owners of receiving sets must pay regular fees intended to provide financial support for broadcasting services.
4. There are two major exceptions to this statement. "Public stations" are prohibited from taking advertising (although they are allowed to solicit corporate "underwriting" for programs). Most of their revenue comes from a mix of local, state, and federal funding. Audience contributions account for about 17 percent of revenues.

    The other exception comprises non-profit FM stations, most of which have religious affiliations and make on-air appeals for audience support.
5. *PM* was sold and renamed *The Star,* which ceased publication a year later. For a fuller account of this noble experiment, see pp. 771–772 of Frank Luther Mott's *History of American Journalism* (New York: Macmillan, 1950).
6. The producers and audience of "The Lawrence Welk Show" experienced a happy ending; the program became one of the pioneers of the syndication market.
7. *'90 Facts About Newspapers.* Reston, Va.: American Newspaper Publishers Association, 1990, p. 2.
8. The biggest advantage results from the tuning mechanism on most sets, which makes it easier to select VHF stations.
9. Vogel, Harold L. *Entertainment Industry Economics.* 2nd ed. New York: Cambridge University Press, 1990, p. 52.

10. Vogel, *op. cit.*, p. 54.
11. Vogel, *op. cit.*, p. 359.
12. *Ibid.*, p. 359.
13. *1991 U.S. Economic Review.* Press Release, Motion Picture Association of America, January 2, 1992.
14. Vogel, *op. cit.*, p. 29.
15. *Ibid.*, p. 80.

PART III

The Changing World of Communication

In the Introduction we advocated a strategy of free thinking about the functions of communication, rather than a strategy focusing on existing media institutions or even the traditional domains outlined by Pool.

Because these institutions have been around for decades and are such familiar parts of our everyday life, we take them very much for granted. After all, newspapers as we know them go back to the mid-19th century. The telephone network was taking shape by the turn of the century as were the recording and movie studios. The broadcasting networks were formed in 1927.

In fact all of these institutions have been in continual evolution, changing because they faced a constant battle for survival against challenges created by new technologies and changing social forces.

An experience of the older author provides a personal example of what such change means for us as individuals. When he graduated with a radio and journalism major from a Texas college in 1951, the "big time" meant a career in AM radio. Four years later, when he got out of the Air Force, television had turned the mass-media world upside down. He hailed the replacement of manual typewriters by IBM Selectrics and has now progressed to word processing on a personal computer. As he prepares for retirement, he is bracing himself for transition into a multimedia world.

Today's undergraduates have had only two decades of change, and yet consider the new technologies and services that have taken place in their lifetime: PPV cable, VCRs, CDs, DAT, the ubiquitous radio/cassette players, solar-powered calculators, personal computers, videotex, digital photography, ATMs, computer games, satellites, optical fiber, cellular phones, telephone answering machines, voice mail and voice information services, fax and uncounted other changes.

In a competitive environment in which change is so rapid and widespread, media and telecommunications institutions must change if they are to survive. And they are changing, as we shall see in the subsequent chapters.

Change is not always sufficient if an institution cannot match the efficacy of the new challenger(s). Newspaper publishers, noting the extremely low readership among young adults, worry about their future. For decades "the telephone company" meant AT&T, once the world's largest corporation. Now AT&T is only one of several companies competing to provide us with long-distance service, and it has nothing to do with local service. Broadcasters openly question the survival of the major networks. Advertising agencies are consolidating, restructuring to accommodate shifts in marketing practices. Newspapers may be gone twenty years from now, but we're willing to predict journalism will survive: it meets the need for the communication of information.

Our competitive economic and political marketplaces will still need channels to persuade people to buy and to vote, but television commercials and display ads in newspapers may no longer be the preferred way.

In an age where knowledge can be stored and retrieved in audio-visual format just as easily as in print, concepts such as literacy, books, periodicals, and libraries will be redefined. The task of relaying to new generations the accumulated wisdom of civilization itself will expand in both scope and importance.

As the pace of change increases, success—individual as well as institutional—will increasingly depend on our ability to anticipate how technologies can be adapted to fit the needs of tomorrow's society for information, persuasion, education and entertainment. The following four chapters set the stage by looking at the past, the present and the immediate future. The pace of change is such that this immediate future will soon be part of the present—and then the past.

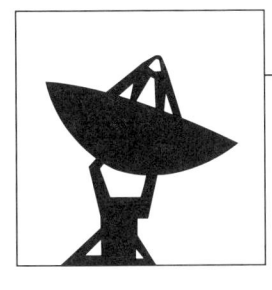

CHAPTER 9

From All the News That's Fit to Print to All the News We Want

As you struggle to wake up, the soft glow of the sun rising over Hawaii's Diamond Head greets you from the video wall of your bedroom. A voice then interjects reality, telling you the outside temperature is 5 degrees Celsius; it's pouring rain, and sleet is expected later in the day.

Diamond Head fades as the wall screen divides into nine pictures, each headlining different categories of news. Using your remote gun, you spot the stories which interest you and then hit audio record. That done, you beam onto sports and, while you drink your coffee and get dressed, watch highlights from last night's NBA games on the big screen.

As you leave for the car, you pick up the audio tape containing the stories you requested so that you can listen to your personally selected news report while you drive to work. You also grab your printout of stock quotations, a list of movie times and the odds on the horses running at Belmont today.

Of course when all these services are available you may be working at home instead of commuting. If you wish, you can spend more time watching video reports of the events that interest you. But this is how you may get your daily news in the future.

GATEKEEPERS, WATCHDOGS AND AGENDA SETTERS

On its front page each day, the *New York Times* announces its goal, first set in 1896 when its new publisher, Adolph Ochs, said his paper would present to its readers "All the news that's fit to print." This motto became the credo for American news editors and publishers.

> ### The Fourth and Fifth Estates
>
> Newspaper people often refer to themselves and their publications as The Fourth Estate. This stems from an 1828 comment by British politician Thomas Babbington Macaulay after reporters had been admitted to view and report the actions of the House of Commons. Macaulay observed: "The gallery in which the reporters sit has become a fourth estate of the realm." (The other three estates were the Lords Spiritual, the Lords Temporal, and the Commons.) The implication was that through its reporting and comment the press becomes an active force in the political process. In an American adaptation of this observation, Douglas Cater titled his 1959 study of Washington correspondents *The Fourth Branch of Government*.
>
> For years broadcasting reporters were treated as outsiders or second-class citizens by press reporters and politicians alike. As television news gained ascendancy over the press in national reporting, the broadcasting industry took its revenge by declaring itself "The Fifth Estate." The weekly trade magazine *Broadcasting*, for example, identifies itself as "the News Magazine of the Fifth Estate."

This credo implies more than simply a commitment to gathering and reporting news; it assumes a responsibility to exercise judgment about what news is "fit to print." In effect news media executives take onto themselves the responsibility to act as the public's agents in the marketplace of daily happenings. From the immense variety of daily events, they decide what is news and what is fit to print.

Along with this responsibility, our journalists also have assumed the role of watchdogs on government. They keep an eye on our public servants, both elected officials and bureaucrats, to make sure that they are doing their jobs honestly and properly. Combining the roles of gatekeepers and watchdogs, news executives establish for us the priority of the day's events and issues. They set the agenda for the audience's daily review of what's going on in the world, what is worth knowing and what is worth worrying about.

For almost a century, the public seemed content with the work of their self-appointed gatekeepers. We were a nation whose people were voracious users of newspapers and, later, broadcast news reports. But now the major news media are in trouble.

SYMPTOMS OF DISSATISFACTION

For the last decade, daily newspaper circulation has not kept pace with population increase, and network-news audiences have declined. Newspaper reading and TV news watching are lowest among those in the 18–30 year-old age bracket, suggesting further audience erosion is ahead. Something appears to be wrong in the functional relationship between these media institutions and the public.

This matter is of both individual and social concern. As individuals we need appropriate information so we can meet the challenges and opportunities confronting us. Democratic societies such as ours depend on a population with adequate information that enables its members to judge the performance of elected representatives and participate intelligently in elections.

The dilemma of our newspapers and network news programs is that they have not kept pace with changing information needs of society. Although the revolutionary technologies offer new opportunities for these media to adapt their operations, they do not guarantee either of these institutions will survive over the long term. These same technologies offer the public new options for fulfilling their information needs.

Loss of audience directly affects the advertising revenues of mass media, and both daily newspapers and network news departments have experienced painful financial pressures. Evidence of increased suspicion and/or antipathy toward journalists and the news media exists throughout large sections of the public.

The declining audiences do not necessarily indicate a declining public interest in news, but it certainly indicates a declining public interest in the news selected and presented by the dominant news media. In today's complex society, the odds are that the information needs of individuals simply cannot be met by news packages put together for a mass, largely undifferentiated audience.

THE FUNCTION IS SURVIVAL

In the Introduction we said that the primary functional role of communication was to provide individuals and groups with surveillance—information to help them meet the challenges, threats and opportunities in their environment. We equated this with news. Until the latter 19th century, most communities were sufficiently small, simple and isolated that gossip and the network of personal conversations could meet the needs of individuals for this news. But as the Industrial Revolution progressed, communities expanded in size and complexity, making it difficult for each citizen to be able to maintain individual surveillance. This change resulted in a need, an opportunity, for institutions to collect and distribute such information. Simultaneously, new technologies—the rotary press, inexpensive paper and the telegraph—allowed these institutions to provide the "organized gossip" that helped members of communities form the public mind. These institutions evolved into today's mass-circulation daily newspapers.

Today we find ourselves living in a multidimensional community where the needs for information seem to constantly expand. No longer can individuals or communities survive in isolation from others. We wear clothes made in Hong Kong, drive cars made in Japan and eat fruit and vegetables grown in Latin America.

The company we work for may be owned by a multinational corporation that moves facilities and staff from one nation to another. Long-range bombers and rockets, radioactive fallout and air and water borne industrial effluent from distant locations all pose threats to our constitutionally guaranteed rights to "life, liberty, and the pursuit of happiness." To maintain our professional status, protect our investments and guard our health, we must stay abreast of research, legislation and market trends on a worldwide basis.

Our environment is expanding, psychologically as well as physically, and mirroring this expansion, the number and variety of news reports constantly increases to the point that many of us feel we suffer from an information overload. People still need news, but the old gatekeepers—daily newspapers and newscasts—have become bottlenecks through which the news we need may or may not get through. The agenda these gatekeepers are setting may be out of touch with the real needs of the public.

DECIDING FOR OURSELVES WHAT NEWS IS "FIT"

The technologies of the Information Age now make it possible for individuals to bypass these institutions that dominated journalism during the era of mass media. We are entering an era of individual access in which each of us can obtain an expanded quantity and variety of news and opinions. If we wish, we can function as our own gatekeepers and agenda setters and decide for ourselves what news is fit, rather than have a forced dependence upon the daily paper or the evening network news.

The technology is available, but it remains to be seen whether or not most people will wish to take on this individual responsibility. In the meantime the traditional news media are undergoing transformation under pressure from both audience and advertisers.

SOCIAL AND ECONOMIC CONDITIONS SHAPE OUR INSTITUTIONS

In both the era of mass media and the new era of individualized access, intrinsic interaction occurs between the organization and operation of information media and other forces within the society.

From the mid-1800s to the middle of this century, the population grew rapidly and increasingly gathered in urban areas. The economy showed similarly dramatic growth, both in size and in the opening of opportunity. Increased levels of education were reflected in the expansion of the political franchise [1] and an expanding interest in news and information among the public.

As if in reaction to the devastating division of our Civil War, the population appeared to seek a common identity of national patriotism and purpose that transcended the debate between political parties. The news media did much to promote the ideals expressed on our coins, "E pluribus unum" and "In God we trust." The unity and divine power propounded by the media in fact reflected the values and culture of the white, Anglo-Saxon, Protestant males who largely controlled the nation's political, business and cultural institutions.

"MANIFEST DESTINY" EXPANDS THE NEWS HORIZONS

It is often said that the Spanish-American War was not only exploited but was actually promoted by William Randolph Hearst and Joseph Pulitzer as part of the circulation battle between their newspapers.² Certainly the news coverage provided by their papers sought to excite the public as well as to solidify opinion in support of the concept of the nation's "manifest destiny," typified by the advice of the great editor-publisher, Horace Greeley, who continually urged: "Go West, young man, go West."

In the pre-television era, the *Saturday Evening Post* was perhaps the medium of greatest national reach and impact. The magazine's covers by Norman Rockwell became icons of the United States that existed in the media, if not in real life: a unified, middle-class, small-town society cleaving to Judeo-Christian ethics and morality.³

PRESSURES FOR OBJECTIVITY

In the period between World War I and World War II, a major change occurred in American journalism. The concept of objective reporting evolved and triumphed in the newsrooms of the great dailies across the nation. Objective reporting was hailed as an advance of civilized communication and a triumph of ethics among journalists who now sought professional status for themselves and respect for their service to society.

More mundane, practical forces were also at work. Despite a strong isolationist sentiment, the policy of manifest destiny and foreign entanglements forced attention, if not interest, on international news. The rising threat of war in Europe riveted the attention of this nation with its millions of immigrants and others who still had close relations in the "old country."

The Great Depression which began in 1929 helped undermine the tradition of home rule as the public turned to the federal government for economic relief. News from Washington acquired a new urgency for local readers. And as newspapers expanded their coverage of non-local events, more of their content came from sources outside their own newsroom. Taking advantage of improvements in telecommunications, the several wire services provided more and more timely reportage of events from Washington and abroad. By 1935 the Associated Press had begun to also distribute news photos by wire to subscribers.

OBJECTIVE REPORTING: THE JOURNALISTIC STANDARD

Wire-service stories expanded the scope of coverage provided by individual papers, but the managements of those papers differed in their editorial outlook on the issues of the day. To avoid offending customers with different points of view, wire services adopted a practice of "objective reporting" and had their reporters and editors attempt to sift out partisan perspective from news stories.

Cornell offered a college certificate in journalism as early as 1875. By 1908 the University of Missouri expanded its course list into the first School of Journalism. The growing number of college journalism programs reflected a drive for professional respectability within the news field. In these college courses objective reporting became the standard taught to would-be reporters and editors.

Newspapers that had begun as "party papers" and for decades had actively promoted their publisher's political views, now sought to convince readers that they were objective, providing fair treatment of people and events in the news, confining opinion to the editorial page. Unfortunately for many newspapers, they had succeeded all too well in establishing their political identity, and public suspicion often continued long after a paper's editorial reform.[4]

THE PUBLIC SHIFT FROM PRINT TO BROADCAST NEWS

The push for objectivity became increasingly important as newspapers struggled to survive the attrition that was the inexorable result of competition with television for audience and advertising dollars. As the number of daily papers decreased, survivors found themselves with increasingly diverse audiences.

Because economic survival depends on advertising, and circulation is necessary to attract the advertising, editors sought to avoid offending any groups. As the use of wire-service stories increased, the front pages of newspapers across the nation became increasingly similar in appearance and in actual content.

The newspaper situation was complicated by the growing competition provided by broadcast news reportage during World War II. This competition became more intense in the mid-1950s when the networks began to broadcast evening news reports on television. In this competition newspapers steadily lost ground to broadcast news. As we became a nation of news listeners and news watchers, the public drifted from being news readers.

By 1969 daily newspaper circulation had stagnated despite continued population growth. The circulation of evening papers in the cities plummeted from 36 million in 1975 to about 26 million today.[5] Although morning circulation grew the net result has been a continued decline of newspaper penetration. Because this decline is most apparent among the younger age groups, further decline is likely in the future.

BROADCASTING AND PUBLIC TRUST

Broadcast news gradually displaced newspapers as the major source of local as well as national and international news. According to a 1991 national survey by the Elmo Roper Organization, the number of people choosing broadcasting as the more credible news medium was almost three times those choosing the newspaper. By the 1960s television had won the objectivity contest. By the end of the 1970s most people not only spent more time watching TV news than reading newspapers, they also relied upon television as their major source for all categories of news.[6]

The most important aspect in broadcasting's perceived credibility was that the audience could see the events, together with the personal trust developed by the news anchors.[7]

Network television news enjoyed an unprecedented claim upon the attention of the nation's citizens for two decades. For most of the nation's families, evening tele-

Table 9.1 Circulation Patterns of U.S. Daily Newspapers (in millions)

Year	Morning	Evening	Total Daily	Sunday	Percentage of Adults Who Read Daily (age 18 and over)
1970	25.9	36.2	61.1	49.2	78
1980	29.4	32.8	62.2	54.7	67
1985	35.4	26.4	62.8	58.8	64
1990	41.3	21.0	62.3	62.4	62

Source: '91 Facts About Newspapers. Reston, Va.: American Newspaper Publishers Association, 1990.

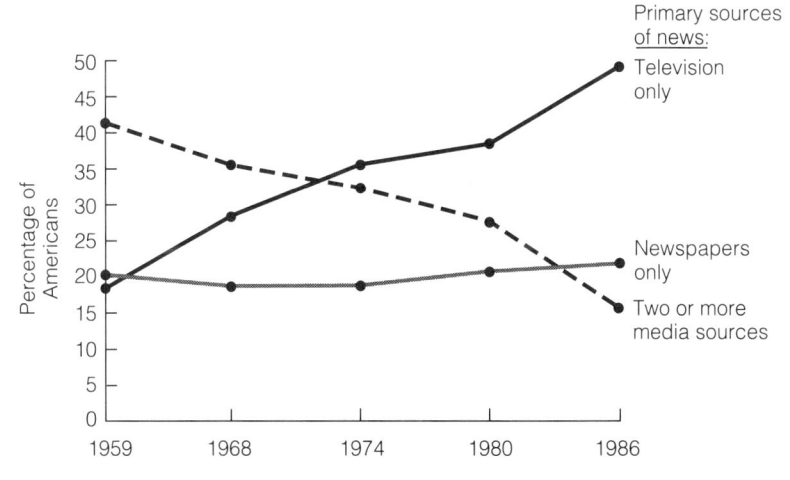

Figure 9.1 Trends in Use of Newspapers and Television News
Source: America's Watching. Television Information Office, 1987, p. 4.

vision viewing began with the news presented by their favored network. For this brief period of each day—first a quarter hour and later a half hour—the nation's attention was focused on the news as defined by the three networks.

AN INTEREST MORE APPARENT THAN REAL

Despite large audiences for the dinner-hour network news, interest may have been more apparent than real for at least some viewers. By 1955 television had become the nation's preoccupation each evening, and television meant the oligarchy networks: ABC, CBS and NBC. There were few independent stations and no cable. The networks chose to compete head on, scheduling their news programs in the same time period. For most families, choice was reduced to which network news program they would watch, not whether they would watch news or some other type of program.

By the start of the 1980s network news was coming under pressure on several levels. Cable penetration was increasing across the nation, expanding the channels competing for audience attention. Cable families did have a choice other than news. Concurrently more households were acquiring second and third sets. If someone in the family wanted to watch the news, others had the option of watching something else on another set.

Network news began to have more competition within the broadcast television field itself. Network affiliates and independent local stations profited not only from an expanded schedule of news programs, but from counter-programming against the network news. Locally produced news programs proved attractive to advertisers and earned major revenue for the stations.

The audience for news was no longer concentrated in the network-news time period but was spread across a broader period in the early fringe of evening prime time. As stations increased their own efforts and earnings in the news field, network news departments began to experience audience slippage.

THE PUSH OF ADVERTISING

Critics of the news media have debated the extent to which advertisers are able to influence the journalistic gatekeepers and the agenda the gatekeepers set with their selection of news. Whether or not advertisers exert overt pressure, news executives generally are part of the power hierarchy of their communities. This status inevitably influences their perspective in deciding what news is fit to pass through their gates.

Whether or not individual advertisers are able to influence what passes through the news media gate, the reliance on advertising for revenue itself restricts the freedom of news executives. Instead of offering a marketplace of ideas, the news media participate in a marketplace in which they compete for audiences as a commodity for advertisers.

OBJECTIVITY: IN THE EYE OF THE BEHOLDER

Newspaper and broadcast news executives must seek the largest possible audience in order to support their advertising rate structure. They must try to appeal to everyone and to avoid offending anyone. Controversial material might offend and drive away some members of the audience, a loss that would increase their CPM—cost per mille (thousand)—and decrease their competitiveness.[8]

In an attempt to attract and keep audiences, they have emphasized objectivity and a middle-of-the-road approach in selecting and reporting news events. Admirable as the intention may be, such a policy can be self-defeating and even perverse. In reality no objective position exists for controversial points of view. The location of the middle of the road depends upon where the viewer or reader stands on an issue. If the public is polarized, an attempt at objectivity is doomed to be judged as biased and offensive by almost everyone.[9]

By striving for neutrality and objectivity the media can create a false sense of consensus and commonality within the population. For decades many, if not most, whites were blissfully (and possibly willfully) ignorant of unrest among minorities in their own communities. In most cities the literally all-white (and all-male) news media simply did not see this as news fit to pass through their gates. The Civil Rights battles that began in the South in the 1950s and spread to other areas in the 1960s exposed this delusion and came as a shock to the white establishment, including journalists.[10]

Protesters adopted the strategy of creating events impossible for the media to ignore, and this news clearly showed the diversity and tension within what had been portrayed as a unified and peaceful public. The long ignored frustrations of the many minorities who had enriched and diversified the nation's population exploded into the news, forcing their way onto the agenda of the white majority. A convergence of conditions, events and technology began to change the picture U.S. citizens had of themselves and their society.

FRAYING THE FABRIC OF PUBLIC CONSENSUS

The national consensus, real or otherwise, seemed to unravel in recent decades. The media increasingly became the focus of public suspicion, resentment and antipathy as many individuals and groups came to view the journalism establishment as arrogant and even venal.

The Vietnam War fueled the development of the counterculture, which had appeared in the 1950s and flourished in the 1960s and 1970s. Underground publications appeared on newsstands in most cities, restoring vitality to the marketplace of ideas even as they raised eyebrows and ire among those of the Establishment.

The kaleidoscope nature of our society became more obvious as cable broke the oligarchy's monopoly control of home video screens. Given a choice some viewers deserted the network evening news block. Some turned to entertainment; others found new sources of news and comment, such as CNN and C-SPAN, which serviced their interests and needs better than the traditional media. Ethnic-oriented news channels appeared on cable; many radio stations, particularly in the AM band, turned to ethnic music and news formats.

SHIFTING FUNCTIONS AMONG THE NEWS MEDIA

By 1990 the managers of the once-dominant daily press and network news programs were in a confused state. Each medium still looms large, but their structures and content increasingly ring hollow as they seek to clarify their function within contemporary society.

Broadcasting and cable pre-empted the newspaper's role as the provider of the day's news. Printed newspapers simply could not match the immediacy and speed of reportage available through video and radio.

Displaced as the purveyor of news, newspapers now allocate an increasing amount of space, even on the front page, to news analysis and comment. Following the lead of *USA Today,* papers are abandoning traditional make-up. They invest in new printing facilities to dress up their pages with color pictures and charts, flexible layout and headlines. Even the traditionalist *New York Times* has prepared for color and change by investing half a billion dollars in a new printing facility.[11]

CHANGES IN THE NEWSPAPER

Centrifugal Forces in Metro Areas

What do these changes mean in terms of function? As daily papers expand news analysis, they also allocate more space to sports and business and to sections on food, homemaking, travel, arts and entertainment and other topics that often are the focus of accompanying advertising.

Even as they battle video on the front lines, metropolitan dailies find themselves attacked on their flanks by increasingly aggressive community papers and shopper publications. The newspaper industry reflects the centrifugal forces in our metropolitan communities—the flight of population to surrounding suburbs. As the number of metropolitan papers decreased in recent decades, community papers appeared and expanded to serve these suburbs, diverting circulation that might otherwise accrue to the metropolitan daily. The battle for suburban readers hastens the adoption of new technologies by metropolitan papers.

Computerization of both the newsroom and the "back shop" makes it easier to produce an expanded schedule of zone editions. Computer editing and on-screen composition facilitates compiling special pages or entire sections for individual suburbs or suburban areas, sections containing news coverage and advertising focused on those communities. Computerization in the press room speeds the changes necessary to produce the different editions and bundle them for delivery to the appropriate communities.

Computer-programmed collating equipment makes possible varied inserts for each community, each neighborhood and even each subscriber. With such flexibility metros can meet the needs of advertisers who want very specific geographic distribution as well as those interested in the entire metropolitan area. A less felicitous effect is that many editions, particularly on Sunday, are increasingly cluttered with the equivalent of junk mail.

The Emergence of National Papers

As the metropolitan dailies battle suburban papers on the home news front, the combination of satellite, computer and flexible printing technologies spawns competition on the national front. As we noted in Chapter 6, the daily press in the United States has traditionally been a local press. The tradition resulted from the vast land area of the nation coupled with home rule. However, in recent years we have seen the emergence of national papers. The *Wall Street Journal* is the real pioneer in this field. It began publishing regional editions in 1929. In 1991 it issued 17 different editions from 18 printing locations. Its combined circulation makes The *Wall Street Journal* the nation's largest paper.

USA Today is actually the first true national paper. Its uniform edition for the entire nation is edited in Alexandria, Virginia, and distributed by satellite to printing plants in almost three dozen locations coast-to-coast. Gannett, the company publishing *USA Today,* avows the paper is intended for a unique, nationally oriented audience of frequent travelers. But Gannett is also the owner of the nation's largest chain of local dailies. In fact, it seems very likely that at least part of the circulation of *USA Today* represents a diversity of people who would otherwise be readers of local daily newspapers.

The *New York Times* not only distributes its New York–based edition from New England to Washington, but distributes a national edition printed in 8 additional locations. The *New York Times,* in straight-forward fashion, promotes its regional editions as an option to readers who want better national and international coverage than they find in their local papers.

The *Wall Street Journal* has expanded into international editions, printed in both Europe and Asia. *USA Today* has a European edition. The *New York Times* produces a fax edition for Japan. And as these papers push abroad the Paris *International Herald-Tribune* is increasingly aggressive in seeking readers in the United States.

Does the Daily News Have to Be a Newspaper?

The expansion of national and even international papers is providing new choices to local readers, but generally these choices are more expensive than local papers. To pay for the new equipment and personnel required by their competitive struggle, local papers are having to raise street and subscription prices.

Experience shows that each price increase results in loss of readers. This loss creates a dilemma for newspaper publishers. It may also create an opportunity to reconsider strategies for publishing the daily news.

The technologies responsible for the emergence of national papers, as well as the expansion of zone editions, make use of the fact that the entire news process is adaptable to computerization. If we separate tradition from function, the substantive function of the newspaper is that of a database. Today this database is largely computerized.

If a newspaper's primary function is to provide access to the day's news and that news is in an accessible database, there really is no need for the physical product—all that newsprint which we must put out for the trash collectors each week. Anyone with a personal computer and a modem can access the news content of over 100 newspapers across the nation.[12]

Why don't newspaper publishers take the jump and abandon their present inefficient format and process and fully embrace the new technology already within their walls? As yet it is neither practical nor economically feasible. In 1990 only about 10 percent of the nation's homes contain a modem-equipped personal computer. Conditioned as we are by the ingrained habit of paying only 35–50 cents for each newspaper, most of us would recoil at the cost of getting our news in this manner. Despite our complaints about piles of paper and inky fingers, the newspaper has characteristics which make it handy: It is user friendly (assuming we are literate), and we can carry it with us and read it on the subway or bus.

Nevertheless some newspaper managements are exploring alternative technologies. As the cost of these services decreases and the cost of daily newspapers increases, an economic crossover point is coming.

New Ways of Getting the News

Several newspapers have experimented with videotex services. Traditionalists somewhat gleefully emphasize that most of these experiments have been disasters,[13] but their glee may be both premature and misplaced. Despite the failures, something like videotex may be a future practical reality. Gannett has pioneered a series of daily summaries covering a variety of news categories available through gateway or kiosk services to those with modems.

In 1989 the Hartford, Connecticut, *Courant* inaugurated a daily afternoon fax edition containing news summaries scheduled to appear in the next morning's regular edition. The *New York Times* publishes a facsimile edition for distribution in Japan and to cruise ships. These have been relatively expensive services,[14] but advertising-supported facsimile dailies are beginning to appear. They may be small and bear little resemblance to their bulky forerunners, but they don't smear people's fingers nor pile up for the garbage, and at least some seem to be making money.

Relatively few homes are equipped now with fax machines, and so potential reach of these publications is limited. But penetration of this technology has shown rapid growth, and if costs continue to decline the fax machine may become as ubiquitous as the answering machine.

Fax-service use might vary. For example, stock-market quotations require a great deal of space but are of interest to only a small percentage of readers. By omitting these from newspapers and offering them by fax, papers may save space and reduce production costs with minimum reader dissatisfaction.[15] When we recall the impact of cable's expanded penetration on broadcast television, we may glimpse the potential impact of fax publications on the traditional newspaper.

Newspapers are also instituting voice information service to provide updates and specialized reports on topics such as weather, sports, stock quotations and events. The great advantage is that this service is easily available to anyone with a push-button telephone. The service can be kept current through frequent updates. By inserting an advertising message, these services can be offered free to users.

The experiments with fax, voice mail and videotex show that, like it or not, newspaper journalists are in a state of transition. They are moving toward a future in which their job will be to compile news that users will access individually, perhaps by using a multimedia machine equipped with a high-speed laser printer and an optical fiber connection to access the newspaper's database.

CHANGES IN VIDEO NEWS

Video news is also in a state of confused transition as new technologies provide greater flexibility to gather and distribute audio-visual coverage. Semiconductor-based miniaturization of video equipment allows a single reporter to provide coverage of events. Satellite transmission facilitates gathering these field reports from practically any location. This capability has been demonstrated most dramatically in the coverage of armed conflicts.

The American public has had little direct experience with war since our Civil War. But in World War II families sitting in their safe homes in the American heartland heard the bombs falling on London as Edward R. Murrow made his nightly reports to CBS using trans-Atlantic telephone lines. News reporting took on new dimensions and new immediacy.

Vietnam became the first "living room war,"[16] thanks to the combination of electronic field equipment and satellite transmission in use during the last years of the war. These early satellite relays added urgency to the reports, changing the public's perception of and attitudes toward our involvement in Southeast Asia. They also began the transformation of the public's expectation of daily news coverage.

As more satellites were placed in orbit and the number of ground links multiplied, the networks expanded their live coverage of events worldwide. Events and the people involved acquired a new psychological immediacy as the audience saw, rather than read or heard about, these events. As the costs of the technologies decreased, their availability and use increased throughout the video news field, not just among the networks.

The Tradition of Network News Dominance

Broadcast news developed along a pattern almost the reverse of that seen in United States newspapers. National reports provided by the networks traditionally dominated broadcast journalism. Individual stations lacked the resources to compete with local newspapers, who for many years effectively blocked station access to the nation's leading wire service, the Associated Press.

On the other hand the networks combined their financial resources and the immediacy of broadcast reporting to capitalize on the public's interest in national and international news which grew as World War II unfolded. The reporting of network journalists from the war fronts did much to make listening to the news a national habit.

As the network oligarchy made the transition from radio to television, their managements continued a tradition developed during World War II: The news departments served as standard-bearers for network prestige. The investment of resources in news departments not only was a matter of pride, but also was pragmatic. The evening news played a major role in gathering listeners and viewers into the network's audience. The news anchors themselves functioned as symbols of the network.

In the turmoil which followed the network management changes of the late 1980s, the news departments were no longer sheltered from massive cutbacks in personnel and operating expenses. In 1990, as the networks sought further economies, network retrenchment extended the cuts to include not just overseas news bureaus but domestic ones as well.

This move reflected a new reality in which the network news departments were undergoing functional challenge both within their own systems and within the larger area of video news generally.

Shifting Patterns of Video News

The majority of United States households continue to watch news in the dinner-hour period. The late news at 10 or 11 p.m. remains the television nightcap for many viewers. The pattern of choice, however, has changed. By the 1989–1990 season, only 31 percent of U.S. households watched one of the three network evening-news presentations, and their combined audience share (of homes viewing at that time) was just under 60 percent.[17]

Network news traditionally provided the foundation to which affiliates added their local reports. News is almost the sole production activity of most stations. Although news production means expense, many stations found that they could generate profits from good newscasts. Coupling their local news programs to network news, the stations had large audiences providing the base for selling advertising time within their news program.

The network news helps attract and anchor the audience, but the local news programs constitute a block of a half-hour (or more) from which the affiliates derive all advertising income. As these programs began to produce strong profits for the stations, affiliates resisted network proposals to expand their news programs to a full hour. The additional half-hour had become too valuable to the affiliates for them to give it up.

Expanding Ability to Cover Local News

Technological developments helped stations expand the scope of their news coverage. The miniaturization of field equipment made it possible for more from-the-scene reporting, with little or no increase in news staff. Whereas field production previously required a crew of three plus access to a major power source, now a single person with a minicam and a lightweight powerpack can cover the action.

By the mid-1980s more than three dozen satellites with 750 transponders in orbital positions provided service to the United States. With this much capacity, the cost for satellite relays came within the reach of individual local stations. Stations began to invest in electronic news vehicles (ENVs), self-contained mobile production facilities that can establish direct transmission back to the station via microwave links. Computer animation and graphics made it possible for local news programs to acquire the polish previously associated with network news.

As local stations expanded their efforts in news production, they also began to widen the scope of their reportage. No longer did they function strictly as a local supplement to the networks' national and international coverage; they began to develop comprehensive programs. The networks themselves unintentionally abetted this development.

Stations Join Satellite News Coverage

One of the great advantages of telecommunications satellites for the broadcasting industry has been the flexibility they provide for gathering news from distant points. As satellite technology became more efficient and dish size diminished, their use could be extended to remote locations.

Adding dishes and appropriate transmitting equipment to ENVs has transformed them into satellite news vehicles (SNVs). Field crews can up-link their reports via satellite directly to the control center of either the station or the network.

Network news executives recognized that SNVs allow local news staff to provide flexible and economic coverage of breaking news anywhere in the nation. And so the networks implemented a policy whereby they shared the $400,000 cost of SNVs with local affiliates.

Even with network support, SNVs represented a major investment by stations. Management sought to put this investment to use through more live event coverage, to gain an edge on their competitors for audience and advertising support.

As satellite transponders increased, costs for satellite relays decreased, and local TV news editors grew more ambitious. To provide special coverage tailored to audience interests, they dispatched their SNVs to events farther afield. The 1988 conventions of both the Republican and Democratic parties saw a new phenomenon: parking lots filled with SNVs from all over the country. Stations were learning to supplement network convention coverage with interviews and stories focusing on the activities of local convention delegates. National events could now be localized with satellite feeds of special coverage by individual stations.

Because they provide full-time program schedules, the networks each lease multiple transponders for program feeds and communication to and from affiliates. But because individual stations make only sporadic use of satellite links, it is not economical for them to have their own transponders. They must have some method for obtaining access to such links on an ad hoc basis. Brokers match the needs of short-term users with time available on various transponders that are not dedicated to single users. One such agency, CONUS, has evolved into a satellite news co-operative.

CONUS, News Co-ops and the All-News Channel

CONUS was developed by Hubbard Broadcasting, a broadcast group headquartered in Minneapolis. With its own transponders, CONUS has evolved into a multifaceted full-time operation providing flexible services through which local stations can enrich their news productions.

Through CONUS's nine regional cooperatives, 150 broadcast and cable member organizations in Japan, Australia, Europe and the United States can coordinate coverage of distant events, sharing the benefit of one another's SNVs. For example, if the mayor of Boston is making a major speech in Dallas, the news director of a Boston station can have coverage without dispatching a crew. Arrangements are made for a Dallas station to send a news crew to the event, transponder time is booked to relay the coverage to Boston, and the local station edits it for the evening news.

CONUS also organizes eight daily national news feeds compiled from reports of member stations, including cut-ins for breaking news stories. It has White House and Capitol Hill bureaus to provide special coverage upon request by members, and it also sends crews to cover presidential trips and other major international political events. Through a joint venture with the Associated Press, members can obtain a variety of live and taped news feeds as well as still photographs.

The All-News Channel draws upon the CONUS resources and, in partnership with Viacom International, provides an ongoing cycle of six updated news reports to subscribing video outlets throughout each 24 hours. Subscribers can either rebroadcast entire sections or take segments and edit them into their own local programs.[18]

With such far-flung resources, local stations can create comprehensive newscasts combining community news with national and international coverage not only competitive in scope with that of the networks, but with additional detail for specific local interests.

The CNN Phenomenon

The erosion of network news dominance by their own affiliates and other local stations comes on top of an even greater shock: CNN, Cable News Network, which used satellite technology to develop the world's first full-time video news service, a phenomenon which gave new dimensions to cable television as well as to video news itself.

Just as the networks had to fight the established Washington press corps for access and status, CNN had to fight the networks as well as other skeptics, including the advertisers essential to provide operating revenues. CNN's success is measured by the fact that today it is an international service with distribution in Europe, Africa and Asia, as well as a Spanish-language service for Latin America. Its coverage of the 1991 Gulf War together with that of various important congressional hearings has given it prestige to match its growing list of advertiser clients.

CNN not only pioneered satellite distribution of news but has also pushed the development and use of more portable equipment for field coverage. This includes fly-away kits for satellite coverage from remote areas. All the equipment needed to establish a field control center with up-linking capability is stored in foot-locker-sized containers easily carried to any location.

CNN also makes aggressive use of amateurs with minicams to obtain coverage of unexpected events. Coverage can be up linked from a local or regional center to the Atlanta headquarters for review and editing. CNN's staff continues to explore new ways to add flexibility and depth to coverage, including provision for viewers with personal computers and modems to go online for questions, answers and comments, interacting with the CNN staff.

CNN has also taken advantage of the increased interest in national and international reportage by local television news editors. It now sells broadcasters a syndicated video news report compiled from its worldwide staff.

Following the lead of CNN, other satellite-delivered services have been developed to provide specialized news reports. The most successful, perhaps, has been

ESPN, the sports channel, but others specialize in news of finance, health and religion. The success of ESPN encouraged the start of regional sports news services.

Increasing the Depth of Video Reportage

These new technologies have greatly expanded the variety and scope of news available to the public. Viewers obtain greater depth of information about events and issues.

One of the most interesting and significant cable news innovations was the formation of C-SPAN, the Congressional Satellite Public Affairs Network. Funded by the National Cable Television Association, C-SPAN provides ongoing coverage of the actions in both houses of Congress as well as of major committee hearings.

The service now includes background reportage of political campaigns and the discussion of timely issues. C-SPAN has become video's medium of record for national government and affairs.

Another pioneer, Satellite Communications for Learning (SCOLA), operates from Creighton University in Omaha, Nebraska. Using a variety of satellite dishes, SCOLA receives news programs from 35 nations. These programs are distributed in their original format and language by satellite to subscribers—mostly school organizations and cable systems—throughout the United States. The 24-hour daily schedule includes live relays of news from some countries (France, Japan, Mexico, and Russia), same day relay from others and delayed broadcast (as much as six days) from the remaining nations. "Outwrite" service, available by fax and by mail, provides the original text and English translation.

Widening the Video Marketplace of Ideas

While CNN, CONUS, C-SPAN and SCOLA have expanded the national and international news available to cable subscribers, access and origination channels have become cable vehicles for local reporting. In some communities the cable franchise stipulates that the system will provide production facilities and training to help local groups make use of the access channels. True, these channels are often poorly used and seldom watched. But they do provide the potential for expanding the marketplace of ideas, and, when community interest runs high on an issue or event, they may attract an audience significant in its composition if not in numbers.

Cable managements have not been blind to the financial success of local television news. More aggressive cable operators have begun to fashion their own local news programs. Because most cable systems service areas much smaller than the signal area of broadcast stations, their programs can have a neighborhood focus in terms of both news coverage and advertiser appeal. The premier example of this focus is News 12 on Long Island, which functions as an ongoing local news channel.

The combination of network and local news from both broadcast and cable services means that the average cable system itself now provides a marketplace of news with breadth undreamed of by Thomas Jefferson. "Time shifting" by recording programs on the VCR for later viewing has given us additional freedom to decide what and when we will watch.

THE FUTURE: GETTING OUR OWN NEWS

Moving Toward the Digital Newsbase

Print news media, as we have seen, are already well along the way to digitization. Digital sound is already well-established in recorded music and has been introduced at least experimentally in broadcasting. The new laser video disks use digital technology for audio-visual materials, as do experimental CD-ROM recordings, which can also be played back on a video screen. Video news coverage may also be digitized.

The prototype already exists in an experimental program of the Massachusetts Institute of Technology's (MIT) Media Lab. Researchers there have been working for several years to develop an interactive video news format functioning in a fashion similar to videotex. Audio-visual news reportage is recorded digitally, indexed and stored in a computer.

Today we can make our way through videotex menus to fashion a news and information package to suit our own needs and interests. In the digital video future, we will be able to select items and depth of detail from video reports gathered by satellite and brought upon command to our home through fiber optics.

The Technology Is Ready, but Are the Users?

As we saw in the section on revolutionary technologies, most of the technology for these processes already exists. What is needed is to put the pieces together and have the service available to a sufficiently large market for economic viability. Human nature presents two major stumbling blocks.

The remote tuning wand and the VCR have begun a process of changing video viewing into an interactive process, in which the audience exercises active choice in selection of content and schedule. The VCR illustrates our first stumbling block, what we might call "technology phobia." The inability of many adults to deal with the VCR emphasizes that any multimedia news service must be exceedingly user friendly.

Undoubtedly a generational difference affects the ease with which various members of the audience make this transition. Unlike their parents, younger viewers easily manipulate the VCR, drawing upon experience gained from exposure to high-tech products at an early age. In another decade most adults will have been using simple media interactivity from childhood.

In the medium-term future, public acceptance of computer-based, personal information media will possibly be much greater than is the case among today's audience. The next generation will be computer-smart, psychologically undaunted by the machines and processes used to access digitally stored information archives.

The Burden of Choice

In addition to the question of user friendliness, videotex illustrates the second hurdle to personalized interactive news services: the decision-making placed on the user. One of the banes of the Information Age is the flood of material flowing past us each day. Most of us do need and desire gatekeepers to help us sort through this mass to find what is of interest and importance to us.

But editors can provide the same service through videotex. The Gannett services already do this. If after reading the summary service(s) we want more details on individual items, a simple request provides these. This process is more efficient than scanning items in newspaper pages or watching a 30-minute video news program without knowing what the topics will be.[19]

Keeping the Emphasis on Function

Let us again emphasize that ultimately the function—not the form or format—counts. The function of news is to provide the public with the information they individually and collectively need and want. How that is done has changed through the centuries. For today's adults using the newspaper is an ingrained habit. But the newspaper as we know it is a relatively modern phenomenon, developed in the 19th century as technological change provided a new way to service information needs within the social and economic conditions of the period.

The broadcast media have already displaced the newspapers in fulfilling some informational functions. Cable now gives broadcast news functional competition, and other technologies are ready to test the market. The nature of news that we need and desire may change, and the way we obtain that news may change. But the functional need of information for survival will remain.

Worldwide Party Line?

Cooley's description of the newspaper as "organized gossip" not only calls to mind an image of the simpler lifestyle of a long-gone era, but also reinstates the fundamentally personal nature of the communication function of news.

Before 1945 private telephone lines were rare. Many, if not most, non-business subscribers shared a party line with as many as a dozen other families. Much information was shared (sometimes unintentionally) along the party line. In many communities exchanges were still manually operated. When one picked up a telephone, a real, live human being responded—not a dial tone, not a computer synthesized voice. Small-town operators often functioned as the nerve—and news—center of the community.

As telephone service expanded, it revolutionized our habits of exchanging personal and business information and news. We no longer have party lines and all-knowing operators, but with a sequence of touches we can make contact with our own news sources almost anywhere in the world. AT&T's slogan, Reach out and touch someone, is reflected in our daily lives by the way we share happy and sad tidings with those who constitute our community of interest—regardless of where they are.

In fact the telephone is our most basic news-disseminating technology. Cellular and personal phones are already expanding our accessibility to others, while making isolation more difficult. Long distance and international rates have fallen dramatically, and in the age of optical fiber further reductions can be expected.

In the near future we probably will use some combination of telephone, video and computer technologies interconnected by optical fiber and satellites to gather news of all kinds, from all over the world. And we (or our children) will use this technology with the same ease that our grandparents used their party lines to keep up with the gossip of their more geographically circumscribed communities.

Suggestions for Further Reading

For a broad look at how the information function has been served by societies throughout history, try Michael Stephens' *A History of News*.

A seemingly endless stream of books analyze and critique the performance of the information media. The question of who and what influences the work of gatekeepers and agenda setters is the focus of Herbert J. Gans' *Deciding What's News*. Edward Bliss Jr. focuses on the development of radio news in *Now the News,* and Bob Franklin and David Murphy focus on local newspapers in *What News*. One news program, CBS's "60 Minutes," has consistently been near the top of the prime time ratings over the past decade. In *60 Minutes: The Power and the Politics,* Axel Madsen provides a fascinating look at the power and the politics playing a major role in shaping that program.

For an inside look at how new technologies are being influenced by what goes on in newspaper newsrooms, try Philip Meyer's *The New Precision Journalism*.

Perhaps the classic critical commentary on the press is *The Press,* a collection of caustic essays by the long-time columnist of the Baltimore *Sun*, A. J. Liebling, which was originally published in the *New Yorker* in the 1940s. Despite their age Liebling's observations remain as valid as they are fun to read. Norman Isaacs, one of the great American newspaper editors and later an associate dean of Columbia's Graduate School of Journalism, does a similar job with a series of more recent case studies in *Untended Gates*. Leo Bogart provides a comprehensive view of the news audience in *Press and Public*.

Notes

1. Property ownership remained a requirement in some states into the 19th century, and some states imposed a poll tax as recently as the 1950s. Until the ratification of the 19th Amendment to the Constitution in 1920, women were not guaranteed voting rights.
2. Similar criticism of the news media occurred during the events preceding the 1991 Gulf War. Some observers felt that the initial response of the news media exhibited more interest in increasing audience numbers than in providing a balanced report of a complex situation.
3. As the nation has struggled with the stresses of social fragmentation in recent years, Rockwell's pictures enjoyed a renewed popularity as part of a vogue based on nostalgia for the good old days.
4. For examples see Jack Lyle's *The News in Megalopolis*. San Francisco: Chandler Publishing Co., 1967.
5. This drop in circulation has been primarily an urban phenomenon; there are still more evening than morning dailies, but most evening publications are in suburbs, small cities and towns.
6. The Television Information Office (disbanded in 1988) commissioned the Elmo Roper Organization to conduct a series of biennial studies over a period of two decades tracking use of and attitudes toward the media. The Times-Mirror Corporation has also conducted studies on these general topics. Despite differences in the data (the TIO studies show greater preferences for television than do the Times-Mirror studies), the trends are the same. Actual audience estimates can be traced through the accepted measurement agencies of each industry: the Audit Bureau of Circulation for newspapers and the A.C. Nielsen Company's National Television Index.
7. At the height of his career, public opinion polls repeatedly showed that long-time CBS anchor Walter Cronkite was both the best known and most trusted person in the nation.

8. CPM is discussed in Chapter 10. In brief, it is a formula that identifies which station or newspaper delivers the largest audience per advertising dollar spent.
9. The social-psychology literature is replete with experiments that built upon the early work of Gordon and Floyd Alport in which they documented how personal attitudes influence the perception of people and events.
10. The *Los Angeles Times,* for example, dispatched reporters to the Deep South to cover the civil rights struggle in the early 1960s, but no one covered Watts and other predominantly black areas of its own city. Without coverage of the tensions in those areas, the white majority assumed a lack of local race problems—until riots forced Watts into the headlines in 1965.
11. The *New York Times'* new plant demonstrates a classic case of conflict between the new and the status quo. The plant remained unused for months following completion, owing to a combination of a bad economy and the resistance of the paper's unions.
12. Modem users can also access the files of most of the major wire services.
13. Two of the more spectacular of these disasters were the ventures of Times-Mirror Corporation in Los Angeles and of Knight-Ridder in Miami, both of which incurred losses in the tens of millions of dollars over several years of operation.
14. The *Courant* fax edition costs $600 a year.
15. Walt Potter, writing in the August 1991 *Presstime* ("A Modest Role Emerges for Videotext Systems," pp. 12–15), reports that when the Atlanta *Journal* and *Constitution* dropped the commodities and options listings from their financial pages and offered them free by fax, they received about 100 calls daily asking for the service. The papers had been using about three-fourths of a full page each day for information desired by perhaps one percent of their readers.
16. Arlen, Michael J. *Living Room War.* New York: Viking, 1969.
17. Monush, Barry (editor). *International Television and Video Almanac 1991.* New York: Quigley Publications, 1991, p. 254.
18. The service is also available to families with TVROs through Viacom's Showtime Satellite Networks' Extraview program.
19. We might also use hypertext, which is described in Chapter 11.

CHAPTER 10

Selling Ideas, Candidates and Products

Let's say you are a car salesman looking for buyers for the new super-sports convertible, and business is slow. You can have your computer compile a list of all the young, high-income people in your community whose present cars are over two years old—and send them a personalized fax inviting them to dial in for a test drive. If you are one of those young, high-income persons receiving the invitation and you're curious, you don't need to go down to a salesroom. Just dial in the number given in the fax, settle into your virtual-reality lounger, put on the control gloves and the stereoptical color visor and away you go.

If you're trying to decide which candidate to vote for, you can dial the candidate's interaction line, ask your questions and hear personal responses via videodisc.

Years may pass before advertising and campaigning reach these levels of technical sophistication, but our revolutionary technologies are already upsetting many of the existing rules of persuasion, marketing and sales.

HOW DO WE WIN BUYERS AND INFLUENCE PEOPLE?

The continuing popularity of Dale Carnegie's *How to Win Friends and Influence People*[1] attests to the importance of the second category of communication activities, those created to persuade. In our society the decisions we make individually and collectively about products, people and issues are influenced by what we see, hear and read in the media.

Newspapers are two-thirds advertising. A half-hour newscast has only about 23 minutes of news; the rest is advertising and promotion. Advertising is big business—and big money. In 1989 over $118 billion was spent on advertising, and more than half went to newspapers and broadcasters.

We are so inundated with advertising that, like it or not, we have learned to swim through it and even tend to accept this flood of persuasive communication in the media as natural. But this predominance was not the norm as recently as fifty years ago.

In 1940 readers expected newspapers to have 60 percent or more of their space devoted to news, not advertising. Although broadcasting was loaded with commercials, fewer than 1,000 radio stations (all of them AM) existed in the entire nation. Advertising expenditures in 1940 were only $2 billion. Life then was a lot cheaper and simpler—and lacking in most of the conveniences we now take for granted. If you don't believe it, look again at Figure I.2 in the Introduction.

Today's mass media reflect the mass market, both political and economic, that evolved after World War II. Presidential candidates still toured the country on campaign trains, making speeches from the observation car platform to whatever crowds had gathered at each whistle-stop. The advertising jingles and slogans of the 1930s and 1940s may strike us today as quaint, but in their time they represented a highly sophisticated use of the media. The best of today's campaigns no doubt will look just as quaint and dated five or ten years from now.

Persuasive communication evolves to adapt to a changing society and the availability of new technologies. The revolutionary technologies are helping bring about new campaigning and marketing techniques in which products are targeted to specific demographic groups, in which political candidates must respond to growing numbers of special interest groups.

A RELATIVELY RECENT SPECIALIZATION

Persuasion was a major function of the publications in the Colonial and Revolutionary period of our history. Most articles took overt, explicit political positions. After all, printing was so slow in those days that everybody in town knew the news before it could be published. And, yes, these papers contained some advertising, primarily notices such as the arrival of shipments of consumer goods.

Today media executives go to great efforts to convince us that they protect their news from the taint of either commercial or political influence. The codes of both the American Newspaper Publishers Association and the National Association of Broadcasters call for commercial persuasion to be clearly identified as such.

In newspapers we expect that persuasion on political and social issues will be restricted to editorial comment and op-ed page columns, separated from news and entertainment content. Broadcasters use labels such as "editorial" and "paid political announcement" and disclaimers stating that "the management of this station is not responsible for the content of this program," or "the content does not necessarily reflect the policy of this station."

When the president of the United States requests broadcast time, the network executives must wrestle with the question of whether he will be speaking as president or as politician. You can bet that the leaders of the opposition party will take the stand that it is the latter and demand equal time for response.

PERSUASION AND SOCIAL ORDER

Commercial persuasion—advertising—plays an essential role in stimulating the consumer activity which fuels our economic marketplace. Political persuasion plays an essential role in helping to form opinions as well as voting decisions. Both forms of persuasion are integral forces in our social organization.

Social organization allows us to live together in communities. Some degree of direction and agreement is essential to society; otherwise, it will fall into a state of anarchy. But societies use many different patterns to establish rules and persuade the population to abide by them. These patterns range from authoritarian to democratic structures.

In authoritarian societies one person or an elite group makes decisions for the society. In societies with controlled or planned economies, some central authority—not the consumers—decides the nature, amount and price of goods to be produced and made available to the public.

For example, in Indonesia the government's economic development plan pushed investment in basic industries and agriculture, encouraging individuals to save rather than spend. When commercials stimulated demand for consumer products, the Minister of Communication ordered that advertising be banned from television.

Such a situation is inconceivable in the United States. As a democratic nation with a competitive market economy, we rely on an open marketplace of both ideas and products as the mechanism through which we achieve communal decisions for our society. We have periodic elections through which we choose from among candidates and options for public policy. We face an endless series of economic choices: which product, which brand to buy, which store to patronize and which service to use.

MARKETING, ADVERTISING AND PUBLIC RELATIONS

Our consumer economy is driven by marketing. According to one textbook[2] marketing comprises "the four Ps"—price, place, packaging and promotion. Promotion is persuasion, and advertising is promotion very much in the public eye. Advertising tends to be tactical persuasion focusing on specific, immediate goals—making people aware of a product and making them want it. Of course this is exactly what the television commercials were doing in Indonesia.

Public-relations persuasion is generally long-term strategy that builds and maintains product and corporate image and reputation. It also involves crisis management to defuse unexpected disasters.

The Boeing Corporation doesn't buy magazine ads with the expectation that we will run out and buy a 747 or a 767, but it knows that the airlines who do buy the planes appreciate these ads if they make us feel safe in the air. You can be sure that, whatever the cause, when an airplane crashes, the manufacturer's public-relations staff goes into high gear to influence reporters to downplay any mention of their firm.

Public relations relies heavily on personal contacts and behind-the-scenes activity to influence what does and does not pass through the journalistic gates. In any political campaign the press secretary will be working to steer reporters away from subjects that have the potential to embarrass the candidate.

Advertising and public relations overlap, and both make use of a broad range of communications techniques and technologies. The mass media are particularly important in this form of communication because they can extend the reach and impact of messages intended to persuade.

PARALLEL BUT DISTINCT MARKETPLACES

Our society stresses democracy and free enterprise, and that means that we must maintain both a political marketplace of candidates, parties and ideologies and a commercial marketplace of products and services. These two marketplaces may be distinctly different, but it is impossible to keep them totally separate.

For example consider the fact that although it is perfectly legal to sell cigarettes in this country, Congress has banned cigarette commercials from television and required cigarette packages and advertisements to include warnings about the health hazards. Congress has also legislated that broadcasters must make air time equally available to all candidates for federal office.[3]

A more subtle overlap results from the fact that the mass media, including those media with a primary function to provide information, depend upon revenue from commercial persuasion—advertising—for their economic survival.

PARALLELS AND DIVERGENCES BETWEEN THE TWO MARKETS

Political and economic advocacy follow largely parallel paths. Politicians and political activists quickly adopt or adapt techniques that have proven effective in the economic marketplace. However, political and economic advocacy must also reflect some basic differences in the way each marketplace operates.

If you are selling a consumer product, you can survive or even flourish with only a small fraction of the market. But you must work constantly to maintain and improve your competitive situation; any increase or decrease of market share may directly affect your profits.

If you are a politician, the rules are quite different. Politics is a winner-takes-all game, and all players must accept the majority choice. You cannot survive with a fraction of the market; without a majority of votes, you are out in the cold for two, four, six years—whatever the term is for the office you seek.

Election campaigns are tactical battles during which candidates and their parties make use of the same persuasive techniques as the marketers of consumer products.

If You Pay the Piper, Can You Really Call the Tune?

Advertising revenue allows us to have a choice of mass-media institutions independent of control by government. But this does not mean that they are free from external influence.

We have seen that advertising sets many of the parameters for the news media, such as the number of pages a newspaper publishes and the number of newscasts a station schedules. In the battle for survival of metropolitan dailies, the deciding factor is which papers are chosen as the advertising vehicles for the big department stores, not which papers have the largest circulation.

The emergence of "happy talk" news in the 1970s had nothing to do with trying to make television news more effective in informing people. Happy talk was a strategy to attract more viewers and maintain a competitive position in selling commercial time. At the other extreme from "happy talk" is "The MacNeil-Lehrer Newshour" on PBS. This program has lots of prestige, but it would never survive on commercial television. Its ratings are too low to be of interest to advertisers.

Corporations do have vested interest in many public activities and issues. Cases of overt advertiser pressure on the journalistic gatekeepers appear to be rare, but part of the job of corporate public relations is striving for a symbiosis with journalists. Corporate personnel can supply or withhold information or provide access to key company spokespeople. Public-relations personnel can influence what gets through the journalistic gateway and what agenda the news medium presents to the public. That they can do so may reflect the fact that news professionals are just that: professionals whose own self-interest is tied to the business community. Inevitably whoever pays the piper has the opportunity to call the tune.

During the past half century, advertising revenues have skyrocketed, but ownership of media institutions became more concentrated. The corollary of this paradox is that the increased revenues have not resulted in an expansion of the marketplace of ideas insofar as the two major media—newspapers and television—are concerned. This paradox is not the result of conspiracy or policy; rather, it reflects changes within our society.

Candidates may spend tens of thousands, even millions of dollars on advertising to influence the public in the political marketplace.

Although the loss of an election is a real defeat, most advocates, candidates and parties view each election as a crucial milestone in the long-term, ongoing strategic competition for public opinion. Parties and politicians, like businesses and institutions, seek to build long-term good will and consumer or voter loyalty.

A cigarette company sponsors women's tennis tournaments; a manufacturer uses ads featuring a photogenic baseball player wearing nothing but his underwear.[4] The credits for any TV series or even the local evening news show that many public relations people have been at work providing cars, clothes, hair styling, etc.

The handlers of public figures—political as well as entertainment—arrange invitations for their client to appear on the various talk shows, give speeches, receive honorary degrees and appear in public celebrations and parades. Here again we see how persuasion becomes mixed with information and entertainment.

PERSUASION STRATEGIES REFLECT THE TIMES

Persuasion strategies in both markets have changed dramatically over time. Sam Adams, Patrick Henry and the other firebrands of the 1770s roused support for our Revolution primarily through personal persuasion and public discussion. They had little choice: No mass media other than pamphlets and a handful of small papers were available; neither was telecommunications available except a primitive, slow postal service. Despite limited technologies, the firebrands succeeded using the contemporary marketplace of political persuasion to bring about and sustain a popular uprising against the world's most powerful nation at that time.

In that era the political marketplace was far more active than the economic marketplace. Few products were manufactured, and department stores and supermarkets were yet to come. There simply wasn't much to advertise in that period. The consumer market included only essentials and some luxuries for the few wealthy families in each community.

Although the Industrial Revolution produced both the mass market and the mass media, the rapid escalation of expenditures for advertising did not take place until the middle of the 20th century. The growing curve shown in Figure 8.1 was the result of new needs and strategies for persuasion reflecting new economic and political conditions created by demographic changes. The changes taking place in the period 1950–1980 were dramatic, but those in the next several decades probably will be even greater.

SIC TRANSIT E PLURIBUS UNUM?

The mid-20th century was perhaps the apogee of the United States as idealized in the motto appearing on our coins, *E Pluribus Unum*—"many joined into one." Network radio and then television provided a perfect match for a mass-market economy offering new prosperity, comfort and convenience. The mass-market economy also brought large-scale uniformity. A side effect was the decline of local products and retailers and a seemingly endless series of acquisitions, mergers and consolidations. As the nation's collective attention became focused on national mass media, small firms and local products were simply cut out of the market. They could not afford to advertise in the media dominating the market.

The mass market is still there, but it now must coexist with an increasing number of niche markets. To expand their sales, even the manufacturers of mass-market brands have begun to diversify their product lines.

For decades Anheuser-Busch made and marketed one beer, Budweiser. Now there are not only a variety of "Buds" on the shelf, but a series of other labels that also belong to Anheuser-Busch products. The same corporate ownership encompasses the exclusive Henri Bendel shops, the upscale, youth-oriented The Limited and the broader market The Gap stores, which now includes The Gap/Kids.

Manufacturers and retailers speak of "market segmentation." They complement their mass-market product lines with specialty products and services. New brand names are established by large manufacturers, merchandise tailored to service needs of specific consumer groups.

We see a similar development within the political market. There are the Black Panthers and the Gray Panthers. The Hispanics are split into Mexican Americans, Puerto Ricans, Cubans, and other groups. Each community has its distinctive ethnic mix. Groups form around interests in protecting the environment, animals, children or the disabled. Specific groups serve the needs of men, women, heterosexuals and homosexuals. Some groups are for or against gun control, ad infinitum.

Candidates must attempt to assess the importance of each group to try to match the emphasis of campaign rhetoric to the interest of whatever group they are with and to balance their campaign efforts to please as many and offend as few as possible.

RETHINKING COST PER THOUSAND

The shift from mass to segmented markets resulted in new patterns and techniques of persuasion. Because persuasion provides so much media revenue, this shift produced shock waves through those institutions. Advertisers must reconsider one of the basic measures used in selecting advertising media: cost per thousand.

Explore the world of breakfast cereals at your local supermarket. The variations of corn, oat and wheat flakes seem endless. Heavily sugared cereals appeal to sweet-toothed kiddies; unsugared and unsalted cereals cater to the health conscious. A dozen different treatments of bran vie for the choice of the growing market of older people. From one month to the next, old brands disappear, replaced by new versions of the same product produced by the same manufacturer.

Deodorant brands that started with one basic product have been proliferated

Cost per Thousand

For decades, the basic measure used by advertisers in buying media has been "cost per thousand," sometimes referred to as CPM (cost per mille). Cost per thousand is computed by dividing the cost of the advertising unit by the size of the audience expressed in units of 1,000.

If television station WAAA charges $5,000 for a 30-second spot and has an audience of 500,000 viewers, its CPM is $10 ($5,000 divided by 500). If a competing station, WBBB, has an audience of 600,000 viewers in the same time period and charges $9,000 for a 30-second spot, its CPM is $15 ($9,000 divided by 600). If the advertiser simply wants the largest audience, WBBB is obviously the right choice. But if the advertiser is trying to get the most viewers per dollar, the choice is WAAA.

In broadcasting, audience figures are provided by rating services such as Nielsen, Arbitron, Pulse and RADAR. The Audit Bureau of Circulation (ABC) periodically provides certified figures for the paid circulation of daily newspapers. Other types of periodicals have similar types of circulation audit services.

into different shapes, solids, roll-ons, spray-ons and different scents and unscented—each variation tailored to increase sales among different age, sex or environmentally conscious group.

WHY BUY AUDIENCES YOU DON'T NEED?

For years the basic rule in advertising has been to choose the medium offering the largest audience per dollar. That rule makes sense as long as manufacturers are making products for the mass market. Revlon is probably the most widely sold line of cosmetics in the nation. It makes sense for Revlon to spend vast amounts of money to buy commercial time on the major networks and put color ads in leading circulation magazines. The women in those mass audiences are all potential Revlon customers.

Chanel makes expensive cosmetics bought by only a small segment of the public who are willing to pay the extra money. If Chanel buys network time, it spends money to buy an audience that does not correspond to its market. CPM based on the full audience would be an inaccurate representation of its real market.

Advertisers aiming at niche markets must revise their CPM calculations and concentrate on how many appropriate viewers or readers they are getting per dollar. For them the mass media are clumsy, inefficient and uneconomical. Why pay thousands of dollars to advertise to people you know are not going to buy your product or want your service?[5]

General Motors knows that only a certain segment of the audience can afford Cadillacs, but Chevrolets are within the reach of most of the public. Similarly General Mills knows that the people who buy its "natural food" lines are less likely to be big TV watchers than those who buy the standard sugared products. Different media as well as different campaign themes are needed for such diverse target groups.

For decades the mass media were the only game in town, and so the manufacturers had no choice but to pay the big price. The revolutionary technologies now are providing an increasing range of options, making it possible for manufacturers to reach small, specific target groups without having to swallow the high cost of the mass media. Among those learning to thrive through the use of these alternative channels of persuasion are a growing number of small and local shops and manufacturers.

As advertising dollars flow into those alternative channels using the new options, the mass media are experiencing a decline in the growth of their advertising revenues. Their distress is shared by many large retailers and manufacturers who must now adjust to shifting strategies for marketing, including how and where they advertise.

A TRICKIER PROPOSITION FOR POLITICIANS

As usual the political market is quickly adapting the techniques of the economic market. Campaign managers, like promotion directors of the various divisions of General Motors and General Mills, can tailor their persuasive messages and select media to fit target groups while simultaneously mounting mass-media efforts for general visibility and impact.

For politicians the situation is more complex. Ultimately a candidate must be concerned with the full market. Market or voter segmentation creates the danger of getting carried away while playing to each crowd. If statements to one group contradict those to another, the opposition will almost inevitably catch the discrepancy and blow the whistle, to the embarrassment of the candidate and the destruction of his or her credibility.

This potential problem does not negate the advantages of group-specific appeals in political persuasion; it just makes using them a trickier proposition requiring great monitoring and coordination.

CABLE CREATES NEW OPTIONS FOR ADVERTISERS

A late-19th century cartoon shows a wild-eyed demagogue haranguing people all over the world through the wires of Alexander Graham Bell's new invention, the telephone. One wonders what the cartoonist would make of the propaganda potential of satellites and networks of computers now connected by high-bandwidth optical fiber.

Certainly satellite distribution of alternative programming has helped cable crack the networks' hegemony over television advertising as well as programming. Satellites also promoted the formation of ad hoc networks and barter syndication. More recently they have played a major role in on-air marketing, a technique likely to expand as more cable operators switch to optical fiber and make their systems interactive.

TAKING ADVANTAGE OF IMPULSE RESPONSE TO PERSUASION

On-air selling products such as record albums and tapes has been practiced on broadcast television for a long time, particularly in the late-night and early morning hours. Cable carried this a quantum step further with home-shopping channels, which present a nonstop sequence of sales pitches displaying, demonstrating and praising one product after another.

Home shopping, like pay-per-view technology, has not achieved full potential because most cable systems were built for one-way communication. The lack of a feedback loop means that viewers who want a product or service must use another system—usually the telephone—to place an order.

Fortunately for these video hawkers, almost all viewers do have ready access to telephones; 800-number services allow purchasers to place orders to sales operators without charge. But access to a telephone itself does not guarantee an immediate connection and, in home shopping, whether for products or for PPV movies, decisions are often made on impulse rather than reason. Frustration with busy signals can give viewers time for second thoughts about the purchase, possibly killing the desire for products.

PROVIDING FEEDBACK LOOPS

To prevent the loss of impulse sales, cable operators are pushing to rebuild their systems to make them interactive. With up stream capability, subscribers can order products and movies simply by pushing buttons on their converter boxes or remote tuners. The system's computer can keep on file the appropriate information—addresses, credit card numbers, etc.—and pass the information on to the product suppliers.

A combination of computers, microwave and satellite links allows impulse response even without cable. Systems such as "TV Answer" can be used in conjunction with broadcast as well as cable programs. These services require that viewers be equipped with special remote guns and decoder/transmitter boxes on their TV sets.

The TV Answer remote gun is used to spot choices displayed on the TV screen. The signal is relayed by microwave to a local antenna up-linking it to a satellite for relay to a processing center in Virginia where a computer sorts orders and forwards them to the appropriate vendors.

ONLINE COMPUTER SHOPPING AND THE TELCO FUTURE

Another form of home shopping involves the combination of telephones and computers. For example since 1986 IBM and Sears have jointly operated an electronic

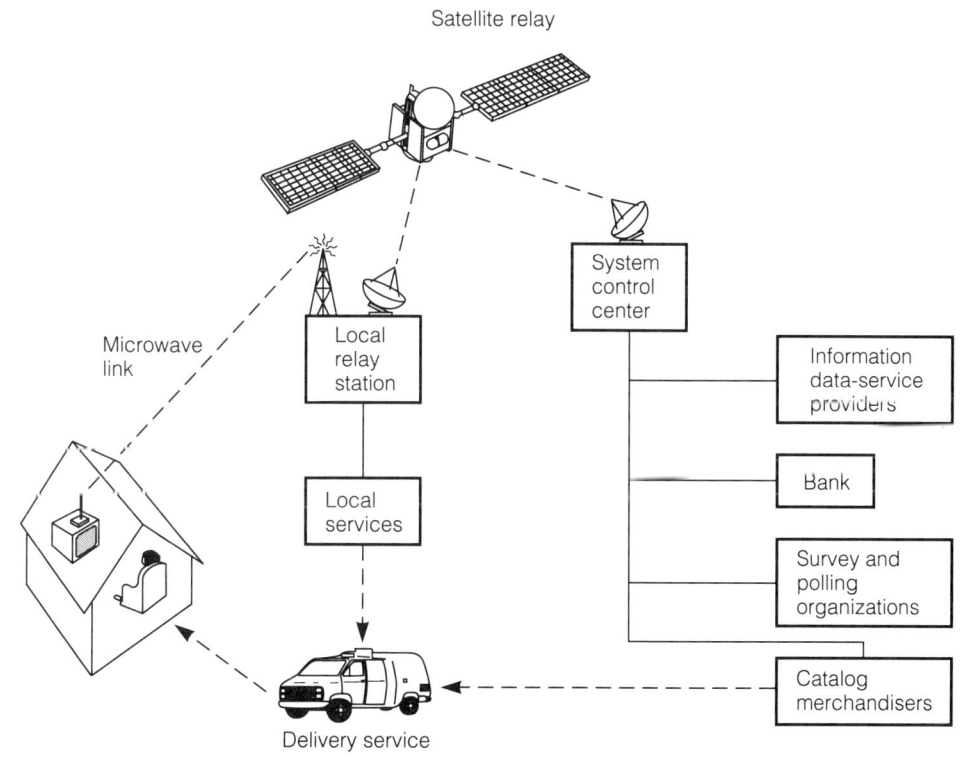

Figure 10.1 Home Shopping via Microwave

information service called Prodigy.[6] Over a million personal computer owners have purchased the software allowing telephone access to Prodigy's various services. Among these services are catalogs of goods that can be ordered directly.

Prodigy is only one of these services, albeit the largest. The involvement of Sears has given Prodigy more emphasis on shopping services than is provided by similar interactional computer services, such as CompuServe, Easy Link, Delphi, etc.

Another form of home shopping lets customers dial up a central computer service and use a bar-code scanner to order groceries and other items. Shoppers are supplied with a catalog listing all the items available, and they simply pass the scanner over the bar code for those they want. As they go along, they are informed of prices and given a running total for their purchases. Upon completing the order the customer can specify desired hours for delivery.

TELCOS ARE KNOCKING AT THE SHOPPING GATES

In his original decision breaking up AT&T, Judge Harold Greene followed the tradition of viewing telcos as common carriers by specifically prohibiting telco participation in the provision of information services over their own lines. Judge Greene modified his original ruling in 1991 and said that henceforth the Baby Bells could go into the business of providing such services to their customers.

For example the telcos can offer interactive Yellow Pages, providing on-demand advertising and catalog service. In effect the Baby Bells and other local telephone companies may now compete with those services being offered by other companies who are using the telcos' systems.

All these services are merely the precursors of online video services, which will be available when we have high-bandwidth connections into the home. Online merchandising will be an increasingly powerful competitor for the rapidly growing field of direct-mail advertising, especially for the catalogs that currently arrive in our mail.

THE GROWING FIELD OF DIRECT MARKETING

The spectacular growth of direct-mail advertising and marketing indicates how campaigns of persuasive communication are changing. Sears Roebuck, Montgomery Ward, and others have been marketing by mail-order catalogs for as long as a century. Originally their big, bulky catalogs came only once or twice a year and then only upon request. Families spent hours planning their winter or summer purchases before the order form was filled out and mother or father went to the post office to buy the necessary money order and send it off. Weeks could go by before the response arrived.

Now most of us find more advertisements than letters in our mail boxes, including elaborate, full-color publications enticing us to order every conceivable type of product and service. Not only are these catalogs unsolicited, but it is almost impossible to get off their mailing lists.

On a dreary winter day you can entertain yourself looking at the swimsuit and cruise catalog or pour over the beautifully illustrated plant and seed catalogs and think of spring. To cheer yourself up, go ahead and order something. Don't bother filling out an order form; just call the handy 800 number. You don't need a money order; your credit-card number will do the trick.

MOVING THE CATALOGS TO MULTIMEDIA

Mail catalogs share the disadvantage of newspapers and other printed periodicals: They are a physical product that has to be delivered and might be discarded without a glance.

Video shopping services suffer from the inherent disadvantage of television: the content must be presented in linear, time-specific fashion. This makes it difficult for the viewer to leaf through the material, to seek out specific items or even types of merchandise.

With electronic shopping we begin to see the potential of multimedia to combine the impact of cable with the convenience of the telephone. A sequence of menus enables us to find specific merchandise and to obtain answers to questions about the merchandise upon demand.

Multimedia Shopping

Try this scenario for multimedia shopping: Checking your multimedia screen for the index of today's incoming messages, you see that the Museum of Fine Arts catalog of Christmas gifts is now available. Using your remote control, you call up the catalog for display on your screen and, from its index, you ask for the display of Christmas cards. As the full-color display of each card is scrolled past, you use your gun to mark those of interest. After looking at all of them, you eliminate some by reviewing the ones you've marked. Now down to two, you display them side by side on the screen.

Once the card is chosen, you run through the list of standard greetings. You don't like any, so you write your own and give instructions for personalization. Then you call up your Christmas card list from computer memory and check through it, eliminating some names and adding new ones. When you're finished, you add that to your order. The Museum then prepares the card and dispatches it by color fax to everyone on your list, simultaneously billing your account for the order.

You'll also be able to browse by scrolling through any of the newest catalogs, somewhat like flipping through the pages of today's mail-delivered print catalogs. If an item catches your interest, you can hit a "describe" button. The scrolling will stop and the item will be described while a full-color demonstration is presented, showing the item from different angles and in different colors and patterns.

If you are looking for a particular item, such as a new lightweight parka, you can call out models from L. L. Bean, Eddie Bauer, J. Crew and Patagonia to compare them in split-screen display. When a selection has been made, the push of a button will place the order. The item will be shipped and your account billed.

The presentation on the current electronic shopping services leaves much to be desired. Often the screen displays little more than an illustration of the product. But multimedia will combine the advantages and eliminate most of the disadvantages of all these systems. Catalogs of audio-visual information on items can be stored in computer memory. You will be able to view the product from different angles, see it operate and try different combinations of colors and accessories. You will be able to compare similar products from different vendors, and the vendor can instantly update information when new models are introduced or when prices are changed.

YOU CAN'T KICK THE TIRES

There are limits as to how far one can carry multimedia marketing. Catalog shopping, even if it incorporated three-dimensional holography and virtual reality, would not be a substitute for kicking the tires, feeling the thickness of wool or the smoothness of silk, pinching the peaches or smelling a melon. Even with the limitations of the current technology, this type of marketing has claimed a large market. As homes acquire multimedia platforms, the market will expand.

Even multimedia won't make it possible to actually kick the tires (although, as we indicated earlier, it may be possible to simulate it with virtual-reality devices). Multimedia still will deliver more kick to the retailer's persuasion because it will provide more vivid, flexible product information, and the delivery will be far more cost efficient.

INTERACTING WITH SOLICITORS AND CANDIDATES

L.L. Bean, Sears Roebuck and Co. and their merchandising peers are not the only ones using direct mail. Colleges press their alumni for contributions; symphony orchestras and repertory theater groups publicize their season subscription ticket packages; politicians and political parties urge voters to the polls. With a little imagination one can see innumerable multimedia possibilities for these types of persuasion.

Political parties as well as corporations already use videoconferencing to introduce new candidates and party platforms as well as new product models and features. Videoconferencing not only lets key people all over the country simultaneously see a lavish presentation, but allows participants to ask questions and make comments. Multimedia will be able to expand participation to more individuals in more locations.

Candidates will be able to prepare presentations voters can select according to their own interests. With videophone conference calls, candidates can conduct question-and-answer sessions with key potential campaign contributors.

Non-profit institutions such as schools, hospitals and museums will be able to use multimedia for fund raising. University alumni may select online presentations by the president, the dean of their college or the football coach. The head of a hospital can set up a videoconference with potential donors to discuss plans for the new pe-

Chapter 10 Selling Ideas, Candidates and Products 173

Polls and Persuasion

Political leaders have always tried to measure the pulse of the public, but one of the dilemmas of representative government is how elected officials balance leadership against representation of their constituents.

Since George Gallup pioneered the "scientific" measurement of public opinion in the early 1930s, surveys have become a standard tool in the political process. Candidates and parties use surveys for strategic planning and, through selective release of results, for persuasion. The media have joined in this process, sponsoring polls then reported as news. Rapid sequences of polls are now used to build suspense, turning elections into horse races between candidates, perhaps at the expense of public attention to the issues and policy choices at stake in the election.

The revolutionary technologies have made it possible to compile and analyze survey data with great rapidity, increasing the temptation for editors as well as politicians to do a quick survey. Newspaper ballots have given way to telephone call ins and overnight surveys. With interactive cable and, in the future, multimedia, instant polls can gauge public opinion.

But are such poll reports actually news, or are they attempts to persuade voters—to create "bandwagon" or "sandbagging" effects? A subtle change in the wording of a question can produce different results. Response categories are arbitrary; by changing how the data are grouped, differences are emphasized or diminished. In any case surveys are samples; they use responses from a small group to estimate how the general population feels.

It is very easy to get responses from a sample of the public, but is the sample truly representative? Many kinds of sample bias—innocent, inadvertent and intentional—may produce measures of public opinion neither reliable nor valid.

Even rigorous sampling procedures produce data that have "errors of estimate," and these errors may be larger than the differences reported between two candidates. Yet survey reports usually downplay or even ignore this fact.

Polls undoubtedly provide elected officials with a reading of opinion within the public they represent. But is there a danger that overuse of polls can lead to a preoccupation undermining the exercise of leadership? One hopes our legislatures are deliberative bodies and that our elected representatives do what most of us cannot do: seek out and consider ramifications of issues, in an effort to choose the option providing the greatest long-term public benefit.

A "wired" nation with multimedia in every home could become a new Athens, with direct citizen participation through electronic voting replacing legislative bodies. How ready are you to spend the time this would entail? How much time do you now spend weighing the pros and cons of issues and candidates? And, by the way, how informed is your opinion if you are asked to give it?

diatrics unit. Prospective donors can see a video tour taking them through the proposed sculpture wing of the museum.

LISTS, LISTS AND MORE LISTS

A major advantage of direct persuasion over mass-media persuasion is the opportunity to identify and single out specific targets or audiences. Niche media narrow the mass market into specific socio-demographic groups, but with direct mail, phone and multimedia, one can further narrow the communication to specific addresses and individuals.

The old practice of sending mass-mail items addressed to "occupant" is largely being replaced with material addressed by name. The storing and sorting abilities of computers have created a new specialization: the generation of customized lists for direct persuasion. These lists play a major role in the increased traffic of computer-mediated communication, such as those big envelopes that arrive saying that—your name in big, black type—has won a million dollars.

Information about our personal activities is being recorded and used more broadly and deeply than most of us realize. Our names are compiled by innumerable organizations of government, business and non-business institutions. These lists are sold and exchanged, with the result that we receive personally addressed messages from organizations totally unknown to us.

The storage capacity and speed with which computers can manage information makes it possible to merge and sort different lists to select only the names of persons who meet almost any set of criteria. The ease and low cost of telecommunications allows marketers to combine lists stored a continent apart—or even oceans apart.

Getting to Know You—More Than You Know

Why did the museum-store salesclerk ask you to provide your address and/or phone number on the sales slip? And did you notice all those personal questions on the warranty card for the new personal computer you bought? Having purchased some posters at a museum in, say, Chicago, you soon find you are receiving catalogs not only from that museum but also from museums in half a dozen other cities. And almost before you've unpacked your new personal computer, you're receiving information about various software packages.

Isn't it convenient that your neighborhood video mart provides you with the membership card that has all the information to print out the rental slip? Included in the public discussion around the unsuccessful nomination of Robert Bork to sit on the Supreme Court was a "character analysis" based on the videocassettes he had rented.

Computers make it possible to store and sort names, addresses and selected descriptive information so that an infinite variety of specialized lists can be compiled. For instance your address can be checked against census data on the socio-demographic characteristics of your immediate neighborhood to decide if you are a good prospect for a luxury product or someone who might vote for a candidate who favors reducing the capital-gains tax.

Inexpensive telecommunications makes it easy to exchange and transfer such information as well as to set up centralized bull pens from which platoons of telephone-sales staff can contact prospects anywhere in the nation.

Information about you is traded and sold by all kinds of organizations—businesses, political groups, charities and institutions. This ability to compile and access personal information portends future crises on the issue of privacy. If you want to read some horror stories of what is and what might be possible, you can start with David Burnham's *The Rise of the Computer State* or Leonard Lee's *The Day the Phones Stopped*.

It also makes possible centralized operations from which sales or solicitation staff use WATS (wide area telephone service) lines to contact potential customers, donors, or voters all across the country. That person calling you to solicit a subscription or a contribution is probably sitting at a computer terminal in some place such as Des Moines, Iowa, or some other community where labor costs are low. They disarm you by asking for you by name, and it turns out they know a lot about you. On the terminal screen is a display of various items of personal information about you: whether you have given before and, if so, how much; an estimate of your income; your age; etc. With this information he or she has a head start in trying to persuade you to buy or give.

CHANGING THE TRADE-OFF

Think of all the personally addressed junk mail you receive and all the phone calls where an unknown person greets you by name and goes into a sales pitch. If you have a fax machine or use an electronic mail service (EMS), you've also received junk mail through those channels. Similar persuasive tactics will evolve for multimedia.

Traditionally the public has accepted or tolerated advertising for its intrinsic informational value and for the trade-off it provides by subsidizing newspapers, magazines, television, radio and other mass media. Where is the trade-off in direct persuasion? This question is particularly vexing with regard to advertising that comes to us through communication systems, such as the telephone and cable's pay tier, for which we pay access fees. Unsolicited fax messages use the receiver's equipment and paper; unsolicited EMS can add to the receiver's line charges.

The U.S. Postal Service is required by law to deliver all material posted. Although devices have been developed to screen incoming telephone calls, they have encountered legal challenges (on the basis of restricting freedom of speech), and the situation remains problematic. Undoubtedly the technology will exist to screen multimedia messages, but the experience of the U.S. Postal Service and telcos suggests that before they are available to us changes in legislation and regulatory policy will be needed.

A MASS MEDIA TAILSPIN?

Just as going to the movies is qualitatively different from seeing a movie on videocassette, going shopping remains functionally different from shopping by catalog. Despite the segmentation, those planning persuasive campaigns still rely on the mass media to introduce new products, stimulate consumer interest and create brand-name recognition.

The irony is that as market segmentation, direct mail and catalog sales increase, they divert advertising expenditures and audience from the mass media. As we have seen the major mass media, both print and broadcasting, are experiencing unprecedented economic pressures. Newspaper and major magazine circulations have been stagnant; the audience of the television networks shrank by about one-third in just a few years.

If these media cannot maintain their advertising incomes, the scope and quality of their content is bound to suffer. A decline in program quality and quantity there will cause further audience loss. Conceivably the mass media could go into a tailspin that could prove fatal to some or all. Where would the persuaders turn when they do need to reach the mass audience? Persuasive campaigns already have increased in complexity, but in the future they will require new strategies to adapt to the still wider choice of channels with increased user specificity.

GETTING THE PUBLIC'S ATTENTION

When the three networks monopolized the attention of the nation in prime time, a presidential news conference, major speeches at the nominating conventions and debates by presidential candidates were seen by most families because no alternative programs were available. Now that most people have 50 channels offering entertainment in the same time period, even the president finds it rough going to get a good rating.

Declining readership of daily newspapers, the proliferation of video channels and the splintering of the audience have made it both more difficult and more expensive for advertisers and politicians to get the public's attention. The burden is particularly heavy for political persuasion. As media choices proliferate, it becomes ever easier for the public to ignore the marketplace of political debate.

CHANGES EVERYWHERE

Despite all the gloom and doom, at least some networks and programs with mass appeal will remain in the future. However, they will never again have the dominance enjoyed by prime-time television shows before 1985; the revolutionary technologies provide too many other exciting options for distributing and receiving communication. The gloomy concerns about limitation we may face with the decline and possible disappearance of major networks and publications may reflect the myopia of the older generations and the discomfort that accompanies changed practices.

Many niche markets have the potential to support their own specialized, national networks. In fact international niche markets and multinational organizations are profiting from these specialized networks. Visit shopping centers in Tokyo, Honolulu, Jacksonville, Montreal, London, Paris or Rome and you will find many of the stores in each occupied by now familiar names: The Gap, Benetton, Crabtree and Evelyn, Louis Vuitton, etc.

The dominance of the now-fading networks was based on channel scarcity, and so the networks benefited from mass marketing. The revolutionary technologies can provide a cornucopia of networks to aggregate the niche markets and provide viable funding for content.

The dominance of the survivors among the big metropolitan dailies resulted from the desire of advertisers to reduce audience duplication. The revolutionary technologies can provide the ultimate in targeting publications. It will be economically and technically possible to provide publications—whether printed or on screen—on an individual basis.

FRAGMENTING OR ALREADY FRAGMENTED?

It is one thing to let manufacturers and vendors segment themselves ad infinitum, but what about the majority-rule concept on which our representative democracy is premised? In a multimedia world of seemingly infinite content choice, the political marketplace might become so fragmented that our traditional two-party system could disintegrate. Would such a change necessarily be bad?

Actually our two-party system is unique. Most democracies are multi-party marketplaces, and their governments frequently depend on coalitions of two or more parties. Coalition governments can be unwieldy and unstable, but they can also be more responsive to the diversity of opinion within a population.

In fact our two dominant parties are themselves coalitions which have become increasingly tenuous. For example Senators Edward Kennedy and Lloyd Bentsen are both Democrats, but they are worlds apart on many issues. George Bush began as a liberal Republican, but as president he constantly worried about maintaining the support of the conservative wing of his party.

The presidential campaign of H. Ross Perot in 1992 illustrated a major change in the role of media as well as a groundswell of dissatisfaction with the two major parties. One of the most fascinating aspects of that election was the confusion for media journalists and party professionals as the campaigns made increased use of such unorthodox channels as television talk shows. When Perot suggested that the public be allowed to express opinions through electronic polls, shivers were palpable in Congress as well as in the nation's newsrooms.

Perot's proposal anticipates the world of multimedia. The multiplicity of communication media and audiences in such a world may broaden the opportunity for third, fourth and even fifth party candidates. If such candidates can revitalize the interest and participation of the public in the political marketplace, political organization may be more complicated but more representative than our present structure.

GAINS ARE COMMENSURATE WITH RISK

Stock brokers, entrepreneurs and politicians will all tell you that there is no gain without risk and that the amount of risk is commensurate with the potential gain.

All technologies are morally and politically neutral. It is the way we use them, the content we put into them, which gives them values. The revolutionary technologies offer dangers as well as exciting opportunities related to the economic and political marketplaces.

One thing is certain: Increased work and vigilance on the part of regulatory agencies and the public will be essential to grasp opportunities while guarding against forces that would curtail or destroy the openness of our economy and our democracy.

Suggestions for Further Reading

If you're interested in a comprehensive survey of the role of the persuasion industry in our society, try *Advertising in Society,* compiled by Roxanne Hovland and Gary B. Wilcox.

If your interest is primarily in politics, Doris A. Graber has put together a set of thoughtful essays by professionals and academics in *Media Power in Politics*. Richard Joslyn's *Mass Media and Elections* covers the same general topic but from the standpoint of an academic who is a political consultant.

Sig Mickelson covered politics and politicians for forty years as a network newsman. In *From Whistle Stop to Sound Bite* he traces the changes he has seen and speculates on the role of television in changing our political processes.

Another leading professional in his field, Irving Crespi, takes a similar look at the role of surveys in *Public Opinion, Polls, and Democracy*.

Notes

1. Carnegie, Dale. *How to Win Friends and Influence People*. Revised ed. New York: Simon and Schuster, 1982.
2. Kotler, Philip. *Marketing Management: Analysis, Planning, Implementation and Control*. 6th ed. New York: Prentice-Hall, 1988.
3. This does not require that stations give time to candidates, only that if they sell time to one candidate they must let the opponent buy equivalent time at equivalent rates at the opponent's request.
4. The manufacturer is well-aware that many, if not most, wives buy their husbands' underwear.
5. In the early 1990s, a small English store, The Body Shop, was so successful in identifying and marketing to a niche audience that it grew into an international chain of outlets with almost no advertising at all, using on-site promotion and the word-of-mouth referrals of its enthusiastic customers.
6. CBS was originally a partner in Prodigy but pulled out early in its development.

CHAPTER 11

The New Renaissance and the Liberation of Learning

When the class of 2010 arrives at dear old Matriculata College, the students will have it made: no registration lines. Instead, students will register on the multimedia terminal in their dorm rooms. Students no longer will take dreary 9 a.m. classes about the antecedents of the Renaissance in Europe or Principles of Physics. Instead of listening to Professor X drone on while he shows those terrible out-of-focus slides from his 1956 European tour or watching Professor Y while she works out equations on the chalkboard, students will use interactive multimedia presentations. Students will be able to call for close-up shots or go back for another look at color presentations and will work through equations with prompting and checking from the terminal.

Coursework will be done at the student's own pace to accommodate whatever combination of courses he or she is taking. At intervals self-correcting tests will pop up, providing the student with immediate feedback on performance.

For the seminar on ethics, a half-dozen students will gather in a videoconference room and proceed to discuss the assigned topics with similar groups at one campus in California and another in Wisconsin. The seminar leader may be in Chapel Hill, sitting at a console where he or she can call up audio-visual material appropriate to the topic.

At the end of the session, next week's reading assignments will be "dumped" into students' terminals, which will give periodic reminders until the student has actually completed the assignments. The teacher can check during the week to see which students have and haven't done their work.

For term papers there will be no more frustration and worries with card catalogs, lost books and missing pages from journals. Students will do their bibliographic search at their dorm desks and will electronically organize and cite references without ever having to trudge through the dusty reference stacks. With a little extra effort, the student can wrap up everything early and add a couple of weeks to spring break.

NEW LITERACY FOR THE INFORMATION AGE

These changes may sound wonderful, and they will be possible. Actually many are possible right now. But something is amiss in our educational system. SAT scores are lower than a generation ago. Reading skills have declined; writing and spelling are the focus of constant complaint among teachers. And how many college students can calculate a percentage without a calculator?

The mention of the calculator serves as a springboard for diving into a really murky pool: What is the real meaning, the real importance of traditional learning skills for the society of today—and tomorrow?

Is penmanship important in an era when we do most of our writing on a keyboard? Is spelling important when our word processing software includes spelling checkers and even grammar checkers? How important is reading in the era of voice-response storage and retrieval and of iconic imagery for personal computer applications? Do we really need to memorize the multiplication tables and know how to extract a square root when calculators are ubiquitous?

If anything, "naive intelligence"—informal knowledge of worldly phenomena—may be greater today than ever before. The concern over declining learning scores may be misplaced, even counterproductive. The real educational issue is what kinds of skills the students of today and tomorrow will need to contribute productively to society. We need to reconsider the relative importance of traditional literacy and other standard measures of education.

PUBLIC EDUCATION: A PRAGMATIC CONCERN

Schools, education and literacy are practically sacred concepts in contemporary society and are laden (indeed, burdened) with philosophical and moral values. Yet the emphasis on national literacy rates and the provision of a standard curriculum by public schools are relatively modern phenomena, dating back little more than a century.

One need not be a cynic to suggest that the economic need for workers who could read and "do numbers," not humanitarian impulses, led our society to invest in public education and make "schooling" compulsory. From the societal standpoint, the functions of this schooling were to create an efficient work force with the appropriate skills for the Industrial Age and to equip students to contribute to and advance within a national industrial economy.

Read any of the many essays now being written about the educational "crisis," and you will see that most have this emphasis: We need, they say, educational reform and improvement so that the United States will have the proper type of work force to remain competitive in the future international market.

Chapter 11   The New Renaissance and the Liberation of Learning   181

At its best "schooling" became education, liberating the joy of learning that encourages individuals to inquire and expand their scope of knowledge, not merely to acquire skills.

For most people education has been seen as a stairway to advancement. College admissions staffs and faculty are none-too-subtly reminded of this at open houses. Parents of prospective students spend more time asking about job placement and job opportunities than about the qualitative aspects of the education provided by the school.

The revolutionary technologies offer the vision of educational systems that can train, liberate and reinforce the joy of learning. Why, then, is there a crisis? Why don't we just move ahead in fulfilling this vision?

STATUS QUO ROADBLOCKS

In addition to being one of society's largest institutions, the educational establishment is also one of the most entrenched and reactionary. More than 4.5 million teachers in our public schools constitute the largest single occupational group in the nation. Altogether more than 7 million persons are employed in our educational establishment. The combination of size, conservatism and quasi-mystic status helps this establishment become a classic case of Pool's "resistance of the status quo."

We must not forget the very important question of money: Designing and implementing curricula based on the revolutionary technologies will be expensive. It will mean abandoning or modifying existing facilities, will require the production of immense amounts of software and will demand staff retraining. Taxpayers already dig in their collective heels at increased assessment rates to support schools.

Even parents pose problems. Our current school year is not only said to be creating an inefficient teaching schedule, but also makes inefficient use of school facilities. But more efficient use proposals inevitably raise protest from parents and students because they interfere with the traditional rhythm of family vacations.

FROM HORACE MANN'S LOG TO MULTIMEDIA EXCHANGE OF KNOWLEDGE

Horace Mann, the great pioneer of our present system, described the ideal educational situation as a student and a teacher sitting on a log together. Mann proposed that such physical proximity and the one-on-one relationship would give the student direct, interactive access to the knowledge stored in the teacher's mind. Note the importance this juxtaposition places on the teacher as a repository of knowledge.

Well, not many logs are around today, and the student-to-teacher ratio is more likely to be 30 or 40 to one. But something else has also changed: the sheer quantity and complexity of knowledge. In Mann's era, the 19th century, a single individual could still encompass the corpus of knowledge for an entire field. Scholars such as Charles Darwin and Alexander Humboldt could synthesize across different fields of study and individually produce magnificent new theories and compendia of knowledge. Brilliant innovators such as Thomas Alva Edison could produce inventions as diverse as the electric light bulb, the kinetoscope [1] and the phonograph. In those times a single teacher sitting on a log could be expected to know all the things a student needed to know, which is to say, the things the society thought they should know.

Today the all-knowing wise teacher has been replaced by area specialists who know "everything" about a limited area, but who are often embarrassingly ignorant of other fields. Research and invention are most often the work of teams, not of individuals. The bounds of knowledge have exploded, and they are expanding with still-increasing momentum.

CHANGING THE RELATIONS AMONG STUDENTS, TEACHERS AND KNOWLEDGE

A computer-literate student may actually be able to sort through the storehouse of knowledge faster and more broadly than the learned senior professor, who would still prefer to be sitting on Horace Mann's log.

Scholars on South Pacific islands are no longer limited to small, inadequate local libraries; they can use satellite links to access data archives in Cambridge, Mass., or Cambridge, England. Videoconferences enable students to participate in seminars with faculty and students on other campuses literally around the world. Using interactive videodiscs or CD-ROMs allows each student to work at the individual pace appropriate to his or her skills and prior knowledge.

To suggest that the student–teacher relationship and structured curricula are passe would be simplistic. But it also would be foolish to deny the need for radical restructuring of curricula and the present pattern of teacher–student relations.

RE-EXAMINING FUNCTIONAL GOALS

The function of education is the transgenerational transfer of knowledge. How this is done, in what context and the assignment of content priorities will change in the future, just as it has in the past. Data stored in computer memory are becoming the substitute for the wise professor, and telecommunications links make this knowledge more accessible than the teacher at the other end of the log.

Education and training require that people change not only what they know, but also how they synthesize what they know. Encouragement and example facilitate overcoming the fear of change and acquiring the motivation to change. Although reinforcement can be built into programmed instruction, some distinctive qualitative difference remains in the encouragement and example provided by personal contact with good teachers.

Personal experience and perspective provided by older guides can help liberate and deepen the joy of learning for novice scholars. Those who have experienced this joy know its intrinsic value. But we repeat what we said earlier: most people seek knowledge for practical reasons, primarily as a means of achieving material rewards.

THE CLIENTS AND SPONSORS OF THE EDUCATIONAL SYSTEM

In medieval times students paid their teachers directly. In effect education operated on a straightforward rewards basis. Private schools today approximate this system; if they do not maintain their reputation (and acceptance of graduates into major colleges), parents shop the education marketplace and find a "better buy" for their children. However, public schools struggle with multiple clients. They are supported by taxes paid by all individual and corporate property owners, all of whom then feel they have a say in setting the goals and evaluating the performance of students, teachers and the educational system. Today several major streams of dismay and dissatisfaction concerning the educational achievement of today's youth reflect the variation in view held by the different clients of the system.

Among the general public, concerns reflect generational differences as well as ethnic and gender differences. Parents decry increasing class sizes while grandparents on fixed incomes vote against tax increases. Minority parents want more emphasis on their cultural heritage with special instruction for students for whom English is a second language.

The educational establishment focuses on the results of standardized tests that show a decline compared with those of the past. The economic establishment focuses on the lack of appropriate skills among those entering or already in the work force. Despite overlaps among the concerns of each, the dissatisfaction of the economic establishment with the products of the educational establishment is growing.

As the educational establishment dithers and agonizes, some corporations are making their own educational and training initiatives. Private, for-profit organizations are increasingly aggressive with proposals to operate community schools on a basis of guaranteed performance according to specific objectives.

Entrepreneurs are getting into the act, too. Whittle Communications has installed—at no cost to schools—televisions and video equipment in thousands of public school classrooms nationwide. In return for the equipment, Whittle provides programming—and commercials. It sells two minutes of commercials to major advertisers, which are provided along with 12 minutes of current events programming to the schools every day. In addition Whittle is planning to establish a network of private schools that rely heavily on television and other relatively new teaching tools.

Criticism of these efforts is varied and highly polarized. Some critics feel that the classroom should be kept completely free from all commercials. They feel the presence of Whittle's commercials is just the beginning of the selling of the classroom to the highest bidder. Others feel that the growth of privately funded projects simply highlights the broad failure of the public school system to embrace potentially helpful teaching methods.

The Industrial Age demanded radical expansion of our concepts of education and the creation of new institutions to perform these functions. The expansion and

Limits on Educational Innovation

Past experiences suggest that our enthusiasm concerning the potential of new technologies for educational innovation should be tempered. One handicap for innovators is the size and decentralized nature of our educational system: over 4.5 million teachers work in more than 83,000 different school districts, each of which is free to establish teacher and classroom standards and to select texts and other teaching materials.

We continue to operate schools on a nine-month schedule designed to accommodate the needs of an agrarian society long since gone. Our school facilities are largely unused and teachers are unemployed for a quarter of each year. Attempts to change to year-round curricula create budgetary as well as administrative problems, all of which are exacerbated by the multiplicity of independent districts.

In the last forty years there has been a sequence of new educational technologies: audio-visual materials, felt boards, instructional television, programmed instruction, videorecorders, computer-aided instruction and personal computers and language labs. Innumerable studies have shown that classroom teacher skill and enthusiasm is key to the successful use of innovative methods and equipment. In most situations it is difficult (if not impossible) for technology to carry the full burden of the instructional process.

Some teachers have made extraordinary use of one or more of these technologies; others effectively have ignored them. Motivated teachers are frequently frustrated by inadequate logistical and technical support. Other demands on their time, energy and resources—as well as lethargy and self-interest—can discourage teacher acceptance of any change, particularly if it involves learning even simple technological skills.

The extreme decentralization of education in the United States greatly hinders coordinated development and implementation of educational innovation on a national basis. Curricula, texts and teaching materials and teacher requirements vary from one district to another. In such confusion teacher-training programs have difficulty establishing basic curriculum requirements. Lacking a stipulation of requirements, it is not surprising that few programs prepare either the existing or future teaching staff to use new technologies.

---

reform necessitated by the Information Age will be even greater and more radical. The revolutionary technologies have great potential to facilitate and support such reform. They give us the technical ability to transfer knowledge across time and space in new and exciting ways. Whether these technologies are adopted by mainstream educational institutions or used only as alternatives to existing methods of teaching remains to be seen.

FROM A TRICKLE TO A FLOOD OF KNOWLEDGE

The world's many streams of cultural heritage began with oral tradition, in which insights and experiences were passed on through rote memory and recitation. This is just as true of the Judeo-Christian tradition, which undergirds the Western European culture on which so many of our own institutions are based, as it is of Samoan culture, where cultural histories and lineages are still guarded and passed on by "talking chiefs."

The first written records preserved date to the Archaic Sumerian civilization of 3100 B.C., and the oldest surviving printed book dates from A.D. 700 in China. Printing with movable type was introduced to Europe in 1455, about a century after the technique appeared in Korea. Photography and the phonograph appeared in the late-19th century. Magnetic recording tape was invented in the mid-20th century, and the use of magnetic cores and discs to record data in digital format dates from the late 1950s. Each of these new inventions expanded our ability to share information between individuals who may live in different places and who lived in different eras.

In 1638 the donation of a personal collection of several hundred books was such a munificent act that the authorities of the Massachusetts Bay Colony gave John Harvard's name to the college they had established two years earlier. But with new technologies the accumulation of knowledge has grown from a trickle to a veritable flood threatening to inundate our great repositories.

Today over 90,000 book titles are published each year in the United States. Harvard's Widener and ancillary libraries now contain over ten million volumes plus millions of other items.

THE STOREHOUSES OF KNOWLEDGE: BURSTING AT THE SEAMS

By 1990 our great national repository, The Library of Congress, contained 19 million volumes plus 33 million other items, which fill two giant annexes and the stately 1897 edifice facing the Capitol. The challenge of physically storing, cataloging and maintaining this collection so that it can be used is daunting.

Knowledge, the storehouse of human experience and thought, grows at an amazing rate. Of the various functions of the media, perhaps none is a better fit to the new technologies than the pure storage and retrieval of information, an act which lies at the very core of the educational process. Computers can be instructed very simply to store, retrieve and display huge amounts of information. They do this at astounding speed. The revolutionary technologies allow the communication of this information anywhere, anytime. From a distance it would seem that the new technologies should only improve the function of education.

LITERACY, MEDIA LITERACY AND COMPUTER LITERACY

The development of new technologies has also changed the form in which we produce and store information and has added complications to the indexing process. These changes add problems to the educational process. Until two or three decades back, traditional literacy skills—reading and writing—sufficed. But now a different, expanded mix of skills are needed. The many cries we hear for retraining of our work force emphasize that one of these skills is adaptability, or the ability to change.

Because children and adults receive so much of their information and culture from audio-visual technologies, some educators now advocate adding media literacy to the curriculum. The growing use of personal computers and word processors brings forth proposals for computer literacy. Indeed being computer illiterate is almost as deadly as being traditionally illiterate for those seeking to move into clerical and professional careers.

THE CHANGING FORMATS OF KNOWLEDGE

The concept of the free lending library open to the public was one of the great innovations of American democracy, dating back to the establishment of the Boston Public Library in 1852. Andrew Carnegie, whose coal operations ravaged much of western Pennsylvania in the 19th century, salvaged his reputation (for history, if not for his contemporaries) by using many of his millions to endow the public libraries that still enrich hundreds of our cities and towns.

The "hush and shush" aura that clung to libraries until recently now gives way to efforts to make these institutions user friendly. Libraries still include long, high, dark stacks, row after row of multi-tiered shelves laden with books. But today's library also offers phonograph, audio cassette and videocassette players; microfiche and microfilm readers and, more recently, computer and CD-ROM terminals.

This proliferation of retrieval technology reflects the changing formats of information and the problems attendant to such change. Newspapers can be microfilmed for convenient storage and retrieval by scholars compiling history, but how do we manage the video documentation that can allow scholars to view the events rather than just read about them?

Novels are easily stored and circulated, but what about creative expression in film and video? In the 1960s one of the networks offered UCLA its library of videotaped programs. With considerable anguish the university librarian declined because the bulk and weight would have required a specially constructed storage facility, with no existing economical means of indexing and retrieving the information.

Vanderbilt University did develop a unique facility for codifying, storing and retrieving information from the evening network news programs. This development was an important work but one that dealt with an extremely limited portion of the total content of the medium. In 1991 the Library of Broadcasting moved into a larger facility to facilitate research and study of the content of that medium—if you can be in New York City.

SWITCHING CONCEPTS FROM VOLUMES TO BITS

The situation is even more daunting in the sciences. For example consider just one scientific phenomenon: global warming. Instead of a single bound volume on, say, the presence of fluorocarbons at upper levels of the atmosphere, today the information is more likely to be stored as raw data. It may be 50 trillion bits of statistical data stored on complexes of massive magnetic disks located all over the world.

By itself the data is meaningless, but it can be available to scores of different scientists, each in a different location, who interpret and synthesize the data. Until recently this process was slow and tedious. Now computers make it possible to create innumerable statistical analyses that can be used to produce models and simulations brought to life with full-color animations.

Not only is more information available, it is a different type of information. Anyone can walk into a library and read a scientific book, but computer data are useless without a computer. When one element of a system changes, the entire system is affected. We must have new ways of editing, indexing, storing, retrieving and displaying data to cope with the information explosion.

Change must go even further. As every student knows, just providing information hardly guarantees knowledge or learning. Much has been written of the misapplication of information and of information overload, the proliferation of all types of information bombarding us daily, much of which is spurious or superfluous. Perhaps the greatest promise of the new technologies works to solve these types of problems.

Advancements in two key areas, indexing and artificial intelligence, open new vistas for information management that will help individuals cope far more easily with the information that now seems poised to inundate them.

LEARNING TO SHARE INFORMATION

Throughout much of human history, the basic means of recording events and accumulating knowledge has been the oral tradition. In order to record its basic history, a society turned events into long stories, songs or poems that more or less captured basic facts. The process of storing, accessing and saving information was easy. The repository of this information was the human brain. Passing it on from generation to generation involved rote learning through repeated recitation. This system was easy to use but limited in capacity and reach, and it had a high probability of transmission error.

Next came the written symbol and with it the collection of written material into archives and libraries. But the accumulation and spread of content was severely limited by the speed with which documents could be individually copied. The invention of movable type and the press set the stage for the printed word. The vast majority of all raw information today (stored as handwritten, drawn, typed, magnetic tape, CD-ROM, film or computer data) consists of alphanumeric characters.

Parents are bombarded with "what" and "why" questions as children begin to organize and understand the world, all of which is new to them. But because parents are not omniscient, more comprehensive sources are needed, and so the kids are packed off to school.

THE IMPORTANCE AND VARIETY OF LIBRARIES

As our need for information expands to incorporate specialized sources, we learn to use dictionaries, encyclopedias and indexes to find specific facts. But the single most important repository for information has been the library.

Libraries get a bad rap. They may look like places where nothing happens, but in fact "library science"—analysis of the most efficient means of indexing, storing and retrieving information—is an academic discipline of rapidly expanding importance and complexity. In considering what goes on in libraries, it helps to divide their functions into two broad areas: (1) processing and indexing and (2) storing and accessing. Together these functions provide the means through which libraries manage information.

Information pours into libraries from every imaginable source in many different forms: reference volumes, periodicals, statistical abstracts, maps, books on every topic imaginable, recordings, film and tape in a variety of formats, documents and statutes and ephemera such as posters and catalogs. Each new item must be processed and its subject(s), origin, and author(s) must be determined. Every time we broaden or add to the formats in which we record and transmit information, we also increase the demands made on our libraries and their staffs.

For centuries the heart of a library has been the stacks, where dusty publications are stored in row upon row of shelves. The size and scope of the contents of the collection in the stacks has defined the capacity of the library. Now libraries and librarians use computer terminals and magnetic storage to supplement and bypass the physical records in the stacks. Satellites and high-capacity optical fiber interconnections liberate libraries from the limits of their own collections. Users in one library can have instantaneous access to information in a library halfway around the world.

ADDING DIMENSIONS TO INFORMATION STORAGE

Information can be raw data describing changes in virtually any physical system. Consider a region's weather pattern. We describe the weather by measuring specific physical things—for example, temperatures at different altitudes, barometric pressures and humidity. These measurements are information. Because each measurement undergoes constant change, the information is constantly changing.

Consider a city's traffic system. We can make the same kind of measurements to describe it, measuring different variables—for example, the number of vehicles, vehicle type and rates of stop-and-go travel or high-speed travel.

If appropriate sensors are installed, we can communicate the measurements as soon as we record them. The measurements flow like oil through a pipeline. Using a stream of data we can describe or model the original system we measured. We can build a mirror image of the physical world just by measuring physical things and communicating data.

In this case the library—the information repository—becomes much more than an archive. It is a living replication of the outside world. Surely the old methods of managing information in this type of library will no longer suffice.

KEEPING TRACK

After this processing a destination for storage must be established. Every book (we'll say "book," but remember the actual variety of items involved) must be evaluated to determine its place among any similar books previously published. Similar books should be stored together, but what constitutes similarity between books? Authorship? Subject matter?

Agatha Christie wrote dozens of mystery novels. She also wrote *Come Tell Me How You Live,* which detailed her experiences in Turkey with her archeologist husband, Max Mallowan. Do we put this book with the other Agatha Christie books? With books on archeology? With books on Turkey? With books on travel? Wherever the book is stored, there must be some cross referencing in the catalog so that, whichever the interest, the reader will be alerted to the book's existence and be able to find it.[2]

At one time individual libraries developed their own cataloging systems, but as collections expanded and inter-library loans increased, most librarians accepted the idea of standardized cataloging systems.[3]

DEWEY DECIMAL GIVES WAY TO LIBRARY OF CONGRESS

In 1876 Melvil Dewey first anonymously published his "Dewey Decimal System," a system of classifying all types of information still used by some libraries. The continued expansion of collections led to the creation of the Library of Congress system, which is the leading standard today in the United States.[4] Now books are published with a bar-code identification for computer scanning.

In effect a library's catalog is an index to its content. It helps us find specific books without having to physically search through the thousands of volumes in the stacks. As any student knows from gathering information for a term paper, information on a topic is usually scattered not only among many different books and periodicals, but also is scattered within the content of individual publications.

Without an index, we have the dreary task of reading or skimming an entire book to find the few paragraphs we actually need. Similarly if we need to trace news coverage of an event or person, we are thankful if major news media have an index so that we do not have to peruse edition after edition of publications or videotapes. We may still have the daunting task of checking many different indexes—those of individual publications and comprehensive indexes such as *Readers' Guide to Periodical Literature*.

THE CRITICAL ROLE OF INDEXING

Items can be cataloged or indexed using various parameters. The most usual categories are title, author and subject. The subject index is the most troublesome but provides the most versatile guide to knowledge.

If you're trying to locate a street, a standard procedure is to consult a city map.[5] You can search all over the map trying to find the street or you can find the street name in the street index, which provides the coordinates for locating the street on the map. The latter is obviously far more efficient. A book without an index is like a map without a list or index of street names. To find something in such a book, you must skim through the entire contents.

In compiling the index for this book, we followed a standard procedure, trying to anticipate topics that might hold specific reader interest. Reading the page proofs, we progressively compiled a list of subject topics with a notation of pages on which each topic appears. We tried to make the original topic list as comprehensive as possible; a topic added halfway through the compilation would require backtracking to seek the earlier citations.

Having gone through the entire book, we assessed topics and cross-references in an effort to streamline the index. Not only did we try to anticipate the topics of importance to readers, but the labels or titles readers would have in mind when they searched the index.

It didn't seem necessary to include vacuum tubes but certainly an entry for CD-ROM was required. Was it necessary to cross reference the terms *transistor* and *semiconductor*? Yes. Compiling an index includes the cross pressures of the need for simplification and streamlining and the need to guard against omitting a critical entry. Indexing may be boring, but a good index is critical; a book without one handicaps the serious reader.

OVERLOAD, OVERUSE AND THEFT

The storage and retrieval of books and other items in libraries presents many problems. The shelves are filled with many unneeded volumes that have remained untouched for years.[6] But there they sit, taking up space and collecting dust, just in case someone does need them.

Library books may be lost in several ways. Popular books may quickly deteriorate through heavy use. Providing evidence of the commodity value of information is the sad fact that libraries must take extreme measures in an often unsuccessful effort to protect their collections against vandalism. Most students have had the experience of requesting a book only to be told that it can't be located, or a student may obtain a book and discover critical pages or illustrations have been removed.

The various colleges and universities in the Boston area (like those elsewhere) cooperate to reduce the costs of acquisition and the burden of processing and storage. The Boston Public Library (BPL) has similar cooperative arrangements with major suburban libraries. Collections of periodicals and more eclectic titles and reference works are cross-listed and are available through interlibrary loans and privileges. A Boston University student may obtain a specialized technical book from MIT; residents of Cambridge can obtain items from the BPL.

PRESSING THE LIMITS OF STORAGE

By sharing and scattering seldom-used items over many locations, the cost of acquisition and processing and the burden of storage can be shared. Nevertheless great libraries are bursting at the seams. For example Harvard now stores its more esoteric and least-used materials in warehouses on the periphery of the Boston metropolis. Such efforts may reduce the strain on finances and facilities, but they increase the difficulties and delays experienced by those seeking to use storehouses of knowledge.

Another problem is the increasing variation in how knowledge is recorded. As we noted earlier libraries must now accommodate more than just books and periodicals. This problem is compounded by the growing number of multimedia products. Some publications are produced in large type as well as standard editions. Braille editions for the blind have been joined by recorded "talking" editions in audiocassette format. Some magazines now publish video editions. Some books are published with ancillary video and audio packages, with programmed materials on personal computer floppy disks or in CD-ROM format. Each innovation storing knowledge exacerbates problems of processing, storing and accessing. Is the personal computer software on 5.25-inch or 3.5-inch disks? In a DOS or an Apple Macintosh format?

INTRODUCING THE DIGITAL ARCHIVE

Digitization provides a way to resolve the dilemma of the information explosion and storage formats. Digital storage will provide far easier indexing and information retrieval. Ultimately people will be able to make greater use of even wider sources of information. But digital storage will change the way society keeps its records. Rather than hundreds of different formats for tens of different media, translation and storage of all information forms will occur in the digital format.

Digital storage is already happening: Many publications—newspapers, magazines and books—are compiled, edited and stored in digital form; most new music recordings are in digital form, and digital still and motion photography is rapidly expanding. The majority of the HDTV technologies competing to become the new video standard for this country are also digital. Converters have already been developed to scan information in traditional analog form and convert it to digital form.

REDEFINING AND REDESIGNING LIBRARIES

What do these changes mean for libraries? Libraries and archives can replace their dust-collecting, space-eating stacks and files, because all information can be stored in a single format on optical and magnetic disks. Instead of interlibrary loans, the contents of one collection can be accessed and shared by users anywhere through optical fiber connections and the appropriate terminals. True, such collections may be damaged or destroyed by power surges or disk or other system failures. But present-day collections suffer from fire and water damage and the decay and disintegration of paper, tape, film, etc. Backup digital systems will be far easier and less expensive to maintain than the present duplication of traditional formats.

Consider the quantum leap in the speed with which information may be stored and retrieved in digital format. Physical transportation of books, films and records requires hours or days to move items, with several points of transfer; and the entire transport holds increased risk of damage. In digital format the same content can be relayed at the speed of light through an optical fiber network without having to endanger the original. Even with signal redundancy as a safeguard against static in transit, the transfer time will still be measured in seconds.

MORE GOOD NEWS

These advantages are spectacular, but the speed advantages of digital technology for indexing are absolutely breathtaking. Digital storage revolutionizes the concept of indexing. Recall the laborious exercise by which the authors compiled the index for this volume. With digital storage, forget the whole process. Instead, if you are interested in *transistors,* just enter that as a key word, and the search program will quickly sift through the entire book and locate each and every reference.

This book was written on an IBM PS/2 using WordPerfect 5.1. The entire contents can be stored on a single 3.5-inch disk. If you had a copy of that disk, access to an IBM or an IBM clone and WordPerfect 5.1, you could do such searches.

If you have had experience using Nexus, Easy Link's Infomaster, or similar archival accessing services, you are ahead of the game. Such services permit searches through entire collections of periodicals and other sources. The trick is figuring out the most appropriate individual or combination of key or search words to produce the information you desire. A service will, in a matter of minutes, produce a list of all the articles available on your topic, giving author, date and source together with how many times the search words are used. You can select those for which you would like to see abstracts and narrow your list to those for which you wish full text. If you wish (and can afford it), you can have the texts downloaded onto your system.

SEARCHING FOR OTHER KINDS OF INFORMATION

As digital storage broadens, as we switch from our present copper wires to optical fiber connections and as our personal computers become more powerful, we will be able to search larger collections of material to obtain information faster and more cheaply.

Such indexing and retrieval works for more than just words. Remember that all types of information can be stored digitally. Interspersed among the pictures, frames or sounds can be key words, symbols, frequencies or other video, film or sound clues. For example, if you did a search for information on the part of Albert Einstein's relativity theory pertaining to gravity's influence on the behavior of light waves, you would be presented with a long list of text references. But you might also find a visual simulation of light waves bending as they weave through a solar system or as they wrap around the curved space buckled by a massive white dwarf star. You might hear and watch the late Richard Feynman, excerpted from a videotaped classroom lecture, describe why each photon was thus affected. You might also view reproductions of the actual drawings Einstein himself used to describe the phenomenon.

HELPING THE COMPUTER TO HELP US

Digital storage creates another important advantage: computer-aided manipulation of information. Rather than manually entering search commands, why not make the computer do it? With the practical application of artificial intelligence (AI) and the availability of hypertext, which electronically links text in new and useful connections, why not indeed?

AI describes a broad range of computer applications exhibiting human intelligence and behavior. It also implies the ability to learn or adapt.[7] Computer software that has the ability to learn is one type of AI. Robots and voice recognition systems are some others.

AI software operates in several ways, primarily by recognizing patterns and drawing inferences built from programmed instructions. For example AI has been successfully used to help doctors perform complex diagnoses. The AI program will compare hundreds of different data points (in this case, symptoms) against thousands of existing cases. It then will ask for more data, depending on the comparisons. This ability to mimic human interaction (making judgments based upon the data and asking for more information in specific areas) gives AI its name. The combinations of statements allow the software to make very simple decisions, but some types of AI-based systems actually learn on the basis of past performance.

When AI is applied to managing information (such as that we receive from various media or from a library), it is a software entity we will call an agent. An agent is a combination of AI and a personal interest profile (PIP).

A PIP is a list of topics about which you have requested information. It is also a set of basic rules for using the list. For example, "when scanning daily newspapers, search for 'Kenya.' When scanning Dow Jones' Business Wire, search for 'Apple Computer.'" The PIP of one of the authors of this book would include such interests as mysteries, Japan, broadcasting, opera and squash (the sport); that of the other author would include science fiction, Africa, computers, guitar and squash (the sport).

Agents direct the computer to manipulate information according to your individual needs. If your interest in Einstein's book was focused on producing a paper on gravity, your agent would already have flagged the portions of the text where relativity and gravity are discussed. It might even search out related documents (brought to its attention by hypertext links throughout the digitally stored Einstein text) and produce a list of related material.

If this leaves you somewhat breathless or, worse, skeptical, remember that the National Academy of Sciences report mentioned in Chapter 4 showed how quickly early computers reduced the time, effort and expense required to do calculations. As the power and speed of microchips continue to expand, the use of AI and hypertext will become common, something we take for granted.

WHAT'S POSSIBLE, AND WHAT'S PRACTICAL?

The process of reformatting all the information, persuasion and entertainment communication produced by humankind is no small chore. But it may not be as unrealistic as you think. In fact, since the majority of historical knowledge is in book form, it can be translated very simply.

A decade ago most digital conversion of text required manual inputting, typing the text on a key board. That was a great improvement over the earlier technologies requiring that the text be keypunched onto 3- by 8-inch Hollerith cards, which were

Parallelism and Hypermedia: The Future of Information Storage and Retrieval

The human brain has a wonderful capacity for problem solving and remembering. Much of that ability is innate; we are born with it. Our brains have developed the ability to store and recall information on the basis of incredibly complex relationships and at lightning-quick speeds.

Consider this scenario: You meet a new professor for the first time. You may remember her name, where she's from, where she received her Ph.D., what she studied, what her voice sounded like, or what her hobbies are but you don't do it consciously. You don't actually say to yourself, "I am going to remember that Ms. Jones studied etymology at La Sorbonne in Paris, where she picked up a distinctive accent, and that she enjoys mountain climbing with her son."

Suppose, though, that in the course of researching a term paper in the library, you find yourself in the biology section. In a flash you recall your new acquaintance because you remember her interest in insects, and then you remember other things: Her alma mater, her hobbies and many seemingly unrelated things about her are suddenly in your head.

Or you're watching television and a commercial comes on picturing two mountain climbers fighting both a cold and the mountainside—a similar flash, and the same memories come flooding back. In another flash you remember the name of a distant relative who's studying in Paris. Or you suddenly remember why you felt like you knew Ms. Jones upon first seeing her: Her accent resembles that of a classmate you hadn't heard from in weeks.

Without your conscious knowledge your brain was hard at work assimilating the new information. It organized the new information and set it aside for potential later use. It even indexed the information according to your personal hierarchy of interests, so that it could get the information quickly. These processes happen in milliseconds millions of times every day.

No one knows how the human brain does it. While you were not consciously and deliberately attempting to seek out and track down all the relevant information in your brain about zoology or mountain climbing, something else was happening. Another thought process was working in parallel with your conscious thought to store and retrieve the information about Ms. Jones that your brain decided to store.

This ability to process many different types of information concurrently sets the human brain "head and shoulders" above every computer ever designed by humans. The ability to automatically contextualize and index information and the existence of millions of independent, parallel and concurrent thoughts are truly remarkable phenomena. Even more remarkable is that they work so well. Computers, on the other hand, are not born with the same capacity. They must be told very specifically what to do and how to do it. Often they do not even do that very well. The ability to have access to so many wide-ranging bits of disparate information comes at a huge price in terms of speed. With everything-to-everything connectivity, acquiring any information can take a long time. If the system is not fabulously well designed, it will eventually bog down into complete inaction.

Coordinating the operation of parallel-processing computers contributes one problem. Until very recently all computers were driven by a single very fast processor. New parallel processors and massively parallel processors are only barely beginning to approximate the parallelism of the brain. These computers—still cabinet-sized and unwieldy—contain only 64,000 processors working in tandem. The human brain contains billions of neurons.

Hardware engineers have already designed computers with more discrete processors hooked together. But that is not the real problem. The hardest part is designing software to make all the processors pull together in the same direction.

Consider the challenge of making thousands of independent-minded processors work together. First the program must understand the problem. It figures out how big the discrete problem chunks need to be in order to solve the whole problem as smoothly as possible. This may involve creating problem sets and sets of sub-problems, linked in a strict hierarchy. For example in dealing with all the new information about Ms. Jones, the program must break all the data into its constituent elements: name, friends, relationship, interests, age, other personal information, appearance characteristics, ambitions and so on.

Once it has parsed the problem into smaller chunks, it can assign different individual processors the job of assimilating that information into what has already been stored. That requires assigning still more processors to sort through the huge body of existing information on file to see where any relevant matches exist. Then it must figure out the exact nature of the relationship between old and new information. Finally the two can be formally linked.

Meanwhile the main program needs to be monitoring the progress of each sub-program. It may have to allocate more resources to particularly slow or hard parts. It may seek to eliminate wasteful duplication by looking for similarities between different portions. If a serious problem occurs, it needs to be able to cut losses and unproductive processing; otherwise, the whole operation may go on forever.

Some standardized programming methods have been developed to help with these problems: hypertext and hypermedia. *Hypertext* is the linking of related data in a specific piece of information. For example by selecting a word in a document, information about that word is retrieved. The term *hypertext* was coined by Ted Nelson in 1964 as a method for adapting computers to the way people think about and use information. It defines different types of relationships individual bits of information can have to each other. It also makes performing operations between bits easier.

In multimedia systems more than just words are linked and indexed. Information in the form of images and sounds and video is linked and indexed together. Then hypertext is called *hypermedia*. For example, instead of just getting a definition of the word *horse* when it is selected from a standard electronic document, one might see a picture of a field filled with grazing horses or a video segment of running horses.

Hypermedia documents allow the reader to explore links. The horse selection might mention horses' importance during the development of the American West. The reader could then select "pony express" and see and read about pre-industrial transportation and mail systems. In this example hypermedia has allowed the reader to explore more information and learn more about the subject of interest.

then read onto computer tape.[8] Today electronic and laser scanners can convert letters, images and sounds into digital format.

The conversion is the easy part. Figuring out what to do with all the information is a problem of monstrous proportions. Coordinating the evolution to digital electronic libraries presents a gigantic challenge in the establishment of standards. The type of remote sharing and accessing outlined above will be possible only with universal standards. Unfortunately, throughout the history of electronic media systems, standards have not come easily.

STANDARDS, STANDARDS AND MORE STANDARDS

First, standards are necessary for storage and retrieval. All digitized forms of text, audio or image information must be stored in some standardized way if they are to be accessed by different people using different retrieval instruments at different locations. This in turn requires the use of standard compression algorithms to insure efficient and economical storage.[9]

Second, standards must be created for indexing schemes. Every word in hypertext documents is "indexed"—that is, retrievable by key-word search—but logic tells us that some words are more important than others. For example in Einstein's book, "*gravity*" is bound to be a highly significant term; "*mother*" may have no significance at all, but if it appears in the text, it is indexed.

Can indexed material be segmented according to such different levels of importance, thereby providing more rapid location of the more important references? How will software from hundreds or thousands of different companies in various nations and languages interact without standard definitions at each level of abstraction? How will indexing schemes be coordinated across different types of data?

Another problem related to standards concerns the use of AI. The rules at the heart of any system that has the ability to learn—be it a human brain or a computer—are quite complex. Integrating the use of PIPs into the AI-based information searches poses still more problems.

THE NECESSITY OF ELECTRONIC PUBLISHING

To take advantage of the opportunities posed by the revolutionary technologies, we must change the way we produce and reproduce communication content. We will have to evolve a system of electronic publishing. In such a system the computer representation of a work—for example, a floppy disk containing the text of this book in digital format—is the end product. All artifacts of knowledge—periodicals and books, posters, film, CDs, DATs, audiocassettes and videocassettes—will become obsolete curiosities.

Why should Mayfield Publishing have to actually print and distribute copies of this book? Why not simply store the digital format in a computer? Those requiring the book could download the text into their multimedia system. They can either read it on screen or have their high-speed laser printer produce a hard copy. For the visually disabled a synthesized voice could read the text. The price of the "book" could be added to their monthly multimedia charge and transferred to Mayfield's bank account.

Such radical changes in the way we store and use knowledge will also require new standards within the educational system. The physical plant and facilities which constitute schools will also change.

Even more basic we must sort out the variety and the level of skills required to insure that the needs of both society and individuals are met. Changes in both the general curriculum and the syllabus of individual courses will be necessary, as well as in the requirements for teacher training and certification. We will have a new concept of literacy.

AS ALWAYS, THE MONEY PROBLEM

In addition to problems of establishing standards, several kinds of money problems relate to these concepts of digital archives, hypertext, AI and educational restructuring. Who will pay?

The school crisis of the 1950s, created by the post–World War II baby boom, helped crack the tradition of education as strictly a local matter. As they sought to accommodate the wave of rising enrollments, the boards of the individual school districts of our decentralized system turned to the federal government for assistance.

Congress authorized the creation of a Department of Health, Education, and Welfare (HEW) and later authorized a separate Department of Education. When the FCC reorganized television channels in 1952, it reserved at least one television channel in each major market for non-commercial educational use. This and earlier FCC actions making a similar reservation of FM radio channels laid the foundation for our present public broadcasting structure.

A series of congressional actions provided massive financial help to local schools. Federal money also helped to build instructional broadcasting facilities and provide schools with other new teaching technologies. The National Institutes of Health built vast new libraries of research materials and underwrote research and development of innovative technologies for the sharing and remote accessing of these materials.

EXCHANGING FREEDOM OF ACTION FOR FINANCIAL ASSISTANCE

Every teenager and college student has learned firsthand the power of parental purse strings. It is axiomatic that money comes with strings attached. The stipulations attached to federal grants and allocations did not result in centralized control and standardization of our educational system, but they certainly brought about a decrease in the variation between districts and curtailed the freedom of action previously enjoyed by local school boards.

During the 1980s voters endorsed Ronald Reagan's campaign to reduce the federal government's size and influence. What they may or may not have counted on was that this also reduced federal assistance to local programs, including the schools. By 1990 most school districts were facing a new wave of problems requiring money, as federal assistance had been pared, and local taxpayers were in rebellion against rising property taxes.

Public concern likely will lead to more federal allocations, and those allocations will continue the erosion of local control and difference. This seems particularly likely if those allocations are for the types of new educational communication systems we have been discussing. The level of standardization required by these technologies alone would promote such a trend to centralization.

We should not overlook the trend mentioned earlier of expanded private-sector interest in education. At least three levels of private-sector interest exist. An increasing number of companies are operating their own in-house courses for employees. Entrepreneurs are contracting to operate community schools on a for-profit basis. Most important of all, investors are always interested in new growth markets, and the new educational communications systems may be one of the greatest growth industries of the coming decades. If standardization is necessary to fulfill that growth potential, the financial market itself will provide a push in that direction.

HOW WILL WE PROTECT AND REWARD INTELLECTUAL PRODUCTS?

Assuming that these systems are designed and built, two questions will remain. First, what will we do about protecting the rights of individuals and groups to own and profit from intellectual property? As we noted in Chapter 6, we have patents and copyrights to stimulate individual and group creative contributions to the social good. But now our concepts and procedures related to copyright (already antiquated and unsatisfactory) will have to be revised.

Teachers photocopy materials for class handouts. They tape programs off-air or off-cable and replay them in class. These efforts to provide their students with expanded substance are laudable and legal—within limits. Wholesale copying of entire books or articles denies authors and publishers revenue protected by copyright. Off-air taping of programs can reduce the sales of copies the producer is planning to market to help earn additional revenue to offset the cost of production. Because software is marketed on floppy disks, it is very hard to prevent illegal copying, which reduces sales.

These problems might be eased by the digitized systems we have outlined. Certainly such systems could provide means to accurately track users, bill them and allocate the income to the copyright holder. As a matter of fact, prototype systems already exist in the library world.

When a library buys a book, like all other buyers it contributes royalty income to the author. But if 100 people then check out the book, the author has lost royalty payments from 99 readers (assuming that they would have bought the book if it were not available in the library). In Great Britain and Germany, library authorities are assessed contributions to a pool used to recompense authors for this lost income. Computerized circulation records provide the basis for allocating the pool to individual authors on the basis of the readership of their books. In this country somewhat similar situations exist to allocate compensation to performing artists and producers for broadcast-radio and cable-television use of certain types of content.

Multimedia educational systems would present far more complex problems of compensation. Would someone who does a computer search pay for access? Would someone who downloads a hard copy pay more than someone who only views it on-screen? What about the creator's right to protect the product? What about new forms of plagiarism, where bits and pieces are lifted from a variety of sources, and then altered and manipulated through the use of easily available editing equipment?

PROBLEMS OF INFORMATION FRAGMENTATION

The second question is a general concern about the trend for information to become increasingly fragmented. What are the relationships of individual facts to larger concepts? These exciting new educational communications systems effectively fragment the body of phenomena underlying concepts, theories and art. This fragmentation allows us to organize phenomena in new ways, but it may also increase the danger that we lose sight of the forests as we increase our focus not just on the trees, but on individual tree leaves.

How much fragmentation can we individually handle? What do we as individuals lose if our use of AI and hypertext causes us to stop browsing, that random wandering through information that is "only" interesting, rather than critically important. Most of us can remember instances when, in the midst of such browsing, we stumbled onto an exciting idea or insight.

One might reply that Darwin focused on such esoteric and eclectic phenomena as the earthworms in his garden and the finches of the Galápagos Islands. True, but would he have come to his ideas about biological evolution if he hadn't also signed on for that long voyage on the *Beagle,* a period of several years during which he surveyed a broad scope of flora and fauna in many different geographic environments?

Is there a societal cost if our educational communication technologies, purposefully or inadvertently, undermine the generalists while encouraging and facilitating the work of specialists?

NEITHER AN EASY NOR A RAPID RECONSTRUCTION

Answers to these and other questions may be years, even decades, in the making. Once again every change affects and is affected by a status quo. The existing educational system with its millions of dedicated teachers, the parental expectations based largely on their own experience, an existing infrastructure of buildings and equipment representing an investment of billions of dollars, the necessity to convince millions of taxpayers that the expenditures related to change are justified—all of these issues contribute to a massively large and potent status quo.

On the other hand, growing concern and demand already exists within the economic sector for radical measures to realign the educational system to the new needs of business in the Information Age. The cornerstones of the technical infrastructure for a boundless digital library and other educational resources are only now being laid. Whole sets of standards still must be explored and developed. We are now only beginning to build the data communication superhighways needed to carry the information. More advanced software technologies are still more talk than action. The complete system will take years to develop, but it is worth noting that the trend in recent decades has been for change to come faster than predicted.

What's not in doubt is that the educational functions of communication are being expanded even as the technological means of performing these functions are revolutionized. In the coming decades the classroom will be an exciting place to be—for teachers and for students.

Suggestions for Further Reading

A good overview of what is happening with new technologies in our schools is provided by *The Electronic School,* an October 1991 supplement to *The American School Board Journal* and *The Executive Educator* produced by the Institute for the Transfer of Technology to Education in Alexandria, Va.

In *Smart Schools, Smart Kids* Edward B. Fiske includes descriptions and discussion of some examples in which new technologies are being used to innovate and improve classroom education. Two books more specifically focused on new technologies in education are Elizabeth L. Useem's 1986 *Low Tech Education in a High Tech World: Corporations and Classrooms in the New Information Society* and the 1990 *Cooperative Learning and Educational Media: Collaborating With Technology and Each Other* by Dennis Adams, Helen Carlson and Mary Hamm.

Those who want to know more about the fascinating world of AI and hypertext should try *Mapping Hypertext* by Robert E. Horn or *Intelligent Tutoring Systems: At the Crossroad of Artificial Intelligence and Education,* edited by Claude Frasson and Gilles Gautheir.

Notes

1. The kinetoscope was a hand-cranked device through which individuals could view motion pictures. They are still sometimes found in penny arcades and amusement parks.
2. Actually, Dame Agatha published *Come Tell Me How You Live* under her married name, Agatha Christie Mallowan, adding a further complication to the problem of cross references (New York: Dodd, Mead and Company, 1946).
3. One of the authors once worked in an Air Force library and remembers the visit of an inspector general, who, in all seriousness, suggested that the books be arranged by size of volume. The suggestion possibly reflected the general's experience as a student at West Point, where he had had to arrange the books on his desk in this manner. But try to imagine the difficulty of finding specific books if tens of thousands of volumes were so arranged. The civilian librarian, who had a wry sense of humor as well as no fear of generals, responded respectfully that perhaps the books should also be grouped by color.
4. The Library of Congress is provided with a copy of all published material. The classification assigned by the library is often included with the copyright information on the backside of the title page, and pre-printed catalog cards are also available. This greatly facilitates the work of individual libraries in processing new acquisitions.
5. You can, of course, ask somebody. But they (1) may not know the location, (2) may give you confusing directions owing to their complexity and/or use of reference points unknown to you or (3) may give you incorrect information. If you are lucky, they may give you clear, straightforward instructions.
6. Quinn McNemar, an outstanding professor of psychological statistics for many years at Stanford, told his students that upon finishing his doctorate, he went into the university's

library, found the bound copy of his dissertation and put a $10 bill in it. Ten years later he went back and retrieved the bill.
7. According to Alan Freedman's *The Computer Glossary* (New York: The American Management Association, 1991), the term "intelligence" is used to denote the ability to process information. Therefore, every computer uses intelligence. Artificial intelligence implies human-like intelligence, an ironic twist in terminology.
8. When we say "punched" we mean it literally. Each card contained 90 columns into which a bit of information was denoted by punching a single hole or a combination of holes denoting previously established code symbols.
9. Library of Congress and several small personal computer companies are recommending the adoption of a standard known as Z39.50 for the purpose of storage and retrieval.

CHAPTER 12

Entertainment Unlimited

So you've mastered Super Mario Brothers IX. It's time to move on to Sons of Mario Brothers. The scene of action is projected before you by holograph in three dimensions so you can chase and be chased up and down, from side to side *and* from front to back.

Or go into a "virtual reality" mode and project yourself into a James Bond Adventure.

If you're tired of the way *Gone With the Wind* ended, the next time you watch it, select from several alternate endings—created by computer simulation with Clark Gable and Vivian Leigh still playing Rhett and Scarlett.

In the unlikely event that you are an opera freak and you don't like the soprano in the Metropolitan's video of *Tosca,* you can create your own cast. It doesn't matter that Maria Callas died years ago, the computer synthesizer will recreate her performance for you.

If you are curious about what it would be like to have Madonna singing with Mick Jagger, the synthesizer will create a holographic performance right in your living room.

If all this sounds extreme and even silly, it may be—or it may not be. Remember that 20 years ago the Mario Brothers didn't even exist, and fifty years ago television didn't exist. Seventy years ago there was no radio, and eighty years ago there were no feature films. The first music recordings were made 100 years ago.

ENTERTAINMENT REFLECTS GROWTH OF LEISURE TIME

The concept of an entertainment industry is an invention of the 20th century. Of the plethora of mass-media entertainment choices available to us today, only a few primitive ancestors were available at the turn of the century—acoustic recordings, nickelodeon programs consisting of several one-reel silent movies, dime novels and popular magazines that often featured serialized stories.

Leisure time is also a recent invention. Prior to 1900 most people—including many children—worked long hours six days a week for low wages. Insufficient numbers of people had the leisure time and the discretionary income to sustain professional entertainment on a mass-audience level. And something else was lacking: home electrification.

ELECTRICITY TO LIGHT AND LIGHTEN OUR LIVES

The incandescent light bulb was not invented until 1879. Lamps and candlelight may be romantic, but they're pretty hard on the eyes when it comes to reading. In his Menlo Park, N. J., laboratories, Edison and his assistants produced an amazing variety of inventions and applications. Among them were basic mechanisms related to the development of motion pictures (the kinetoscope) and broadcasting (DeForest's audion tube) and, of course, recordings (the phonograph). Many other creative people made major contributions to these technologies, but the breadth of Edison's contributions exemplifies the excitement of these frontier days of the entertainment media—and of the Age of Communication.

All these devices would ultimately depend upon easy and inexpensive accessibility to electrical current. Even in 1920 fewer than half the residences in urban areas were wired for electrical service; two-thirds of the nation's households were still, electrically speaking, in the dark. By 1940 nine out of ten urban homes had electricity, and by the mid-1950s the nation effectively was electrified—98.8 percent of our homes had electrical power.

LIGHTENING OUR LIVES

As electrification expanded, our lives were lightened literally and in other ways as well. Factories converted to electrical power and became cleaner, quieter and more efficient. Concurrently unions won gains for employees. The work week was reduced to 48 hours, then to 44. Wages increased. Child labor laws ended the worst exploitation of youngsters, and expanded compulsory education raised education levels. Appliances such as vacuum cleaners, washing machines and refrigerators were appearing in homes, and the public was being offered new options for filling its expanding leisure time.

Hollywood and its feature films were known worldwide, and the bright lights of cinema arcades shone in every community. The wax disks of Edison's early phonograph had been replaced by 10- and 12-inch shellac "platters" pressed from electrically processed masters. Records were still expensive, but no longer a novelty. David Sarnoff's 1916 idea of the "home music box" was becoming a reality in the 1920s as wireless was transformed into radio broadcasting. By the 1930s, families across the nation gathered around console radios, listening to drama, comedy and music.

These new entertainment media changed concepts, expectations and standards for entertainment. Star professional talent was now available on local movie screens and from the radio speakers in homes, towns, villages and cities. During the painful depression years of the 1930s, these inexpensive diversions helped ease public anxiety.

After World War II ended in 1945, we entered an era of unprecedented expanding prosperity and leisure that included the 40-hour, 5-day work week; minimum-wage legislation; Social Security and veterans' benefits. These benefits and other social legislation combined to help fuel an unprecedented economic growth for the entire population, not just the wealthy few.

The expansion of prosperity and leisure was paralleled by development of new entertainment technologies: FM radio, black and white television followed by color television, universal use of color and wide-screen movies, LPs, stereo radio and recordings, cable television, and tape recordings for sound and pictures.

EXPANDING CHOICE AND USE

When we look at the changes in media entertainment over the last half century, two general trends stand out: First is the expanding choice of media and of choice within media; second is the expanding and diversified use made of the video screen. Our television sets today have sprouted wires running to auxiliary units—cable converters, VCRs, computers and video CD players—enabling us to see an expanded range of content on what is now a video screen.

Cable, which originally provided little more than reliable pictures of local stations, now provides scores of channels with entertainment of every kind. VCRs and videodiscs fill the screen with our own off-air recordings and home videos, recordings of concerts as well as movies, and video editions of magazines, such as *National Geographic*. With Nintendo and other adapters, the video becomes the display for interactive games. The expanding use of video for all kinds of music performance increases the demand for better stereo sound quality in our television sets.

NON-TELEVISION PRESSURES FOR HDTV

We watch all this material on NTSC-format screens developed to display television programs, and most of the public is apparently satisfied with the picture and sound quality this screen provides. But NTSC technology unquestionably degrades the image quality of movies and it provides inadequate detail for display of graphic and textual material. The impetus for the development of HDTV will come from these other uses of the video screen, not from broadcast television.

Many of us may not wish to have wall-sized video screens in our homes, but such screens will be welcomed in public places—theaters, bars and clubs. The push for conversion to HDTV will come from those who are supplying non-television material seen over the video screen. The introduction of HDTV likely will be part of a larger change from analog to digital technologies throughout the entertainment media.

DIGITAL CONVERSION: AESTHETIC AND ECONOMIC COSTS

The change to digital will not be without aesthetic and economic costs. CDs are a case in point. Purists point out that, while CDs eliminate surface scratch and tape hiss, they reproduce a rapid series of samples rather than the continuous line of melody provided by analog recordings.

For some the extremely clean sound of digital recording also removes something of the reality of the performance. The use of digital technology to alter and edit recorded music seems to blur the borderline between music created by human performers and that created by electronic and mechanical synthesis. However, sampling is not new to the visual recording field. Both film and NTSC video technologies, analog technologies though they are, use sampling in the recording and re-creation of the visual field through visual persistence. This is not to say that there are not aesthetic differences between digital photography and film or video photography.

The controversy over digital "colorization" of movies originally produced in black and white is indicative of the depth of feeling creative artists and critics have about the transposition of material produced in one technology to another.[1] It is safe to anticipate considerable hue and cry over aesthetic loss as the use of digital photography increases.

FUNCTIONAL COSTS, NOT AESTHETICS, DRIVE THE MARKET

Popular taste and consumer expenditures, not aesthetics, supply the driving force in the entertainment marketplace wherein decisions are made regarding technological change.

In only four years CD sales matched those of LPs, and after seven years CDs had captured 40 percent of the recorded music market. At that point most record companies stopped producing LPs. Turner Broadcasting has reported that colorization has increased viewer interest as well as cassette sales and rentals of old films originally released in black and white.

These examples suggest that music and movies as entertainment are not necessarily the same thing as music and movies as art. In the case of movies, further support for such a conclusion is provided by the success of movies on broadcast television where they are interrupted by commercials and entire scenes are eliminated to make the movie's running time fit the program schedules of stations and networks.

The aesthetic argument is already compromised because some creators in both film and video not only cross over from one technology to the other, but also make use of computers. Many television commercials have been shot on film because it provides higher visual quality than current NTSC video technology. Some movie directors convert film footage to video for economy and ease in editing and reconvert to film. Computers are widely used for animation and special effects. A competitive market in computer equipment and editing programs reduces their cost and increases their availability in the film and video fields.

AESTHETICS, ARTISTIC LICENSE AND MARKET PRESSURES

When we discuss aesthetics in media entertainment we run the risk of lapsing into pretension. We must remember that feature films have always been composites of selected takes of individual scenes filmed in sequences to fit economic considerations and the availability and convenience of cast members. Part of the creativity exercised by the director is selecting and sequencing the individual takes into a single entity, the final feature we see on the screen. But most directors will alter that selection and sequence if previews yield unfavorable audience response. If the director isn't willing, studio heads may force the changes anyway, because their overriding concern is box office.[2]

Television producers abandoned live performance when videotape made recording practical. Prerecording eases logistical problems of production, and makes it possible to repeat and select scenes and shots.

In the music field recording producers began to take advantage of splicing master tapes almost as soon as tape began to replace stylus recording. The egos of performers encouraged the practice of editing out missed notes and replacing them with correct ones. What is presented as a complete performance or even a single number is often a composite in which a selection of the best takes from a sequence of repeated performances is skillfully spliced together.

The general public apparently accepts and perhaps even welcomes the perfection of these synthetic performances. In an ironic reversal the artificial recordings have become the reality, and artists use them in live-performance concerts to sidestep possible audience disappointment. Digital technology merely makes such practices easier.

DIGITAL TRADE-OFFS

Making the transition to digital means expenditures for new equipment in production, transmission and reception. Psychological and monetary costs are incurred to retrain performers and technicians. And there is the question of maintaining the value of existing inventory of feature movies, syndicated video series and musical recordings.

In the music field the transition was sequential. It began with the use of digital technology for recording; distribution and playback continued to be in analog disk and tape formats. The transition to digital playback in tape, DAT, has not matched the success of the CD—not necessarily through lack of consumer interest, but through political and legal maneuvers to protect performance rights.[3] This concern will spread as digitization progresses throughout the entertainment industry.

EMBRACING THE DIGITAL FUTURE

Whether or not anyone else is enthusiastic about a transition to digit technologies, the manufacturers of electronics equipment are ecstatic. This change will bring them billions of dollars in sales as studios, distribution systems and the audience accelerates the purchase of new equipment.

One of the most significant signs of the digital future was an announcement made by Eastman Kodak, a firm practically synonymous with film, that it is preparing for a market in which digital photography will be an option for both professional and private use. Actually Kodak had no choice; this move was essential for it to maintain its competitive position in the field of photography.

The competition among Kodak, Polaroid, Fuji and others will inevitably speed development and improvements in cameras and display technologies. The competition will also result in lower costs for users.

We needn't worry about losing access to all those old classics produced in analog technologies. Remember how quickly old films have become available on videocassette. Similarly scanning mechanisms are already in development to convert sound waves and printed text as well as film images to digital format.

The change to digital distribution will challenge traditional practices and relationships in the entertainment industries. Owners and operators of both cinema and broadcast television stations must brace for change, but each faces a different set of challenges.

DIGITAL FORMATS, OPTICAL FIBER, VIDEO AND TELCOS

We can distribute digital signals perfectly well through terrestrial and satellite radio signals as well as copper and optical fiber networks. Optical fiber seems particularly well-fitted to the digital future. Thus telcos and the movie and broadcast industries mutually benefit in the building of optical fiber networks and the conversion to digital signalling and storage of communication content. The telcos must be included in consideration of the mass-media future because they have been in the vanguard of both digital signalling and fiber optics.

The great capacity of optical fiber expands the challenge faced by those who operate optical fiber networks as they seek the volume of traffic providing the greatest return on the hefty investment required to extend fiber into our homes. Everyone agrees that broadband services can provide the means of meeting that challenge. For all practical purposes, broadband services means the distribution of video material.

The prospects for a "fibered" nation are very enticing, but they are also formidable. Imagine an interactive system that will provide individuals with access to an unprecedented variety of entertainment. If, as Neil Postman[4] says, we are already "amusing ourselves to death," think of what we can do with the options provided by fiber!

MOVIES AS THE DRIVING FORCE FOR FIBER

If history is any guide, movies will provide the greatest impetus for broadband services on optical fiber. Recount all those who have vested interests in movies—studios, cinemas, broadcasters, cable operators and video-store operators. With so many people having a stake in a single product, any change in its format and its distribution is bound to produce tension and conflict. But the promise of an El Dorado created by new, expanded revenue streams is enough to give everybody pause and to make even present antagonists cooperate. In Washington the lawyers and lobbyists representing cable, telco, broadcaster and publisher interests wage war against one another for the support of Congress, the FCC and other key bodies in the law and regulatory field. Even as this war goes on, the largest cable MSO (TCI) has joined the telcos in a marketing experiment to explore the best methods of exploiting the new technology. Similar cooperative efforts are underway in other markets.

It is not so much a question of whether fiber will bring us access to movie archives, but how the access will be provided, how viewers will be billed and how the revenue will be divided. Managements of broadcast television, video stores and cinemas have cause to worry about the impact of this service on their own future operations and revenues.

MOVIE ARCHIVES AT OUR FINGERTIPS

A look at *TV Guide* or the TV magazine in our Sunday paper provides us with a graphic reminder of just how many movies are already available each week via broadcast and cable TV. We can use our VCR to time shift for more convenient viewing, but we have no control over the selection of titles. The digital and optical fiber future will give us expanded control over both selection and schedule. Experiments in providing "script it yourself" options will allow viewers to decide on the ending of a drama.

Consider this possible scenario for the movie future. Feature movies for the popular market are produced with digital cameras and editing equipment. Instead of a film print, the data containing the picture are stored in the digital headend, an online, electronic archive of the studio's output. Existing libraries of old films are converted to digital format by scanning devices. Digital storage saves space, making cataloging and retrieval easier. Perhaps even more importantly, features in digital format do not suffer the wear and tear that deteriorates film and video copies.

We sit in our home video room and explore the menu of new releases. If we prefer we can call up a listing of all the movies by a favorite star and make a selection or scroll through menus listing musicals, comedies, etc. When we've made a selection, we enter the appropriate code and the feature is instantaneously available. The fee for viewing is added into our monthly bill.[5]

This scenario is already technologically feasible. The lasers that drive optical fiber transmission could signal 3.5 billion bits per second in 1991 and were still gaining speed. Compression devices can download a full-length feature in 20 seconds. Combining even the present transmission speed with fiber's great capacity means that tens of thousands of requests can be handled simultaneously with little or no delay—if there is adequate switching capability. AT&T engineers have been quoted as saying that switching for such online services is really not a problem. Just imagine 50 million families each watching a movie of their own choice!

LOCATION ALTERS IMPACT

What would this mean for the cinema theaters? It seems inconceivable that cinemas could disappear. As we observed in Chapter 6, going to the movies is functionally different from watching a movie at home. It is a social occasion; it takes us out of our homes and into the company of others. Humor, horror and sorrow are contagious; and our emotional reactions are intensified by experiencing the content with others.

In contrast watching a movie may be an isolating experience, a way of filling empty time. Even if we watch with others at home, the viewing experience is altered by the greater informality of the ambience. We feel freer to make comments, and extraneous factors, such as a ringing telephone, may cause us to stop and restart the film. We may replay scenes we especially enjoy (or don't understand) or fast forward through those that bore or offend us. We come and go from the room, breaking the spell of the story.

DIGITAL AND HDTV CINEMA EXHIBITION

Video may have already done its worst to the cinema, but these theaters also will be affected by the digital transformation and the introduction of HDTV. If production makes the transition, economic pressure will build to convert cinemas to digital HDTV technology.

Consider the problems of current film distribution and exhibition. The several reels required for a feature movie must be shipped to each of hundreds of individual cinemas and then shipped back at the end of the film's run. The logistics of distribution are complex and expensive, and the prints can be lost or can be diverted briefly to pirates who make quick copies for illegal distribution.

Film is also susceptible to damage. Each reel of a feature film must be run and rewound several times every day. Each scratch or tear adds to an accumulating number of visual and aural distortions that detract aesthetically from the audience's pleasure at each subsequent showing.

New technologies are already being used for cinema exhibition. In Japan NHK has constructed video cinemas that use large-screen HDTV for projecting movies, bypassing the use of film. Present-day HDTV technology is of doubtful adequacy for large auditoria, but most cinemas today are clusters of a number of small theaters. In theaters seating under 200, the picture quality of large-screen HDTV projection is competitive with 35-mm film—and is not subjected to the scratches and dust that deteriorate film quality.

Some American cinema chains and campus film clubs are using satellite distribution of video-formatted movies to theaters scattered over several states. Digital formatting will facilitate movie distribution via either satellite or optical fiber to theaters and homes.

In summary strong logistic and economic factors argue for a conversion to digital cinema distribution and exhibition.

A MATTER OF MONEY

True film fans will recoil from the idea of abandoning film in favor of digital technology. Even less-sensitive moviegoers may recognize the distinct aesthetic quality of film. But if the primary function of movies is popular entertainment rather than art, economics will push the industry into the digital path.

In *The Liveliest Art,* Arthur Knight makes the following observation:

> The artist, however, has no control over the inventor, nor over the technological advances that come into his medium. Often the inventors work alone, outside the industry. Their discoveries are incorporated into the film by the businessmen, the "front office" that must, of necessity, worry less about artistic achievements than financial stability.[6]

Perhaps film will evolve as a form of high culture as have other previously popular forms of entertainment, such as opera. Already major art museums throughout the nation routinely present film series together with lecture series to analyze individual movies and movie genres.

VIDEO AND TELEVISION

What about technological change in video entertainment? We've said earlier that U.S. television broadcasters have been perfectly content with NTSC and have shown muted enthusiasm for HDTV at best. However, optical fiber delivery of movies in HDTV format will create inexorable pressure on television programmers to join in the transition. Just as competitive pressure forced all TV stations to make the move to color, the need to maintain image comparability between their programs and other video-screen content will force the television industry to make the move to HDTV.

Again we can anticipate that the men and women in the front office will be pushing technological convergence. Conversion to digital HDTV will offer an opportunity for studios producing both television series and feature films to use a single technology, rather than juggle film and video as they do now.

If we have movies stored in computer archives, why not do the same with individual video programs and series? If we do this, video programs can be accessed online and on demand rather than being tied to the schedules of broadcast and cable operators.

In effect we could construct individualized program schedules of video series as well as movies. This may be going farther into individual control—and effort—than most of us wish. However, it is only a step or two beyond the "VCR Plus" technology that permits use of number codes to preselect video programs for automatic recording of our VCR.[7]

A RESTRUCTURED TELEVISION INDUSTRY?

Such a scenario suggests nothing less than a restructuring of today's television industry. In the most extreme case, such a restructuring could result in the eventual elimination of broadcast television. Politics, if nothing else, makes this an unlikely possibility. Even in less extreme scenarios, the television industry will be fundamentally altered. At the start of the 1990s, the industry was developing cracks from the additional 30–40 channel choices provided by existing cable systems. Broadcast television must now brace itself for the impact of optical fiber systems offering 150 or more channels.

During the 1980s the big audience losers were the oligarchy networks and their affiliates, as can be seen from Table 12.1. The relationship between these networks and their affiliates has become strained as the networks have sought to adjust to the economic consequences of increased competition and declining audience shares. Network decline has consequences extending throughout the industry. If the dream of a "fibered" nation is realized, the need for broadcast television will be questioned on both political and economic grounds.

Table 12.1 Where Has the Television Audience Gone?

Average share in prime time, 1990–91 Season. (Multiple television set households account for total exceeding 100 percent.)

Networks/Affiliates 54%
    ABC 18%
    CBS 17%
    NBC 19%
Independents 15%
Cable 39%
    Basic Services 31%
    Pay Services 8%

Source: Cabletelevision Advertising Bureau.

NEW NETWORKS TO CHALLENGE THE OLD

From 1927 until the mid 1970s, *network* was synonymous with the oligarchy of ABC, CBS and NBC.[8] As we saw in Chapter 6, the scarcity of channels itself effectively limited the number of full national networks. Then satellite-delivered program services such as CNN, Discovery, Arts and Entertainment, ESPN, USA and Fox expanded the meaning.

Now some of the big MSOs, such as TCI, operate what in effect are their own networks. They put together a schedule of programs and deliver by satellite to each of their local cable systems across the nation. The MSO itself sells as many availabilities as possible to national spot advertisers, and the local cable system tries to sell the remaining slots to local advertisers.

The ability to aggregate a large national audience has been the unique advantage of the broadcast networks in the national advertising market. The present audience reach of the cable satellite networks does not compare to that of the broadcast networks. However, their combined impact has shaken the dominance and complacency of the broadcasting industry, particularly that of the networks and their affiliates. The networks now find themselves in a perplexing dilemma. The erosion of their audience shares has had a dual impact on relations with affiliates and advertisers.

THE UNRAVELING OF THE NETWORKS

The power of the broadcast networks has always depended on the unique ability to provide national coverage. In turn the networks themselves have been dependent upon local affiliates in cities across the nation. The relationship between a network and its affiliates has been symbiotic and mutually profitable. But, as we saw in Chapter 8, the dynamics of the network and affiliate relationship are changing.

As networks reduce or eliminate their compensation to affiliates and their audience shares decline in individual time periods, affiliates must reassess the value of the network to their own operation. Some affiliates find it to their advantage to pre-empt some program slots from the network and fill them with programming and advertising from other sources.

Every time an affiliate pre-empts from the network's feed, a hole appears in the blanket coverage the network has promised to its national advertisers. As the holes increase, the network's bargaining position with advertisers weakens. As that happens the network's financial situation is further weakened with a comparable reduction in its ability to maintain dominance in the competition for programs and talent.

In 1990 the oligarchy structure was showing tatters, if not signs of unraveling. CBS announced plans to discontinue station compensation; NBC announced that it would discontinue its program feed during some weekday daytime periods. Disappointing, if not disastrous, earning reports prompted a new round of staff reductions.

REDEFINING THE SHAPE OF NETWORKS

Just as it is inconceivable that cinemas would disappear, so is it inconceivable that available program choices will not include some major, national program services.

However, that is not to say all three of the major networks will survive or survive in their present form.

Networks have thrived by combining two separate but related functions. Most of the audience is conditioned to having someone structure a selection of video entertainment for them each evening, just as they are conditioned to expect to be told what news is important. The public may be happy to have the multiplicity of choices provided by cable, but people also find it convenient and reassuring to know they can turn to the networks for consistent programming. And the majority still do so.

Despite marketing trends emphasizing target demographics, major manufacturers still need a reliable way to reach a mass audience on the national level. So long as the networks attract dominant shares of the audience, they provide the most efficient means of doing this.

Advertisers don't care how the network delivers programming; they just want large national audiences. The networks feasibly could fulfill these two basic functions without affiliates by using a national optical fiber system. Their program schedules could be available online. No more problems and tensions would be related to affiliates. The networks could even sell the adjacencies between programs rather than letting this income go to affiliates.

AN END FOR BROADCAST TELEVISION?

What about the 2,000 or so local television stations? With the great capacity of fiber, no reason prevents these, too, from distribution within their respective market areas, just as many currently are distributed to most of their viewers by cable.

Under the 1934 Communications Act, station licensees have a special obligation to provide programming for the convenience, interest and necessity of their local communities. Just as the oligarchy faces competition from new national rivals provided by cable, local stations now face competition in fulfilling this function for their communities. Access channels and some of the new cable stations now provide more locally oriented programming than most broadcast television stations.

In a "fibered" nation all the functions of television conceivably could be filled without using broadcasting. Federal authorities might be tempted to reallocate the very large stretches of the electromagnetic spectrum currently reserved for broadcast television to accommodate the increasing number of new technologies clamoring for access. However, any functional displacement of broadcast television must address two critical factors of program accessibility:

> Optical fiber must be able to deliver programs to as many or more homes than currently receive off-air television signals.

> Entertainment services on fiber must accommodate or overcome the public's expectation of free or heavily subsidized content.

THE QUESTION OF PENETRATION

If optical fiber is to replace broadcasting as a delivery system without an outcry from public and national marketers alike, it must provide comparable audience penetration.

But comparing the ability of the several delivery systems to reach the public is complicated.

Almost all American homes, 98 percent, possess a television set; and, thanks to the skill and patience of the FCC's engineers and planners, the average family has a choice of five or more off-air television signals. But the networks individually have a somewhat lower penetration, just over 90 percent each.

Most of our families now watch the programs of television stations, affiliates and independents alike via cable, which on average brings them three dozen or more different channels. Because only about 60 percent of U.S. families subscribe to cable, the penetration of any network that relies solely on cable distribution is much less than that of the major broadcast networks.

More than 90 percent of American families do have a telephone, and so it would seem that the telephone system has a higher penetration than the cable system. The current infrastructure of cable systems, however, passes almost as many homes as does that of the telephone companies. The difference is that almost a third of those who have the option of subscribing to cable have chosen to remain unconnected. Therefore the potential penetration of cable systems is almost equal to that of the telephone systems, which, in turn, is more or less equal to that of any of the major networks at the present time.

THE QUESTION OF MONEY

Families decide not to subscribe to cable for various reasons. They may be content with the choice available to them from the free off-air signals of local stations, and so the additional services have insufficient value to these viewers to justify the monthly cable fee. As with most statistical data, other interpretations are possible. For example parents simply may not wish to deal with the pressures extended channel choice can create within the family.

The official policy set forth in the 1934 Communications Act states that broadcast programming shall be free, but that policy has little relevance to the current market, which encompasses video—not just broadcasting. In fact most American families are voluntarily paying monthly service fees to get channels in addition to those they can receive off-air. Having said that, we must remember tens of millions of voters and potential cable customers still rely on free broadcast television.

THE DILEMMA OF BEING IN BETWEEN

With cable penetration at only 60 percent, the traditional economic operation of the broadcasting industry is already coming under pressure. Station and network executives who have been accustomed to extraordinary profits for half a century are having to adjust to more modest, but still attractive, expectations. What will happen if cable penetration increases to 80 or 90 percent and the number of channels continues to multiply?

Network executives bravely predict that most new channels will take audiences from other cable channels, not from the networks. Even if they are correct, networks are unlikely to dominate audience shares as they once did. Already they have had to adjust to lower operating costs to maintain profitability.

This raises the question of whether the reduction in their financial base will reduce the broadcast networks' ability to dominate the competition for programming. In early 1992 one of the major producing studios (Paramount) announced they would sell two major series in the first-run syndication market, bypassing the networks. Cable networks have run up the bidding for major professional and collegiate sports and have captured some of these contracts from the networks. Some of the large MSO and cable organizations, as well as the upstart Fox network, have acquired major feature movie packages and have joined in underwriting production of original video series. As major programs shift to other channels, the networks will have a harder time maintaining even their reduced audience shares. Programming, audience, advertising and resources make up the dynamics of the industry; a change in one produces similar changes in the others.

Network executives hope they will be allowed to compete in the off-network syndication market to develop new revenue sources. However, these efforts face intense resistance from the American Motion Picture Producers Association, other production organizations and the cable industry.

THE EXTENDED CYCLE OF TELEVISION ECONOMICS

The erosion of the network audience has set into motion a cycle of effects extending beyond networks, stations and cable systems. This cycle involves the production studios and talent as well as the off-network syndication business.

Similar to the situation in the movie industry, recent years have seen a continuing escalation of television production costs. It is not unusual for studios to spend a quarter of a million dollars or more producing a single half-hour segment of a popular series. Like movie stars of established box-office appeal, stars of series with proven audience appeal demand and receive high fees and a share of off-network syndication sales.

The inflation in costs originally reflected the high-flying profits that prevailed in network broadcasting. Program buyers for the three networks did not hesitate to bid prices higher and higher; they knew they could pass the cost on to the advertisers who were waiting in line to buy prime-time slots.

In that era production houses recovered 90 percent or more of a series' cost through the original sale to the network. Income from subsequent off-network syndication was almost all profit; as the demand for syndicated material expanded, profits soared.

With the decline of network ratings two trends developed. Each network increased the number of reruns within the season, thereby reducing the number of programs they buy each season. Networks have also moderated their bids for all but the top-rated programs. This means that even if a production studio does score with a network sale, the studio doesn't recover its costs and begin to earn a profit until the series is also successful in the syndication market. In other words syndication income is now essential to studio profitability.

Fortunately for the producers, an explosion of video outlets in Europe has expanded the international syndication market in addition to expansion of the domestic market from the growing number of broadcast, cable, MMDS and DBS channels. The growing importance of the syndication market reduces the dominance of the networks within the overall programming market.

Just as cinemas provide promotion for feature movies to help stimulate subsequent video viewer interest, network exposure creates audience interest and recognition for syndicated series. Some form of national program schedules seems essential for audience, advertisers and producers.

FINDING MATERIAL FOR ALL THOSE CHANNELS

If you look at the channel listings in any market over a period of one week, you will see a high level of material redundancy. The redundancy is even greater if you extend the analysis over the entire season.

In the past summer was rerun season. Now prime-time network series may run as many repeats as new shows during the regular fall-to-spring season. The same old series and feature movies run again and again and again on local stations and cable services. If such high redundancy already exists with 50 cable channels, what will the situation be with 150 channels?

More channels will not necessarily mean expanded program choice. The operational plans of the new, expanded cable systems call for using several channels for each PPV service. For example, by having the same feature start on a different channel at half-hour intervals, the system can reduce the loss of impulse viewers who do not want to wait an hour or so for the feature to begin.

With current technology this makes economic sense. But with fiber and multimedia systems that can download features in 20 seconds upon demand, even greater flexibility can be offered within a single channel. This provides the potential for greatly expanding the program choice.

MORE CHOICE, MORE DIVERSITY?

Both broadcasters and cinema operators survive on high numbers of viewers or of tickets sold. Except in large metropolitan markets, minority and most special-interest groups are not large enough alone to provide sufficient traffic to support cinema or broadcast programs. Similarly, cinema operators and broadcast programmers are reluctant to exhibit unknown talent for fear of losing audiences to their competitors. Such fears also inhibit the exhibition of foreign productions.

Cable satellite services have proved that groups too small within a single locale can be combined into national audiences of considerable size, large enough to be viable if operating costs can be kept low.

Community-access channels on local cable systems generally do not attract many viewers, but they do provide a unique opportunity for individuals and groups to obtain experience in video performance. And occasionally they may attract popular and critical attention.

In their search for new or unique material to fill channels and attract more subscribers, some cable operators have added programs of foreign broadcast services. These may find favor with local ethnic groups, but they also provide others with an opportunity to practice foreign language comprehension and sample the video culture of other nations.

In a "fibered" nation these types of services could be expanded. Digitally formatted feature movies of independent and foreign producers could be inexpensively stored and offered for on-demand PPV. Over time they might attract sufficient orders to enable the producers to recover costs. Any viewing might generate word-of-mouth promotion to stimulate interest by others, creating interest in future work by the same artists.

GAMES AND SPECIAL SERVICES

The revolutionary technologies are already changing the world of games. The type of interactivity provided by games such as Nintendo will be expanded by online game choices. You will be able to play alone or to challenge known and unknown players all over the country. You will be able to participate in team and league play with other enthusiasts all over the world.

These technologies can also expand the entertainment options for people with various kinds of disabilities. Voice-sensitive digital encoders could caption the news and program dialogue for the hearing impaired. The blind could use a voice-synthesized menu to select from an online library of recorded books.

WHAT ABOUT MUSIC?

Most of our new records already are produced with digital technologies. With fiber connections and the appropriate in-home terminals, we could directly access computer archives of the various music labels to construct our own libraries recorded on CD ROM disks, DAT or other storage devices.[9]

For example you could select from a menu of current hit albums or select individual songs or numbers. Say you're a real fan of Ella Fitzgerald. You could compare her renditions of a favorite song over the course of her career. If you don't know which rendition of a favorite song to choose, you could call out the recordings by a half-dozen of the best performances and compare them.

If you were getting ready for a special date, you could program an entire evening of special selections by dozens of different performers that either could run in sequence or could vary by a voice command, depending on how the evening develops.

MTV has already gained worldwide popularity for music video. The recording industry has experimented with adding video to some CDs, but the amount of information required has limited the practice. Fiber could easily provide online access to video and sound recordings.

THE UNIQUENESS OF AM AND FM RADIO

Our cable services generally offer us a selection of FM channels. The great bandwidth of fiber could certainly allow the inclusion of many, if not all, current AM and FM stations. But radio broadcasting has a unique functional capability that probably insures its survival, although not necessarily as either AM or FM.

Today much of our radio listening occurs on-the-go. We listen in our cars as we commute; we use personal radio and cassette machines as we jog or sit on the beach and as we come and go around the house and yard. Both cable and fiber depend on wire connections and so cannot provide this service, leaving a market to be shared by radio and recordings. Radio now is in a transition to digital technology, compelled by the joint impact of digital recording and the threat of digital audio satellites (DAS).

From its early days radio has had a symbiotic relationship with the recording industry. Records have provided a major portion of radio content, and playing recordings "on air" has been critical in promoting the sale of individual recordings and the careers of artists. High-fidelity LPs played a major role in raising listener expectations regarding sound quality, and those raised expectations helped FM capture the music audience. As digital recordings replace LPs, the listening public's expectations are again being raised.

The FCC has authorized the use of DAS. DAS will provide digital transmission of a choice of music services to subscribers supplied with special decoders all over the nation. Because music is such an important factor of broadcast radio programming, station managers individually and collectively are being forced to meet this competitive threat by accelerating a changeover of their equipment to digital transmission.

But such a transition is a problem for radio broadcast licensees. As with HDTV additional bandwidth will be needed, at least for the transition period, so that stations may continue their present service until digital receivers penetrate the market.[10] In the face of ever-increasing demands for spectrum space, getting the FCC to make such an allocation will be difficult.

Another problem is that the transition to digital service will eliminate the present technical differences between AM and FM stations as well as technical advantages some stations currently enjoy over others in the same service category. These advantages translate into competitive advantage which in turn translates into more revenue. The dominant stations now enjoying these advantages will resist efforts that reduce or eliminate their competitive edge.

NEW TECHNOLOGY, OLD QUESTION

The technical conversion of the entertainment industries to digital will be relatively simple and straightforward. The market and policy questions will be more difficult, particularly answering the question, Where will the money come from? Given our competitive free-enterprise economy, money inevitably will end up the focus of many of the problems.

The entertainment that will be available to us through the revolutionary technologies represents an enormous investment. How will this wealth of entertainment be financed? How will we pay for entertainment? How much are we willing to pay?

Since 1930 the share of personal disposable income spent on entertainment has not only increased (from about 5.3 percent to about 7.1 percent), but those expenditures have increasingly gone to services rather than hard goods.[11] Will this growth be sustained in a future in which we are faced with rising costs for health care, education and housing?

The vigor of our economy is such that we can confidently predict that the money will be there. Perhaps the bigger challenge will be figuring out how to sell and collect the tickets. In the end somebody has to pay the creative talent who provide the available material to entertain us through the revolutionary technologies.

THE MULTINATIONAL DIMENSION

Protection of copyrights may be a problem within our domestic market, but it is a major dilemma at the international level. Since the 1920s the products of the United States entertainment industry—feature movies, television series and music—have enjoyed worldwide popularity. During the 1980s when our trade deficit grew, entertainment (along with aircraft) was one of the few sectors in which our exports vastly exceeded imports.

The size and wealth of our domestic market allowed U.S. studios to recruit the best talent, foreign as well as domestic. The products of these studios became de facto standards for technical and artistic performance throughout the world.

American movies and TV programs have an economic advantage. For example foreign broadcasters can obtain U.S. programs in the syndication market far more cheaply than they can produce programs in their own studios. Because American producers have recovered most or all their costs in the giant domestic American market, they can be extremely competitive in the international syndication market and still make a profit.

But a solely economic explanation oversimplifies the issue. American features and TV series usually are genuinely popular wherever they play. Even in as xenophobic a market as Paris, U.S. features dominate the cinema box office. The success of American movies and TV series abroad may indicate that the multinational talent employed by U.S. studios has created an international style that transcends the American market.

PREPARING FOR A MULTINATIONAL MULTIMEDIA FUTURE

The purchase of United States movie, television and recording companies by foreign interests suggests a tacit acceptance of this thesis by some extremely large and powerful corporations interested in guaranteeing a steady supply of popular content for the technologies they operate and manufacture.

At the same time that European nations are creating a new, unified political and economic community, they are wrestling the problem of maintaining unique cultural identities. The European Community (EC) has voted common restrictions on video imports together with measures intended to encourage co-production and exchange within the community. Almost as soon as the measures were adopted, the media of the individual nations began to make exceptions.

In the meantime American studios—many now owned by foreign interests—were taking steps to establish or expand their European operations so they can operate from within the EC.

National politics prevented the realization of Arthur C. Clarke's vision of a global satellite system, but with growing multinational corporate ownership and control, it may not be possible to similarly contain multinational multimedia. The battles to prevent local cultural identities from being overwhelmed by foreign entertainment have been severe in the past—and they are probably just beginning.

Suggestions for Further Reading

Mass Media: A Chronological Encyclopedia of Television, Radio, Motion Pictures, Magazines, Newspapers, and Books in the United States is somewhat more than its title suggests. This compilation by Robert V. Hudson is a compact and comprehensive single volume providing some historical context. It attempts to tie things together from one period to the next.

Perhaps the best one-volume history of American broadcasting is Erik Barnouw's *Tube of Plenty*, 2nd revised edition. *Empire of the Air* by Tom Lewis is a history of early radio written to accompany the 1991–92 PBS documentary by the same name. As devastating as it is fascinating, *Three Blind Mice* by Ken Auletta details how inept the sophisticated executives have been in managing the three networks.

Tino Balio has edited an excellent overview, *The American Film Industry*, which was updated in 1985, and the more recent (1990) *Hollywood in the Age of Television*. Arthur Knight's *The Liveliest Art* has not been similarly updated but remains a useful and readable book on the movies.

One general overview of entertainment is John Fiske's *Television Culture*. In *No Sense of Place*, Joshua Meyrowitz takes a unique and rather provocative stance concerning the impact of the electronic media.

Notes

1. In addition to digital compression, which reduces signal capacity by eliminating redundant information from one frame to the next, compression pumps make adjustments in the running time of visual recordings. They are used to trim a few seconds from a commercial or a few minutes from a feature film. The adjustment is very small relative to the total running time, but even such small changes may distort the aesthetic intention of the producer.
2. The release of restored prints of a number of classic films often includes the reinsertion of scenes deleted when the feature was originally released.
3. The lack of a universal standard and continuing announcements of new playback technologies have also played a major role by creating consumer uncertainty.
4. Postman, Neil. *Amusing Ourselves to Death*. New York: Penguin, 1986.
5. AT&T has taken steps to be ready to offer extended credit charge services with its "Universal Card."

6. Knight, Arthur. *The Liveliest Art*. New York: New American Library, 1959; revised ed., 1979, pp. 2–3.
7. This service provides identification numbers for programs listed in the TV schedules of major daily papers and magazines. With a special adapter, viewers punch in the appropriate numbers, and their VCR automatically records the selected programs (assuming they have remembered to put a cassette in the machine).
8. During the era of radio dominance, the Mutual Broadcasting System (MBS) straggled along as a fourth network, with the status of a poor cousin.
9. Some large chain outlets, such as Tower Records, have experimented with a comparatively primitive form of such technology that permits customers to put together cassettes containing a personal selection of individual musical numbers.
10. The National Association of Broadcasters proposes a 20-year transition period during which licensees would simulcast in digital and their present service.
11. Vogel, Harold L. *Entertainment Industry Economics*. 2nd ed. New York: Cambridge University Press, 1990, pp. 15–24.

CONCLUSION

Bringing the Revolution Home: A Survey of the Communication Landscape of the Future

What could happen and what will happen are two different things. We will live somewhere in the middle. But where is that? How will things change? When will things change, and what will the change mean to individuals and to society at large?

Change has been a central element of much of this book. Yet change is disruptive, inevitable and confusing. It is difficult to nail down all the change we've tried to isolate and impossible to trace all the implications. Change always seems to move faster, and it is neither always bad nor always good. Often agents of change are double-edged swords. Evaluating their impact can be difficult, because their effects are rarely apparent until well after individuals, institutions and regulatory bodies have been set into motion. One important goal of this book has been to make the process of benefiting from change easier. We have tried to do that by examining a host of new technologies that threaten—or promise—to change the status quo. By understanding why and how change is occurring, society can take appropriate steps to maximize the benefits of change and minimize its threats.

The revolutionary technologies will create new information and communication products and services. But not all of them will be functional; consequently, not all will be successful. Some products made with the flashiest of the flashy new technologies will fail. Others will meet our changing needs for information. They will engender new models of popular communication and will spur change to threaten the status quo.

Media institutions—giant media companies in the information business; advertisers financing the media pyramid; the creators of popular art forms like film, music and prose; regulatory bodies and regulators—are on the verge of chaos. Some institutions may be pushed into obsolescence by the new products. Other institutions will benefit from the change. They will capitalize on the opportunity by learning to teach more effectively, for example, or to reach customers more efficiently.

The imminent changes in information-based products and services pose serious social questions, too:

> How can society insure that all its members have access to information? How can we guarantee media literacy for poorer nations and for poorer portions of individual countries?
>
> How can society use the new media to improve our educational and training institutions, to truly make people's lives better?
>
> How can society insure that the new technologies will be used to spur individual creativity and used not only to increase large bureaucracies' involvement in our daily lives?

A second goal of this book has been to build a framework for making a distinction between threats and opportunities. That goal can be accomplished by identifying the basic trends driving the development of future information-based communication systems. From there we can begin to evaluate the change process.

An even broader goal has been to examine the growing fuzzy regulatory areas between different communication systems. These are the tensions between the borders of Pool's regulatory models. By examining those tensions, we can begin constructing newer regulatory paradigms to allow for more equitable access to information sources.

This isn't a test; there are no sure answers. There is a fine line to walk while the game changes, and it will change with acceleration. By distinguishing between change and threat, and by considering new regulatory opportunities, predicting the future may become somewhat simpler.

A FRAMEWORK FOR PREDICTING EFFECT

In the introduction and the first four chapters, we looked at specific enabling technologies that have changed and continue to change the face of modern communication systems. Then we looked at how institutions have evolved to construct and deliver functional communication. In so doing, we learned something about what the revolutionary technologies threaten. We saw that if those new technologies, systems and standards are to become ubiquitous, something else in the communication system must change. Throughout this book we have set the stage for even greater change in our daily lives as a result of new communication technologies. Nowhere in these discussions have we said "this will be." Throughout this book we have touched on some of the reasons why it's difficult to pinpoint the changes and their effects. These roadblocks include the high cost of installing fiber optics, the need for standards, the desire to control content, the challenge of accessibility for all, changes in political leadership and agendas, the allure of great potential profitability and the threat of lost profitability. These factors combine to make predicting the future of new technologies and new communication systems a difficult task.

This book is a request for students to break down existing barriers and radically rethink the current wisdom. Media systems and structures of tomorrow *will* be radically different. If thirty years ago a professor of communication (or journalism or the social sciences) said that during the 1990s CBS would have trouble turning a profit and might go out of business, he or she would have been ridiculed. Thirty years ago broadcast television from at least one of the three networks was beamed into almost every home in the country. Free television news was a nightly ritual. It was taken for granted. If the same professor said that in the 1990s only a small portion of all Americans—the most affluent—would be able to afford the multitude of pay-tier television and information services available to them, he or she would have gained more ridicule. Yet that's exactly what's happening.

New technologies show real potential to widen the gap between the information-rich and the information-poor. Not all members of society have access to the revolutionary technologies. Similarly, seemingly unassailable institutions are showing the earliest signs of vulnerability. Anyone who expects to work in the information business, or who expects to ride or duck under the next waves, had better be able to understand why the changes are happening. That requires radically different thinking.

Media forms of tomorrow will also be radically different. If television stations and networks must change, what will happen to the nightly network news? As people watch and participate in interactive digital video forums, what will happen to popular art forms such as newspapers, magazines and books? As mass-audience broadcasting gives way to specialized pay-service narrowcasting, what are the implications for the poorest members of society, who are effectively locked out of gaining some important information? What will those changes mean for those of us who use the media or who want to work in the media?

One way to project ways the technological building blocks can be thrown together into a new media pyramid is to say "what if." We can start with some specific technological forecasts. Then we can examine the products and services those technologies can be used to create, and we can evaluate their functionality. Next we can look at the structures themselves: How well do they serve society's goals of a marketplace of ideas and non-discriminatory universal access to sources of information? And then we also can evaluate the relative ability of existing institutions to drive or survive in such a system.

Here's an example: What if personal computer screen technology developed tomorrow to the point that everyone could carry around a feather-light HDTV screen that instantly could contract to ultra-miniature or expand to wall size in seconds? What if every individual could purchase a single high-bandwidth multimedia telephone number that followed them from office to home to car to beach and back again? What if they could just whip out the magic screen when they heard that number ring and receive a call? What type of services might result? How would people use—and want to use—that kind of technology? Which of their needs might it serve? What are the societal implications of such a system? Does the system truly provide opportunity to all? Or is it constructed, financed and operated by a ruling elite? What does the system do to propagate the pluralist, libertarian ideals to which our society ascribes?

And finally, how would this system affect today's institutions? Which would prosper? Which would wither? Which types of industry, institution and society would you rather work with, in and for?

FORECASTING TECHNOLOGY

To begin to ask those questions and trace their implications, we need a simple communication-technologies forecast. The first step is to state some fundamental technological assumptions. The next is to examine the systemic implications of those assumptions. Next, the functionality of the new communications system or service must be examined. Finally we can develop several likely scenarios. They might prove fallible; only portions of them may bear out. But the process of technological assessment is the important part. It allows us to build yardsticks of how systems, institutions and society will change. Then measuring change is a little easier.

Assessing the future of a technology isn't as hard as it might seem. But it does require a little creativity and a little blind faith. It is foolhardy to begin debunking future possibilities if one hasn't stretched one's imagination to the limit. It's important to derive as many future scenarios as possible. Often the process of intellectual stretching sheds new light on how completely different subsystems may match up to create synergy or may clash to create disharmony. Only after one has described the glitziest of the possible technoglitz does the time come to chop it down to size. Only after pushing the technology to its realistic limits can one say, "But what about . . . ?" Then the constraints described in the middle portions of this book—such as regulatory, financial and those caused by consumer apathy—can be used to distinguish between likely and unlikely scenarios.

We begin by identifying three areas where technological change in communication systems occurs: at the source of communication messages, along the channel and at the message's destination.

THE DIGITAL HEADEND: NEARING CYBERSPACE

All information to be communicated to and among members of society will soon be stored digitally. This includes text, sounds, moving images and projections of reality. Eventually only the most basic of sensory inputs—words directly spoken by another human, human touch, smell and some sight—will remain as analog-based information.

Such a sweeping statement needs several caveats. The transition to digital information structures is not necessarily an all-or-none change. Some media will slowly push digital codes through their system. Many already do. Consider a CD played over an FM broadcast station. The music is digitally mastered, digitally stored, digitally recalled, converted to analog radio waves and transmitted in analog format to our radios. Ultimately all information must be converted back to analog waves, because our sensory organs understand only analog input.

This too may change. Researchers have had moderate success helping blind people "see" by means of specialized video cameras. Neurologists understand more every day about how sensory receptors in our brains recognize and process stimuli. But for the foreseeable future all information still needs that final conversion to analog, no matter how it has been gathered or transmitted.

Digitalization is slowly infiltrating every type of media system. But the changes will not happen overnight. The transition will progress slowly over the next fifty years. Some types of information—telephone transmission, for example—will be all-digital within the next ten years. Some will take only slightly more time, such as photographs and still images. Other information types, such as moving images as represented by NTSC, PAL, SECAM, HDTV and film standards and signals will take much longer—decades, not years.

What does this first assumption, that all information will be stored digitally, imply? One implication is that conventional, analog storage systems will no longer be used: no more cassettes, no more videotape, no more film, books or newspapers. Everything will be stored on the floppy disks of the future. But they won't be floppy disks; they will be credit-card size memory packs. Slip them into a camera, a multimedia terminal, a stereo speaker system or an in-the-round conglomeration of HDTV screens. Information will be communicated across time and distance in digital format.

A second implication is even more important: eventually it will be much simpler to share information across what are now distinct technologies. Information shared between scholars used to be hand-copied or photocopied. Now it may be retrieved from an electronic bulletin board, or stored and retrieved on a magnetic disk. Consider how easy it is to get information about the status of your bank accounts from an ATM. In the past that sort of information could only be gained by standing in line at the local branch, asking the teller for the information, waiting while he or she pulled up your records and finally receiving the information.

REALITY REDEFINED BY DIGITAL MEDIA

So what? What does all-digital really mean? One way of looking at it is to recognize that cyberspace is becoming reality. Cyberspace is what people experience when they use huge, next-generation computers to travel about great computer and data networks. It has been defined as "an artificial reality that projects the user into a three-dimensional space generated by computer."[1] The term was coined by science fiction writer William Gibson[2] to refer to a computer network that people use by plugging their brains into it.

Cyberspace has traditionally been the fictional domain of futurists. But cyberspace is becoming more palpable every day. Where do we go when we flip through 70 or 100 cable channels? How do we define "reality"? An individual's world used to extend no farther than he or she could see, hear, smell or feel. Early communication systems changed that. The world grew to encompass far-away places, the very large and the very small.

Electronic media have had a more radical effect. The very distant became commonplace. The far reaches of our worlds expanded to include the whole globe in real time. If members of a society spend one quarter of their waking hours watching (navigating) cable, their universe is defined not by their own experiences, but by the area traveled by distant information gatherers.

That trend is accelerated in an all-digital world. Ever-larger computer networks will store ever-larger oceans of data. With the right access technology, that data will become a vast, shapeless, boundless library of the past and present—it will become the place to go to define the future.

The multimedia cyberspace network will offer a spectacular panorama of choices. It will not be a frustrating lesson in the difficulty of operating modem and software. The terms *modem* and *computer* will fall out of everyday use as going online infiltrates our daily lives. Those terms will give our children a great deal of curious amusement, the same amusement that we experienced when our parents and grandparents used the term *horseless carriage* to describe the defining invention of their day.

Navigating multimedia cyberspace will be a transparent experience. You often won't know you're using it. When you download music or news to your portable multimedia terminal, you won't be aware of the layers of hardware and software that are making your daily information habit possible.

Sometimes using the network will be very exciting. Turn on the Skydiving Channel or the Jupiter Exploration Channel, and you will experience a completely interactive adventure. You're the boss. Want to explore that cave off to the left? Go ahead. Want to fly upside down? Just flip. Media systems will no longer just decrease distances and shorten time, they will eliminate them through virtual reality.

A NEW REALITY WILL REQUIRE NEW RULES

Of course, many questions remain. How will the cyberspace frontier be settled? Who will the settlers be? By which guiding principles will it be constructed? What type of place will it be—an overtly commercial outpost or a beneficent utopia? Will it really live up to its promise?

Before we can answer these questions we must come to grips with even more basic questions. How will we build cyberspace analogs to the physical laws defining our lives? For example, how do we account for gravity in cyberspace? The difference between what one sees and hears in cyberspace and what one feels in reality—earth's gravity—accounts for much of the nausea the early cyberspace pioneers describe.

We can construct the basic principles that will guide the development of this new community. The challenges are daunting; society must completely redefine current notions of privacy, freedom, human rights and, potentially, the entire human experience. As we develop solutions to these dilemmas we will begin to understand whether virtual reality will be a sort of public library, where anyone curious enough to enter can enter, or a private boardroom, where deals are struck between important movers and shakers.

While those questions remain to be answered, we continue with our analysis, sure in the knowledge that the construction of faster, bigger, more accessible networks and network computing engines promises to provide a radically new definition of reality.

THE ELIMINATION OF SCARCITY: DIGITAL TRANSPORT

Moving away from the source of communication, our next assumption concerns the transportation of digital information. Content-neutral, media-neutral, inexpensive digital transport systems will become ubiquitous. High-speed, digital bandwidth-on-demand services will become as available or even more available than standardized electrical current is today.

This statement contains two important components. The first is the concept of on-demand service. The basic justification for on-demand services is that different types of communication require different transport capacities. The price of a communication service is a direct function of the bandwidth used. Transmitting a simple voice-only telephone call is far less expensive than transmitting video signals, just as moving one banana from California to New York is much less expensive than moving a ton of bananas the same distance.

Consider this example: You're calling the local telephone company to question a recent bill. You know you'll be put on hold for a while. Naturally you will choose the least expensive voice service you can; why pay more just to hear the operator more clearly? But what if it's your mother's birthday? You can assemble a synthesized version of Dean Martin and Frank Sinatra crooning a "Happy Birthday" duet to open up a CD-quality connection, with the highest available fidelity. It costs a little more, but it may be worth it. Or you might want to see your mother, too. In that case after the duet you might want to open up enough bandwidth to make the voice-only, CD-quality call into a full-fledged, two-way videocall.

Some people call this type of service a video dial tone. Want to see a movie? Turn on the movie player (your multimedia HDTV personal computer television ensemble), review a list of new selections, or page through an index of subjects, actors, locations or names and pick one. Your system instantly sees how big it is (in mega-, giga- or terabytes) and figures how much bandwidth it needs to download the movie in seconds (for saving locally and viewing later). Or save on your bandwidth bill by downloading in real time. Better yet download an uneditable version that includes 10 or 20 percent commercial time (commercials, by the way, geared specifically for your buying interests and habits), and save even more on the price of the movie and transmission.

The second important component of this assumption is that transport is technology- and system-neutral. You won't know—and won't care—whether your telephone calls are being carried by copper or optical fiber cables. You won't know—and won't care—whether you're getting your HDTV CNN feed from the phone company, a broadcast common carrier or maybe straight off the satellite or MMDS microwave. You won't know if your mobile telephone call is going over a cellular system or a satellite system. Your communication management software seeks out the least expensive way automatically. In much the same ways that a small, simple computer today constantly monitors and adjusts the operation of your automobile's engine (gas mixture, air flow, temperature, etc.), your personal network manager will take care of bandwidth, media and billing.

PERSONAL COMPUTER OR TELEVISION? OR BOTH? OR MUCH MORE?

Finally we examine technologies that will shape future receivers, the devices people will use to take advantage of the powerful forces unleashed by the previous two trends. The convergence and continued rapid development of personal computer technologies—microchips, displays, storage and software—will allow the creation of a powerful new information terminal that will perform many of the functions paper, appointment books, telephones, radios, televisions and computers do today—and many more.

Technological convergence is a term to describe how advances in different technologies enable new, previously unheard-of creations. For example consider the semiconductor. It required huge leaps in many different technologies: microscopic manufacturing techniques, circuit design, materials handling and heat dissipation, to name just a few. Without any one of them, the semiconductor would never have been built. The inventors of the enabling technologies knew nothing of the semiconductor; it hadn't been invented yet. But each of their contributions was critical. Similar advances are now occurring in four technologies that will allow the creation of the new information terminal: microchip "engines" to manipulate instructions and data, display screens, memory storage of several varieties and software to run it all.

MICROCHIPS

Theologians once debated how many angels could fit on the head of a pin. Today designers of semiconductors have their own debate: Just how many transistors can fit on a tiny piece of silicon? No one knows for sure, nor are they likely to until well into the 21st century. It is clear that the number, already huge, is continuing to grow at a geometric rate, with no end in sight.

For the foreseeable future microchips will continue the incredible, exponential growth in power that has spawned such comparisons as this one: If cars evolved at the rate of semiconductors, we would all be driving Rolls Royces today that go a million miles an hour and cost 25 cents apiece. Microchips have grown with enough speed to spawn Moore's Law to describe the process. First formulated in the 1960s by the founder of Intel Corporation, it initially stated that the number of transistors per chip doubled every two years. In the 1970s the law was amended to reflect the quickening pace of development; it now holds that the number doubles every 18 months and quadruples every three years.

How does that affect our information terminal? Microchips drive the terminal. They are its brains, heart and lungs. As they grow, our small terminal takes on the power of today's supercomputers. They are able to perform hundreds of millions of computer instructions every second; to construct and display multiple, three-dimensional color images in milliseconds; to manage many tasks at once, such as monitoring information channels, scanning news headlines, making appointments and verifying and reconciling financial accounts.

DISPLAY SYSTEMS

Today's display screens are either too big and heavy or not clear enough. A trade-off exists between picture quality (clarity, color and resolution) and portability. But this trade-off will not be necessary much longer.

Already researchers are developing notebook-sized color screens with the resolution of today's most dazzling technical workstations, with thousands of colors and hundreds of thousands of pixels. Some are wall-sized, flat screens that can be neatly hidden in living rooms.

STORAGE

Computers today rely on a spinning magnetic disk to store and save data. That's clumsy, because it requires a power source to drive the motor that spins the disk where data resides in tracks like music on an LP. The combination of power source, motor and disk is heavy and cumbersome. Key developments in memory chips will soon render magnetic disks obsolete. Two-megabyte memory cards (enough to hold hundreds of pages of text) are now widely available. Four-megabit chips are already in production, while 256-megabit chips will be readily available by 1999 at the latest.

Today's palmtop computers hold dozens of megabytes of data on a credit card-size memory card. Tomorrow's portable multimedia terminals will download and store hundreds of megabytes. Inexpensive, easy-to-use, abundant storage is just around the corner.

THE NEW SOFTWARE: TENTACLES CONNECTING EVERYTHING

The operation of multimedia terminals will be coordinated by a new generation of software. It will oversee our different information and entertainment needs and act as our personal assistant. The new software will be so advanced and ubiquitous that it will be to today's software as the supersonic Concorde is to the Wright Brothers Kitty Hawk plane.

Actually the day-to-day responsibility for managing our information and entertainment habits requires hundreds, even thousands, of different pieces of software performing different tasks independently, yet ultimately all working together. All the pieces must be nearly perfect, lightning fast and easy to use—so completely user friendly that we don't even know we're using a sophisticated system. Multimedia terminal software needs to talk to a variety of larger systems. Software at the headend needs to interact with hundreds of different types of digital appliances. This is no small feat.

We have examined some of the problems associated with building this kind of software network in our discussion in Chapter 11. Creating a simple but powerful interface so that our terminals and the multimedia network are easy to use is a daunting challenge. Establishing standardized indexing schemes and standards for the interoperation of different types of hardware (from large and small computers to digital appliances scattered around our homes, cars and offices) will be a huge and very important challenge.

Even the most basic of these challenges is difficult: Software that manipulates many different kinds of data (numbers, pictures, sounds and images) has been developed, but it requires continued refinement. The problems associated with operating many different tasks at once (the way the human brain does) are only beginning to be addressed. Making a computer more closely approximate the operation of the human brain requires great technological leaps.

We are beginning to understand the scope of the challenge, and advances in software technology are beginning to solve these problems. New ways of programming that re-use good programming over and over and allow programmers to insert selections from a program library into their projects promise to help. Building artificial intelligence into programs helps the programs help themselves. The challenge is to build a product that begins to manage information as well as the human brain does. However, because we don't fully know how the prototype works, it's very difficult to build the production models!

THE INFORMATION TERMINAL: THE PERSONAL COMPUTER OF THE FUTURE

Advances in microchips, display technologies, storage systems and software are reshaping the concepts of television and personal computer. One result of the convergence is that top-of-the-line television sets are more like personal computers. What used to be called a television is now a video screen. Tomorrow's screens will incorporate computer functionality. The amazing functionality of the new devices will render today's dinosaurs obsolete.

Windowing and "picture in a picture," for example, will be considered as primitive as rubbing sticks together for fire. Home computers, HDTV sets and communications managers will be video mailboxes, video editors and video postmasters. Television sets will be computers that manage digital information of every type, computers optimized for image processing. The future of television is inexorably tied to advances in computer technology.

The personal computer will rapidly become a personal window into cyberspace, the car by which you navigate information highways. It will be equipped with multiple channel-management devices to allow it to monitor what the news channel is covering while you watch the ball team. It will constantly check your video mailbox, keeping an eye out for any personal messages, or combing through thousands of direct-marketing entertainment and commercials that might interest you, all while you're off elsewhere or watching other things. It will help you manage your finances and will let you participate in international, interactive political and entertainment forums.

How this will all happen is somewhat unclear. That it *will* happen is not unclear. Society is at an information crossroad. The challenge to take advantage of these technologies and changes is at hand, and the gauntlet is down. But it will not be easy. Some industries and institutions clearly stand to win market share (and the potential for long-term profitability), and others are threatened. Some threatened institutions are very powerful; they will do everything they can to resist the changes. But they can do nothing to stop the trends we've identified. Such an attempt would be similar to a quill-pen manufacturer trying to stop the spread of the typewriter. It just won't happen.

What will happen? We'll start by looking at the systemic and structural implications of the technology forecasts.

TECHNICAL ADVANCES AND SYSTEMIC CHANGE

The trend toward media-neutral bandwidth on demand becomes more real every day. But not without a fight: Some of society's largest and most powerful institutions (telephone companies, broadcasters and cable companies) have gained their might based upon the simple existence of bandwidth scarcity—whether spectrum scarcity or the limitations of telephone or cable transmission systems. Unlimited transport is a real threat; they might have competition. Competition, the most fundamental tenet of capitalism, reduces prices to end users to the lowest practical level.

For individual members of society and for many of society's larger organizations (businesses and government bodies), lower prices for communication services is good news. It means the system is working to achieve at least one important result: the greatest good for the largest number. But to threatened institutions, lower prices and competition mean they have to work harder for less per-unit reward. The unnaturally comfortable level of operation they've enjoyed in the absence of competition is threatened. So they resist change, even if the total potential is far greater. That's why some lawmakers have a tough time answering the roll call to the regulatory challenges we discussed earlier. Similar services should be similarly regulated. It's difficult enough simply developing a regulatory system that can work across different technologies. When powerful lobbying organizations start pushing and pulling in different directions, institutional inertia seems to increase, and nothing gets done.

Threatened media and communications institutions are attempting to limit competition, but their efforts are bound to fail. Competition across traditional technological domains will increase. Cable companies will compete with telephone companies for the information pipeline-to-the-home business. Private fiber optic carriers will compete with regional telephone companies. Local broadcasters will feel competition from any carriers who think they can identify, gather and package news better than the established stations. What used to be the sole differentiator, that the local stations could get a signal into your home and onto your television, will become irrelevant. Anyone will be able to hire a carrier—telephone, cable, low-power television, DBS or MMDS. Existing companies must learn to recognize the business they really are in—packaging news and entertainment—before someone comes along to do it better. If they continue thinking along the old lines, they really are in trouble.

Unlimited transport bandwidth will become the new communication paradigm. With transport no longer the bottleneck, what becomes the critical differentiator among information providers? What will separate the mediocre from the great? Consider another way of asking the same question: What's the difference between a good newspaper and a great one? Between a good radio station and the best in a market? Between a so-so magazine and a best seller? We identify two related abilities: knowledge of the audience and creativity, which includes packaging information or entertainment to meet audience needs. Information providers (broadcast stations, television networks, news bureaus, etc.) that can produce the appropriate information for an audience in the way the audience wants it will always be able to sell it.

CAN INSTITUTIONS REDEFINE THEIR BUSINESS MODELS?

The wide-open, transport-unconstrained future requires that today's information providers, carriers and managers undergo a great deal of strategic soul-searching. What got them where they are now may not be enough to keep them there. The systems by which they profited may no longer be profitable. The time-honored relationships between advertisers and carriers may not hold up. Consumers may expect to pay nothing, or they may expect to pay a lot. Changes in the roles of key players in the advertising, publishing and broadcasting industries are equally momentous.

Consider the broadcast networks. Their business may completely change from distribution to packaging. Instead of transmitting information they may need to focus all their energy and finances on becoming production houses that stage, produce and market huge, global "edutainment" and "infomercial" events. Or they may perish.

The changing nature of the business realities of today's broadcasters and newspapers has other systemic implications. In fact it promises to change the very content of forms—artistic, journalistic and entertainment—developed under the old system. Equally important the changes strike at the very core of how media systems are financed. We look first at the implications on expressive forms.

THE EVOLUTION OF ART AND COMMUNICATION FORMS

Communication products and services must change to meet the needs of the people who create and use them. Technology changes how those people can create and use communication. The resulting products are new and different, but the process continues. We call this trend the evolution of art and communication forms.

Consider the concept of journalism. The ability to access online databases simply and easily will likely redefine the role and importance of gatekeepers and journalists. Individuals will no longer be dependent upon gatekeepers to sort out information and to rate the relative importance of news and other information. Newer, more functional forms of communication made possible by the new technologies will evolve to meet society's changing needs.

For example columnists and commentators will take their messages straight to the people over the multimedia network. Neither the national nor the local media outlets will choose who the commentators or columnists, the experts, are. Anyone and everyone will be able to publish and broadcast their views. Individuals will choose who they want to see, hear or read from among a list of millions.

Entertainment forms will also undergo change. Euripides created the first great literary form: drama. It was later refined by playwrights such as Shakespeare to meet the needs of his era. Cervantes invented the novel in the 16th century. Today the short story is a more popular literary form. Television has superseded most others, and it is the most popular of today's entertainment forms. Each form filled a need for entertainment and storytelling, a need that was uniquely defined by the people of the day. While some of the older art and entertainment forms have persisted, they have had to grow and stretch to meet the needs of modern people.

More recently we have seen the growth (and some might say death) of art forms: magazines, the cinema and the situation comedy. Each new form was made possible by new technologies. Each may be superseded as newer technologies allow for the creation of even more functional entertainment forms.

Some of those artistic formats are already emerging. They include interactive fiction, interactive television and interactive video. But hypertext fiction, Nintendo and "Adventure" games (pioneered by early computer gamesters) are just the beginning. They will become far more elaborate and far more engrossing.

Still newer art and entertainment forms are coming, such as virtual-reality universes that operate on creative variations of our traditional social and cultural values. What will they be? Who will develop them? How will they affect the institutions around them—in some cases, the very institutions that created them?

PINPOINT MARKETING

The familiar systems of media financing—advertiser-supported, subscription, one-time fees, etc.—are in for a shake-up. One only needs to look at the impact of cable on network television to get a feel for the implications of our technology forecast on the advertiser–programmer–carrier–consumer relationship. At most, the shake-up literally blows the middle out of that multi-billion-dollar pipeline. At least, it radically alters the balance of power among them. Either way the old way of doing business, of financing programming through broad-based advertising, is in for a change. We call this the trend toward "pinpoint marketing." How will advertising change? Who are the big winners and losers? When will the changes occur? It's still too early to tell. We can make a few educated guesses by examining basic trends.

Networks of media outlets that promise to deliver a national audience must address the new reality: the national market is far less attractive than it used to be. Fragmentation and specialization are the name of the game. That's not to say the desire to advertise to broad, national audiences will ever go away. It won't. Mega-events like the Super Bowl will remain valuable ways of reaching mass, nationwide audiences, although that is still an audience dominated by males. But with communications channels weaving millions of miles across, over and through the United

States, the oligopolist national TV networks can no longer call the shots. Indeed, the networks are turning to negotiation and more creative approaches to sell their space.

The whole concept of advertiser-supported video programming is questionable. Cable television and VCRs were the first technologies to bring programming to consumers unfettered by commercials—much in the same way that books and specialized periodicals such as advertising-free newsletters exclusively brought information to consumers. The trend will continue. The result will be both boom and bust for national advertisers and their carriers. Boom, because carriers, realizing that in some cases people are willing to pay a huge premium for commercial-free programming, will package their programs in ways to deliver what the customer wants—and nothing else. Listen to your customers and you'll succeed; ignore them and you won't. And bust, of course, because many institutions have only recently realized that the rules have changed.

The gulf between commercial-free television and PPV programming will widen. Why buy more than you will watch? Television service will become like electrical service. Turn on a lamp (or a computer or a toaster), and a few weeks later the electric utility sends you your monthly bill reflecting how much electricity you used. In such a billing system, you don't get charged a flat fee just because you *might* want to use the toaster. (But if you did, the cost would be relatively small.)

The same model will apply to communication service. Want to watch HBO? No problem: Watch for 90 minutes and two weeks later your bill for 90 minutes of A-tiered service will arrive in the mail. The concept of pay-per-view as a special option will dissolve, because almost every high-quality TV event will be pay-per-view. Or you will have the opportunity to watch the sponsored version and get commercial credits that reduce your TV bill. This model has serious implications. If the local carrier I use knows which type of programs I like to watch, how much more do they know about me? And what does that mean? Will I like that? Well, they'll know a lot. And the fact that they know it very likely will change the way you live your life.

Growth in the ability of carriers to monitor and track individual consumers' media habits and preferences will have a radical impact on media finance. This is the future of focused marketing. Today advertisements for sports equipment and for cars go on sports channels. Research has determined that men sitting around watching other men play golf are more likely to buy sports equipment and cars than are, for example, children watching animated cartoons on Saturday morning. In its most simple form, that is focused marketing.

CUSTOMIZED, PERSONALIZED ADVERTISING

Suppose an advertising manager at the local carrier could insert specific commercials that will appeal to individuals. You've heard of direct mail? This is direct—pinpoint—marketing. For example carriers will be able to determine that on a specific date a certain person watched a certain type of television show on the history of the European elm trees in New England. The carrier can take that name, and the name of every other person who watched that same show, to a local nursery warehouse and say: "I can guarantee these people have an interest in horticulture. Do you have any trees (fertilizer, tools, seeds, services, etc.) in which you think they might be interested?" The next time that person signs on the TV network, he may get a message saying something like, "Smith's Nursery and Florists is running a special on trowels and Triple Strength Fertilizer. Want to learn more about it? Press 'yes' now!"

That's direct marketing on a show-by-show basis. Not season to season, not channel to channel. Advertisers don't waste money telling something important to people who don't care. Consumers don't waste time listening to something they don't care about. Of course general-purpose, broad-based informational advertising will always be around, but it will be optional. After all, spending a half hour paging through a video catalog from Bloomingdale's or L. L. Bean can be very entertaining and relaxing.

PERSONAL INFORMATION FOR SALE

Suppose that same advertiser could start putting information together from a variety of sources, and consider that an industry of "consumer data brokers" will develop to help him. Today direct marketers buy and sell lists of names that meet specific socio-economic criteria. They're just names and addresses, but that will all change; in the future much more specific information will be traded. Along with names and addresses will be other kinds of information: possessions, media habits, interest areas, education levels, vacation preferences and so on. Instead of the message mentioned above, you might see something like this:

> Mr. Jones, are your solar panels still charging quickly? Is your electronic map up to date? Are your afterburners still firing as precisely as ever?
> The electronics on the 1997 Chevrolet Futura you purchased four years ago are due for regular maintenance.
> Would you like to view some testimonials from your neighbors, or shall we schedule a visit for next week, which is your first available time, according to your appointment calendar?

Or you might see this:

> Mr. Jones, our records show it's been seven months since your 1997 Chevrolet Futura was tuned up. While you're in next week, you may also be interested in our tire sale. Alloy-belted radials for the Futura are usually $125 each, but today we're selling them for only $90. The attached spreadsheet shows how large your monthly payments will be. And we've already figured in your after-tax rebate, for your convenience. Just click "OK" now to look at those payments, or to let our schedulers figure out a convenient appointment for both of us. And don't forget your wife's birthday. Shall we send a dozen roses, or would you prefer some of those African violets she purchased last summer?

In short, mass marketing will give way to the most focused marketing of all: a target of one. If you own a sporty coupe model of the Futura, you might be offered a special deal on high-performance tires. If you had a more economical model, you might be offered long-lasting economical tires.

Obviously, detailed personal information has value to advertisers. It will help them make more sales less expensively. They might even be willing to pay for it. This is the trend toward selling personal information, rather than just giving it away.

To date, advertisers have not had the chance to be so selective. They could only buy broad lists of individuals culled from other lists according to fairly specific socio-demographic criteria. Personal information has been next to impossible to gather and very difficult to act upon if it has been gathered. Instead, we are identified according to broad types of buying behavior. Major advertisers have developed models of different consumer buying patterns (early adopters and laggards, among many others) into which we fall. Then they buy advertising in specific magazines and specific types of television shows that their target market will likely be watching.

A NEW INDUSTRY: DATA BROKERS

In a free-market economy, objects are bought and sold at prices determined by the forces of supply and demand. Their value is largely a function of scarcity. In the future personal information will be viewed as a commodity. And, like pork bellies, it will be sold to the highest bidder. In the future consumers will have the ability to sell their attention to advertising to advertisers. A byproduct of pinpoint marketing will be turning personal information into a commodity.

A new industry of personal-data brokerage will develop to intermediate between individuals and advertisers. Data brokers will be able to offer consumers credit for watching commercials between plays of the football games. Before sitting down to watch the game, the consumer will run through a range of offerings on the screen. With no commercials the game will cost $15.95. With ten minutes of halftime commercials, it will cost $4.95. With regular 30-second spots between possessions, the game will be free. The football fan, depending on whether friends will be coming over, the importance of the game or on his other plans for the evening will choose whichever edition of the game is most convenient.

Individual advertisers will not be able to keep all this information about consumers. To do so would require an uneconomically huge investment in computer equipment. Instead, personal information warehouses will emerge. These businesses (data brokers) will guard and maintain all information about specific individuals. They will sell appropriate portions of individual profiles to appropriate advertisers, based on their clients' (consumers) requests. Data brokers will tailor advertising to individuals' very specific needs. They offer advertisers the ability to reach the right audience more easily, lowering advertisers' costs, increasing marketing and market efficiency. Once the fan has decided which version of the game he wants—the advertiser-supported or the $15 version—he will send that choice to his data broker. The broker will notify appropriate advertisers who have previously indicated a desire to communicate with that fan.

These won't be the low-involvement commercials we're used to today. These commercials will demand attention. They will ask questions based on the information the advertiser already has assembled. The advertisements will be focused, personalized appeals about products in which you've already shown an interest. You will not be able to avoid the advertisements by sneaking into the kitchen for a snack, because your participation will be required. The advertiser will be able to recognize if you do not respond to certain questions or fill in certain blanks on the electronic forms. If you do not respond, the advertiser will not be receiving the one-on-one contact it had been promised by the data broker. As a result the advertiser will receive some kind of "make good" from the broker. And you probably will be charged a higher fee by the broker for the programming you had been watching, because you didn't live up to your end of the original agreement. The question for the consumer: Is it worth it?

PRIVACY FOR SALE

Programmers will offer their products with advertising or without. Consumers will sell the use of their name to advertisers for programming credits. If a consumer chooses to avoid all advertising, that's fine. He or she must simply pay more for access to programming. But the specter that data brokers keep all this information about individuals has implications. Most implications are rather frightening, particularly when information from different sources is assembled into an entire consumer profile. Armed with information about what types of cars, appliances, clothing and food we prefer, companies may gain an uncomfortable degree of understanding of our personal lives.

What might happen if information falls into the wrong hands? What if a data broker specializes in tracking where and when we like to vacation, how we're likely to return from vacation and what we're likely to buy upon returning? With little ingenuity that data broker can schedule precise robberies. Other data brokers could conveniently let information leak between databases to their own advantage.

While dozens of safeguards will be built into the brokerage (such as "smart" home-alarm systems and data "firewalls" that would prevent sharing of certain types of data) the opportunity for egregious abuse does indeed exist. Is this really what we want? Where can society draw the line? How will society define personal privacy? The way direct mail now floods into our mailboxes and homes, is it unreasonable to wonder whether the system will be abused? Will it be possible for an individual to draw the line? If so, how?

JUST THE RICH?

Will the full range of options for financing one's media habits be open to all members of society? Just as families at higher levels of socio-economic standing can afford to buy and eat fancy South American fruit or beluga caviar and can shop at expensive markets, so will they have the choice to pay a little more for their information to increase personal convenience. A greater number of information options will be open to more affluent members of society. Consider another segment of the economy, retail clothing. Only a few members of society can make use of the personal shopping consultants offered by upscale boutiques and shops. These consumers pay more for their clothing because they attach enough value to the extra services they receive in those shops.

THE FORK IN THE ROAD

The trends toward unconstrained bandwidth, the evolution of art and communication forms, the development of pinpoint marketing and the establishment of value for personal information create opportunities, not just threats. Perhaps the most important challenge is one of balance. How can we as a society use these new technologies to our best advantage? In other words, which regulatory systems and models can we employ to achieve that goal? At the heart of this question is another, deeper question of balance: How can society maximize individual creativity while concurrently insuring that the new technologies serve the greatest social good?

While some of these questions will remain unanswered, we know that change is in the wind. How we will use technology to communicate, what we will expect to communicate and how and what we learn will all change. A knowledge of the underlying forces causing the surface changes allows us to judge the implications for individuals in society who will continue to rely on communication services.

What about those who have decided to seek careers working for media and communications organizations? They, like all people, in part define themselves through their work. If their jobs change fundamentally, so may they! These changes may have very significant implications for them, their careers and their decisions to enter the media.

The trends we've identified here will allow and even require us to change how we live our lives. As we have seen, for journalists, broadcasting professionals, publishers, writers, artists, actors and dozens of other professionals the revolutionary technologies and their subsequent systemic changes may require that they change how they view themselves and their livelihoods.

Even more broad-based changes are at hand for individuals, changes that will affect anyone who uses communications media. With digital messages coming to us over wider and wider communications channels (messages that often are directed directly at individuals because the sender knows something about us), the concepts of media management and media literacy will become increasingly important. That means more than just knowing how to negotiate the electronic frontier. Media literacy means knowing how to gather information: identifying what information is required, selecting it, retrieving it and presenting it. It means controlling information, instead of being controlled by it.

THE CHALLENGES OF MEDIA LITERACY

Members of society are as challenged by the new technologies of communication as is any institution. How we gather, discard and use information will need to be changed. The amount of information is increasing exponentially. To learn to manage our use of information efficiently, we need to be media literate.

Media literacy is more than just a liberal dose of skepticism. To be passive is to be illiterate. A member of society used to be able to ignore the dominant media of the day if he or she so chose: Avoid reading the paper; don't watch the evening news. But in an increasingly interactive, intrusive world, that's no longer an option. The world—people, places, prices, products and rules—will change too fast without you.

To be media literate is to possess the ability to separate the information wheat from the chaff. The challenge is twofold. The first challenge concerns individuals. Media literacy means changing individual habits. Media-literate people will understand how to use the mammoth information resources around them to make the process of identifying and responding to change natural and simple, not a trial and tribulation. Media literacy means embracing change, not recoiling from it.

Knowing what technology can do and how to use it are part of being media literate. The growing use of AI agents will certainly help. The overwhelming amount of information must be proactively managed—not just reactively managed. To that end media-management software systems become important extensions of ourselves.

The second challenge of media literacy is broader in scope. It entails providing appropriate education to insure media literacy at all levels of society. In this light continuing education takes on a sudden and dramatic new importance. When we say continuing education, we're not talking about basket weaving for senior citizens anymore; we're talking about the difference between feeling helpless and feeling powerful. The revolutionary technologies are changing so quickly that ongoing educational maintenance is universally important.

Sometimes the future is viewed as a threat to our own personal status quo. Indeed the potential exists for technology to be used to suppress individual thought, creativity and freedom. The "Big Brother" of Orwell's *1984* is not completely farfetched. But the trends we've identified here can mean a new and better world. It can mean using information to make society more efficient. The media literate will not only have the will to change the world, but the power to change their parts of it. The revolutionary technologies are every bit as much opportunities as threats—but only if that is how we choose to use them.

SOCIETY'S CHALLENGE: INSURING EQUITABLE ACCESS TO ELECTRONIC INFORMATION

How can society use the new technologies to effect positive change? How can we use them to shape a fairer, more responsive and more efficient society? The United States has a great tradition of egalitarianism. Throughout our history the ideal by which almost all public policy was created has been the individual. The basic unit of policy making has been the individual, not peoples, regions or governments. Those policies have sought to maximize the rights, protections and possibilities for individual thought, creativity and responsibility.

No other country has a tradition like the American dream, which implies that the aspirations and goals of every member of society are equally important, from the top to the bottom, from the most privileged to the least.

Our society has protected these ideals with such laws as the First Amendment. As a result our social institutions—creative, structural and regulatory—attempt to foster and expand upon those ideals. Today's communication systems openly and freely provide information that people can use to form opinions, to coordinate response to outside actions, to build consensus and to motivate action and change. They help people build a better society.

As the form of information and communication has changed, so has society. Beyond just guaranteeing free speech, our society has gone to great lengths to insure access to all types of information. The vast public library system represents openness and availability of information to all members of society. The land-grant colleges were built for the sole purpose of making information and education available to underprivileged and underrepresented members of society.

Making those decisions was never easy. In fact, our country's founders made many courageous decisions. The First Amendment was just one of them. The decision to allocate public tax funds to make information accessible to more people through public libraries and land-grant colleges are just two examples. And neither of those choices was particularly easy.

Our country's founders had several choices in 1789, just as we do now. It might have been easier for them to select a lesser route than the path they chose. They could have chosen to imply freedom of speech but not state it directly and clearly. Perhaps they could have stated the importance of free speech but then not provided the funding for a network of public libraries and institutions of higher education.

Our society has today arrived at a similar fork. We must now choose to travel the long road bounded by the very ideals which shaped this nation or the path of least resistance. If our commercial, educational, legal and social institutions fail to recognize the opportunity that now exists, access to the newest electronic media might become a privilege, rather than an individual's birthright.

The challenge at hand is to insure that all of society has equitable access to electronic information through the revolutionary technologies. The challenge is every bit as fundamental as the decisions facing James Madison and Thomas Jefferson 200 years ago. Applying quick fixes might protect specific interest groups, but they are not long-term solutions. Simply removing some of today's restrictions on competition, or merely introducing market competition within specific technological domains, will not insure the equitable distribution of the new information services. Free, fair access to information will be achieved only by regulatory mandate, prescient public thinking and the wise deployment of public funds.

The chance to change the world is a fleeting one. The chance to change the shape of a new communication system usually arrives too late—when the medium is frozen in place. Today a rare opportunity exists to shape this new communication system in the public interest without sacrificing access, diversity or financial return. If we act now to be inclusive, rather than exclusive, we can create an open and free electronic community in America. To fail to do so and to lose this opportunity, would be tragic. To seize the opportunity and establish the technical and legal framework for a new communication era—the Information Age—would be an achievement no less revolutionary or heroic than the work of Madison and Jefferson.

Notes

1. Freedman, Alan. *The Computer Glossary.* 5th ed. New York: The American Management Association, 1991.
2. Gibson, William. *Neuromancer.* New York: Berkely Publishing Group, 1984.

Glossary

access channel—A cable-systems channel that the operators make available for programming by local groups.

addressable system—A cable-television computer system that can activate each subscriber converter box. The cable operator instantly can scramble or unscramble the picture for pay-tier and pay-per-view channels within individual homes.

adjacency—A time period between broadcast programs during which a station inserts a commercial.

advanced television (ATV)—A term used interchangeably with HDTV or high-definition television.

Advanced Television Test Center (ATTC)—The facility in Alexandria, Va., that conducts comparative on-air testing of HDTV systems proposed for adoption as the new U.S. television standard.

agent—A software program that seeks out news and information for a person or for another software program.

amortize—An accounting term used to describe the process of spreading the cost of a capital project (such as upgrading a copper-based network to fiber) over the life of the project, rather than having to absorb the cost all at once.

analog code—A signal code that corresponds directly to message content; for example, sound waves, which are the direct result of the vibration on vocal chords, guitar strings, etc.

artificial intelligence (AI)—A broad range of computer applications that exhibit human intelligence and behavior. AI also implies the ability to learn or adapt by examining repetitious patterns and recognizing links between seemingly unrelated elements of information.

audion tube—The name Lee de Forest gave to his adaptation of Edison's incandescent light bulb, which made it possible to amplify and tune electrical signals. Audion tubes became generally known in the United States as *vacuum tubes*, which were the basic component of broadcast transmitters and receivers until the development of the transistor. In England they are called *pumps*.

availability—Unused inventory of commercial broadcast time; in other words, an unsold spot for commercials.

bandwidth—A measure of a communication channel's capacity; for example, the bandwidth of a twisted-pair copper telephone cable is 20 kHz and that of an FM radio station is 200 kHz. The greater the bandwidth of a channel, the greater the amount of information it can carry simultaneously.

barter syndication—An arrangement whereby television program syndicators reduce or waive the fee a station pays for a program or series in exchange for the right to sell and retain the income from some of the availabilities during the program.

billing kiosk—A service through which users may access a menu of content choices or transactions, which provides the user with a comprehensive bill and allocates revenues to the various service providers.

binary—A language composed of only two pieces of information, *0*s and *1*s. Meaning is generated by building complex arrangements of the two digits, which can be used to describe other information.

bit—The most elemental form of digital information: an "on" or "off" signal corresponding to high or low voltage in a semiconductor; the *0*s and *1*s of computers.

Boolean algebra—A mathematical model based on series of statements involving combinations based either on *and* or *and/or*.

broadband service—A term used to describe any communication service that requires more bandwidth than voice (telephone) service. Typically it is used to indicate a cable television service, but it also refers to interactive video services such as home shopping or video catalogs.

broadcasting—The dissemination of radio communications intended to be received directly by the public or by the intermediary of relay stations (as defined by the Communications Act of 1934).

bypass—The practice of using a private communication channel to avoid paying premium prices charged by local telephone companies. For example, a company with two office buildings located one mile from each other might place a small microwave dish on each. Then, rather than buying or leasing fixed lines between the two buildings from the local telephone company, voice, data and video signals can be transmitted between the two over the microwave.

byte—A combination of 8 bits, used to create digital "alphabets." (*See* digital code.)

cathode ray tube (CRT)—An electronic tube that provides the viewing screen of standard television sets and computer terminals.

Carterphone decision—A 1968 Supreme Court decision that forced AT&T to allow customers to own their equipment and to buy equipment from companies other than AT&T.

C band—One of the range of frequencies of the electromagnetic spectrum used for satellite communications. The C band allocations are in frequencies between 1 and 10 GHz.

CD-ROM—An optical storage medium that can store thousands of pages of text, tens of hours of audio, up to several hours of video or any other type of digital information.

cellular telephone—Within a geographic area (a cell) mobile users on land are linked by microwave to computers connecting them into the local telephone switching system. The systems are coordinated so that as the user moves, the call is handed off from one system to the next with no interruption of service.

channel—Arbitrary boundaries incorporating a specified range of frequencies of the electromagnetic spectrum or wired communication system. When different users are assigned to such discrete channels they can share the capacity of the system without interfering with one another.

circulation—A measure of audience size. In print media it generally means the number of copies sold or distributed. In broadcast media it refers to the total number of viewers or listeners who tuned to a station during a week-long period.

common carrier—A communication system that is regulated to insure fair treatment of all customers. To insure fairness common carriers are prohibited from generating content themselves, and must provide carriage to any paying customer (except those sending grossly misleading or indecent services). The best-known common carriers include railroads, truck lines and telephone operating companies.

compression—A process whereby unnecessary or redundant information is eliminated from a message. This reduces the bandwidth requirement and allows more messages to be carried within a channel.

co-op advertising—Advertising paid for by more than one entity. For example, a national manufacturer may pay part of the cost of a local department store advertisement that features its product line.

CPM—Cost per mille (thousand), a comparative measure of how much it costs to reach 1,000 people using different media.

CRT—*See* cathode ray tube.

cyberspace—A term used to refer to the illusion of reality created when computer-generated stimuli are used to replace the naturally occurring stimuli that surround us.

database—Any electronically stored collection of information; a set of interrelated files that is managed and stored by a central software system called a database management system.

DBS—*See* direct broadcast satellite.

decoder—Any device that translates encrypted information into a usable form.

dedicated line—A telecommunications link for the private use of a single company or group of companies or individuals.

demographics—In the mass media, this term is used for statistics that describe the composition of an audience by sex, age, etc.

digital audio broadcast (DAB)—The use of digital signals for either AM or FM radio broadcasting.

digital audio tape (DAT)—Tape recordings that use digital signals, rather than the analog signals used in conventional audiocassettes.

digital code—A language comprising only two pieces of information, *0*s and *1*s. Meaning is generated by building complex arrangements of the two digits, which can be used to describe other information. In constructing such a digital language, each 0/1 choice is a *bit*. By using different combinations of eight choices (a *byte*), we can establish digital "letters" to enable us to encode the letters, numbers and editing symbols in our alphabet.

digital service—A communication channel purchased from a local or long-distance carrier using digital codes as a basic transport mechanism. It does not require a digital-to-analog conversion in order to transmit digital data.

direct broadcast satellite (DBS)—System designed to use satellites to distribute programs to individual users, bypassing broadcast stations and cable systems.

disk drive—A device that stores digital information on spinning magnetic platters.

download—The process of requesting and receiving information from a central host computer. In today's electronic mail systems, for example, your messages can be downloaded from your central mailbox to any remote terminal from which you call. In the future information such as feature films may be stored digitally in a central location and downloaded in seconds to your television or personal computer.

D-RAM—Dynamic random-access memory; microchips used to store information in computers.

electromagnetic spectrum—The range of electromagnetic energy waves, part of which includes the waves used for the various forms of radio communications: AM, FM, TV, microwave, etc.

electronic mail service (EMS)—Sending and receiving written messages via the telephone by using personal computers and modems.

electronic news vehicles (ENV)—Specially equipped vans that contain video cameras, simple editing equipment and a microwave transmission tower that relays video signals to a central receiver.

encryption—The encoding or "scrambling" of information in order to prevent its unauthorized use.

enhanced television (ETV)—A method of reprocessing the NTSC signal to improve the image quality. The number of scanning lines is increased by 50 percent.

Eureka—The name given to the HDTV system being developed for use within the European Economic Community.

Fairness Doctrine—An FCC regulation, rescinded in 1986, requiring broadcasters to seek out spokespersons for opposing points of view on issues broadcast in the station's editorials. The FCC action led to congressional attempts to legislate the doctrine, but President Reagan and President Bush successfully overrode the measures.

feed—External source of information (usually audio or video) that arrives at local stations for use in news or entertainment programming.

fiber optics—*See* optical fiber.

first-run syndication—Producers may put a program or series into syndication to stations or cable services for the initial showing, rather than selling the first and second performance rights to a major network and then putting it into off-network syndication.

fly away—A compact collection of satellite equipment (camera, editing gear, uplink and downlink) that can be stored in several airline-ready trunks for transportation to any remote event.

footprint—The geographic area covered by transmission of a satellite signal.

function (of communication)—Communication facilitates four basic functions: information, persuasion, education and entertainment.

gallium arsenide (GaAs)—A material that carries electric current faster and with less resistance than silicon. New computers built using GaAs chips will be faster than the silicon-based computers of today.

gatekeeper—A media professional who determines what types of information constitute news: editors, producers and journalists. More broadly gatekeepers include the institutions that set the agenda for what types of information will be considered news.

geosynchronous orbit—An orbit 22,300 miles above the earth's equator in which an object such as a satellite moves such that it remains above the same point relative to the earth's surface at all times.

hardware—The mechanisms and devices used in computer and communication operations; e.g., personal computers, modems, printers, microphones, cameras, switchboards.

HDTV—*See* high-definition television.

Hertz—The term used to denote the frequency or cycles per second of electromagnetic energy waves. The use of this term honors Heinrich Hertz, the German physicist who experimentally confirmed the existence of radio waves in 1887.

hierarchy of switches—The successive series of points at which information messages may be switched for transfer from one point to another.

high-definition television (HDTV)—Television that provides pictures of a quality rivaling that of projected 35-mm film.

Hi Vision—The term used by NHK of Japan to denote its operational HDTV system.

homes passed—The number or percent of television households passed by a cable system, including those households not subscribing to the service.

horizontal integration—Owning or controlling similar companies or institutions, such as newspaper chains, cable MSOs or broadcast groups.

HUT—Households using television; the number of homes watching television at any given time. The figure is used as the base for calculating broadcast shares.

hypertext—A form of organizing information in computers that permits the linking of any place in text (or other media) to any other place and the rapid retrieval of information by following trails of these associative links.

impulse PPV—An interactive service allowing cable subscribers to order special charge programs with the punch of a button of their remote tuner.

information service—Any type of interactive source of information that can be accessed through a telephone, personal computer or other means.

integrated circuit—Single pieces of silicon—microchips—onto which transistors, diodes, resistors and capacitors are formed and then interconnected by electrical paths provided by a film of aluminum. By using a photochemical process, the design pattern can be reduced so that hundreds of thousands of components can be printed onto a single microchip.

intelligent network—A network comprising a complete infrastructure (switches, transmission lines, etc.) that will enable advanced functions such as bandwidth management and universal personal telephone numbers.

INTELSAT—International Telecommunication Satellite Organization.

interexchange carrier—A company that provides long-distance telephone service between local service areas.

inventory—The amount of space (such as pages in a publication or broadcast time) available for sale to advertisers.

ISDN—Integrated services digital network; a system for managing different types of messages on a single network. ISDN provides a standardized, interoperable, digital, broadband communication service that anyone with the appropriate adapter can use anywhere. ISDN provides "plug and play" communication between personal computer and video terminals.

ITU—International Telecommunications Union, the United Nations organization coordinating use of the electromagnetic spectrum and standards in electronic telecommunications.

K bands—Two of the ranges of frequencies of the electromagnetic spectrum used for satellite communications. The Ku band allocations are in the frequency range between 12 and 14 GHz; those of the Ka band are between 20 and 30 GHz.

key word—A word or symbol in a hypertext document that has been indexed to facilitate the formation of hypertext links for extremely rapid search procedures. A key word is also a search term in any computerized information system.

liquid crystal display (LCD)—A technology used on small personal computers for displaying information. LCDs may eventually be developed as an alternative to cathode-ray tubes for displaying television signals.

local loop—The network of cables used to connect individual subscribers to the public telephone network. Local loops feed into local switching centers, where trunk lines connect to the rest of the public network.

local operating company (LOC)—A telephone company that has been granted authority to provide telephone service within a specific area. The company's physical network allows callers to make local connections within the area, or to connect to interexchange carriers that then connect to other telephones anywhere in the world.

long lines—High-capacity (usually fiber optic) cables used to connect long-distance switching centers to each other.

massively parallel processors (MPP)—*See* parallel computers.

microchip—*See* integrated circuit.

MIPS—Millions of instructions per second, a measure of computer or microprocessor calculation speed.

modem—A device serving as a conversion interface between digital technology and transmission systems that use analog signaling. For example modems allow us to use the analog telephone system for transmitting digital data from one personal computer to another.

multichannel, multipoint distribution system (MMDS)—A microwave service that can deliver 30 or more channels of television to subscribers equipped with special antennas and decoders.

multimedia—Universally available, standardized audio, image, video or data communication based on a single technical standard and network.

multimedia communication—The use of a multimedia system to achieve the transfer of printed, audio, video, image or other types of information. It is the product that is made possible by the use of a multimedia platform.

multimedia platform—A system combining four computer technologies: personal computers, a communication channel, storage capability and software.

multiple systems operator (MSO)—A company that owns and operates more than one local cable television franchise.

multiplexer—A device that can combine two or more signals within a single communication channel; for example, FM stereo is accomplished by multiplexing.

narrowcasting—A programming strategy that targets specific audience segments and in which sheer audience size is considered less significant than the homogeneity of the target audience.

niche audience or market—A group identified by shared interests, characteristics or behavior; for example, working mothers, teenagers, hockey fans, country and western aficionados or people wanting to lose weight.

NTSC—The current broadcast television standard in the United States and most of the Western Hemisphere nations, as well as Japan, Korea and the Philippines. Although more nations use the PAL standard, NTSC sets outnumber those of all other standards combined.

off-network syndication—Networks normally purchase the right for the first and second showing of a program. After the second showing on the network, the producer puts the program into off-network syndication and anyone—other networks, cable networks or individual stations—may bid for the right to show the program for a specified number of times, after which the program is again available to bidders.

online service—The name given to a variety of (usually) personal computer–based services making use of modems and a central host computer. These are usually available through a kiosk service such as Prodigy, CompuServe, Easy Link, etc.

optical drives—A device that stores digital information on spinning platters triggered on and off by high speed lasers; for example, CDs.

optical fiber—Very fine wire made of high quality glass or, in some cases, plastic through which flashes of light generated by extremely high speed lasers may be transmitted.

PAL—Phase alternating lines; a broadcast television standard developed in West Germany and also adopted by Great Britain. Because most Commonwealth nations and former British colonies followed the British example, PAL is used by more nations than any other standard.

parallel computers—Computers comprised of thousands of small processors rather than just one or two very fast processors. By working together, parallel computers can accomplish some kinds of computing far more efficiently than traditional computers can.

pay tier—The cable channels that are not included in the basic monthly service and for which viewers must pay an additional monthly surcharge; for example, HBO, Disney, Playboy.

pay to basic—The ratio of subscribers who take one or more pay-tier channels to the cable system's total subscriber base.

performance fees—A fee paid for the right to use a creative production. As programs go into syndication, the performance fee is based on a sliding scale reflecting the size of the market, the age of the production and the number of times it has already been used.

personal interest profile (PIP)—A list of topics and relationships assembled by an individual that are used to guide searches for news and information through databases.

pinpoint marketing—Any marketing effort that is aimed at specific people, not groups of people; a step beyond marketing that aims at specific socio-economic or demographic segments of the population.

pixel—An individual element making up a picture. The greater the number of pixels per units of area, the finer the picture quality. A frame of 35-mm color film contains some 500,000 pixels, as does a fully scanned picture in HDTV.

POTS—"Plain old telephone service," the term applied to basic telephone service.

Prime Time Access Rule (PTAR)—A regulation promulgated by the FCC in 1974 that forces affiliates to forego network entertainment programs for one hour at the beginning of the evening prime time period during the week.

radio communication—The Communications Act of 1934 defines radio communication as using the waves of the radio bands of the electromagnetic spectrum to transmit writing, signs, signals, pictures and sounds of all kinds.

rate averaging—Regulatory agencies allow common carriers to have a varying rate of return on different classes of services so that a higher rate of return on high-traffic, efficient exchanges is used to offset losses from low-traffic, high-cost exchanges.

rating—The percentage of all television-equipped homes in which a set is turned on and tuned to a specific station or program.

redundancy—Repetition or duplication of information within communication signals; the continuation of the same information from one frame, scan or phase of a sequential communication.

Regional Bell operating company (RBOC)—Any one of the seven "baby Bells," which are the primary providers of local telephone service in various parts of the nation. They include NYNEX, Bell Atlantic, BellSouth, Ameritech, Southwestern Bell, USWest and Pacific Telesis.

release cascade—The sequential release of a movie for exhibition in different media, such as cinema theaters, videocassette, pay-per-view, network TV, etc.

residual fee—A fee paid to creative talent as a share of the income from repeated play of a commercial or from program syndication.

satellite news vehicle (SNV)—A truck equipped with video newsgathering equipment and a satellite uplink to transmit video signals.

scanning line—Television cameras transmit pictures by dividing the image into lines (525 in NTSC), each of which is scanned by an electronic eye 30 times per second to create the transmission signal.

scarcity—Because orderly use of the spectrum requires its division into a limited number of channels, spectrum space or channels is said to be a "scarce" commodity. This premise is used to justify the licensing and regulation of spectrum users by the government.

SECAM—Sequential Colour Avec Memoire, a broadcast standard developed in France and used by other nations with close cultural ties to France as well as in much of Eastern Europe.

semiconductor—Glasslike material that conducts electricity and that can be sliced into tiny wafers, into which are etched tiny circuits. Semiconductors form the basis for all types of memory chips, integrated circuits and microchips.

share—A measure of audience computed as a percentage of only the homes in which the television set is turned on, in contrast to the *rating*, which is based on the total number of television households. Therefore the share for a program, station or network will always be larger than the rating.

signal area—The geographic area with dependable reception of the signals emitted by a broadcast transmitter.

sine wave—The periodic waveform that results from oscillatory motion. For example this can be displayed by attaching a pen to a pendulum and then passing a roll of paper beneath the pendulum at uniform speed. The pen, tracing the movement of the pendulum, would draw a sequence of sine waves.

slot—A specific point in the geosynchronous orbit at which telecommunications satellites are stationed.

software—(1) A set of instructions, encoded in a distinct language, that guide the operation of a computer. The instructions contained in the software set up the necessary switching paths within the microchips for performing some function such as data calculation, word processing or graphics. (2) In station programming, entertainment material prerecorded on film, videotape or some other medium.

spot beam—A beam that results when satellite transmitters are focused on relatively small signal areas; the resulting increase in signal strength may reduce the size of dishes required at the point of reception.

technological convergence—The result of advances in two or more different technologies that produce new breakthroughs, products or services that could not be achieved by advances in a single technology.

telco—Term used to denote any type of telephone company: carrier, manufacturer or local operator.

television households (TVHH)—The total number of homes with television, the number used as the base for calculating broadcasting ratings.

television receive only (TVRO)—A satellite dish installation used to intercept the satellite distribution of video networks.

transistor—A device that combines several semiconductors to perform a specific type of function through which the power of selected electrical currents can be increased.

transponder—One unit of the electronic components within a telecommunications satellite.

trunk line—A high-capacity (usually fiber optic) cable used to connect telephone switching centers to one another.

twisted pair—The type of copper cables most prevalent in the local loop of the public telephone network. Twisted-pair cables currently have the capacity to carry two telephone conversations concurrently but have been shown ultimately to be able to carry much more.

upstream—The direction from subscribers' homes to the headend in an addressable cable television system. Programming travels downstream, from the headend to subscribers. Pay-per-view requests travel upstream.

vertical integration—A strategy for reducing a business's costs by controlling all aspects of operations, from supplies and production to distribution and sales.

video dial tone—A proposed telecommunication service that would make placing video telephone calls as simple as placing voice-only telephone calls is today.

videotex—A system providing access to alphanumeric and graphic information via telephone lines or interactive cable systems. Users must have appropriate display screen to receive information and numeric keypad for indicating choices from menu selections.

virtual reality—A computer-simulated reality that can interact with more than one of the senses, usually touch, sound and sight.

visual persistence—The phenomenon that produces the perception of motion when we watch television or motion pictures.

voice information service—Recorded or synthesized messages provided by telephone.

voice mail—The application of computers to the processing of telephone-mediated communication; a computer designed to function as a telephone answering machine.

VSAT—Very small aperture terminals; small satellite receiving installations used primarily for business and data communication.

window—A specific time period during which one medium has protected access to program material; e.g., cinemas have a three-month window before movies are released in either videocassette or PPV channels.

Bibliography

1991 U.S. Economic Review. Press Release, Motion Picture Association of America, January 2, 1992.

'89 Facts About Newspapers. Reston, Va.: American Newspaper Publishers Association, 1989.

'90 Facts About Newspapers. Reston, Va.: American Newspaper Publishers Association, 1990.

'91 Facts About Newspapers. Reston, Va.: American Newspaper Publishers Association, 1991.

Adams, Dennis M., Helen Carlson and Mary Hamm. *Cooperative Learning and Educational Media: Collaborating With Technology and Each Other.* Englewood Cliffs, N.J.: Educational Technology Publications, 1990.

America's Watching. New York: Television Information Office, 1987.

Andrews, Edmund L. "F.C.C. Report Predicting Gloom for Broadcast TV," *New York Times,* June 27, 1991, p. D26.

Arlen, Gary H., with Suzan Prince and Mark Trost. *Tomorrow's TVs.* Washington: National Association of Broadcasters, 1987.

Arlen, Michael J. *Living Room War.* New York: Viking, 1969.

Armand, Mattelart. *Advertising International.* New York: Routledge, 1991.

Asker, James R. "Upstart Satellite Companies Press for New Telecommunications World Order." *Aviation Week and Space Technology,* October 7, 1991, pp. 50–54.

Augarten, Stan. *Bit by Bit.* London: Unwin Paperbacks, 1985.

Auletta, Ken. *Three Blind Mice.* New York: Random House, 1991.

Bagdikian, Ben H. *The Information Machines.* New York: Harper & Row, 1971.

———. *The Media Monopoly.* Revised ed. Boston: Beacon Press, 1990.

Balio, Tino. *The American Film Industry.* Revised ed. Madison: University of Wisconsin Press, 1985.

———. *Hollywood in the Age of Television*. Boston: Unwin Hyman, 1990.

Barnouw, Erik. *A Tower in Babel*. New York: Oxford University Press, 1966.

———. *Tube of Plenty*. 2nd ed. New York: Oxford, 1990.

———. *The Golden Web*. New York: Oxford University Press, 1968.

———. *The Image Empire*. New York: Oxford University Press, 1970.

Bennett, W. Lance. *News: The Politics of Illusion*. 2d ed. New York: Longman, 1988.

Bingham, Joan Carol. "PC Graphics and Video Products." International Data Corporation Reports 5451, March 1991, and 5544, April 1991.

Bliss, Edward, Jr. *Now the News*. New York: Columbia University Press, 1991.

Block, Alex Ben. *OutFoxed*. New York: St. Martin's, 1990.

Blumenthal, Howard J., and Oliver R. Goodenough. *This Business of Television*. New York: Billboard Books, 1991.

Bogart, Leo. *Press and Public*. 2d ed. Hillsdale, N.J.: Lawrence Erlbaum Associates, Inc., 1989.

———. *Silent Politics*. New York: John Wiley, 1972.

Boorstin, Daniel J. *The Americans: The Colonial Experience*. New York: Vintage Books, 1958.

Bortz, Paul I., Mark C. Wyche and James M. Trautman. *Great Expectations*. Washington, D.C.: National Association of Broadcasters, 1986.

Bryson, Bill. *The Mother Tongue*. New York: William Morrow, 1990.

Budd, Richard W., and Bent D. Ruben. *Beyond Media*. Revised ed. New Brunswick, N.J.: Transaction Press, 1991.

Bureau of the Census. *Historical Statistics of the United States Colonial Times to 1970*. White Plains, N.Y.: Kraus International Publications, 1989.

Burnham, David. *The Rise of the Computer State*. New York: Vintage Books, 1983.

Byron, Christopher. *The Fanciest Dive*. New York: Norton, 1986.

Carnegie, Dale. *How to Win Friends and Influence People*. New York: Simon and Schuster, 1936.

Carroll, Glenn. *Publish or Perish: The Organization Ecology of Newspaper Industries*. Greenwich, Conn.: Jai Press, 1987.

Carter, T. Barton, Marc A. Franklin and Jay B. Wright. *The First Amendment and the Fifth Estate*. Mineola, N.Y.: The Foundation Press, 1986.

———. *The First Amendment and the Fourth Estate*. Mineola, N.Y.: The Foundation Press, 1984.

Cater, Douglas. *The Fourth Branch of Government*. Boston: Houghton Mifflin, 1959.

Chaffee, C. D. *The Rewiring of America*. New York: Academic Press, 1987.

Chiles, James R. "Goodbye Telephone, Hello to the New Communications Age." *Smithsonian*, February 1992.

Clarke, Arthur C. "Extraterrestrial Relays: Can Rocket Stations Give Worldwide Radio Coverage?" *Wireless World*, Vol. LI, January-December 1945.

———. *2001: A Space Odyssey*. New York: New American Library, 1982.

Coll, S. *The Deal of the Century*. New York: Atheneum, 1986.

Comstock, George. *The Evolution of American Television*. Newbury Park: Sage Publications, 1989.

Cook, Philip S., Douglas Gomery and Lawrence W. Lichty, eds. *American Media*. Washington: The Wilson Center Press, 1989.

Cooley, Charles H. *Social Organization*. Glencoe, Ill.: Free Press, 1956.

"Counting on Technology." *Wall Street Journal,* October 21, 1991, p. R15.

Crespi, Irving. *Public Opinion, Polls, and Democracy*. Boulder: Westview, 1989.

De Sonne, Marcia L. *Satellite Issues: 1987*. Washington, D.C.: National Association of Broadcasters, 1987.

———. *Television Satellite Newsgather*. Washington, D.C.: National Association of Broadcasters, 1988.

Dizard, Wilson P., Jr. *The Coming Information Age*. 2d ed. New York: Longman, 1985.

Donnelly, William J. *The Confetti Generation*. New York: Henry Holt, 1986.

Donow, Kenneth R. *HDTV: Planning for Action*. Washington: National Association of Broadcasters, 1988.

Dordick, Herbert S. *Understanding Modern Telecommunications*. New York: McGraw-Hill, 1986.

Douglas, Susan J. *Inventing American Broadcasting, 1899–1922*. Baltimore: Johns Hopkins University Press, 1987.

The Electronic School. Alexandria, Va.: Institute for the Transfer of Technology to Education. Special supplement to *The American School Board Journal* and *The Executive Educator,* October 1991.

Fiske, Edward B. *Smart Schools, Smart Kids*. New York: Simon and Schuster, 1991.

Fiske, John. *Television Culture*. New York: Routledge, Chapman and Hall, 1987.

Franklin, Bob, and David Murphy. *What News*. New York: Routledge, 1991.

Fraser, J. T. *Time: the Familiar Stranger*. Amherst: University of Massachusetts Press, 1987.

Frasson, Claude, and Gilles Gautheir, eds. *Intelligent Tutoring Systems: At the Crossroads of Artificial Intelligence and Education*. Norwood, N.J.: Ablex, 1990.

Freedman, Alan. *The Computer Glossary*. 5th ed. New York: The American Management Association, 1991.

Gans, Herbert J. *Deciding What's News*. New York: Vintage, 1980.

Gantz, John, and Jack Rochester. *The Naked Computer*. New York: William Morrow and Co., 1983.

Gassée, Jean-Louis. *The Third Apple*. New York: Harcourt Brace Jovanovich, 1985.

Gibson, William. *Neuromancer*. New York: Berkely Publishing Group, 1984.

Gilbert, John K., Annette Temple and Craig Underwood, eds. *Satellite Technology in Education*. New York: Routledge, 1991.

Gilder, George. *Microcosm: The Quantum Revolution in Economics and Technology*. New York: Simon & Schuster, 1989.

Gitlin, Todd. *Inside Prime Time*. New York: Pantheon, 1983.

Graber, Doris A. *Media Power in Politics*. 2d ed. Washington, D.C.: Congressional Quarterly, Inc., 1990.

Graham, Margaret B. W. *RCA and the VideoDisc: The Business of Research*. New York: Cambridge University Press, 1986.

Haigh, Robert, George Gerbner and Richard B. Byrne. *Communications in the Twenty-First Century*. New York: John Wiley & Sons, 1981.

Head, Sidney W., and Christopher H. Sterling. *Broadcasting in America*. 6th ed. Boston: Houghton Mifflin Company, 1990.

Horn, Robert E. *Mapping Hypertext*. Lexington, Mass.: The Lexington Institute, 1989.

Hovland, Roxanne, and Gary B. Wilcox. *Advertising in Society*. Lincolnwood, Ill.: NTC Business Books, 1989.

"How Powerful Will Computer Chips Be in the Year 2023?" *New York Times*, December 29, 1991, Sec. 3, p. 1.

Hudson, Heather. *Communication Satellites: Their Development and Impact*. New York: The Free Press, 1990.

Hudson, Robert V. *Mass Media: A Chronological Encyclopedia of Television, Radio, Motion Pictures, Magazines, Newspapers and Books in the United States*. New York: Garland Publishing, 1987.

Inglis, Andrew F. *Behind the Tube: A History of Broadcasting Technology and Business*. Boston: Focal Press, 1990.

Isaacs, Norman E. *Untended Gates*. New York: Columbia University Press, 1986.

Joslyn, Richard. *Mass Media and Elections*. Reading, Mass.: Addison-Wesley, 1984.

Kahn, Frank J., ed. *Documents of American Broadcasting*. New York: Appleton-Century-Crofts, 1968.

Kellner, Douglas. *Television and the Crisis of Democracy*. Boulder, Col.: Westview, 1990.

Kidder, Tracy. *The Soul of a New Machine*. Boston: Atlantic-Little, Brown, 1981.

Knight, Arthur. *The Liveliest Art*. New York: New American Library, 1959; revised ed., 1979.

Kotler, Philip. *Marketing Management: Analysis, Planning, Implementation and Control*. 6th ed. New York: Prentice-Hall, 1988.

Lee, Leonard. *The Day the Phones Stopped*. New York: Donald I. Fine, 1991.

Lewis, Justin. *The Ideological Octopus*. New York: Routledge, 1991.

Lewis, Tom. *Empire of the Air*. New York: Harper Collins, 1991.

Lichtenberg, Judith, ed. *Democracy and Mass Media*. New York: Cambridge University Press, 1990.

Lichter, S. Robert, Stanley Rothman and Linda S. Lichter. *The Media Elite*. New York: Hastings House, 1986.

Liebling, A. J. *The Press*. New York: Ballantine Books, 1961.

Lowell, Robert T. S. "Once to Every Man and Nation." *The Hymnal of 1970*. New York: Church Publishing House, 1970.

Lowenstein, Ralph L. and John C. Merrill. *Macromedia*. New York: Longman, 1990.

Lucky, Robert W. *Silicon Dreams—Information, Men and Machines*. New York: St. Martin's Press, 1989.

Lyle, Jack. *The News in Megalopolis*. San Francisco: Chandler Publishing Co., 1967.

Madsen, Axel. *60 Minutes: The Power and The Politics*. New York: Dodd Mead, 1984.

Mallowan, Agatha Christie. *Come Tell Me How You Live*. New York: Dodd, Mead and Company, 1946.

Markoff, John. "Denser, Faster, Cheaper: The Microchip in the 21st Century." *New York Times*, December 29, 1991, p. F5.

McLuhan, Marshall. *The Medium Is the Massage*. New York: Random House, 1967.

Meyer, Philip. *The New Precision Journalism*. Bloomington: University of Indiana Press, 1991.

Meyrowitz, Joshua. *No Sense of Place*. New York: Oxford, 1985.

Mickelson, Sig. *From Whistle Stop to Sound Bite*. New York: Praeger, 1989.

Minsky, Marvin Lee. *The Society of Mind*. New York: Simon and Schuster, 1986.

Mirebito, M. and B. Morgenstern. *The New Communication Technologies*. Boston: Focal Press, 1990.

Monush, Barry, ed. *International Television and Video Almanac 1991*. New York: Quigley Publications, 1991.

Moran, James. *Printing Presses: History and Development from the Fifteenth Century to Modern Times*. Berkeley: University of California Press, 1973.

Mott, Frank Luther. *History of American Journalism*. Revised ed. New York: Macmillan, 1950.

Newsroom Management Handbook. Washington, D.C.: American Society of Newspaper Editors, 1985.

Noll, A. Michael. *Introduction to Telecommunication Electronics*. Boston: Artech House, 1988.

———. *Television Technology: Fundamentals and Future Prospects*. Boston: Artech House, 1988.

Paper, Lewis J. *Empire*. New York: St. Martin's Press, 1987.

Parenti, Mochal. *Make Believe Media*. New York: St. Martin's Press, 1992.

"Phone Companies Could Transmit TV Under FCC Plan," *New York Times*, October 25, 1991, page A1.

Picard, Robert G. *Media Economics*. Newbury Park: Sage Publications, 1989.

Pierce, John R. *Signals*. San Francisco: W. H. Freeman and Company, 1981.

Pierce, John R. and A. Michael Noll. *Signals, the Science of Telecommunications*. New York: Scientific American Library, 1990.

Pool, Ithiel de Sola. *Social Impact of the Telephone*. Cambridge: MIT Press, 1977.

———. *Technologies of Freedom*. Cambridge: The Belknap Press of Harvard University, 1983.

———. *Technologies Without Boundaries*. Cambridge: Harvard University Press, 1990.

Postman, Neil. *Amusing Ourselves to Death*. New York: Penguin, 1986.

Potter, Walt. "A Modest Role Emerges for Videotex Systems," in *Presstime*, August 1991, pp. 12–15.

Powe, Lucas A., Jr. *The Fourth Estate and the Constitution*. Berkeley: University of California Press, 1991.

Prendergast, Curtis. *The World of Time Inc*. New York: Atheneum, 1986.

Prentiss, Stan. *Satellite Communications*. 2d ed. Blue Ridge Summit, Pa.: TAB Books, 1987.

Ramsey, Douglas K. *The Corporate Warriors*. Boston: Houghton Mifflin Co., 1987.

Rice, John F, editor-in-chief. *HDTV: The Politics, Policies, and Economics of Tomorrow's Television*. New York: Union Square Press, 1990.

Rivers, William L., Wilbur Schramm and Clifford G. Christians. *Responsibility in Mass Communication*. 3d ed. New York: Harper & Row, 1980.

Robinson, John P. "TV's Impact on Everyday Life: Some Cross Cultural Evidence," in *Television and Social Behavior,* volume IV. Eli Rubinstein, George C. Comstock, and John Murray, eds. Bethesda, Md.: National Institute of Mental Health, 1972.

Rochester, Jack and John Gantz. *The Naked Computer*. New York: William Morrow & Co., 1983.

Satellite Communication. Untitled special insert on satellites in geosynchronous orbit. July 1991.

Schramm, Wilbur. *The Story of Human Communication: Cave Painting to Microchip*. New York: Harper & Row, 1988.

Siebert, Fredrick S. *Four Theories of the Press: The Authoritarian, Libertarian, Social Responsibility and Communist Concepts of What the Press Should Be and Do*. University of Illinois Press, 1956.

Smith, F. Leslie. *Perspectives on Radio and Television*. 2d ed. New York: Harper and Row, 1958.

———. *Perspectives on Radio and Television*. 3d ed. New York: Harper and Row, 1988.

Squire, Jason E., ed. *The Movie Business Book*. New York: Simon and Schuster, 1983.

Stephens, Michael. *A History of News*. New York: Penguin, 1988.

Statistical Abstract of the United States 1989. Washington, D.C.: Bureau of the Census, 1989.

Statistical Abstract of the United States 1990. Washington, D.C.: Bureau of the Census, 1990.

Statistical Abstract of the United States 1991. Washington, D.C.: Bureau of the Census, 1991.

Tebbel, John and Mary Ellen Zuckerman. *The Magazine in America*. New York: Oxford, 1991.

Turow, Joseph. *Media Industries*. New York: Longman, 1984.

Useem, Elizabeth L. *Low Tech Education in a High Tech World: Corporations and Classrooms in the New Information Society*. New York: Free Press, 1986.

Vogel, Harold L. *Entertainment Industry Economics*. 2d ed. New York: Cambridge University Press, 1990.

Weinstein, Stephen B. *Getting the Picture*. New York: Institute of Electrical and Electronics Engineers (IEEE) Press, 1986.

White, Adam, ed. *Inside the Recording Industry*. Washington, D.C.: Record Industry Association of America, 1988.

Wiese, Michael. *Film and Video Financing*. Studio City, Calif.: MW Productions, 1991.

———. *Film and Video Marketing*. Studio City, Calif.: MW Productions, 1989.

Williams, Frederick. *Technology and Communication Behavior*. Belmont, CA: Wadsworth, 1987.

Willis, William James. *Surviving in the Newspaper Business: Newspaper Management in Turbulent Times*. New York: Praeger, 1988.

Winston, Brian. *Misunderstanding Media*. Cambridge: Harvard University Press, 1986.

Wright, Charles R. *Mass Communication*. 3d ed. New York: Random House, 1986.

INDEX

ABC Television, 121, 124
Access channels. *See* Cable
A. C. Nielsen Corp., 158n, 166
Advanced television (ATV). *See* High-definition television
Advanced Television Test Center (ATTC), 72, 76
Advertising
  barter syndication, 168
  broadcasting, 120, 124, 161, 212
  cable, 130, 212
  content in media, 160–161
  cost per mille (thousand) (CPM), 146, 166–167
  demographics, 121, 123, 165–166
  expenditures, 121–123, 161, 167, 175
  influence on news media content, 120, 164
  interactive, 168–169
  multimedia, 133, 233, 234
  newspaper, 120, 123
  niche markets, 124, 165–166, 176, 178n
  pinpoint, 234
  restrictions, 92
  See also Persuasion
Aesthetics, 205–206, 209
Alpha Lyracom, 37
Alport, Floyd and Gordon, 159n
AM (amplitude modulation). *See* Radio
American Federation of Musicians, 131
American Motion Picture Producers Association, 215
American Newspaper Publishers Association (ANPA), 51, 161
American Society of Composers, Authors and Publishers (ASCAP), 131
Ampex, 79
Analog energy waves, 23
Analog environment, 26
Anheuser Busch Corp., 165
Apple Computer, Inc., 57–58, 99
Archives. *See* Libraries
Arianne, 42n
Armstrong, Scott, 13
Artificial intelligence (AI), 192–193, 196, 199, 200n, 231, 240
Artistic license, 206
Aspect ratio, 69–70
Associated Press (AP), 143
AT&T (American Telephone and Telegraph Company), 20, 48, 66n, 90, 113, 119, 157, 170, 209, 220n
  infrastructure change, 107–109
Athens, 82
Atlanta *Journal* and *Constitution*, 159n
ATS-1 satellite, 41
Audience measurement, 101, 158n, 166
Audion (tube), 21
Audit Bureau of Circulation, 158n, 166

Babbage, George, 55
"Baby Bells," 108, 170
Bandwidth, 74
  high-definition television, 73–75
  on demand, 232
Battle of New Orleans, 29
Bell, Alexander Graham, 26, 168
Bell Laboratories, 20
Bit, 23
Black market. *See* Piracy
Body Shop, The, 178n
Books
  copyright problems, 198–199
  electronic publishing, 196–197
  number published, 185
  variety of formats, 191
  See also Libraries
Boolean algebra, 23
Bork, Robert, 174
Broadband services, 120, 132, 208
Broadcasting
  advertising, 118, 120, 212

259

Broadcasting (*continued*)
   audience, 145–146, 211
   characteristics, 101
   definition, 101
   financing, 214
   First Amendment, 101
   multimedia, 232
   news, 144–146, 151–152, 164
   non-profit, 135n
   ownership restrictions, 91
   policy, 85–86, 91–92, 101, 214
   program sources, 131
   public broadcasting, 135n
   See also Networks; Radio; Television
"Bugs." *See* Computers
Byte, 23, 28n

Cable, 89
   access channels, 155, 216
   advertising, 212
   audience, 211, 216–217
   Bronx (New York) franchise, 53
   cross-ownership, 91
   history, 106–107
   interactive, 169
   multimedia, 232
   multiple system operator (MSO), 88, 130, 208, 212, 215
   must-carry provision, 97n
   networks, 212
   news, 146, 154–155
   optical fiber, 49
   pay-per-view (PPV), 130, 132, 168, 216, 217, 235
   penetration, 130, 214
   piracy, 42n, 113–114, 115, 131
   policy and regulation, 51, 88, 91–92, 96n, 97n, 106–107
   program sources, 131, 214
   revenue, 130, 132, 134
   satellite delivery, 212
Cable Communications Act of 1984, 51, 92, 96n
Carnegie, Andrew, 186
Carterphone decision, 108
Cater, Douglas, 140
Cathode Ray Tube (CRT), 69–70
C Band, 40
CBS television, 124, 178n, 212, 223
CD-ROM, 25, 156, 186, 190, 191
CDs. *See* Recording industry
Cellular mobile. *See* Telephone
Chain Broadcasting Rules of 1941, 91
Change
   barriers to, 232
   individual, 239

   mass media institutions, 4, 239
   societal, 4–5, 223, 239–241
Channels. *See* Electromagnetic spectrum
Christie, Agatha, 189, 200n
Cinema. *See* Movies
Clarke, Arthur C., 1, 3, 30, 37, 220
CNN (Cable News Network), 95, 109–110, 114, 147, 154
Codes
   analog, 7
   digital, 7–9, 23, 26–27, 205–207, 225
   digitization, 196, 225–226
   Morse, 46
Colorization, 205
Commodity value of information, 3
Common carrier
   characteristics, 102
   multimedia, 228–229
   new services, 102
   policy, 86–87
   rate structures, 119
Communication functions, 5
Communication process, model of, 99–100
Communication Revolution, 1, 2, 5, 9–10, 13, 15, 87, 96
Communications Act of 1934, 72, 84, 85, 87, 91, 101
   Section 315, 92, 213, 214
Community antenna TV (CATV), 88
Compression, 75, 209, 220n
Computers
   "bugs," 56
   computer literacy, 185
   data inputting, 193–196
   digitization, 193–196
   history, 55–57
   storage, 230
Constitution, 83
   First Amendment, 82, 84, 85, 87, 91, 92, 97n, 103, 133, 241
   Interstate Commerce Clause (Article I, Section 12), 82
   Patent Provision (Article I, Section 8), 82, 84
CONUS, 153–155
Copyright, 82, 84, 89, 131, 198, 219
Cost per mille (CPM). *See* Advertising
Cronkite, Walter, 158n
Cross-ownership, 91, 109
C-SPAN (Congressional Satellite Public Affairs Network), 147, 155
Cyberspace, 225–227, 231

Data brokers, 237–238
de Forest, Lee, 21, 203
Demographics. *See* Advertising
Dewey Decimal System, 189
Digital Audio Broadcasting (DAB), 102, 218
Digital Audio Satellite (DAS), 218
Digital audio tape (DAT). *See* Recording industry
Digitization, 193–196, 205–207, 217, 225–226
Direct broadcast satellites (DBS). *See* Satellites
Domains, of telecommunication, 100
   broadcasting, 102–103
   common carrier, 102
   crossover between, 102, 232
   press, 100–102
   resistance to change, 232
Dordick, Herbert S., 11, 15, 27
Douglas, Susan J., 11
D-RAM, 24
Duopoly Rule, 91

Eastman Kodak, 207
Edison, Thomas Alva, 21, 26, 106, 182, 203
Education
   artificial intelligence, 192, 196, 199, 200n
   electronic publishing, 196–197
   expansion, 184–185
   financing, 197–198
   hypermedia, 194–195
   information storage and retrieval, 188–195, 196, 198–199
   learning skills, 180, 185–186
   literacy, 185, 239–240
   purposes, 180–181, 182–183
   technologies, 184–185
   See also Libraries; Schools
Einstein, Albert, 192
Electrical signals, 47
Electrification, 203
Electromagnetic energy, 17–18
   use of, 20–21
Electromagnetic spectrum, 17–18
   channels, 18, 74, 84, 86, 91, 218, 232
   international issues, 89
   interstate commerce, 84
   new users, 88
   policy, 85–86
   satellite use, 40
Electronic news vehicle (ENV), 152
Electronic publishing, 196–197

E-mail, 133, 175
Encryption, 45
Enhanced television (ETV), 69, 77n
Entertainment
　expenditures, 219
　history, 202–204
　industry, 202
　market factors, 205–206, 219
　multimedia, 234
ESPN, 155
Eureka, 72
European Economic Community (EEC), 72, 95, 114, 220

Facsimile. *See* Fax
Fairness Doctrine, 92
Fax, 89, 132, 159n, 175
Federal Communications Commission (FCC), 52, 72, 77n, 84–88, 91–93, 96n, 103, 114, 208, 218
Feynman, Richard, 192
"Fibered" nation, 213
Fifth Estate, The, 140
Film industry, 10, 95. *See also* Movies
First Amendment. *See* Constitution
FM (frequency modulation). *See* Radio
Fourth Estate, The, 140
Franklin, Benjamin, 17, 28n
Functional displacement, 105
Functions of communication, 223

Gallium Arsenide (GaAs), 52
Gallup, George, 173
Games, 217
Gannett Corporation, 149, 150, 157
Gatekeepers, 140
Geosynchronous orbit, 9, 29, 38–40
Greene, Harold, 48, 51, 90, 113, 132, 170
Gulf War (1991), 29, 158n

"Hackers," 114
"Hal," 7, 15
Hardware, 9
Hartford (Conn.) *Courant*, 150, 159n
Harvard University, 185
HBO (Home Box Office), 36
Hearst, William Randolph, 142
Hertz, 17
High-definition television (HDTV)
　ATTC, 72, 76
　bandwidth requirements, 73–75
　broadcaster resistance, 73, 210
　cost, 118, 133
　digital technology, 76, 210, 226

Eureka, 72
　foreign trade, 93
　Hi Vision, 71, 72, 118
　market demand, 72–73, 204–205
　movies, 209–210
　multimedia, 230
　optical fiber, 51
　picture quality, 69
　standards, 71–72, 76, 112
Hi Vision. *See* High-definition television
Hollerith card, 193, 200n
Holograms, 59
Hopper, Grace Murray, 56
Horizontal integration, 109–110, 118, 131
Hubbard Broadcasting, 153
Hypermedia, 195
Hypertext, 193–195

IBM, 99, 169
Indexing, 189–190
Indonesia, 162
Industrial Age, 2, 15, 183
Industrial Revolution, 94, 103, 165
Information Age, 1, 2, 5, 8, 13, 15, 96, 142, 199, 242
Information function
　advertiser influence, 146
　database, 156–157
　gatekeepers, 140
　history, 141–142
　information terminal, 231–232
　multimedia, 233
　news media, 144, 145, 147–148, 155
　objective reporting, 143–144, 146–147
　telephone, 157
　VCR, 155–156
　See also Journalism
Information as commodity, 3
Integrated circuit, 9, 22. *See also* Microchip
Integrated services digital network (ISDN), 63–64
Intellectual property. *See* Copyright
Intelligence
　definition, 200n
　storing and sorting, 16
　in technology, 15
　See also Artificial intelligence
Intelligent network. *See* Integrated services digital network
Interference, signal, 47, 94–95
International Herald Tribune, 114, 149

International policy, 95
International Telecommunication Satellite Organization (INTELSAT), 36, 37
International Telecommunications Union (ITU), 38, 40, 94–95, 113
Interstate Commerce Clause. *See* Constitution

Jefferson, Thomas, 103, 155, 241, 242
Jobs, Steve, 57–58, 79
Journalism, 10
　education, 143
　multimedia, 233
　See also Information function
Joy, William, 59
Joyce, James, 97n
Justice, Department of, 85

K Bands, 40, 48
Kinetoscope, 200n
Kiosk services, 132
Knight, Arthur, 210
Knight-Ridder, 49, 118, 159n
Kodak. *See* Eastman Kodak

Lasers, 46, 209
"Lawrence Welk Show," 121, 135n
Leisure time, 203
Libraries
　Boston Public Library (BPL), 186, 190
　computer use, 185–187, 191
　copyright problems, 198
　function, 187–188, 191
　Harvard University, 185, 190
　Library of Broadcasting, 186
　Library of Congress, 185, 189, 200n
　UCLA, 186
　Vanderbilt University, 186
Lifestyle changes, 4
Light signals, 47
Liquid crystal display (LCD), 70
Lists. *See* Marketing
Localism, 84, 86
LOCs (local operating companies). *See* Telephone
Los Angeles *Times*, 109, 159n

MacNeil-Lehrer Newshour, 164
Madison, James, 103, 241
Mann, Horace, 181, 182
Marconi, Guglielmo, 21

Marketing
  catalogs, 170–171
  computer, 170, 174
  data brokers, 237–238
  direct, 171–175
  home shopping, 168–169
  lists, 173–175, 236–238
  mass market, 165
  multimedia, 171–172, 234
  niche markets, 124, 165–166, 173, 176, 178n
  segmentation, 165–167
  telephone, 170
  See also Advertising; Persuasion
Mason, George, 103
Mass media
  advertising, 118
  change, 4, 222, 224
  conversion to digital codes, 9
  credibility, 144, 145
  displacement, 6, 105
  functions, 6, 147
  revenues, 95
Mayfield Publishing Co., 196–197
Mayflower Doctrine, 92
MCI, 49, 108
McLuhan, Marshall, 30
Media literacy, 239–240
Microchip, 17, 22–25, 229, 230. *See also* Integrated circuit
MIPS (Millions of Instructions per Second), 59
MIT Media Laboratory, 156
Modem, 27, 53
Moore, Gordon, 59
Moore's Law, 229
Movies
  aesthetics, 205–206, 209
  box office revenues, 127
  cinema attendance, 126–127
  cinema operations, 129
  colorization, 205
  digitization, 207–210
  distribution, 208–210
  film characteristics, 209
  finances, 124–125
  high-definition television (HDTV), 209–210
  industry organization, 125–126, 210
  optical fiber distribution, 208
  release cascade, 128
  satellite distribution, 210
  on television, 208–209
MTV, 114, 217
Multichannel multipoint distribution system (MMDS), 52, 88, 89, 103, 134, 216
Multimedia, 9, 49, 60–62, 94, 216, 224
  advertising, 133, 233, 234, 235–236
  art, 234
  display screens, 230
  effects, 227
  entertainment, 234
  journalism, 233–234
  marketing, 171–173, 234–236
  pay-per-view, 235
  platform, 61, 62
  politics, 172
  software, 230
  standards, 60
Multinational corporations, 95, 220
Multiple system operator (MSO). *See* Cable
Music. *See* Recording industry
Mutual Broadcasting System (MBS), 221n

Narrowcasting, 224
NASA (National Air and Space Administration), 42n
National Academy of Sciences, 55, 193
National Association of Broadcasters (NAB), 161, 220n
National Cable Television Association (NCTA), 155
National Institute of Standards and Technology (NIST), 116n
National Telecommunications and Information Agency (NTIA), 84–85
Natural monopoly, 86–87
NBC television, 121, 124, 212
Networks, broadcast
  advertising, 124, 212–213
  audience, 124, 211, 214, 215
  finances, 215
  management and structure, 211–213
  multimedia, 233
  news, 151–152
  optical fiber, 212–213
  owned and operated stations (O&Os), 96n
  syndication, 215
News, 12, 155. *See also* Information function
Newspapers, 10, 89
  advertising, 120, 123
  circulation, 101, 140, 144–145, 158n
  computer use, 148
  content, 149–150
  credibility, 144–145
  cross-ownership, 91
  delivery, 116n
  fax editions, 150, 159n
  format, 149–150
  history, 103–105
  national papers, 148–149
  organization, 104
  ownership, 92
  voice information services, 102, 150
  See also Press
New York Times, 139, 148, 149, 150, 159n
NHK (Nippon Hoso Kyokai), 77n
  Hi Vision, 71, 72, 77n, 93, 210
Niche markets. *See* Marketing
Nielsen. *See* A. C. Nielsen Corp.
Noll, A. Michael, 27
NTSC, 69, 71, 73, 74, 77n, 93, 112, 204

O&Os. *See* Networks
Obscenity, 97n
Office of Telecommunications Policy (OTP). *See* National Telecommunications and Information Agency (NTIA)
Optical fiber, 9, 41, 89
  advantages, 44
  cable, 49, 51, 52, 216
  capacity, 44, 45, 48
  competition with satellites, 44, 48
  components, 47
  costs, 48, 118, 134
  digitization, 45, 207–208
  high-definition television (HDTV), 51
  lasers, 46
  music, 217
  multimedia, 94
  newspaper, 51
  penetration, 52, 213
  telephone, 48, 49–51, 52, 93

PAL, 69, 71, 112, 114
PanAmSat, 37
Patent Provision. *See* Constitution
Pay-per-view. *See* Cable; Multimedia
PCs (personal computers)
  history, 57–59
  information terminal, 231
  multimedia, 59, 61, 224, 229

Index

optical fiber, 49
penetration, 53
software, 64–66
uses, 58
Performance fees, 131
Perot, H. Ross, 177
Personal interest profile (PIP), 193, 196
Persuasion
history, 161–162
politics, 163–164, 167–168, 176, 177–178
polls, 173
public relations, 163–164
societal impact, 162
strategies, 165
See also Advertising; Marketing
Photography, 207, 226
Piracy, 42n, 113–114, 115, 131. *See also* Cable; Recording industry; Satellites
Pixels, 73
Plain old telephone service (POTS). *See* Telephone
PM (newspaper), 135n
Policy
advertising, 92
broadcasting, 72, 84–87, 91, 92, 101, 213–214
cable, 51, 88, 91, 92, 96n, 97n, 106–107
common carriers, 86–87
film industry, 85
international, 38, 40, 94–95, 113
interstate commerce, 83–84
market regulation, 90–91
National Telecommunications and Information Agency (NTIA), 84–85
Supreme Court, 91, 96n, 97n
See also Constitution; Copyright
Politics. *See* Persuasion
Polling, of public opinion, 173
Pool, Ithiel de Sola, 79, 84, 85, 87, 100, 103, 112, 181, 223
Postal service, 97n, 115n, 175
Postman, Neil, 220n
Potter, Walt, 159n
Press, 100–101. *See also* Film industry; Movies; Newspapers; Recording industry
Prime Time Access Rule (PTAR), 92
Prodigy, 133, 170, 178n
Public broadcasting, 135n
Public relations. *See* Persuasion

Radio
AM (amplitude modulation), 74
definition, 101
digitization, 218, 225–226
FM (frequency modulation), 74
functional displacement, 123
niche audience, 123
nonbroadcast services, 22
survival, 6
See also Broadcasting
Radio Act of 1912, 85–86
Rate averaging, 119
Ratings, 101
RCA (Radio Corporation of America), 6
Reagan, Ronald, 84, 197
Recording industry
CDs (compact disks), 205, 207, 217, 225
copyright, 89
digital audio tape (DAT), 106, 131, 133, 206–207, 217
digitization, 206–207, 217, 220n
history, 105–196, 203
optical fiber, 217
piracy, 113–114, 131
See also Press
Recording Industry Association of America (RIAA), 113–114
Residuals. *See* Performance fees
Reuters News Agency, 3
Roper, Elmo, 144, 145, 158n

Sarnoff, David, 6, 203
Satellite Communications for Learning (SCOLA), 155
Satellites, 89
advertising, 168
antennas, 31–32, 34
capacity, 48
competition with optical fiber, 44, 48
direct broadcast satellites (DBS), 32, 37–38, 52, 88–89, 103, 114, 134, 216
disadvantages, 40–41
footprint, 30, 32, 34, 42n
impact, 34–36
low orbiting, 42n
piracy, 42n
redundancy, 41
satellite news vehicles (SNV), 153
spotbeams, 34
system components, 31–34
television receive only (TVRO), 32, 36

very small aperture terminal (VSAT), 32, 38
weather, 29
See also Geosynchronous orbit
Saturday Evening Post, 106, 116n
Schools
clients, 183
educational establishment, 181, 183
private efforts, 183
purposes, 180–181
roadblocks, 181, 184
student-teacher relations, 181–182
See also Education
Schramm, Wilbur L., 11, 55
SECAM, 69, 71, 112, 114
Section 315. *See* Communications Act of 1934
Semiconductors, 9, 16–17, 18
development of, 20
impact on miniaturization, 25
impact on switching, 23, 25
storing and sorting information, 16
Showtime, 159n
Sine wave, 17, 23
SkyPix, 75
Satellite news vehicle (SNV). *See* Satellites
Social effects of technologies, 93, 223–224, 240–241
Software, 9, 57, 64–66, 230
Sony Corp., 113
South Pacific, 29
Spanish-American War, 142
Special services, 217
Spectrum. *See* Electromagnetic spectrum
Sprint, 108
Sputnik, 30
Standards
broadcast, 71, 112
economic importance, 113
high-definition television (HDTV), 112
international, 114, 220n
need for, 110–111
resistance to change, 112–113
television, 69, 71
variety, 112
Status quo, 10, 232
Supreme Court, 91, 96n, 97n
Switches, 18–20, 25
Switching hierarchy, 19, 102
Syndication, 215–216, 219
copyright problems, 89

TBS (Turner Broadcasting), 110, 205
TCI, 66n, 208, 212
Technological convergence, 229
Telephone
  broadband services, 120, 132, 208
  cellular mobile, 97n, 103, 120
  content, providing of, 89, 132
  cross-ownership, 91
  history, 107–109
  local operating companies (LOCs), 49–50
  long-distance service, 90
  marketing, 169–170
  multimedia link, 63–64, 232
  optical fiber use, 48, 49–51, 93, 207, 208
  penetration, 214
  plain old telephone service (POTS), 64, 107, 109
  revenues, 95, 119, 132, 228
  satellite use, 35, 48
  voice mail, 120
Television
  audience, 211
  market saturation, 67
  movies, 208
  multimedia, 232
  networks, 211–213
  penetration, 214
  See also Broadcasting
Television receive only (TVRO). *See* Satellites
Time, Inc., 109
Times-Mirror Corp., 109, 158n
  Gateway, 49, 118, 158n
Time-Warner, 53n, 109
Time shifting, 144
Transistor, 17, 20
Turner, Ted, 109
TV Answer, 169

Ulysses, 97n
United Press International (UPI), 85
USA Today, 148–149
Utopia, 10

Vacuum tubes, 21
Vanderbilt University, 186
VCR (videocassette recorder), 73
  beta, 113
  impact on cable revenue, 134
  movies, 208
  piracy, 89
  standards, 113

VCR Plus, 211, 220n
Vertical integration, 109–110, 118, 131
Very small aperture terminal (VSAT). *See* Satellites
VHS (vertical helican scan), 113
Video. *See* Television
Video dial tone, 103, 228
Videotex, 49, 51, 89, 118, 159n
Vietnam War, 147, 151
Virtual reality, 227
Visual persistence, 68
Vogel, Harold L., 125, 127
Voice information services, 102, 150
Voice mail, 120

Wall Street Journal, 149
WalMart, 3
Warner Communications, 109, 119
Western Union, 109
Whittle Communications, 183
Wireless Ship Act of 1910, 85
Wireless telegraphy, 21
World War II, 144, 151
Wozniak, Steve, 57–58, 79
Wright, Charles, 11

P 96 .T42 L95 1993